U0945253

总 主 编： 林大津

主　　编： 龚帆元

编　　写： 龚帆元　龚龑珑

翻　　译： 龚帆元　蔡江云　林　艳　方　璐　王绪伟　龚龑珑

外籍审校： Andrew Werling, Michael Potts, Jane Haasnoot

Series Editor-in-Chief: Lin Dajin

Chief Editor: Gong Fanyuan

Compiled by: Gong Fanyuan, Gong Yanlong

Translated by: Gong Fanyuan, Cai Jiangyun, Lin Yan,
Fang Lu, Wang Xuwei, Gong Yanlong

Proofread by: Andrew Werling, Michael Potts, Jane Haasnoot

龚帆元同时负责本分册的主编、统稿和审校工作。

福建省高校“一带一路”跨文化研究丛书

NINGDE

◎ 林大津　总主编
◎ 龚帆元　主　编

(宁德分册)

福建应用翻译大全

A Panorama of Fujian

C-E Translations for Practical Reference

厦门大学出版社 XIAMEN UNIVERSITY PRESS
国家一级出版社
全国百佳图书出版单位

序
Preface

壬辰龙年正月初二那天，我无意间被CCTV-9正在播映的纪录片《玄奘之路》吸引，从下午看到晚上7点多。多年时光飞逝而去，然而其中内容久久挥之不去。玄奘十九年的西天取经，十九年的佛经翻译，令我浮想联翩、感慨万千。坦率地说，现行的学术评价体系和瞬息万变的时代节奏已无法容忍“十年磨一剑”，因此充分发挥团队精神，形成“众人拾柴火焰高”的集体攻关态势，各有分工，重点突破，统为一体，形成系列，如此大概可弥补无法单枪匹马“十年磨一剑”之缺憾。

谈及翻译，一般认为应用翻译(也可统称为实用翻译)是相对于文学翻译而言的，其范围涵盖经济、政治、文化和社会的方方面面，既涉及传统发展脉络，更展现时下风貌；大至区域政治组织构架，小至地方特色产品。这一切构成对外交流应用翻译的广阔天地。

然而综观全国应用翻译领域，我们既看到赏心悦目、富有启发性的亮点，也看到不少汉英翻译垃圾，有的贻笑大方，有的触目惊心。

正是这一现实问题催生了《福建应用翻译大全》系列，全省九大地市各分册陆续面世。此系列丛书服务地方跨文化交流，是汉英应用翻译规范样本，却不是唯一正确的样板。说是规范，因为眼下应用翻译的劣质产品往往是译者信手取自还不发达的电脑翻译软件，如果译者勤奋点，查查《福建应用翻译大全》，的确可以从中得到借鉴和启发，会大大避免“国际玩笑”；说它不是唯一正确的样板，是因为翻译离不开对语境因素的充分考虑，译者可能需要根据特定语境，对各分册提供的翻译表达法进行必要的创造性调整。

综上所述,《福建应用翻译大全》可以是工具书,供译者查阅参考,也可以是应用翻译教材,供师生讨论互动。希望这双重目的在读者的批判性阅读过程中得以实现,由此进一步提高《福建应用翻译大全》修订版的水平。

“一带一路,语言铺路”,虽然不是严格意义上的逻辑推演,但翻译跨语言、跨文化交流的桥梁作用却是显而易见的。在“一带一路”宏伟蓝图中,我省外语界同仁携手谱写语言、文化和翻译新篇章,必定大有作为。

是为序。

林大津

2018 年 12 月 21 日

目　录
Contents

第一章　自然地理与行政区划　Chapter 1　Natural Geography and Administrative Divisions …… 1
第一节　自然地理　1.1 Natural Geography …… 1
一、地理地貌　1.1.1 Physical Geography …… 1
二、气候条件　1.1.2 Climatic Conditions …… 2
三、自然资源　1.1.3 Natural Resources …… 3
第二节　行政区划　1.2 Administrative Divisions …… 17
一、建制沿革　1.2.1 Evolution of the Organizational Systems …… 17
二、行政区划　1.2.2 Administrative Divisions …… 20

第二章　历史与时政　Chapter 2　Ningde：Past and Present …… 48
第一节　历史　2.1 Past of Ningde：Facts and Figures …… 48
一、宁德的历史发展　2.1.1 Historical Development of Ningde …… 48
二、宁德九个县市名称的由来　2.1.2 Origins of the Nine Counties/Cities/Districts …… 53
三、宁德历史大事记　2.1.3 Historical Events in Ningde …… 57
四、宁德历史名人　2.1.4 Historical Figures in Ningde …… 67
第二节　时政　2.2 The Present Ningde：Facts and Figures …… 84
一、宁德城市性质与发展目标　2.2.1 Characteristics of Ningde and Its Goals for Development …… 84
二、宁德的城市精神　2.2.2 The City Spirit of Ningde …… 85
三、宁德市政府工作重点　2.2.3 Work Focus of Ningde Municipal Government …… 87
四、宁德市委主要党政机关　2.2.4 Major Municipal Party and Government Departments …… 91

五、中央、省驻宁德机构 2.2.5 Branches of the Central and Provincial Organs Stationing in Ningde …… 93
六、宁德市新闻媒体 2.2.6 News Media in Ningde …… 95

第三章 宁德经济 Chapter 3 Economy in Ningde …… 96
第一节 经济概况 3.1 Overview …… 96
一、综合实力 3.1.1 Comprehensive Strength …… 96
二、经济结构 3.1.2 Economic Structure …… 99
第二节 现代农业 3.2 Modern Agriculture …… 101
一、新农村建设 3.2.1 A New Countryside Construction …… 101
二、农业和农村经济 3.2.2 Agriculture and Rural Economy …… 103
三、粮食生产 3.2.3 Grain Production …… 106
四、副业生产 3.2.4 Subsidiary Production …… 107
五、重点企业 3.2.5 Key Enterprises …… 116
六、宁台农业合作 3.2.6 Agricultural Cooperation Between Taiwan and Ningde …… 119
第三节 现代工业 3.3 Modern Industry …… 122
一、工业招商 3.3.1 Industrial Investment Promotion …… 122
二、产业集群 3.3.2 Industrial Clusters …… 124
三、以港兴市 3.3.3 City Development Through the Port Construction …… 126
四、重点产业 3.3.4 Key Industries …… 128
五、高新技术产业 3.3.5 High-Tech Industry …… 137
六、重点企业 3.3.6 Key Enterprises …… 142
七、品牌战略 3.3.7 Brand Strategies …… 146
第四节 现代服务业 3.4 Modern Service Industries …… 147
一、社会服务业 3.4.1 Community Service …… 147
二、商贸物流业 3.4.2 Trade Logistics …… 148
三、文化创意产业 3.4.3 Culture and Innovation …… 150
四、金融保险证券业 3.4.4 Finance, Insurance and Securities …… 151
五、邮电通信业 3.4.5 Postal and Telecommunication Service …… 153
六、交通运输业 3.4.6 Transportation …… 154
七、会展业 3.4.7 Convention and Exhibition …… 156
八、旅游业 3.4.8 Tourism …… 157
九、房地产业 3.4.9 Real Estate …… 158

第五节 对外经济合作 3.5 Foreign Economic Cooperation …… 159
一、对外经济贸易 3.5.1 Foreign Trade …… 159
二、利用外资 3.5.2 Utilization of Foreign Capital …… 160
三、国际经济技术合作 3.5.3 International Economic and Technological Cooperation …… 161
四、宁台经贸交流与合作 3.5.4 Economic Exchange and Cooperation Between Ningde and Taiwan …… 161
五、贸易合作平台 3.5.5 Major Trade Cooperation Platforms …… 163
六、宁德国家级、省级对外开放产业基地 3.5.6 National and Provincial Foreign-Invested Industrial Bases in Ningde …… 165

第四章 社会事业 Chapter 4 Public Welfare …… 172
第一节 教育 4.1 Education …… 172
一、历代大事记 4.1.1 Major Events …… 172
二、书院及教会学校简介 4.1.2 Academies and Missionary Schools …… 175
三、基础教育 4.1.3 Elementary Education …… 179
四、中等教育 4.1.4 Secondary Education …… 183
五、高等教育 4.1.5 Higher Education …… 195
六、民办教育 4.1.6 Private Education …… 197
第二节 体育 4.2 Sports …… 201
一、体育设施建设 4.2.1 The Construction of Sports Facilities …… 201
二、群众性体育运动 4.2.2 Public Participation in Sports …… 202
三 、竞赛成绩 4.2.3 Medals and Awards …… 203
四、宁德市体育明星 4.2.4 Sports Stars from Ningde …… 204
第三节 医疗卫生 4.3 Health and Medical Care …… 206
一、建设成就 4.3.1 Major Achievements …… 206
二、主要医疗机构 4.3.2 Major Hospitals in Ningde and Their Addresses …… 208
三、主要医院简介 4.3.3 Profiles of Major Hospitals …… 210

第五章 文化特色 Chapter 5 Culture in Ningde …… 215
第一节 宁德特色文化 5.1 Distinctive Ningde Culture …… 215
一、宁德文化历史 5.1.1 Cultural History of Ningde …… 215
二、宁德市十大名片 5.1.2 Ten Highlights of Ningde …… 217
第二节 民间艺术 5.2 Folk Arts …… 231

一、戏剧 5.2.1 Opera …… 231
二、曲艺 5.2.2 Folk Art Forms …… 233
三、音乐与舞蹈 5.2.3 Music and Dance …… 235
四、武术与杂技 5.2.4 Martial Arts and Acrobatics …… 238
五、工艺与技艺 5.2.5 Arts and Handicrafts …… 240
第三节 民俗民风 5.3 Local Festivals …… 246
一、节俗 5.3.1 Major Festivals …… 246
二、习俗 5.3.2 Folk Customs …… 252
三、农时节令 5.3.3 Agricultural Seasonal Customs …… 258
四、信俗 5.3.4 Traditional Beliefs and Worships …… 259
五、食俗 5.3.5 Dietary Customs …… 262

第六章 宁德旅游 Chapter 6 Traveling in Ningde …… 265
第一节 风景名胜 6.1 Scenic Spots and Places of Historical Interest …… 266
一、宁德风景名胜 6.1.1 Scenic Spots and Places of Historical Interest in Ningde …… 266
二、宁德名人故居 6.1.2 Former Residences of Famous People in Ningde City …… 285
第二节 宁德旅游线路 6.2 Traveling Routes in Ningde …… 291
一、宁德蕉城区旅游线路 6.2.1 Inner Traveling Routes of Jiaocheng District …… 291
二、宁德市周边景点自驾游路线 6.2.2 Self-Driving Traveling Routes Around Ningde …… 291
第三节 宁德交通指南 6.3 Ningde Transportation Information …… 295
一、航空 6.3.1 Air Transportation …… 295
二、铁路 6.3.2 Railway Transportation …… 295
三、公路 6.3.3 Highway Transportation …… 296
四、水路 6.3.4 Waterway Transportation …… 297
五、公交车 6.3.5 Public Bus Service …… 298
第四节 宁德主要酒店 6.4 Major Hotels in Ningde …… 298
一、宁德主要五星级酒店 6.4.1 Major Five-Star Hotels in Ningde …… 298
二、宁德主要四星级酒店 6.4.2 Major Four-Star Hotels in Ningde …… 301

三、宁德主要三星级酒店 6.4.3 Major Three-Star Hotels in Ningde …… 307
四、其他三星级酒店 6.4.4 Other Three-Star Hotels in Ningde …… 309
五、宁德主要经济型酒店 6.4.4.5 Major Budget Hotels in Ningde …… 311
第五节 美食特产 6.5 Gourmet Foods and Local Products …… 312
一、宁德美食 6.5.1 Ningde Local Gourmet Foods …… 313
参考文献 References …… 316

第一章　自然地理与行政区划

Chapter 1　Natural Geography and Administrative Divisions

第一节　自然地理

1.1　Natural Geography

一、地理地貌

宁德俗称闽东，是海峡西岸经济区东北翼正在崛起的一座新兴滨海城市，位于长江三角洲、珠江三角洲、台湾三大经济区的中间位置，地处北纬26°18′～27°40′，东经118°32′～120°43′。东望台湾岛，西邻南平，南连福州，北接浙江温州。东西横距235千米，南北纵距153千米。全市陆地面积1.35万平方千米，海域面积4.46万平方千米。海岸线长1 046千米，居全省各设区市之首。

宁德市在福建省地层区划中属华南地层区东南沿海地层分区。境内除福鼎大部分和柘荣一部分地域属温州地层小区外，其余均属青田漳州地层小区。在地质构造带中，宁德位于闽东燕山火山岩断裂带北部，处在东南沿海火山岩带。其地貌基本轮廓形成于燕山运动末期，在福建省地貌区划中属闽中火山岩系中山地貌区和东部沿海花岗岩丘陵与平原地貌区。境内西北部有洞宫山、鹫峰山两大山脉，千米以上山峰697座，最高峰山尖海拔1 649米；中北部和中南部有太姥山和天湖山两条山脉，千米以上山峰189座，最高峰山尖海拔1 479米；东面濒临太平洋，海域内港湾岛屿众多，构成区内地势陡峻，其间杂有山间盆地，沿海一带夹滨海堆积平原。

1.1.1 Physical Geography

Ningde, traditionally called Mindong (East Fujian), is a fast emerging and thriving coastal city in the northeast of the Western Taiwan Straits Economic Development Zone. It is situated in the central area of the three major economic regions of the Yangtze River Delta, the Pearl River Delta and Taiwan with its geographical location between 26°18′-27°40′ north latitude and 118°32′-120°43′ east longitude. It faces Taiwan in the east and borders Nanping in the west, Fuzhou in the south, and Wenzhou of Zhejiang Province in the north. Its east-west span reaches 235 kilometers and the north-south span is 153 kilometers, with a land area of 13 500 square kilometers and a sea area of 44 600 square kilometers. Its coastline is 1 046 kilometers long, topping that of all the cities in Fujian Province.

In the stratum divisions of Fujian Province, Ningde is a part of the southeastern coastal sub-zone of the southeast stratums of China. Within Ningde, most of Fuding City and a part of Zherong County belong to Wenzhou Stratum, and the rest are a part of Qingtian Zhangzhou Stratum. As to the geological belt, Ningde is located in the north of the broken volcanic belt of Yanshan Mountain of East Fujian, and in the volcanic rock belt of the southeast coast of China. Ningde's landform came into its innitial shape at the end of the Yanshan Mountain Movement. In the landform divisions of Fujian Province, Ningde is a part of the mountain landforms of the volcanic rock areas of Fujian as well as a part of the plain landform zone and the coastal granite hills of East China. In Northwest Ningde, there are Donggong Mountain Range and Jiufeng Mountain Range, within which there are 189 mountains over 1 000 meters high. The highest mountain peak reaches 1 479 meters. Ningde is on the Pacific Ocean in the east with many ports, bays, islands and islets. Thus, its landforms are steep. Among them, there are basins among mountains and accumulated plains along the coast.

二、气候条件

宁德属亚热带海洋性季风气候，冬少严寒，夏少酷暑；气候湿润，雨量充沛；夏季最长，秋季最短；无霜期 235～300 天，年日照时数 1 711.7～1 916.0小时，由于有 4 个高海拔山区县，气象要素的地理差异较大。全市年平均气温 17.8℃，年极端最高气温出现在 8 月上旬，以福安的 40.4℃ 为最高，全市极端最低气温除蕉城区出现在 11 月 9 号外，其余均出现在 12 月 28 号，山区各县寿宁最低 - 5.8℃，沿海各县、市福鼎最低 - 1.7℃。年降水量 1 811.1 毫米，降水集中两个时段，即 5—6 月的雨季(前汛期)和 7—9 月的台风季(后汛期)。年平均有 3.5 个台风影响，暴雨日数年平均 5.7 天。特大暴雨和台风来临之际，给沿海渔民近海养殖、船泊作业及生命财产带来严重影响和巨大的损失，最佳旅游季节为 4—12 月。

1.1.2 Climatic Conditions

Ningde has a marine, subtropical and monsoonal climate. There are few extremely cold days in winter, and few extremely hot days in summer. Summer here is the longest season, and autumn is the shortest. The frost-free period lasts 235-300 days and the amount of sunny hours ranges 1711.7-1916.0 hours. Because of the four high-altitude counties, different areas differ a lot in their climate. The average temperature of the city is 17.8℃; the extremely high temperature occurs at the beginning of August, at 40.4℃, which occurs in Fu'an City. The lowest temperature in Ningde is on December 28th each year except Jiaocheng District which is on November 9th. The lowest temperature among the mountainous counties is at - 5.8℃ in Shouning County. Along the coastal counties, the lowest temperature is - 1.7℃ in Fuding City.

The annual precipitation averages 1 811.1 millimeters and falls mainly during two periods: the rainy season from May to June (the first flood period) and the typhoon season from July to September (the second flood period). There are 3.5 typhoons and 5.7 extremely stormy days a year on average. The extreme storms and typhoons severely affect the coastal sea farming and shipping operations, causing huge losses as well as damage to life and property. The best time for tourism in Ningde is from April to December.

三、自然资源

1.1.3 Natural Resources

(一)土地资源

宁德市素有“八山一水一分田”之称。全市土地面积 13 452平方千米，其中山地面积8 522.3平方千米，占总面积的 63.6%，主要分布在境内的西部、西北部、中北部、中南部地域，丘陵面积3 699.5平方千米，占全区总面积的 27.6%，主要分布在山地边缘，平原面积5 106平方千米，占 3.8%，主要分布在溪河两岸和丘陵地下部，沿海溪河入海口，山间盆谷面积 224.8 平方千米，占全区总面积的 1.7%，零星分布在山地之间和溪谷之中，滩涂面积 439.7 平方千米，占全区总面积的 3.3%，分布于沿海岸线一带(即潮间带)。

2013 年，根据年度土地利用变更调查结果，土地总面积 134.32万公顷，其中农业用地面积 117.42万公顷，占土地总面积的 87.42%；建设用地面积 5.3 万公顷，占土地总面积的 3.95%；未利用地面积 11.6 万公顷，占土地总面积的 8.63%。

1.1.3.1 Land Resources

Ningde features 80% mountains, 10% waters and 10% paddy fields. The total land area of the city is 13 452 square kilometers, in which the mountainous land takes up 8 522.3 square kilometers, i.e. 63.6% of the whole area of the city. The mountainous land is mainly located in the west, northwest and central north and south of the city. The hill areas covers 3 699.5 square kilometers, taking up 27.6% of the whole area of the city, mainly situated in the mountainous land margins. The plain area is 5 106 square kilometers, which accounts for 3.8% of the total area of the city. It is mainly distributed along the banks of rivers, the lower reaches of hills, and the mouths of the rivers to the sea. The basin area is 224.8 square kilometers, which accounts for 1.7% of the total, sporadically located between the mountainous land and the valleys. The inter-tidal beach covers 439.7 square kilometers, which takes up 3.3% of the total area of the city, mainly located along the coast (i.e. the inter-tidal zones).

According to the annual survey on the changes of land utilization in 2013, Ningde had a total usable land area of 1.3432 million hectares, of which the agricultural land area was 1.1742 million hectares, which took up 87.42% of the total land area, and the land area for infrastructural construction was 53 thousand hectares, which covered 3.95% of the total land area, and the unexploited land area was 116 thousand hectares, which accounted for 8.63% of the total land area.

(二)物产资源

宁德物产丰富，粮食作物主要有水稻、甘薯、马铃薯、大麦、小麦、大豆、杂粮等。经济作物主要有蔬菜、水果、茶叶、食用菌、水产品等众多名优特产，已形成规模与特色。其中蕉城区飞鸾镇、三都镇一带，独特的地理、气候条件，成就了晚熟荔枝、龙眼、水蜜桃、四季柚、油柰、刺葡萄和脐橙等优质水果。

宁德拥有辽阔的海域，沿海岛屿众多，水产资源 600 多种。有鱼类 500 多种，常见的海水鱼类约 72 种，淡水鱼类约 38 种。经济价值较高的有鳗鱼、石斑鱼、梅童鱼、大黄鱼、黄菇鱼、凤尾鱼、草鱼、鲢鱼、鲤鱼、鲫鱼、香鱼等 30 多种。其中官井洋大黄鱼、东吾洋对虾、二都蚶、沙塘剑蛏、沙江牡蛎等闻名海内外。

虾、蟹类：区域内约有 60 多种，以热带、亚热带沿岸虾蟹类为主。经济价值较高的虾、蟹类有长毛对虾、中国对虾、日本对虾、斑节对虾、新对虾、仿对虾、管鞭虾、鹰爪虾、毛虾、锯缘青蟹、梭子蟹、河蟹、日本眼蟹等 10 多种。

贝类：区域内约有 70 多种，以瓣鳃类和复足类占优势。经济价值较大的种类有缢蛏、牡蛎、近江牡蛎、菲律宾蛤子、杂色蛤子、泥蚶、结蚶、文蛤、厚壳贻贝、紫贻贝、翡翠贻贝、泥东风螺、栉孔扇贝、寻氏肌蛤等 20 多种。

水果：适宜种植的果树品种达 200 余种。福安、古田的水蜜桃，福鼎的四季柚，福安的芙蓉李，蕉城区、霞浦的晚熟荔枝和晚熟龙眼，屏南的无核柿，寿宁的板栗，周宁的雪梨等等，居水果之上乘。

食用菌：全市有真菌类上百种，已被开发利用的食用菌有银耳、香菇、蘑菇、草菇、金针菇、凤尾菇、茯苓、竹荪、猴头菇、灵芝等。

茶叶：宁德茶叶种质资源丰富，拥有国家级良种 11 个，省级良种 19 个，全市无性系良种普及率达 95%以上，每年繁育良种茶苗 2.5 亿株，市内的福建省茶叶研究所保存茶树种质资源达 2 000多份。

宁德特产有大黄鱼、剑蛏、二都珠蚶、紫菜、三都澳晚熟荔枝、晚熟龙眼、古田银耳、茶叶、红曲、柘荣太子参、惠泽龙黄酒、穆阳线面、福鼎槟榔芋、水蜜桃、油柰、福安葡萄、魔芋、金丝扣等。

1.1.3.2 Local Products

Ningde is abundant in agricultural products. The main food crops are rice, sweet potato, potato, barley, wheat, bean and millet, etc. The main cash crops are of a large scale, including vegetables, fruits, teas, edible fungi, aquatic products, etc. The unique geography and climate in Feiluan Township and Sandu Township of Jiaocheng District help to grow excellent fruits like late-in-season lyche, longan, honey peach, four-season pomelo, younai plum, thorny grape, and tangerine, etc.

Ningde possesses a wide sea area with many coastal islands and islets. There are over 600 kinds of aquatic products, among which are more than 500 kinds of fishes. There are about 72 sea water fishes and 38 fresh water fishes. Those of high economic value are over 30 kinds, such as eel, rudd, baby croaker, larger yellow croaker, nibea albiflora, anchovy, grass carp, chub, carp, crucian, catfish, Epecially the large yellow croaker from Guangjingyang Bay Area, the pair-prawns from Dongwuyang Sea Area, the cockle from Erdu

Township, the mussel from Jiantang Area, and oyster from Shajiang, are well-known at home and abroad.

There are over 60 kinds of shrimps and crabs, mainly tropical and subtropical coastal ones. Those of high economic value are more than 10 kinds, such as hairy shrimp, Chinese shrimp, Japanese shrimp, monodon, Metapenaeu, etc. and crab and mud crab and Japanese crab, etc.

Shellfish: There are over 70 species of shellfishes in Ningde. The shellfishes with lamella gills and gastropoda are the main kinds . There are over 20 kinds with higher economic value, namely: razor clam, oyster, Jinjiang oyster, Philippine clam, parti-colored clam, mud blood clam, striped clam, thick-shell mussel, purple mussel, snail, scallop, and muscular senhousei, etc.

Fruit: Ningde is suitable for growing over 200 kinds of fruits. The honey peach grown in Fu'an and Gutian counties, the pomelo in Fuding, the plum in Fu'an, the late-in-season lyche and longan in Jiaocheng District and Xiapu County, seedless persimmon in Pingnan, nut in Shouning, pear in Zhouning all are considered to be high quality fruits.

Edible fungi: There are over 100 kinds of fungi in Ningde. The grown edible fungi are tremella (ear-shape fungi), fragrant mushroom, mushroom, grass mushroom, gold-needle shaped mushroom, phoenix-tail shape mushroom, poria coco, monkey-head shaped mushroom, ganoderma and so on.

Tea: Ningde is abundant in tea germplasms, boasting 11 fine national varieties of tea, 19 of provincial level. The clonal fine breeding rate has reached 95% and 250 million fine tea seedlings are cultivated each year. The Fujian Provincial Tea Research Institute, located in the city, keeps over 2 000 fine species of tea germplasm resources.

The specific unique local products in Ningde are as follows: yellow croaker, cockle in Erdu Village, nori, late-in-season lyche and longan in Sandu Bay, fungi, tea, and red yeast rice in Gutian County, Taizi Ginseng in Zherong County, Huizelong-Brand rice wine, thread noodles in Muyang Township, taro, honey peach, and plum in Fuding, grape in Fu'an, magic taro, sweet potato starch noodles, etc.

(三)森林资源

境内森林资源丰富,植物有 189 科,2 163 个种,其中孢子植物 27 科,67 个种;种子植物 162 科,2 094个种。在地形、气候、土壤等环境因素的综合影响下,垂直分布与水平分布比较明显，大致可分为三个带：东南部海拔 500 米以下滨海丘陵平原地带，西北部和西南、东北部海拔 800 米以上中山地带，中部海拔 500～800 米的低山地带。全市典型的森林植被类型有常绿阔叶林、常绿针叶林、针阔叶混交林、山地常绿矮林、竹林、荒草山植被、海岸植被 7 种。其中常绿阔叶林是重要的水源林和特种用材林。常绿针叶林是本市主要的用材林和薪炭林。

常绿阔叶林：乔木层优势树种以壳斗科的甜槠、米槠、丝栗栲、青岗栎为主，其次为樟科、山茶科、杜英科、冬青科等；林下灌木有黄瑞木、柃木、乌药等；草本有狗脊、地念等；层外植物有猕猴桃、金花、葛藤等。

常绿针叶林：遍布全区各地，有纯林、混交林。主要有马尾松、杉木、柳杉、黑松、黄山松等。针、阔叶混交林有原生天然针阔混交林和人工营造的混交林。人工混交林中有杉木与檫木、杉木与油桐、杉木与松木、柳杉与马尾松等混交林。

山地常绿矮林：主要种类有青岗栎、石栎、丝栗栲等，林冠层低，仅 3～4 米，一般残存于山谷或陡坡上。

宁德市还有许多奇特且价值连城的森林资源，也是珍贵的旅游资源。有国家公布的珍稀濒危保护古树 12 种，占省内分布的保护树种的 26.7%，其中有被誉为“活化石”的银杏，有距今 200 多万年的濒危树种水松、桫椤树、鹅掌楸、香果树、半枫荷、福建柏、凹叶厚朴、天女花、沉水樟、天竺桂、红豆杉等，还有分布在宁德福鼎市部分海湾内的红树林，主要为秋茄，树高一般为 6～7 米，被誉为“海底森林”。

荔枝王：霞浦县沙江镇涵江村东吾洋有棵荔枝树，高 7 米，主干直径 1 米多，树龄 400 多年，年产果千余斤。

四季杜鹃：屏南县棠口乡龙源村有株杜鹃花，已有 400 多年树龄，高 4 米，冠幅 5 平方米，如今枝叶繁茂，生机盎然，一年四季开花。

红花油茶：霞浦县水门畲族乡八斗丘有一片 10 公顷的红花油茶林，树龄 120 年，仍花红果硕。

古罗汉松：古田县大甲乡前桃村岩富，现存一株约 3 000年的古罗汉松。树高 5 米，胸径 134 厘米，为全国之最。

四季千年桐：霞浦县溪西水库旁有株千年桐，树高 5.5 米，雌雄同株，一年开花 4 次，结果 2 次。

枫香吊莲：柘荣县宅中乡所在地村口有一株生命力旺盛的大枫香，树高 27 米，胸径 4.65 米，冠幅 21 平方米，相传植于清同治年间。树干顶部寄生一棵大吊莲，闻名方圆百里。群众采莲煎水为药，清凉退火，治疗小儿麻疹效果颇佳，现由村委会保护。

榕抱樟竹：福鼎市硖门乡石兰村水库边有一株古榕树，树龄达 800 多年，树高 22.7 米，树围 9 人合抱。树杈中生一株竹子和一株樟树，树围 2.5 米，高 7.5 米，树中有树，抱为一体。

秃杉巨树：古田县杉洋镇楼下村村头和平湖镇南岭村南阳小学旁边，有11株国家一级重点保护树木——秃杉，其中胸径1米以上的巨树有7株。

榕抱银杏：宁德市九都镇扶摇村有株大榕树，树干旁长出一株银杏，外为榕树根，内为银杏身，冠为榕、杏混合交叉，苍劲挺拔。

据统计，2013年全市林业用地面积99.4万公顷万亩，林地面积87.3万公顷万亩，活立木总蓄积量4 371.61万立方米，重点生态公益林34万公顷，森林覆盖率66.99%，林地绿化率90.94%。拥有国家级森林公园2个（宁德支提山、屏南天星山）、省级森林公园13个，国家级湿地公园1个（东湖）。

1.1.3.3 Forest Resources

Ningde is abundant in forest resources. There are 189 families and 2 163 species of plants, of which there are 27 families and 67 species of spore plants, and 162 families and 2 094 species of seed plants. Under the comprehensive influences of topography, climate and soil, there are distinctively vertical and flat distribution of forests. Roughly, they can be divided into three belts: the coastal hills and plains below 500 meters in the southeast of China, the medium mountainous belt over 800 meters high in the northwest, southwest and northeast, and the low mountainous belt ranging 500-800 meters in the central area. The seven typical forest vegetation types in Ningde are: evergreen broad-leaf forest, evergreen coniferous forest, mixture of coniferous and broad-leaf forests, mountainous evergreen dwarf forest, bamboo forest, wild mountain grassland vegetation and coastal vegetation, of which evergreen broad-leaf forest is the important water source and special timber source, and evergreen coniferous forest is the main timber and charcoal sources.

Evergreen broad-leaf forest: the major species of this category are mainly Castanopsis eyrei, carlesii, Castanopsis fargesii, and oak of the Fagaceae; these are followed by Lauraceae, Theaceae, elaeocarpaceae, and Ilex. Besides there are shrubs such as yellow Ramu, Eurya aggregata; for the herbaceous there are Woodwardia, Dinian herb and so on. The extrastratum plants are kiwis, Golden flowers, kudzu, etc.

The evergreen coniferous forests grow all over the city. There are pure woodlands and mixed ones. The main trees are horse-tail pine, fir, Japanese cedar, black pine, Yellow Mountain pine and so on. Besides, there are coniferous and broad-leaf forests mixed together with both natural and cultivated ones. The cultivated mixed forests are of fir and Sassafras, fir and Tung tree, fir and pine, Japanese cedar and horse-tail pine.

Mountainous evergreen dwarf forest: the main types are Green oak, rock oak, and Castanopsis. The canopy layer is low, just 3 to 4 meters high, generally remaining on the valleys or steep slopes.

Ningde boasts many unique and priceless forest resources, which are also precious tourism resources. There are 12 rare and endangered ancient species that are listed for protection by the National Government, which account for 26.7% of the total in Fujian Province. Of them, ginkgo is known as a "living fossil". There are other endangered species that are over 2 million years old, like water pine, Cyathea, Liriodendron, Emmenop-teryshenryi, Semi liquidambar cathayensis, Fujian cypress, Magnolia officinalis, sieboldin, micranthum, Cinnamomum pedunculatum, Chinese yew and candel of the mangrove mainly with a height of 6 to 7 meters. The latter is known as "seabed forests" growing along some bays of Jiaocheng and Fuding.

King of Lychees: In Dongwuyang, Hanjiang Village, Shajiang Town, Xiapu County, there is a "Lychee King" which is 7 meters high with a diameter of over 1 meter. It is over 400 years old and bears more than 500 kilos of fruit annually.

Four-season azalea: In Longyuan Village, Tangkou, Pingnan County, there is an azalea which is over 400 years old. It is 4 meters high and covers an area of 5 square meters. It still flourishes and blossoms during all seasons.

Camellia tree with red flowers: in Baidouqiu She Ethnic Village, Shuimen of Xiapu County, camellia trees with red flowers cover an area of 10 hectares. These trees are over 120 years old, yet they still blossom and bear fruit.

Ancient Yacca Tree: In Yanfu, Qiantao Countryside, Dajia Village, Gutian County, there is an ancient yacca tree of over 3 000 years old. It is five meters high with a circumference of 1.34 meters, which exceeds that of any other one in the whole country.

A unique Tung tree, which is over 1 000 years old and blossoms for four times per annum: By Xixi Reservoir of Xiapu County there is a Tung tree of 5.5 meters. It is monoecious and blossoms four times annually and bears fruit twice a year.

A sweetgum with a Live-on Lotus: In Zazhong Village of Zherong County lives a vigorous sweetgum, 27 meters high and with a circumference of 4.65 meters. Its top branches extend over 21 square meters. It is said to be planted in the Tongzhi Period of the Qing Dynasty. At its top, there is a hanging lotus which is famous in the surrounding villages. The residents there used to pick its leaves to boil herbal water to rid the body of heat or to cure a child's rashes. It is now protected by the Village Committee.

A Banyan Hugging a Camphor and a Bamboo: By Shilancun Reservoir in Xiamen Village of Fuding City lives an ancient banyan tree, more than 800 years old and 22.7 meters high. It takes nine people to encircle it. On its bough lives a bamboo tree and a camphor tree, 2.5 meters wide and 7.5 meters high. The two trees grow on another tree and mingle together.

Taiwania Flousiana Gausse: By Nanyang Primary School in Nanling Village of Pinghu Township and at the entrance of Louxia Village of Shanyang Township of Gutian County grow 11 firs (Taiwania Flousiana Gausse), which have been listed in the national key protection priority. Seven of them have a circumference of over 1 meter.

A Banyan Tree Hugging an Ginkgo: In Fuyao Village of Jiudu Township of Ningde City grows a huge banyan, by which grows a ginkgo. Outside are the roots of the banyan and inside is the ginkgo. At their tops the banyan and ginkgo branches co-exist together and grow vigorously.

In 2013, there were 994 thousand hectares of land for forestry-related purposes in Ningde. The forest land alone covered 873 thousand hectares with a total timber reservation of 43.7161 million cubic meters. There were 34 thousand hectares of key ecological forests. The forest coverage was 66.99%. The forestation rate was 90.94%. In the city there are 2 national forest parks (Zhiti Mountain and Tianxing Mountain of Pingnan), 13 provincial forest parks, 1 national wetland park(Donghu Lake).

(四)矿产资源

宁德市非金属矿比较丰富,金属矿次之,能源矿产贫乏。截至2014年底,境内已发现矿产资源51种,其中能源矿产3种(铀、钍、泥煤),金属矿产18种,非金属矿产20种,水气矿产2种(矿泉水、地热水)。列入福建省矿产资源储量表的固体矿产有银、钼、铅、锌、镉、铁、铜、金、钨、锰、高岭土、叶蜡石、明矾石、冶金用白云岩、冶金用脉石英、硫铁矿、饰面石材等;优势矿种为银、钼、饰面石材。探明固体矿产矿床(非建筑砂石粘土类)120处,其中饰面石材81处、银矿7处、钼矿5处。当年,发现飞鸾地热。全市探矿权总数62个,主要勘查银、钼、金、铁、铜、锰(多金属)等矿产。采矿权总数108家,开采钼、银、铁、饰面石材、建筑石料、叶蜡石、矿泉水等矿产。

1.1.3.4 Mineral Resources

Ningde is comparatively rich in non-metal mineral resources and metal mineral resources, but poor in energy resources. By the end of 2014, 51 minerals had been discovered, of which there are three energy minerals (uranium, thorium, and mud coal), 18 metal minerals, 20 non-metal minerals and 2 groundpower and gas minerals. The solid minerals listed on the Table of Mineral Reserves in Fujian Province are as follows: silver, molybdenum, lead, zinc, cadmium, iron, bronze, gold, wolfram, manganese, kaolin, pyrophyllite, alunite, metallurgic quartz and pyrite, decorative stone, etc.

Discovered solid mineral beds (non building sand and clay) reached 120, of which 81 are decorative stones, 7 silver minerals, 5 molybdenum minerals. In 2014, geothermal heat was found in Feiluan. The total number of the prospecting miners in the city was 62, mainly in exploration of silver, molybdenum, gold, iron, copper, manganese (polymetallic) and other minerals. There are a total of 108 mining companies in the city that are entitled to deal with mining of molybdenum, silver, iron, stone, building stone, pyrophyllite, mineral water and other minerals.

（五）海洋资源

全市海洋水域总面积44 565.8平方千米，占全省海洋总面积的35.6%。大陆岸线北起福鼎市沙埕镇的虎头角，南至蕉城区三都镇的大沙头，长达1046千米(不包括岛屿岸线)，大陆岸线长度在全省地市级中最长，占27.88%，可利用岸线222.9千米，其中天然良港三都澳是世界少有、全国唯一可全天候靠泊50万吨级巨轮的优良港湾。区域内有大小岛屿307个，占全省岛屿总数的21.3%。岛、礁、沙滩、岬角、水道、河口共1 215个，大小港湾29个，40～100米等深线近海区面积12 113.7平方千米，40～100米(大陆架)等深线外海区面积26 603.5平方千米。全市有四个港区，分别为三都澳、赛江、三沙和沙埕港区，共16个作业区。

三都澳港区属半封闭海湾，湾内大小岛屿星罗棋布，四周为海拔300米以上的山脉环抱，外海波浪难以直接进入湾内，形成大风浪。澳内主航道水深30～115米，且口小腹大，避风条件好，可规划12个10米以上水深的理想锚地(现已有5个)。随时可供锚泊大吨位巨轮，河床为泥质，锚着力强，终年不冻不淤，50万吨级巨轮可全天候进港，符合世界航运船舶大型化、航道深水化的趋势。在我国18 000多千米的海岸线上很难再找到这样一个深水港湾，世界罕见。

赛江港区:位于福安市赛岐镇至下白石镇的赛江沿岸。水路至上海438海里、至香港554海里。1982年赛江港区成为外贸起运点，1984年为国轮外贸物资装卸点,1985 年与香港正式通航。目前为宁德港重要的船舶修造基地。

三沙港区:三沙港区位于福宁湾北端,地处霞浦县三沙镇东北 3 千米外的小古镇,陆路距霞浦县城 35 千米,是我省最大的渔港,对台直接小额贸易点,霞浦台湾水产品集散中心,2007 年 5 月三沙港区口岸对外开放。

沙埕港区:沙埕港区位于福建省沿海最北端闽浙交界处的沙埕湾内,水路至温州 81 海里、至福州马尾 125 海里、至台湾基隆 142 海里,外海货运远及香港、上海、山东、浙江沿海。

1.1.3.5 Ocean Resources

Ningde has a total ocean area of 44 565.8 square kilometers, accounting for 35.6% of that of Fujian Province. Its coastline starts in Hutoujiao of Shacheng Township in Fuding City in the north and extends to Dashatou of Sandu Township of Jiaocheng District and reaches over 1 046 kilometers (excluding the coastlines of islands and islets). Its coast length is the longest among the cities and counties in Fujian, taking up 27.88% of the province's total and with an exploitable coastline over 222.9 kilometers. Of them, Sandu Bay is a super fine harbor, rare in the world and unique in China, which can berth 500 000 ships all the year round. In Ningde there are 307 islands and islets of various sizes, accounting for 21.3% of those in Fujian.

There are in total 1 215 islands, reefs, beaches, capes, water courses, river mouths and 29 harbors and bays. The offshore isobathic area, ranging from 40 to 100 meters deep, covers 12 113.7 square kilometers and the external isobathic sea area ranging from 40 to 100 meters (continental shelf) takes up 26 603.5 square kilometers. There are four ports, namely: Sandu Bay Port, the Saijiang River Port, Sansha Port and Shacheng Port, with a total of 16 operation zones.

Sandu'ao Port Zone is largely an enclosed bay with many islands and islets of various sizes inside. Its surrounding areas are mountains over 300 meters high, which serve to protect the bay from large waves. The main navigation routes are from 30 to 115 meters deep. What is more, the bay is huge inside with a small exit with excellent sheltering conditions that can accommodate approximately 12 ideal anchoring docks over 10 meters deep. (So far there have been five.) Huge ships can berth anytime in a year. The bay bed is of mud with strong anchoring capacity and will not freeze, so 500 000-ton super ships can operate all the year round. Therefore, the area can meet the shipping development trend of huge ships and deeper navigation routes. It is hard to find such a deep-water harbor on the 18 000 kilometer coast in China or even in the world.

Saijiang Port Zone: It is located along the banks of Saiqi Township to Xiabaishi Township of Fu'an City. It is 438, and 554 nautical miles away respectively to Shanghai and Hong Kong. In 1982, it was officially designated as a shipping port for foreign trade. In 1984, it was a loading and unloading port for national foreign trade ships. In 1985, it was officially open to shipping from Hong Kong. It is now an important ship repairing and building base in Ningde City.

Sansha Port Zone: It is located in the north part of Funing Bay, 3 kilometers away from Sansha Township, an ancient town in the northeast of Xiapu County. It is 35 kilometers away from Xiapu County proper. It is the largest fishing port of Fujian Province, a direct and small trial trading spot with Taiwan, as well as a distribution center of aquatic products of Taiwan and Xiapu. From May 2007, it is open to the outside world.

Shacheng Port Zone: It is located in Shacheng Bay in the northeast sea areas between Fujian and Zhejiang provinces. It is respectively 81 125 and 142 nautical miles away to Wenzhou City, Mawei of Fuzhou City and Jeelung Port of Taiwan. Its shipping scopes include Hong Kong, Shanghai, Shandong and Zhejiang, etc.

(六)水利资源

境内水系发达,河流密布,较大的河流有 24 条,流域总面积 1.19 万平方千米,其中最大的交溪和霍童溪两条水系和干流及其 10 条较大的支流,控制面积 0.78 万平方千米,占全市流域总面积的 65.5%;地下水资源约占水资源总量的 14%左右,分布于全市各地,特别是西部、北部和中部地区。全市的水资源总量在丰水年为 204.35 亿立方米,平水年为 144.69 亿立方米,偏枯年为 117.84 亿立方米,枯水年为 98.45 亿立方米。水能资源理论蓄存量 191.64 万千瓦,可开发利用装机容量 131.09 万千瓦,占蓄存量的 68.87%。降水是本市水资源的主要来源,由于季风气候以及地质、地形、植被等影响,境内水资源在时间和空间上的分布同降水量大致吻合,但很不均匀,地表径流形成了高值区和低值区。

交溪(原名长溪)是福建省第五大河流、宁德市最大河流,发源于洞宫山脉和鹫峰山脉,由 14 条较大的河流组成,其中穆阳溪、东溪、双溪、斜滩溪、管阳溪、柘荣溪、茜洋溪、七步溪是其中 8 条较大支流。交溪流经 11 个县,流域面积 5 549平方千米,占全市河溪流域总面积的 46.63%,河流总长 868 千米,年均径流量 69.69

亿立方米。多年平均水资源量56.5亿立方米，水能理论蕴藏量为94.94万千瓦。可开发量为89.28万千瓦，平均年电能为29.08亿千瓦时。

霍童溪是宁德市第二大河流，发源于鹫峰山脉，上游自北而南有后垅溪、棠白溪、金造溪和黛溪4条水系，流域面积2 244平方千米，占全市诸河流域总面积的18.86%，河流总长225千米，年均径流量27.25亿立方米。天然落差815米，可利用水头676.5米，多年平均水资源34.45亿立方米。水能理论蕴藏量为37.81万千瓦时，可开发的水力资源为61.09千瓦，平均年电能17.82亿千瓦时。市内除交溪和霍童溪外，自成系统的河流还有古田溪、霍口溪、赤溪、水北溪、七都溪、杯溪、罗汉溪、柏源溪、长桥溪、大金溪、溪头溪、百步溪、武步溪等14条溪河，流域面积共4 107平方千米，占全区诸河流域总面积的34.5%，河流总长539千米，多年平均产水量52.1亿立方米。水能理论蕴藏量58.89万千瓦，可开发量108.57万千瓦。多年平均电能17.62千瓦时。

1.1.3.6 Water Power Resources

Ningde boasts many rivers. There are 24 large rivers here that flow over an area of 11 900 square kilometers, of which the largest Xiaoxi River and the Huotongxi River and their 10 larger branches flow through an area of 7 800 square kilometers accounting for 65.5% of all the watercourses of the city.

The underground water resources take up 14% of the total water resources, and are distributed all over the city, especially in its westerw, northern and central area. The total amount of the water resources of the city in an abundant year is 20.435 billion cubic meters while the number are 14.469, 11.784 and 9.845 billion cubic meters in a rich year, a slightly drought year and a drought year respectively.

The theoretical reserves of water resources in the city are 1.9164 million kilowatts, of which 1.3109 million kilowatts i.e. 68.87% of the reserves can be exploited for installed capacity. Rainfall is the main source of the water resources in the city. Because of the influence of the monsoon climate, geology, landforms and vegetations, the amount of water resources in Ningde goes in time and space with rainfall roughly, but very unequally so that there are high value and low value zones of the flowing areas.

The Jiaoxi River (formerly known as the Changxi River) is the fifth largest river in Fujian Province and the largest in Ningde. It originates from the Donggong Mountains and the Jiufeng Mountains, and consists of 14 major rivers, of which 8 major ones are the Muyangxi River, the Dongxi River, the Shuangxi River, the Xietangxi River, the Guanyangxi River, the Zherongxi

River, the Qianyangxi River and the Qibuxi River. It flows through 11 counties with a flowing area of 5 549 square kilometers, equal to 46.63% of the total flowing area of rivers in Ningde City. It is 868 kilometers long with a flowing quantity of 6.969 billion cubic meters. For many years its annual average flowing quantity is 5.65 billion cubic meters. Its theoretical hydro power in reserves is 949 400 kilowatts and its exploitable amount is 892 800 kilowatts with an average annual electric power of 2.908 billion kilowatt hours.

The Huotongxi River, originating from the Jiufeng Mountains, is the second largest river in Ningde. Its upper reaches flow from north to south consisting of four water systems, namely, the Houlongxi River, the Tangbaixi River, the Jinzaoxi River and the Daixi River, with a flowing area of 2 244 square kilometers, accounting for 18.86% of the total flowing areas in the city. The total length of the river is 225 kilometers with an annual flowing amount of 2.725 billion cubic meters. Its natural fall is 815 meters with a usable water head of 676.5 meters high. Its annual average flowing quantity is 3.445 billion cubic meters. Theoretically, its hydropower in reserves is 378 100 kilowatts. Its exploitable hydro resource is 610 000 kilowatts with an annual average electric power of up to 1.782 billion kilowatts/hour.

Beside the Jiaoxi River and the Huotongxi River, there are 14 other complete water systems, i.e. the Gutianxi River, the Huokouxi River, the Chixi River, the Shuibeixi River, the Qiduxi River, the Beixi River, the Luohanxi River, the Baiyuanxi River, the Changqiaoxi River, the Dajinxi River, the Xitouxi River, the Baibuxi River and the Wubuxi River. They flow over an area of 4 107 square kilometers which accounts for 34.5% of that of the city, with a total length of 539 kilometers. Its annual average potential hydropower quantity is 5.21 billion cubic meters, with a theoretical hydropower in reserves of 588 900 kilowatts/hour. Their exploitable quantity is 1.0857 million kilowatts/hour with an annual hydropower potential of 176 200 kilowatts/hour.

（七）其他能源

宁德市海岸线长，蕴藏着丰富的潮汐能源和风电能源。可开发总装机容量潮汐能源 245.96 万千瓦，其中三沙湾潮汐可开发利用 129.34 万千瓦，为全省之最。

霞浦大京风电，位于霞浦县长春镇大京至斗米的沿海山地上，此处风力资源丰富，风向稳定，该项目安装 28 台并网型风力发电机组，单机容量 1 500千瓦，装机容量达 4.2 万千瓦，自 2011 年建成投产至 2015 年 9 月已累计发电 2.2 亿千瓦时，成为霞浦重要的绿色能源基地，同时也是该县沿海岸线上的一道美丽风景线。

大唐国际宁德发电公司是第一家落户宁德市的中央直属企业，投产总装机容量 252 万千瓦，2014 年 1 月，完成发电量 10.7 亿千瓦时，实现利润数千万元，该企业已经连续 5 年上榜福建省纳税百强企业，今年至今已纳税 3.86 亿元，预计全年可纳税近 5 亿元。

宁德核电站，项目规划总容量为 6 台百万千瓦级机组，是目前国内自主化程度和国产化比例最高的在建核电项目之一。2014 年，已投产的 1 号、2 号机组全年实现上网电量 108.02 亿度（相当于福建省全社会年用电量的 5.96%）。电运营安全标准化达到 7 级（世界先进水平），工程安质环标准化达 6 级（世界良好水平），已通过国家能源局电力安全生产标准化一级评审。2015 年 3 月 8 日 12 时 30 分，宁德核电 3 号机组成功首次临界，标志着 3 号机组反应堆正式进入运行阶段。

1.1.3.7 Other Resources

Ningde has a long coastline which leads to abundant tidal and wind resources. The amount of the exploitable tidal resources for installed capacity is 2.4596 million kilowatts, of which Sanshan Bay takes up 1.2934 million kilowatts, which is the No.1 in Fujian Province.

Dajing Wind Power Farm in Xiapu, located on the coastal hills in Changchun Township from Dajing to Doumi, enjoys abundant wind resources and stable wind directions. The farm has 28 wind power generators of grid-connections with a single unit capacity of 1 500 kilowatts and an installed capacity of 42 000 kilowatts. Since its operation from 2011 to September, 2015, the farm generated a total of 220 million kilowatts hours of electricity. It has become an important green energy base and at the same time also a beautiful scene along the coast in Xiapu.

Ningde Power Company of Datang International Group is the first affiliated enterprise to the central government settled locally with a total installed capacity of 2.52 million kilowatts. In January, 2014, it generated 1.07 billion kilowatts hours of electricity with a profit of over tens of millions of yuan. The company has been listed on the Top 100 Enterprises that Pay the Most Tax in Fujian for five years in a row. So far it had paid 386 million yuan by the time the book was written and it was predicted that it would pay 500 million yuan of tax in the whole year.

Ningde Nuclear Power Station was planned with 6 sets of million-kilowatt generators, being one of the most autonomous and localized stations under construction. In 2014, an output of 10.802 billion kilowatts was generated (equivalent to 5.96% of the total electric consumption of Fujian Province in the same year). Its generation safety standard reaches Class 7(the advanced level in the world). And its engineering safety standard was up to Class 6(the good level in the world) and passed Class-I appraisal test of electric power production by National Energy Bureau. At 12:30 of March 8, 2015, Generator 3 successfully reached its first critical point, indicating the No.3 reactor officially entered the operation stage.

第二节 行政区划

1.2 Administrative Divisions

一、建制沿革

先秦时期宁德为闽越族驻地，晋太康三年(282)开始设县，设温麻县，属晋安郡。隋开皇九年(589)撤温麻县入原丰县。唐武德六年(623)改为长溪县，属泉州(州治今福州)。唐开成年间，将长溪县的宁川和古田县东北划为感德场。后唐长兴四年(933)升场置县，取宁川之"宁"、感德之"德"为之命名，而有宁德县，属长乐府。宋淳祐五年(1245)增设福安县，与长溪、宁德皆属福州。

元至元二十三年(1286)长溪县升为福宁州，辖福安、宁德两县，属福州路。明洪武二年(1369)福宁州降为县，成化九年(1473)恢复福宁州。清雍正十二年(1734)，福宁州升为福宁府，隶属福建闽浙总督府，辖福安、宁德、霞浦、寿宁4县。乾隆四年(1739)增设福鼎县，共辖五县。民国元年(1912)，废府、州厅建制，实行省、道、县3级地方政制，区内古田、屏南、霞浦、福鼎、宁德、福安、寿宁7县并东路道。民国三年，东路道改称闽海道，区内7县并闽海道。民国十四年废道，区内7县属省政府。民国二十二年福建划分为4省2市，区内7县同属闽海省。民国二十三年，福建省政府实行行政督察区制，闽东划为第二行政督察专员公署；民国二十四年，闽东并入第一行政督察专员公署；民国三十二年，闽东被划为第八行政督察专员公署；民国三十六年，闽东又被划为第一行政督察专员公署。期间，闽东所辖境域几经变动。

1949年6月—12月，区内各县相继解放。中华人民共和国成立后设福安专区，专署驻福安城关，辖福安、福鼎、宁德、霞浦、寿宁、周宁、柘荣七县。1956年划进原属闽侯专区的长乐、连江、罗源三县,撤柘荣县。1959 年划长乐、连江二县归闽侯专区,增进原属南平专区的松溪、政和二县。1961 年恢复柘荣县。1962 年划罗源归福州市,撤销松政县,恢复政和、松溪二县。1970 年专署迁驻宁德城关,改称宁德地区,同时划松溪、政和二县归建阳地区,增进原属闽侯地区的连江、罗源、古田、屏南四县,再次撤销柘荣县。1975 年重新恢复柘荣县,1983 年划连江、罗源为福州市管辖。1988 年原宁德县改设为宁德市。1989 年福安县改设为福安市。1995 年福鼎县改设为福鼎市。1999 年 11 月 14 日,国务院批准宁德撤地设市,成立宁德市人民政府,2000 年 11 月 14 日正式挂牌。宁德市人民政府驻新设立的蕉城区,全市辖 9 个县(市、区)。

1.2.1 Evolution of the Organizational Systems

Before the Qin Dynasty, Ningde was already a settlement for the Minyue people. In the third year (282AD) of the Taikang period of the Jin Dynasty, Wenma County was established in Ningde and a part of Jin'an Prefecture. In the ninth year (589AD) of the Kaihuang period of the Sui Dynasty, Wenma County was abolished and joined with Yuanfeng County. In the sixth year (623AD) of the Wude period of the Tang Dynasty, it was changed to Changxi County and was a part of Quanzhou(Fuzhou today).

During the years of the Kaicheng period of the Tang Dynasty, Ning Chuan Township of Changxi County and the northeast of Gutian County were joined together to be Gan De Chang Township. In the fourth year (933AD) of the Changxing period of the later Tang Dynasty, "Ning" in Ningchuan Township and "De" in Gan De Chang Township were taken out to name Ning De (Ningde) which was a part of Changxing Prefecture. In the fifth year (1245AD) of the Chunyou period of the Song Dynasty, Fu'an County was added to counties of Changxi and Ningde, all under administration of Fuzhou. In the 23rd year (1286AD) of the Zhiyuan period of the Yuan Dynasty, Changxi County was promoted to Funingzhou Prefecture in charge of Fu'an and Ningde counties, both a part of Fuzhou. During the second year (1369AD) of the Hongwu period of the Ming Dynasty, Funingzhou Prefecture was lowered to county administration, and in the ninth year (1473AD) of the Chenghua period, Funingzhou Prefecture was restored. In the twelfth year (1734AD) of Emperor Yongzheng's reign of the Qing Dynasty, Funingzhou Prefecture was promoted to Funing Larger Prefecture, directly under the jurisdiction of Fujian and Zhejiang Governor Administration in charge of counties of Fu'an, Ningde,

Xiapu and Shouning. Fuding County was added in the fourth year (1739AD) of Emperor Qianlong's reign, so the five counties were under the jurisdiction of Funing Larger Prefecture. In the first year (1912AD) of Republic of China, Fu, Zhou and Ting administrations were abolished, and Provincial, Prefectural and County Administration was implemented for the local areas. The seven counties including Gutian, Pingnan, Xiapu, Fuding, Ningde, Fu'an, Shouning were under the jurisdiction of Donglu Prefecture. In the third year of Republic of China, Donglu Prefecture was changed to Minhai Prefecture, and all the seven counties were put under its administration. In the 14th year of Republic of China, Minhai Prefecture was abolished, and all the seven counties were put under the jurisdiction of Fujian Provincial Government. In the 22nd year of Republic of China, Fujian was divided into 4 provinces and 2 municipalities. The seven counties in Ningde were put under the jurisdiction of Minhai Province. In the 23rd year of Republic of China, Fujian Government implemented Administrative Inspection Zone System and Ningde was put under jurisdiction of the Second Administrative Inspection Zone. In the 24th year of Republic of China, Ningde joined with the First Administrative Inspection Zone. In the 32nd year of Republic of China, Ningde was put under the jurisdiction of the Eighth Administrative Inspection Zone. In the 36th year of Republic of China, Ningde was put under the jurisdiction of the First Administrative Inspection Zone. During this time, Ningde's jurisdiction changed again and again.

From June to December of 1949, all the counties in Ningde were liberated from the rule of the ROC one by one. After the liberation, Fu'an Special Prefecture was established with its location set in Fu'an and its jurisdiction over the counties of Fu'an, Fuding, Ningde, Xiapu, Shouning, Zhouning and Zherong.

In 1956, the three counties, Changle, Lianjiang, Luoyuan, which were formerly under the jurisdiction of Minhou Special Prefecture, were added to Ningde, and Zherong County was abolished. In 1959, Changle and Lianjiang Counties were put back under jurisdiction of Minhou Special Prefecture while Songxi County and Zhenghe County of Nanping Prefecture were included. In 1961, Zherong County was reestablished. In 1962, Luoyuan County was put back under Fuzhou Municipal Government's administration, and Songzheng County was abolished, Zhenghe County and Songxi County were restored again. In 1970, the location of Fu'an Special Prefecture was moved to Ningde County and promoted to Ningde Prefecture. Meanwhile, Songxi County and Zhenghe County were put back under the administration of Jianyang Prefecture, and four counties of Lianjiang, Luoyuan, Gutian and Pingnan from former Minhou Prefecture were put back under the jurisdiction of Ningde Prefecture. Zherong County was abolished. In 1975, it was restored again. In 1983, Lianjiang and Luoyuan were put back under Fuzhou's administration. In 1988, Ningde County was promoted to Ningde City. In 1989, Fu'an County was promoted to Fu'an City. In 1995 Fuding County was promoted to Fuding City. On November 14, 1999, Ningde Prefecture was abolished and Ningde Municipal Administration was set up with the approval by the State Council. On November 14th, 2000, Ningde Municipal Administration was formally launched. It is located in the newly established Jiaocheng District and has jurisdiction over 9 counties (cities).

二、行政区划

"宁德"的意思,来自唐朝中期划长溪县宁川及古田县东北部设感德场。后唐长兴四年(933)升场置县,取宁川之"宁"、感德之"德"为之命名,而有宁德县。广义的闽东指福建东部地区,包括福州、宁德两市,两地方言同属闽东语。狭义的闽东是福建省宁德市的俗称,位于福建省东北部。

2014年,宁德市总面积1.3452万平方千米,市人民政府驻蕉城新设立的东侨开发区,下辖蕉城区、东桥开发区和福安、福鼎、古田、霞浦、周宁、寿宁、屏南、柘荣8个市县、47个乡、65个镇、13个街道、183个居委会、2 138个村委员会。

截至2014年全市户籍总人口为3 522 387人,户数为1 033 624户,常住人口为285万人,人口密度227人/平方千米。人口自然增长率7.0%。全市有36个少数民族16.87万人,其中畲族人口15.4711万人,约占全省畲族人口的二分之一,全国的四分之一。少数民族千人以上的村镇58个,占乡镇总数的47.2%,少数民族人口占全村总人口30%以上的民族村235个;民族自然村986个。全市设1个畲族经济开发区(福安畲族经济开发区)、9个畲族乡。

1.2.2 Administrative Divisions

The name of Ningde (Ning De) County was coined from Chinese character Ning in the name of Ning Chuan Township of Changxi County and the other character De in the name of Gan De Chang Township in the northeast of Gutian County in the mid-period of the Tang Dynasty. In the fourth year of the

Changxing period in the later Tang Dynasty, county administration was established. The general meaning of "Min Dong" (East Fujian) refers to the east area of Fujian including Fuzhou and Ningde cities. Their dialects are both the Mindong dialect. The narrow meaning of Mindong refers to Ningde City located in the northeast of Fujian Province.

By 2014, Ningde covers an area of 13 452 square kilometers with its municipal government located in newly established Jiaocheng District and its jurisdiction over Jiaocheng District, Dongqiao Development Zone, Fu'an City, Fuding City, Gutian County, Xiapu County, Zhouning County, Shouning County, Pingnan County, and Zherong County, and administrates 47 villages, 65 townships, 13 sub-districts and 183 residential committees and 2 138 village committees. By 2014, Ningde has a registered population of 3 522 387 and 1 033 624 households. Its permanent population was 2. 85 million with a population density of 227 persons per square kilometer and a natural population growth at 7%. There are 36 ethnic minorities in the city with a population of 168 700, of which the number of the She ethnic people totals 154 711 making up half of that of Fujian Province and one fourth of the nation. There are 58 villages or townships that have a She ethnic population over 1 000 and that number amounted to 47. 2% of that of the City. There are 235 villages with the ethnic population exceeding 30% of the total. Besides, there are 986 ethnic sub-villages and one She Ethnic Economic Development Zone(in Fu'an) and 9 She ethnic villages in Ningde.

(一)蕉城区

蕉城区是宁德市政府所在地，是闽东的政治、经济、文化中心。位于北纬26°31′～26°58′，东经119°08′～119°51′。全区总面积1 709. 96平方千米，土地面积1 537平方千米，海域面积172. 96平方千米，海岸线总长211千米，户籍总人口为457 492人，户数为140 680户，常住人口44. 09万人，人口密度274人/平方千米，人口自然增长率7. 3%，辖2个街道、4个乡(其中1个民族乡)、10个镇、41个居委会、281个村委会。

蕉城区地处闽东山地北部，地势西高东低，自西向东呈阶状下降，大部地区海拔500米以上，为沿海地势最高的县市。全区最高峰第一旗海拔1 479米，岛屿20多个。主要河流有霍童溪，干流长126千米(境内68千米)，流域2 244平方千米(境内517. 5平方千米)，支流有赤溪等，流域334平方千米。主要湖泊东湖，面积3平方千米；人工湖金涵水库面积72公顷。

区内有沈海高速公路、温福铁路、宁武高速公路及104国道,宁德火车站是温福铁路(福建段)最大的旅客站。有漳湾等码头、三都澳城澳港作为国家一类口岸可泊10~50万吨的轮船,外轮海面交货可全天候作业。

另外,花岗石、高岭土等非金属矿产丰富。林、果、茶、牧、山场别具特色;溪河密布、水量充足,水电资源丰富;海域滩涂辽阔,水产养殖品种繁多。

旅游资源有省级重点风景名胜区支提山,被佛教界视为"海山第一禅林"国家级重点佛教寺院华严寺,被誉为"福建第一水"霍童溪。中国畲族同胞朝圣地"中华畲族宫",和被著名诗人郭沫若誉为"三都良港举世无,水深港阔似天湖"的三都澳。

2014年蕉城区,东侨开发区、街道(乡镇)基本情况一览表

街道(乡镇)	面 积 平方千米	人 口		居委会(行政村) 个
		户数 户	人口数 人	
蕉南	5	13 341	50 000	11
蕉南	6.8	11 800	35 000	7
城南镇	34	13 376	45 143	3+12
漳湾镇	55	14 592	53 204	1+25
七都镇	78	6 904	21 557	1+19
八都镇	105	4 696	12 248	1+25
九都镇	90	2 405	6 211	13
霍童镇	166	7 481	23 285	1+25
赤溪镇	168	4 979	12 158	1+26
洋中镇	163	6 517	13 255	33
飞鸾镇	102	7 386	24 108	2+19
三都镇	162	7 753	29 553	2+27
金涵乡	62	7 934	29 746	16
洪口乡	104	923	2 105	11
石后乡	60	2 536	6 846	14
虎坝乡	155	3 284	13 154	17
东侨开发区(东侨新区,享有县一级的经济、行政管理权限)	19.7	8 522	21 844	8

1.2.2.1 Jiaocheng District

It is the location of Ningde Municipal Government and also the center of politics, economy and culture of Ningde. It lies between a latitude of 26°31′-26°58′ north, and a longitude of 119°8′-119°51′ east, covering a total area of 1 709.96 square kilometers with a land area of 1 537 square kilometers and a sea area of 172.96 square kilometers as well as a coastline of 211 kilometers.

Its total population is 457 492 with a registered household number of 140 680 with a permanent population of 440 900. Its population density is 274 persons per square kilometer and its natural population growth at 7.3%. It administrates 2 sub-districts, 4 villages (one of them is of ethnic people), 10 townships, 41 residential committees and 281 village committees.

Jiaocheng District is located in the northeast mountainous area of Ningde and its topology is high in its west and low in its east, gradually declining from west to east. Most of its areas are about 500 meters above the sea level and it is the highest coastal county in China. The highest peak in the district is Diyiqi Peak at 1 479 meters high. There are also over 20 islands and islets. The main river is the Huotongxi River, with its main stream flowing over 126 kilometers and its flowing area of 2 244 square kilometers; and the part in Jiaocheng District is 68 kilometers long, having a flowing area of 517.5 square kilometers. Its branches are the Chixi River and others with a flowing area of 334 square kilometers. The main lake is the Donghu Lake of 3 square kilometers, and also there is an artificial Jinhan Lake of 72 hectares.

Through the district run Shengyang-Hainan Expressway, Wenzhou-Fuzhou Railway, Ningde-Wuyi Mountain Expressway No. 104 National Highway, etc. Ningde Railway Station is the largest station in Fujian on the Wenzhou-Fuzhou Railway. There are also ports, such as Zhangwan Port and Cheng'ao Port of Sandu Bay which is a national Class A harbor and allows 100 000 to 500 000-ton ships to berth there and the foreign ships to operate all the year round.

Resources of non-metals like granite and kaolin are very abundant. The forests, fruits, teas, and husbandry and mountainous farms are unique; the rivers here supply abundant water and hydro power resources; in addition, its mud flat area is wide with many aquatic products.

Jiaocheng is also rich in tourism resources. There are Zhiti Mountain, a key provincial level scenic spot; the Huayan Temple, a key national level temple regarded as "No. 1 Temple by the Coast Mountain" in the Buddhist circles; the Huotongxi River is regarded as "No.1 River" in Fujian Province; China She Ethnic Palace, a pilgrimage place for the She ethnic people; Sandu Bay which was praised by Guo Moluo, a famous poet, in a poem that goes, "Sandu Bay finds no match in the world. It is deep and wide like a sky lake".

Table of Basic Data of Sub-districts and Towns/Townships in Jiaocheng District and Dongqiao Development Zone

Name of Subdistrict/Town	Area (square kilometer)	Population		Number of Residential Committees /Villages
		Number of Households	Number of Residents	
Jiaonan Township	5	13 341	50 000	11
Jiaobei Township	6.8	11 800	35 000	7
Chengnan Township	34	13 376	45 143	3+12
Zhangwan Township	55	14 592	53 204	1+25
Qidu Township	78	6 904	21 557	1+19
Badu Township	105	4 696	12 248	1+25
Jiudu Township	90	2 405	6 211	13
Huotong Township	166	7 481	23 285	1+25
Chixi Township	168	4 979	12 158	1+26
Yangzhong Township	163	6 517	13 255	33
Feiluan Township	102	7 386	24 108	2+19
Sandu Township	162	7 753	29 553	2+27
Jinhan Viuage	62	7 934	29 746	16
Hongkou Viuage	104	923	2 105	11
Shihou Viuage	60	2 536	6 846	14
Hubei Viuage	155	3 284	13 154	17
Dongqiao Development Zone	19.7	8 522	21 844	8

(二)福安市

福安是宁德市辖市,1989年撤县设市,1993年被列为沿海开放城市,地处闽东地理中心,位于北纬26°41′~27°24′,东经119°23′~119°51′,全市总面积1 795平方千米,海岸线长145千米,总户数195 645户,总人口670 912人。常住人口56.85

万人,人口密度 318 人/平方千米,其中畲族人口 6 万多人,是全国最大的畲族人口聚居地,下辖 2 个开发区、4 个街道、5 个乡、13 个镇、46 个居委会、439 个村委会、108 个少数民族村,素有“中国中小电机之都”“全国第二大民间船舶修造基地”“中国茶叶之乡”“南国葡萄之乡”等之誉。

境内沈海高速公路、温福铁路、宁武高速公路、湾坞半岛铁路支线、规划中的福泰高速公路和宁衢铁路交叉贯穿全境,构成铁路、公路、港口三位一体的交通体系。水力资源丰富,全省五大水系之一的交溪从南至北贯穿全境,流域面积 5 638平方千米,水能资源蕴藏量 34.1 万千瓦。

全市探明金属和非金属矿 15 种,其中钼矿储量 6 500吨。森林植被类型多样化,有刺桫椤、水松等 60 多种珍稀树种。白马港为国家一类开放口岸、货物吞吐量居闽东之首,是福建开发最早的深水良港之一。

旅游资源丰富,有世界地质公园白云山,我国最低纬度地区保存最多、最好和发育最典型的第四纪古冰川遗迹——冰臼群,保存完整的廉村宋代古城堡建筑群,古朴奇特的柏柱洋明清古民居,别具风情的溪塔葡萄沟,绚丽多彩的仙岫畲族风情以及闽东苏维埃旧址。

2014 年福安市,街道(乡镇)基本情况一览表

街道(乡镇)	面 积 平方千米	人 口		居委会(行政村) 个
		户数 户	人口数 人	
赛岐镇	77	15 924	53 206	7 + 24
穆阳镇	13	3 629	14 110	6 + 2
甘棠镇	91	9 072	36 279	1 + 32
下白石镇	117	7 820	30 505	1 + 41
溪柄镇	130	5 943	23 163	1 + 24
上白石镇	79	4 701	17 980	1 + 21
社口镇	102	4 828	18 830	24
潭头镇	168	7 505	30 192	29
晓阳镇	96	1 721	6 831	10
溪尾镇	65	3 305	10 730	1 + 14
溪潭镇	115	5 785	20 818	1 + 34
湾坞镇	116	7 216	28 318	24
城阳镇	161	8 827	34 628	4 + 31
范坑乡	114	4 880	13 660	17
松罗乡	87	5 064	10 790	19

续表

街道(乡镇)	面积 平方千米	人口		居委会(行政村) 个
		户数 户	人口数 人	
坂中(畲族乡)	76	8 026	31 287	3+19(8个畲村)
穆云(畲族乡)	119	3 873	15 103	33(14个畲村)
康厝(畲族乡)	114	5 300	20 846	32(7个畲村)

1.2.2.2 Fu'an City

Fu'an City, under the jurisdiction of Ningde Municipality, was established in 1989 after its county administration was abolished. In 1993, it was put on the list of the open coastal cities to the outside world. It is between a latitude 26°41′-27°24′ north and a longitude 119° 23′-119°51′ east with an area of 1 795 square kilometers and a coastline of 145 kilometers long. Its total household number was 195 645 and its total population was 670 912 with a permanent population of 568 500. Its population density was 318 persons per square kilometer. Of the permanent population, 60 000 are the She ethnic people who make Fu'an the largest residential area for the She ethnic people in China. Fu'an has jurisdiction over 2 development zones, 4 sub-districts, 5 villages, 13 townships, 439 village residential committees and 108 ethnic villages. It gains such reputations as "the Capital of Medium & Small Motors in China","the Second Largest Private Ship Repairing and Building Base in China","the Hometown of Teas in China", "the Hometown of Grapes in South China", etc.

Through Fu'an City run Shenyang-Hainan Expressway, Wenzhou-Fuzhou Railway, Ningde-Wuyishan Expressway, Branch of Wanwu Peninsula Railway, Fu'an-Taishun Expressway and Ningde-Quzhou Railway. A traffic hub of railways, expressways and ports has been formed.

Fu'an enjoys rich water resources. The Jiaoxi River, one of the five major rivers in Fujian runs through it from north to south with a flowing area of 5 638 square kilometers. There are hydro power reserves of 341 000 kilowatts.

In the city, 15 metal and non-metal mines ane ascertained, of which molybdenum ore reserves reach 6 500 tons. Its forest vegetations are various with over 60 rare species such as Alsophila Spinulosa Tryon and glyptostrobus, etc. Baima Port here is a national Class-I open port. Its handling capacity is the top in Ningde City and is one of the earliest and finest deep water ports constructed in Fujian.

Fu'an City is abundant with tourism resources: There are White Cloud

Mountain, a global geopark; the Moulin Clusters, ancient glaciers of the Quaternary Age that are well kept in the lower latitude areas of China and one of the best and the most typical areas; the well preserved ancient castle buildings of the Song Dynasty in Liancun Village; the unique and ancient residential buildings of the Ming and Qing Dynasties in Baizhuyang Village; the exotic Xita Grapes Brook; and the colorful She ethnic traditions in the Xianxiu Mountain as well as the remaining site of the former Soviet-style government of the Red Army, etc.

Table of Basic Data of Sub-districts and Towns/Townships in Fu'an City

Name of Subdistrict/Town	Area square kilometers	Population		Number of Residential Committees /Villages
		Number of Households	Number of Residents	
Saiqi Township	77	15 924	53 206	7 + 24
Muyang Township	13	3 629	14 110	6 + 2
Gantang Township	91	9 072	36 279	1 + 32
Xiabaishi Township	117	7 820	30 505	1 + 41
Xibing Township	130	5 943	23 163	1 + 24
Shangbaishi Township	79	4 701	17 980	1 + 21
Shekou Township	102	4 828	18 830	24
Tangtou Township	168	7 505	30 192	29
Xiaoyang Township	96	1 721	6 831	10
Xiwei Township	65	3 305	10 730	1 + 14
Xitang Township	115	5 785	20 818	1 + 34
Wanwu Township	116	7 216	28 318	24
Chengyang Township	161	8 827	34 628	4 + 31
Fankeng Village	114	4 880	13 660	17
Songluo Village	87	5 064	10 790	19
Banzhong(She Village)	76	8 026	31 287	3 + 19 (8 She Villages)
Muyun(She Village)	119	3 873	15 103	33 (14 She Villages)
Kangcuo(She Village)	114	5 300	20 846	32 (7 She Villages)

（三）福鼎市

福鼎是宁德市下辖的一个县级市，1995 年撤县设市，地处福建省东北部。位于北纬 26°52′～27°26′，东经 119°55′～120°43′。全市土地总面积 1 526.3平方千米，海域面积 14 959.7平方千米，海岸线长 432.7 千米，有大小港湾 41 个，大小岛屿 81 个，最大为嵛山列岛，陆地面积 25.65 平方千米。台山渔场是闽东的主要渔区。最高峰青龙山海拔 1 141.3米，太姥山主峰覆鼎峰海拔 917.3 米。辖 3 个乡、10 镇、3 个街道、34 个居委会、251 个村委会。总户数 163 275户，总人口 597 965 人，常住人口 53.5 万人，人口密度 350 人/平方千米，福鼎先后荣获“中国白茶之乡”“中国化油器名城”“中国合成革名城”等称号。

境内 104 国道、沈海高速公路和温福铁路纵贯全境，水陆交通便捷。溪河纵横，主要河流有水北溪、赤溪、溪头溪、百步溪、照澜溪等 5 条溪流，主河道总长 158.5 千米，流域面积达 978.3 平方千米，鱼类有 500 多种，可供海洋捕捞的经济鱼达 100 多种。蕴藏丰富的潮汐能，国家水电部专家曾到八尺门考察，并拟在此建造年发电量可达 1 亿千瓦时，世界排名第二、亚洲排名第一的潮汐电站。

境内已探明主要矿产有 14 种。其中白琳大嶂山的玄武岩储存量 5 000万立方米，矿石裸露地表，呈墨黑色、色调凝重高雅，是中国罕见的高级建筑板材，属中国建筑石材基地之一，被国务院建材总局命名为“福鼎黑”，是全国十大石板材出口基地之一。

主要景点有太姥山、管阳雁溪、九鲤溪、小白鹭滨海浴场、翠郊古民居等。其中太姥山成功入选世界地质公园、国家自然遗产和 5A 级景区，并与嵛山岛同时获评“中国青年最喜爱的海西旅游目的地”，管阳雁溪入选“海西之美十佳景点”。

2014 年福鼎市，街道（乡镇）基本情况一览表

街道（乡镇）	面　积	人　口		居委会（行政村）
	平方千米	户数（户）	人口数（人）	个
管阳镇	198	9 367	29 980	27
贯岭镇	79.45	6 488	21 965	12
前岐镇	99.4	14 856	38 953	2+19
点头镇	120	11 529	34 760	3+18
白琳镇	130.33	11 130	30 175	1+20
店下镇	155	18 319	53 058	2+22
沙埕镇	38.12	9 862	23 954	3+19
太姥山镇	114.4	21 396	56 931	5+26
磻溪镇	224	7 364	20 965	18

续表

街道(乡镇)	面 积 平方千米	人 口		居委会(行政村) 个
		户数(户)	人口数(人)	
嵛山镇	26	1 548	3 588	5
叠石乡	80	5 639	13 210	14
佳阳乡	73	4 923	10 661	12
硖门乡	56	4 324	17 250	9

1.2.2.3 Fuding City

Fuding is a county-level city under the jurisdiction of Ningde Municipality. Its city administration was established after its county establishment was abolished in 1995. It is located in the northeast of Fujian province between the latitude of 26°52′-27°26′ north and a longitude of 119°55′-120°43′ east. Its total land area is 1 526.3 square kilometers with a sea area of 14 959.7 square kilometers and a coastline of 432.7 kilometers long. There are 41 bays and 81 islands of various sizes. The largest island is Yushan Island with an area of 25.14 square kilometers. Taishan Fishery is a major one in Ningde. Qinglong Mountain, with an altitude of 1 141.3 meters, is the highest in the local, and Fuding Peak, a major peak of Taimu Mountains, is 917.3 meters. Fuding City governs 3 villages, 10 townships,34 residential committees and 251 villages. The total household number is 163 275 with a population of 597 965 and a permanent population of 535 000. The population density is 350 persons per square kilometer. And Fuding City is awarded honors like "the Hometown of White Tea", "the Famous City for Carburetors in China", "the Famous City for Leather Products in China".

National Highway 104, Shengyang-Hainan Expressway and Wenzhou-Fuzhou Railway run through the city with convenient land and sea transportation. There are also many rivers intersecting Fuding City. The major ones are the Shuibeixi River, the Chixi River, the Xitouxi River, the Baibuxi River and the Zhaolanxi River, etc., with a total length of 158.5 kilometers and a total flowing area of 978.3 square kilometers. There are over 500 kinds of fish and more than 100 are economic fishes. Abundant tidal power is reserved. The experts from the National Hydro Power Ministry once inspected Bachimen and planned to build a tidal power station there which annually produces 100 million kilowatts/hour, and will rank the second in the world and the first in Asia.

Fuding is abundant with mineral resources and 14 of them are ascertained, of which the mine of the granite of the over 50 million cubic meters in Dazhang Mountain in Bailin Township is shallow and the granite can be seen and looks black and elegant. It is a high-grade building stone known as "Fuding Black Granite", according to the National Ministry of Construction. The city Fuding is one of the top ten major national stone export bases.

Fuding City is abundant with its tourism resources. The main scenic spots are Mount Taimu, the Yanxi River in Guanyang, the Jiulixi River, Xiaobailu Beach, Cuijiao Ancient Residence and so on, among which Mount Taimu successfully are enrolled onto the list of Global Geoparks, the national natural heritage list, and 5A scenic spot list. Yushan Island is honored "the most popular tourism destination in the Western Taiwan Straits for the national youths". Besides, the Yanxi River of Guanyang is enrolled onto one of "Ten Best Scenic Spots along the Western Taiwan Straits".

Table of Basic Data of Sub-districts and Towns/Townships in Fuding City

Name of Subdistrict/Town	Area square kilometers	Population		Number of Residential Committees /Villages
		Number of Households	Number of Residents	
Guanyang Town	198	9 367	29 980	27
Guanling Town	79. 45	6 488	21 965	12
Qianqi Town	99. 4	14 856	38 953	2 + 19
Diantou Town	120	11 529	34 760	3 + 18
Bailin Town	130. 33	11 130	30 175	1 + 20
Dianxia Town	155	18 319	53 058	2 + 22
Shacheng Town	38. 12	9 862	23 954	3 + 19
Taimushan Town	114. 4	21 396	56 931	5 + 26
Panxi Town	224	7 364	20 965	18
Yushan Town	26	1 548	3 588	5
Dieshi Village	80	5 639	13 210	14
Jiayang Village	73	4 923	10 661	12
Xiamen Village	56	4 324	17 250	9

(四)霞浦县

霞浦县是闽东最古老的县份,是福建最早开放的对台贸易口岸,地处福建省东北部,位于北纬 26°25′～27°9′,东经 119°46′～120°26′,全县土地面积 1 716平方千米,海域面积 29 592.6平方千米。浅海滩涂面积 104 万亩,大小岛屿 194 个,海岸线长 480 千米,大小岛屿 196 个,港口 138 个,辖 6 个乡、6 镇(含 3 个畲族乡)、2 个街道、23 个社区居委会、292 村委会。总户数 162 632户,总人口 554 597人,常住人口 46.3 万人,其中畲族人口 4.4 万人,人口密度 270 人/平方千米,是福建省畲族人口数量第二位的县份,国内著名滩涂摄影基地,素有“中国海带之乡”“中国紫菜之乡”“海滨邹鲁”之誉。

境内河流自成流域,自北向南入海。七都溪、罗汉溪、杯溪、三河、长溪等五大河流蕴藏着丰富的水力资源,总流域面积 635.2 平方千米,河流水能理论蕴藏量 7.42 万千瓦,地下水年蕴藏量近亿万立方米,潮汐能量巨大,开发条件优势。

境内交通条件较好,水路四通八达,内河、内海水道与外海航道贯通,东至台湾,北达沪宁,南抵港澳。福宁高速公路和温福铁路横贯全境,军用机场已投入使用,民用机场建设已启动,三沙港并入宁德港扩大开放,凸现闽东北陆海空立体交通网络的雏形。

境内海拔多在 700 米以上,最高峰目海尖有 1 192.4米,东南港湾岛屿众多,主要有“两洋三湾四港”(东吾洋、官井洋,三沙湾、福宁湾、牙城湾,三沙港、东冲港、吕峡港、盐田港),海洋鱼类 700 多种,滩涂生物 200 余种。

非金属矿产品种众多,硅石、石岗岩、沸石、蛭石、高岭土、紫砂土和石英砂、矿泉水等均占有一定优势。

霞浦县旅游景点富有地方特色,有唐贞观十二年日本空海高僧入唐求法的登陆点赤岸,人称海国桃源的杨家溪,省级文物保持单位大京城堡,名列《中国名胜词典》的塔岗虎镇塔,全国十大最美海岛之一、“海上明珠”——嵛山岛,佛教沩仰宗创立者灵佑禅师的出家修行之地东关建善寺,闽东小普陀之称的三沙留云洞,中国道教名山之一葛洪山,摄影宝地——北岐滩涂,畲族小说歌发祥地白露坑以及各具特色的沿海天然沙滩、岛屿、港湾。

2014 年霞浦县,街道(乡镇)基本情况一览表

街道(乡镇)	面　积	人　口		居委会(行政村)
	平方千米	户数(户)	人口数(人)	个
三沙镇	66	12 596	36 210	27
牙城镇	115	8 189	26 893	1+25
溪南镇	149	9 876	38 303	1+24

续表

街道(乡镇)	面 积	人 口		居委会(行政村)
	平方千米	户数(户)	人口数(人)	个
沙江镇	137	10 678	32 113	1+20
下浒镇	101	10 049	26 966	1+21
长春镇	202	15 688	41 727	27
柏洋乡	173	5 039	10 058	28
海岛乡	31	2 680	7 035	6
北壁乡	72	5 246	13 842	11
盐田(畲族乡)	154	7 850	18 371	1+22
水门(畲族乡)	150	5 094	10 188	23
崇儒(畲族乡)	142	5 131	10 557	27

1.2.2.4 Xiapu County

It is the oldest county in Ningde Municipality, and also the earliest trading port with Taiwan. It is located in the northeast of Fujian between a latitude of 26°25′-27°9′ north and a longitude of 119°46′-120°26′ east with a total area of 1 716 square kilometers. Its land area is 1 489. 6 square kilometers and its sea area is 29 592. 6 square kilometers, with 1. 04 million mu of shallow mud flats. There are 194 islands of various sizes and 138 ports with a coastline of 480 kilometers long. It governs 6 villages, 6 towns/townships (including 3 She ethnic minority villages), 2 sub-districts, 23 residential committees and 292 village committees, with total households of 162 632, a total population of 554 597, a permanent population of 463 000 and a population density of 270 persons per square kilometer, of whom 44 000 are the She ethnic people, which makes Xiapu second in number of the She ethnic people in the province. Xiapu is a popular place to take photos for its shallow mud flats, and enjoys honors like "the Hometown of Kelp", "the Hometown of Laver (Seaweed)" and "the Coastal Hometown to Scholars".

The rivers inside the county are complete with their systems flowing from north to south into the sea. The five rivers, the Qiduxi River, the Luohanxi River, the Beixi River, the Sanhe River and the Changxi River, contain rich hydro power resources with a flowing area of 635. 2 square kilometers. Their theoretic hydro power reserves are 74 200 kilowatts and the underground hydro power reserves annually reach nearly hundreds of millions cubic meters. In addition, Xiapu has huge tidal power and enjoys advantages for development.

Xiapu enjoys well developed transportation routes. The water routes reach out in all directions. The rivers and the bay routes and the outer navigation channels are well connected and can reach Taiwan in the east, Shanghai and Ningbo in the north, and Hong Kong and Guangzhou in the south. Fuzhou-Ningde Expressway and Wenzhou-Fuzhou Railway run through the county. A military airport is operational and the other civil airport is under construction. Sansha Port was integrated with Ningde Port, which highlights the early shape of the dimensional traffic networks by "land, sea and air" in northeastern Fujian.

Most of Xiapu is over 700 meters above the sea level with Mount Muhaijian being the highest at 1 192.4 meters. In its southeast, there are many ports, bays, islands and reefs. They are mainly Dongwuyang Bay, Guanjingyang Bay, Sansha Bay, Funing Bay, Yacheng Bay, Sansha Port, Dongchong Port, Lvxia Port and Yantian Port. There are over 700 kinds of fish in the sea there and 200 species living in shallow mud flats.

Xiapu is abundant with non-mental ores. There are some advantages here for developing silica, zeolite, vermiculite, kaolin, purple clay, quartz sand and mineral water, etc.

Xiapu enjoys unique local tourism resources: Chi'an, the landing spot by Kukai, a famous Japanese monk coming to China to learn Buddhism scriptures in the 12th year of Zhenguan of the Tang Dynasty; the Yangjiaxi River, a Shangrila by the coast; Dajing Fort, a provincial level protected scenic spot; Yushan Island, one of the ten most beautiful islands in China as well as "a bright pearl at sea"; Jianshan Temple, a pilgrimage place for Buddhist monks; Liuyun Cave in Sansha, a mini Putuo Temple in East Fujian; Gehong Mountain, one of the famous Taoist mountains in China; Beiqi Shallow Mud Flats, a photographer's precious designation; and Bailukeng Village, a birthplace for the unique She ethnic songs. In addition, there are also many characteristic coastal beaches, islands and bays.

Table of Basic Data of Sub-districts and Towns/Townships in Xiapu County

Name of Subdistrict/Town	Area square kilometers	Population		Number of Residential Committees /Villages
		Number of Households	Number of Residents	
Sansha Township	66	12 596	36 210	27
Yacheng Township	115	8 189	26 893	1 + 25
Xinan Township	149	9 876	38 303	1 + 24
Shajiang Township	137	10 678	32 113	1 + 20
Xiahu Township	101	10 049	26 966	1 + 21
Changchun Township	202	15 688	41 727	27
Baiyang Village	173	5 039	10 058	28
Haidao Village	31	2 680	7 035	6
Beibi Township	72	5 246	13 842	11
Xiantian(She's)	154	7 850	18 371	1 + 22
Shuimen(She's)	150	5 094	10 188	23
Congru(She's)	142	5 131	10 557	27

(5)古田县

古田是千年古县，是闽东土地面积第一山区农业大县，地处闽中部偏东北方，位于北纬 26°26′～26°63′，东经 118°，全县土地总面积 2 377 平方千米，总户数 131 241 户，总人口 432 112 人，常住人口为 32.67 万人，人口密度 170 人/平方千米。下辖 2 个街道、8 个镇、4 个乡，12 个居委会，275 个村委会。旅外华侨、外籍华人达 20 多万人，古田溪水电站为全国第一个地下电站，食用菌生产居世界第一，曾分别被评为全国体育先进县和全国文化模范县，素有“水电之乡”“食用菌之乡”“华侨之乡”“体育之乡”之称。

境内矿藏种类有金属矿和非金属矿 20 多种。经开发利用的金属矿有铁砂矿、铅、钨、锌及银等；非金属矿有砖瓦粘土、砂、石及高岭土和近年正在开发的花岗岩岩石板材、叶腊石等。古田境内交通便利，有外福铁路、闽江航道，316 国道和 203 省道贯穿境内，合肥高铁，京台高速公路等。

水力资源人均人均居全国之首，除闽江主干流外，还有古田溪、霍口溪和武步溪，主要溪河 25 条，主河道长 301 千米，流域面积 1 498.7 平方千米。水能理论蕴藏量 33.13 万千瓦，可开发水力资源 12 万千瓦。

旅游资源十分丰富，有 1 200 多年历史，国内外临水宫的祖殿国家 3A 级旅游景区翠屏湖，杉洋白溪草场，“八闽第一药泉”卓洋廖厝温泉，是休闲度假的好去处。

2014 年古田县，街道（乡镇）基本情况一览表

街道（乡镇）	面　积 平方千米	人　口		居委会（行政村） 个
		户数（户）	人口数（人）	
平湖镇	147	9 516	33 083	29
大桥镇	202	9 198	31 094	36
黄田镇	212	6 666	21 512	2+16
鹤塘镇	261	9 286	30 871	23
杉洋镇	259	7 993	24 286	22
凤都镇	164	6 207	20 140	17
水口镇	122	2 601	8 203	2+6
大甲镇	111	4 421	13 960	16
吉巷乡	201	8 941	27 330	24
泮洋乡	145	2 536	8 102	15
凤埔乡	196	4 227	14 035	13
卓洋乡	95	4 097	12 220	16

1.2.2.5 Gutian County

It boasts a history of county establishment over 1 000 years and is also the No. 1 agricultural county as the mountainous area is concerned. It is located in the middle area and a bit toward the northeast of Fujian Province between a latitude of 26°26′-26°63′ north and a longitude of 118° east with a total land area of 2 377 square kilometers. There are total households of 131 241, with a total population of 432 112, a permanent population of 326 700, and a population density at 170 persons per square kilometer. Gutian County governs 2 sub-districts, 8 towns/townships, 4 villages and 12 residential committees, 275 village committees with over 200 000 overseas Chinese. Gutianxi Hydro Power Station is the first national underground station. The production of mushrooms and fungi there is the best in the world. Gutian was awarded many honors like "the National Advanced County for Sports", "the National Model County of Culture", "the Hometown of Hydro Power", "the Hometown of Edible Fungi", "the Hometown of Overseas Chinese", "the Hometown of Sports" and so on.

There are reserves of over 20 mental and non-mental ores. Those exploited metal ores include iron, aluminum, tungsten, zinc, silver, etc. And the non-mental ones are clay for bricks and tiles, sand, stone, kaolin and so on. Recent years have seen much exploitation of all kinds of granite, pyrophyllite, etc. Transportation in Gutian is convenient. Waiyang-Fuzhou Railway, the shipping route of the Minjiang River, National Highway 316, Provincial Highway 203, Hefei-Fuzhou High-speed Railway and Beijing-Taiwan Expressway all run through Gutian.

Gutian County is abundant with hydro power resources and its per capita hydro power resources are the highest in the nation. The Minjiang River flows through it besides the Gutianxi River, the Huokouxi River and the Wubuxi River. There are 25 major rivers. Their main shipping routes are 301 kilometers long with a flowing area of 1 498. 7 square kilometers. The theoretic hydro power reserve are 331 300 kilowatts and the exploitable amount is 120 000 kilowatts.

Gutian is also rich in tourism resources. There are the Cuiping Lake, a national AAA scenic spot; Baixi Grassland of Shanyang Township; and Miaocuo Hot Spring at Zhuoyang Village, boasting to be the "No. 1 Hot Spring with Medical Effect in Fujian", a nice resort for leisure and vacation.

Table of Basic Data of Sub-districts and Towns/Townships in Gutian County

Name of Subdistrict/Town	Area square kilometer	Population		Number of Residential Committees /Villages
		Number of Households	Number of Residents	
Pinghu Town	147	9 516	33 083	29
Daqiao Town	202	9 198	31 094	36
Huangtian Town	212	6 666	21 512	2 + 16
Hetang Town	261	9 286	30 871	23
Shanyang Town	259	7 993	24 286	22
Fengdu Town	164	6 207	20 140	17
Shuikou Town	122	2 601	8 203	2 + 6
Dajia Town	111	4 421	13 960	16

Continued

Name of Subdistrict/Town	Area square kilometer	Population		Number of Residential Committees /Villages
		Number of Households	Number of Residents	
Jixiang Village	201	8 941	27 330	24
Banyang Village	145	2 536	8 102	15
Fengpu Village	196	4 227	14 035	13
Zhuoyang Village	95	4 097	12 220	16

(六)屏南县

屏南县位于福建省东北部，地理坐标为北纬 26°44～27°10′，东经 118°41′～119°13′，全县土地面积 1 485 平方千米，总户数 57 595 户，总人口 190 665 人，常住人口为 13.67 万人，人口密度 114 人/平方千米，下辖 7 个乡、4 个镇、7 个居委会、152 个村委会，海外约有 8 万华人华侨，其中以旅居东南亚的为主。屏南县是福建省 26 个重点苏区和林区县之一、典型的山区农业县、省定 26 个重点侨乡之一、全国唯一的省级鸳鸯猕猴自然保护区。

全县平均海拔 830 米，大小山峰 300 余座，千米以上山峰达 265 座。岭下乡东峰尖海拔 1 627 米，为境内最高峰。有大小溪流 186 条，分霍童溪、古田溪两大水系，流域面积 60 平方千米以上，主要溪流有 7 条。已知的矿产资源主要有铅锌、铁、铜锌、硫黄、锰、高岭土、镁、花岗石、稀土等。

交通便捷，203 省道穿境而过，屏宁二级公路和宁武高速公路的通车更大程度上方便了屏南这个小山城与外界的交流，也把如斯美景带入更多人的眼眸。

旅游资源十分丰富，有鸳鸯溪、白水洋 5A 级国家重点风景名胜区，世界唯一的鸳鸯猕猴自然保护区，每年有数千对鸳鸯来此越冬，有第六批国家重点文物保护单位——万安桥为五墩六孔木拱廊屋桥等。

2014 年屏南县，街道(乡镇)基本情况一览表

街道(乡镇)	面 积 平方千米	人 口		居委会(行政村) 个
		户数(常住)	人口数(常住)	
古峰镇	20	14 488	45 801	5
双溪镇	183	2 656	9 378	1+14
黛溪镇	150	4 500	14 687	22
长桥镇	142	3 308	11 305	18

续表

街道(乡镇)	面积 平方千米	人口		居委会(行政村) 个
		户数(常住)	人口数(常住)	
屏城乡	143	2 428	7 938	1+12
棠口乡	164	3 799	12 762	17
甘棠乡	117	2 556	8 520	17
熙岭乡	102	2 489	8 177	16
路下乡	166	1 847	6 334	11
寿山乡	106	1 396	4 484	14
岭下乡	152	2 161	7 314	11

1.2.2.6 Pingnan County

It is located in the northeast of Fujian Province, with a latitude of 26°44-27°10′ north and a longitude of 118°41′-119°13′ east. Its total area is 1 485 square kilometers. Its household number is 57 595 with a total population of 190 665, of which 136 700 are permanent residents with a population density at 114 persons per square kilometer. It governs 7 villages, 4 towns, 7 residential committees and 152 village committees. There are over 80 000 overseas Chinese from here, mainly settling in southeastern Asia. It is one of the key red army bases and forest counties. It is also a typical mountainous agricultural county and a hometown for overseas Chinese designated by Fujian province. There is a only natural reserve at the provincial level for mandarin ducks and macaques in China.

The average altitude of the county is 830 meters with about 300 mountains of various sizes, of which 265 are over an altitude of 1 000 meters. Peak Dongfengjian within Lingxia Village is 1 627 meters, the highest one in Pingnan County. There are 186 rivers of various length in Pingnan which belongs to two major water systems of the Huotongxi River and the Gutianxi River, of which 7 main ones flowing over an area of more than 60 square kilometers. Besides, the surveyed mineral resources include lead, zinc, iron, bronze, sulfur, manganese, kaolin, magnesium, granite and rare earth, etc.

Pingnan enjoys convenient traffic condition. Provincial Highway 203, Pingnan-Ningde grade-Ⅱ Highway, Ningde-Wuyishan Expressway run through the county.

It is also abundant with tourism resources. There are five-A national scenic spots like Mandarin Duck River Scenic Spot and Baishuiyang River Square, etc. The only nature reserve in the world for mandarin ducks and macaques locates here and attracts thousands of mandarin ducks in winter. There is also the Wan'an Bridge with its 5 columns, 6 arches and covered top; the bridge was enrolled onto the 6th Batch of the National Key Cultural Relics for Protection.

Table of Basic Data of Sub-districts and Towns/Townships in Pingnan County

Name of Subdistrict/Town	Area square kilometers	Population		Number of Residential Committees /Villages
		Number of Households	Number of Residents	
Gufeng Town	20	14 488	45 801	5
Shangxi Town	183	2 656	9 378	1 + 14
Daixi Town	150	4 500	14 687	22
Changqiao Town	142	3 308	11 305	18
Pingcheng Town	143	2 428	7 938	1 + 12
Dangkou Town	164	3 799	12 762	17
Gantang Town	117	2 556	8 520	17
Xiling Town	102	2 489	8 177	16
Luxia Town	166	1 847	6 334	11
Shoushan Town	106	1 396	4 484	14
Lingxia Town	152	2 161	7 314	11

（七）周宁县

周宁县位于闽东北山区，地处北纬 26°53′～27°19′，东经 119°06′～119°29′。全县土地面积 1 047 平方千米，总户数 60 334 户，总人口 212 477 人，常住人口 11.29 万人，人口密度 156 人/平方千米。辖 3 乡、6 镇、7 个居委会、140 个村委会。全县平均海拔 800 米，县城海拔 880 多米，居全省之冠，森林覆盖率达 72%，空气质量达到国家一级标准，县城夏无酷暑，气候凉爽宜人，被誉为“天然空调城”，素有“高山明珠”之称。

境内主要溪流 18 条，最大的龙亭溪境内流长 56 千米，水系发达，天然落差大，可开发利用水能达 57.13 万千瓦，已开发和正在开发的水能资源达 53.87 万千瓦。

交通方便，有宁武和宁上两条高速公路贯穿境内。公路以 302 省道为主干。已探明的矿藏有 16 种，矿藏地 27 处，其中中小型矿床 7 个，矿石 20 个，各类矿化点 28 个。

旅游资源丰富，境内有省级风景名胜区九龙漈瀑布群、中华奇观鲤鱼溪、"八闽首景"滴水岩、省级森林仙风山、人工高山湖泊芹山湖、佛教圣地方广寺、千年古刹灵峰寺、闽东的西双版纳后垄大峡以及蝙蝠洞。纪念地有中共闽东特委旧址、大前坪红军修械所旧址等一批闻名遐迩的旅游景点。

2014 年周宁县县，街道（乡镇）基本情况一览表

街道（乡镇）	面积	人口		居委会（行政村）
	平方千米	户数（户）	人口数（人）	个
狮城镇	58	15 312	24 645	6+8
咸村镇	164	6 700	14 451	1+23
浦源镇	106	8 128	16 290	17
七步镇	115	5 229	10 382	20
李墩镇	89	3 682	9 649	10
纯池镇	208	6 386	13 446	18
泗桥乡	100	4 860	9 322	12
礼门乡	134	4 168	7 500	17
玛坑乡	73	4 485	7 186	15

1.2.2.7 Zhouning County

Zhouning County, located in the mountains of the northeast of Fujian between a latitude of 26°53′-27°19′ north and a longitude of 119°06′-119°29′ east, covers a land area of 1 047 square kilometers. Its total number of households is 60 334 with a total population of 212 477 and a permanent population of 112 900, at a population density of 156 persons per square kilometer. It governs 6 townships, 3 villages, 140 village committees, 7 residential committees. Its average altitude is 800 meters above the sea level, which is the highest in Fujian province. Its forest coverage rate is 72% with its air quality up to Class I National Standard, and the climate is pleasant with no extremely hot summers. It is praised as "A Natural Air-conditioning County in Summer" and "A Mountainous Pearl", etc.

There are 18 major rivers inside Zhouning. And the Longting River is the largest and flows over 56 kilometers with huge natural falls. The exploitable hydro power quantity reaches 571 300 kilowatts, and the amount that is developed or under development has been up to 538 700 kilowatts. In addition, Zhouning has convenient access including Provincial Highway 302 and Ningde-Shangrao Expressway.

Zhouning is abundant with mineral resources. Sixteen kinds of minerals have been ascertained and 27 mines have been found, of which 7 are medium and small mineral beds, 20 are stone mines and 28 are mineral and chemical ones.

There are abundant tourism resources in Zhouning: Jiulongji Waterfalls; Carps Stream, a wonder in China; Dripping Rock, regarded as the No.1 View in Fujian; Xianfengshan Mountain, a provincial-level forest farm; Qinshan Lake, an artificial reservoir; Fangguangshi Temple, a pilgrimage site for Buddhists; Lingfeng Temple, with a history of over 1 000 years; Houlong Canyon and the Bat Cave, a tropical Shangarila in Ningde; former sites of the Mindong Special Committee of the CPC, and Daqianping Weapons Factory for the Red Army and so on.

Table of Basic Data of Sub-districts and Towns/Townships in Zhouning County

Name of Subdistrict/Town	Area square kilometers	Population		Number of Residential Committees /Villages
		Number of Households	Number of Residents	
Shicheng Township	58	15 312	24 645	6+8
Xiancun Township	164	6 700	14 451	1+23
Puyuan Township	106	8 128	16 290	17
Qibu Township	115	5 229	10 382	20
Lidun Township	89	3 682	9 649	10
Chunchi Township	208	6 386	13 446	18
Siqiao Village	100	4 860	9 322	12
Limen Village	134	4 168	7 500	17
Makeng Village	73	4 485	7 186	15

(八)寿宁县

寿宁县地处闽东北部,位于北纬27°11′～27°41′,东经119°14′～119°44′,闽浙两省交界,素有"两省门户,五界通衢"及"九山半水半分田"之称。全县土地面积1 425平方千米,辖8乡、6镇、9个居委会、196个委会村,总户数79 664户,总人口275 090人,常住人口17.63万人,人口密度162人/平方千米。全县夏季均温只有20～25℃,被誉为福建夏季最凉爽的避暑胜地;盛产花菇且产量居全国首位,由此被誉为"中国花菇之乡";拥有保存较完好的明清时代贯木拱廊桥19座,被誉为"世界木拱廊桥之乡";有传承三百多年的北路戏,被称为"戏剧孤本",列入中国国家非物质文化遗产名录。

境内还蕴含着丰富的水力资源。全县大小溪流170多条,其中流域面积在100平方千米以上的河流5条,水能蕴藏量27万千瓦,可开发利用的水力资源达21万千瓦,有水电装机容量4万千瓦,年发电量达1.5亿千瓦时,跻身福建省"水电十强县"之列。

已探明金属和非金属矿产21种,其中,叶腊石、石英石、明矾、白云石储量丰富,南阳镇铁场、坝头的白云石矿是省内最大的炼镁用白云石矿,储量达561万吨;平溪乡湖潭叶腊石矿、坑底乡杨梅州石英石矿、下党乡七宝岗钨矿等,都具有较高的开采价值。

境内有福寿和福泰两条高速公路贯穿境内,公路密度居全省前列,主要公路干经有省枫湖线,县道寿泰线、斜镇线、竹洋线,形成了连接浙江庆元、泰顺、景宁,沟通福安、周宁、政和等地的公路网络。

寿宁县著名的旅游景区有"世界贯木拱廊桥之乡"寿宁廊桥,"海西十佳魅力乡村"西浦村,芎坑原始森林,杨梅洲,仙岩,南山风等。

2014年寿宁县,街道(乡镇)基本情况一览表

街道(乡镇)	面积	人口		居委会(行政村)
	平方千米	户数(户)	人口数(人)	个
鳌阳镇	48	15 887	53 007	6+3
斜滩镇	157	4 955	15 596	1+15
南阳镇	122	5 759	19 124	20
武曲镇	60	2 603	8 360	12
犀溪镇	130	3 119	8 658	12
平溪镇	124	2 503	6 632	18
大安乡	111	4 278	14 222	16

续表

街道(乡镇)	面 积 平方千米	人 口		居委会(行政村) 个
		户数(户)	人口数(人)	
坑底乡	192	2 689	6 766	20
清源乡	79	3 751	10 332	16
竹管垄乡	40	5 551	10 195	9
芹洋乡	86	1 575	4 416	17
托溪乡	122	2 650	7 880	15
凤阳乡	86	2 896	8 762	13
下党乡	68	1 935	2 350	10

1.2.2.8 Shouning County

Shouning County is located in the northeast of Fujian Province along the border with Zhejiang Province between a latitude of 27°11′-27°41′ north and a longitude of 119°14′-119°44′ east. It is well known for being "Gates to two provinces and hubs for five counties" and for its geographic features of "90% mountains, 5% rivers and 5% fields". Its total land area covers 1 425 square kilometers. It governs 8 villages, 6 townships, 9 residential committees and 196 village committees. Its number of households is 79 664 and its population was 275 090 with 176 300 permanent residents at a population density of 162 persons per square kilometer. The average summer temperature is between 20-25℃, so it is praised to be the coolest summer resort in Fujian. Because of its abundant output of flora mushrooms, the largest quantity in the country, Shouning is honored to be the "Hometown of Flora Mushrooms in China". There are 19 well preserved wooden arch bridges of the Ming and Qing dynasties in Shouning, so it is also named the "Hometown of the Covered Wooden Arch Bridges in the World". The Northern Road Play, honored as "the Unique Play", has been performed for over 300 years, and is listed onto the national intangible cultural heritage catalog of China.

Shouning County stores rich hydro power resources in the county with more than 170 rivers of various sizes, of which five major rivers flow through an area of 100 square kilometers each. The hydro power reserve reaches 270 000 kilowatts, of which the exploitable amount is up 210 000 kilowatts. The installed capacity of hydro power is 40 000 kilowatts with an annual output of

150 million kilowatts/hour, so Shouning becomes one of the "Ten Strongest Counties in Hydro Power in Fujian".

There are 21 metal and non-metal ores that have been ascertained in Shouning, of which the reserves of pyrophyllite, dolomite, quartz and alum are abundant. The mines of "White Cloud Ore" in Tiechang Village and Batou Village of Nanyang Township are the largest mines of magnesium in Fujian with reserves of 5.61 million tons. Besides, the pyrophyllite ore in Hutang of Pingxi Village, the quartz ore in Yangmeizhou of Kengdi Village and the tungsten ore in Qibaogang of Xiadang Village, etc., are of high exploitation value.

The density of highways in Shouning ranks top in Fujian. The major highways are Fengyang-Hutangban Highway, a provincial line; Shouning-Taishun Highway, Xietang-Zhenqian Highway, Zhuguanlong-Yangtou Highway and all county lines. They form a road network linking Qingyuan, Taishun, Jingning of Zhejiang Province, and Fu'an, Zhounning and Zhenghe, etc. There are buses in Shouning to cities like Shanghai, Xiamen, Fuzhou, Shaowu, Rui'an and Yiwu, etc.

The famous scenic spots in Shouning are: Shouning Covered Wooden Arch Bridge; Xipu Village, one of the most glamorous villages in the Westem Taiwan Strait Economic Development Zone; the Primitive Forest in Gongkeng; Yangmeizhou Shangrila; Xipu Village; the Immortal Rock and the Nanshan Mountain, etc.

Table of Basic Data of Sub-districts and Towns/Townships in Shouning County

Name of Subdistrict/Town	Area square kilometers	Population		Number of Residential Committees /Villages
		Number of Households	Number of Residents	
Aoyang Town	48	15 887	53 007	6 + 3
Xietang Town	157	4 955	15 596	1 + 15
Nanyang Town	122	5 759	19 124	20
Wuqu Town	60	2 603	8 360	12
Xixi Town	130	3 119	8 658	12
Pingxi Town	124	2 503	6 632	18

Continued

Name of Subdistrict/Town	Area square kilometers	Population		Number of Residential Committees /Villages
		Number of Households	Number of Residents	
Da'an Village	111	4 278	14 222	16
Kengdi Village	192	2 689	6 766	20
Qingyuan Village	79	3 751	10 332	16
Zhuguanlong Village	40	5 551	10 195	9
Qingyang Village	86	1 575	4 416	17
Tuoxi Village	122	2 650	7 880	15
Fengyang Village	86	2 896	8 762	13
Xiadang Village	68	1 935	2 350	10

(九)柘荣县

柘荣县是闽东北的内陆山区县，位于北纬 27°05′～27°19′，东经 119°43′～120°04′，全县总面积 544 平方千米，总户数 34 036 户，总人口 109 233 人，常住人口 8.9 万人，人口密度 168 人/平方千米，辖 7 个乡、2 个镇、4 个居委会、112 委会村。柘荣县是全省人口最少、区域面积最小的一个县，是闽浙两省边界贸易点、国务院批准对外开放的全国 55 个县市之一，是国家级生态示范区，有“中国太子参之乡”“中国民间文化艺术之乡”的美誉。

境内大部分地区海拔在 400～1000 米之间，城关海拔 668 米，平均海拔 600 米左右，水力资源丰富，主要溪流有龙溪、交溪、西溪和东溪等，全县可开发的水资源有 216 处，总装机容量为 10 万千瓦，已开发利用 4.26 万千瓦。

境内蕴含的矿产资源有铁、石英、铅锌、明矾、硫黄。已探明的矿产有高岭土、紫砂陶土、明矾、石英、花岗岩、辉绿岩等 10 多个品种，尤其是紫砂蕴藏量高达 260 万吨，其品质可与江苏宜兴紫砂相媲美，素有“北有宜兴，南有柘荣”之称；辉绿岩、花岗岩成材率较高，年开采量分别可达 1 万立方米。

柘荣县著名的旅游景区有省级风景名胜——东狮山和九龙井景区，也是泛太姥山旅游度假区、闽东北亲水游线路的重要组成部分。此外还有仙屿公园、明游朴墓、凤岐古民居、袁天禄纪念馆，纪念地有闽东独立师兵工厂旧址、闽东苏维埃政府主席马立峰殉难地等。

2014 年柘荣县县,街道(乡镇)基本情况一览表

街道(乡镇)	面 积 平方千米	人 口		居委会(行政村) 个
		户数(户)	人口数(人)	
双城镇	11	12 665	40 023	4+1
富溪镇	48	2 048	5 855	11
城郊乡	72	3 155	10 860	15
乍洋乡	80	1 945	5 120	13
东源乡	123	3 217	9 945	18
黄柏乡	76	1 611	4 894	16
宅中乡	35	1 394	3 541	9
楮坪乡	49	2 184	6 120	15
英山乡	52	1 288	3 676	14

1.2.2.9 Zherong County

Zherong is a mountainous inland county between a latitude of 27°05′-27°19′ north and a longitude of 119°43′-120°04′ east with a total land area of 544 square kilometers. Its total household number is 34 036 with a total population of 109 233 and a permanent population of 890 000 at a population density of 168 persons per square kilometer. It governs 7 villages, 2 townships, 4 residential committees, and 112 village committees. It has the smallest population and covers the least area in Fujian. It is also an experimental trading spot on the border between Fujian and Zhejiang, one of the 55 counties or cities approved by the State Council to be open to the outside world, as well as a national model of ecological development. It wins honors like the "Hometown of Taizi Ginseng in China" and the "Hometown of Civil Arts and Culture in China".

Most of Zherong is between 400-1 000 meters above the sea level with its county proper at 668 meters and an average altitude of 600 meters. It is abundant with hydro power resources. The major rivers are the Longxi River, the Jiaoxi River, the Xixi River, and the Dongxi River, etc. There are 216 spots in Zherong that are worth developing for hydro power. Its total installed capacity is estimated at 100 000 kilowatts and 42 600 kilowatts have been developed.

There are rich reserves in Zherong of mineral resources such as iron, quartz, lead, zinc, alum and sulphur. Those that are ascertained are kaolinite, purple sand clay, alum, quartz, granite, diabase and so on. More than 10 ores, especially the purple clay reserves, are up to 2. 6 million tons, with high quality comparable to those of Yixing, the hometown of purple clay in Jiangsu province in China. Therefore, there is a saying, "Yixing is famous for its purple clay in the north, so is Zherong in the south". Its raw diabase and granite yield higher output with an annual production reaching 10 000 cubic meters.

The famous scenic spot for tourism in Zherong is Dongshi Mountain and Jiulongjing Scenic Spot, both at provincial level. They are an important part of the extended Taimu Mountain Resort Area and the Waterside Travel Routes in the Northeast of Fujian. In addition, there are other sites like Xianyu Park, Graveyard of Scholar You Pu of the Ming Dynasty, Ancient Residence in Fengqi, Memorial Hall to Yuan Tianlu, etc. There are also some memorial sites for the Red Army like the Former Weapon-making Site for the Independent Division of East Fujian and the Sacrifice Place of Ma Lifeng, the former Chairman of the Soviet-style Government of East Fujian and so on.

Table of Basic Data of Sub-districts and Towns/Townships in Zherong County

Name of Subdistrict/Town	Area square kilometers	Population		Number of Residential Committees /Villages
		Number of Households	Number of Residents	
Shuangcheng Town	11	12 665	40 023	4 + 1
Fuxi Township	48	2 048	5 855	11
Chengjiao Village	72	3 155	10 860	15
Zayang Village	80	1 945	5 120	13
Dongyuan Village	123	3 217	9 945	18
Huangbai Village	76	1 611	4 894	16
Zhaizhong Village	35	1 394	3 541	9
Chuping Village	49	2 184	6 120	15
Yingshan Village	52	1 288	3 676	14

第二章 历史与时政

Chapter 2 Ningde：Past and Present

第一节 历 史

2.1 Past of Ningde：Facts and Figures

一、宁德的历史发展

宁德属东南沿海印纹陶文化系统，历史源远流长，早在旧石器时期就有人类活动，新石器时代已有一定规模的闽越族在这里劳动生息，他们主要靠渔猎为生，并从事原始农耕。

历史上宁德在夏、商、周时属古扬州；春秋属越，战国属楚；秦属闽中郡；汉初属闽越国，汉武帝时归会稽；三国时属吴国。晋太康三年(282)，划侯官县(今福州)，温麻船屯设温麻县(治所在今霞浦县沙江镇古县村)，属晋安郡。唐武德六年(623)改为长溪县，属泉州(州治今福州)；唐开成年间(836—840)，将长溪县的宁川和古田县东北划为感德场。后唐长兴四年(933)升场置县，取宁川之“宁”、感德之“德”为之命名，而有宁德县，属长乐府。宋淳祐五年(1245)增设福安县，与长溪、宁德皆属福州。

秦汉时期，闽越族先民曾两次被迫迁往江淮一带，中原汉族则不断迁居境内。三国时期，东吴从建安元年(196)至 257 年加强对闽中的统治。吴国于 260 年实现了以文治代替武人统治的局面。此时，江南汉族居民分别由海路和陆路入境，尤其是闽东和闽北，他们带来的语言奠定了闽东和闽北方言的基础。约公元 3 世纪中叶，孙吴政权在今霞浦沿海开设了造船工场“温麻船屯”，建造了许多海船，它的创办为闽东沿海的开发集聚了一大批精干劳动力和技术人才，开通了沿海航线，辽阔的福宁湾成了闽东人走向海洋的第一站。伴随着迈向海洋的步伐，闽东揭开了有志可考的历史。

王审知入闽时，曾经充当其向导的一支畲族先民也跟随着从闽西经闽南迁入闽东，在今天的福鼎落户。他们在有水源的地方"开山为田"，在"高山无水之处，栽种山苗"，胼手胝足，开发了大量水、旱梯田。闽东农作物出现了不少优良品种。随着流入大量北方移民，人口的大幅度增加，一部分原来从事粮食生产的农民，转而以经济作物为主。如油麻、可以织布的葛、荔枝、龙眼、茶业、杉木等，促进了宁德农业发展。

2.1.1 Historical Development of Ningde

Ningde belongs to the stamped pottery cultural category of the southeast coast in China with a long history. As early as in the Paleolithic Age, there were human beings living here. In the Neolithic Age, there were quite many people of the Minyue Clan living and working here already. They mainly lived on fishing and hunting, and started some primitive farming.

In history, Ningde was a part of Ancient Yangzhou during the dynasties of Xia, Shang and Zhou. During the Spring and Autumn Period, it was a part of Kingdom Yue. In the Warring States Period, it was a part of Kingdom Chu. During the Qin Dynasty, it was a part of Minzhong Prefecture. At the beginning of the Han Dynasty, it belonged to Minyue Kingdom. During the reign of Emperor Wudi of the Han Dynasty, it was a part of Kuaiji. In the period of the Three Kingdoms, it was a part of Kingdom Wu. In the third year (282AD) of the Taikang period of the Jin Dynasty, Wenma County was established (its government is now at Guxian Village, Shajiang Township, Xiapu County), and became a part of Jin'an. During the sixth year (623AD) of the Wude period of the Tang Dynasty, Wenma County was changed to Changxi County, under jurisdiction of Quanzhou (now Fuzhou). During the Kaicheng period (836-840AD) of the Tang Dynasty, Ningchuan Township of Changxi County and the northeast of Gutian County were rezoned together to become Gan De Chang Township. During the fourth year (933AD) of the Changxing period of the later Tang Dynasty, Gan De Chang Township was promoted to county administration. Therefore "Ning" in Ning Chuan and "De" in Gan De Chang were joined together to name NingDe County, which was under jurisdiction of Changle Prefecture. In the fifth year (1245AD) of the Chunyou period of the Song Dynasty, Fu'an County was established, which was under the jurisdiction of Fuzhou City with Changxi and Ningde Counties.

During the Qin and Han dynasties, the ancestors of the Minyue Clan were twice forced to immigrate to the regions around the Yangtze River and the Huaihe River while the Han people in Central China moved to Fujian. In the period of the Three Kingdoms, Kingdom Wu, from its first year of Jian'an to 257AD, enforced its rule of Central Fujian. In 260 AD Kingdom Wu achieved a government governed by intellectuals instead of army men. At this time the Han people from the south of the Yangtze River arrived at East and North Fujian by sea and land. The languages they brought became the foundation of the dialects in East and North Fujian. In about the mid period of the third century AD, Kingdom Wu established a shipbuilding yard called "Wenma Shipyard" in coastal Xiapu and built a lot of ships. The establishment attracted lots of able laborers and technological talents, with coastal routes opened. Since then the wide Funing Bay became the first step for the people in East Fujian to reach the oceans, and Min Dong (Ningde) began to open a new page with a recorded history.

When Wang Shenzhi came to Fujian, a She ethnic group, serving as his guides, migrated from West Fujian to South Fujian and finally came to Fuding of Min Dong (Ningde). They settled down in what is now Fuding. They opened up the land where there was water to be rice paddies. They planted mountainous water-friendly seedlings where there was no water. They toiled and moiled to open up lot of rice paddies and dry terrace lands. After that they cultivated many fine agricultural species in the local places. With the coming of many northerners, the population increased rapidly. Some farmers who grew grains shifted to cultivation of economic products like camellia trees, kudzu vines, lychees, longans, teas and firs, etc. In this way agriculture in Ningde was promoted.

唐末五代时期,王审知上任伊始就致力于黄岐港的开凿、疏浚,历时 6 年,于 904 年竣工。唐昭宗赐名"甘棠港"。甘棠港的开辟,有利于加强福建与中原的联系,改善了福建尤其是闽东地区的交通条件,促进了福建海外贸易的发展,从而推动了福建特别是闽东的开发。甘棠港开通后,海运蒸蒸日上,对外贸易盛况空前,黄岐一跃成为福建名镇,其经济繁荣持续了 200 多年,明代时改称下白石。

元至元二十三年(1286)长溪县升为福宁州,辖福安、宁德两县,清雍正十二年

(1734),福宁州升为福宁府,隶属福建闽浙总督府,辖福安、宁德、霞浦、寿宁 4 县。

光绪二十五年(1899)清廷在三都成立福海关,三都澳正式开放为对外贸易港口,与英、美、德、日、俄、葡萄牙、西班牙、荷兰、瑞典等十三个国家的 21 家公司建立贸易关系,这些国家在此开办洋行或分公司,三都澳由此繁荣起来。到了清光绪二十六年(1900),经三都口岸进口的货物种类有日本、印度的棉纱,有香港产的各色布匹,英国羽毛、煤油、火柴及铁丝、铁钉等。清宣统三年(1911),当时进口的货物主要是火柴、煤油、铁钉、铁丝、铅块以及卷烟、棉布、棉纱等。

辛亥革命后,1913 年废府,闽东先后属东路、闽海道、第二、第一、第八行政督察区。1949 年 9 月 30 日,闽东区成立第三行政督察专员公署,辖福安、宁德、福鼎(11 月划入)、霞浦、寿宁、周宁、柘荣等 7 县,隶属福建省人民政府。1999 年 11 月 14 日,国务院批准宁德撤地设市,成立宁德市人民政府,2000 年 11 月 14 日正式挂牌。宁德市人民政府驻新设立的蕉城区,全市辖 9 个县(市、区)。

At the end of the Tang Dynasty and the beginning of the Five-Dynasty Period, when Wang Shenzhi was appointed, he devoted himself to opening up and smoothing the navigation routes of Huangqi Port for 6 years. The project was completed in 904AD. Emperor Zhaozong of the Tang Dynasty named it "Gantang Port". With its launch, the connection with central China was strengthened and the transportation in Fujian, especially in Min Dong, was improved so that outbound trade in Fujian was boosted and the opening and development of FuJian, particularly Min Dong, was pushed forward. After Gantang Port was open, the shipping industry prospered and the outbound trade boomed. Huangqi Town, where the port was, rapidly rose up and became famous in Fujian with its economy booming for over 200 years. During the Ming Dynasty, its name was changed to its present name: Xiabaishi.

In the 23rd year of Zhiyuan of the Yuan Dynasty (1286AD), Changxi County was promoted to Funing Prefecture, administering Fu'an and Ningde, which were parts of Fuzhou. During the 12th year of Emperor Yongzheng's reign (1734AD), Funing Prefecture was promoted to Funing Fu (Mega Prefecture), affiliated to General Administration of Fujian and Zhejiang administering four counties of Fu'an, Ningde, Xiapu and Shouning.

In the 25th year (1899AD) of Emperor Guangxu of the Qing Dynasty, Fuhai Customs was set up in Sandu Island. Since then, Sandu Port had been opened formally to trade with 21 companies from 13 countries like the UK, the USA, Germany, Japan, Russia, Portugal, Spain, Holland, Sweden and so on.

Foreign banks or branches were established here, which contributed to Sandu Island's prosperity. Till the 26th year (1900AD) of Emperor Guangxu, the imported goods by Sandu Port included the cotton yarn from Japan and India, all kinds of cloth from Hong Kong and those pinions, kerosene, matches, wires and nails, etc. from the UK. In the 3rd year (1911AD) of Emperor Xuantong of the Qing Dynasty, the main items of import were matches, kerosene, nails, wires, lead chunk, cigarettes, cotton cloth and yarn, etc.

After the 1911 Revolution, the Fu Administration was abolished in 1913. Min Dong in time sequence was governed by Donglu Prefecture, Minhaidao Prefecture, the Second, the First, and the Eighth Administrative Inspection Zones, etc. On September 30, 1949, the Third Administrative Inspection Bureau was set up in Min Dong in administration of Fu'an, Ningde, Fuding (which was included in November), Xiapu, Shouning, Zhouning, Zherong. The 7 counties were under the jurisdiction of the People's Government of Fujian. On November 14, 1999, approved by the State Council, Ningde Prefectural Administration was abolished and Ningde Municipal Administration was established with its government location in Jiaocheng District. Ningde Municipality administers 9 counties and cities.

以下是宁德市各行政区划的名称及人民政府所在地：

宁德市辖1个市辖区、6个县，代管2个县级市。

蕉城区：(区人民政府驻八一五中路)

东侨开发：(东侨新区)(直属于宁德市)管委会驻地闽东路。

福安市：市人民政府驻城北街道

福鼎市：市人民政府驻桐山街道

寿宁县：县人民政府驻鳌阳镇

霞浦县：县人民政府驻松城街道

柘荣县：县人民政府驻双城镇

屏南县：县人民政府驻古峰镇

古田县：县人民政府驻城东街道

周宁县：县人民政府驻狮城镇

The following are the names and locations of the administrative divisions of Ningde Municipality.

Ningde Municipality administers 1 municipal district, 8 counties, and 2 county-level cities.

Jiaocheng District: with its government located at 815 Mid Road;

Dongqiao Development Zone: Dongqiao New Zone Administrative Committee, under the direct administration of Ningde Municipality, with its location on Mindong Road;

Fu'an City: with its government located in Chengbei Sub-district;

Fuding City: with its government located in Tongshan Sub-district;

Shouning County: with its government located in Aoyang Town;

Xiapu County: with its government located in Songcheng Sub-district;

Zherong County: with its government located in Shuangcheng Town;

Pingnan County: with its government located in Gufeng Town;

Gutian County: with its government located in Chengdong Sub-district;

Zhouning County: with its government located in Shicheng Town.

二、宁德九个县市名称的由来

2.1.2 Origins of the Nine Counties/Cities/Districts

(一)宁德/焦城/蕉城

唐朝中期划长溪县宁川及古田县东北部设感德场。933年五代闽国升场为县,取宁川、感德各一字定名。1988年底撤县改市,市政府驻地设在蕉城。蕉城区的前身是原县级宁德市。从宋朝到明朝期间,屡遭匪寇毁城。嘉靖四十二年(1563),知县林时芳"召良工,采巨石",重建县城。这次由"纯石"筑成的,故曰"焦城","焦"通"礁",含有"固若礁石"的意思。在1939年拆除焦县城后,翌年又在原城里城外置立一个镇,也叫作"蕉城"。从1943年绘制的宁德县《地籍图》来看,它似乎"呈现南北长,东西狭的""芭蕉叶式"。然而,这个"蕉城"并不是"城"名,而是"镇"名。1991年撤销镇建制,分设蕉南、蕉北两个街道办事处时,"蕉城"这个名字被取消。1999年11月14日,宁德地区撤地设市,新设立的蕉城区为市政府驻地,"蕉城"这个名字被正式起用。

2.1.2.1 Ningde/Jiaocheng

In the Mid Tang Dynasty, Ning Chuan Township of Changxi County and the northeast of Gutian County were rezoned to be Gandechang Township. In 933AD, the Township was promoted to County administration and named Ning De with Ning in Ning Chuan and De in Gan De Chang. That was how Ningde originated. Ningde County remained till 1988 and was promoted to Ningde City (at county level) with its government now located in Jiaocheng District. The predecessor of Jiaocheng District was Ningde City at a county level. From the

Song Dynasty to the Ming Dynasty, Ningde proper was often invaded by coastal pirates and bandits. In the 42nd year(1563AD) of Emperor Jiajing's reign of the Ming Dynasty, Lin Shifang, the magistrate, called upon the talented masons to gather huge reef rocks to reinforce the county proper so the county proper was called Jiaocheng, meaning it was as solid as reef rocks, because in Chinese Jiao sounds like another word referring to reef rocks. In 1939, Jiaocheng was abolished. The next year, another town was established in the suburb to take place of former Jiaocheng area, which was also called Jiaocheng. There was another story about its origin. From the maps of Ningde proper printed in 1943, the town looked like a banana leaf that was long north and south-wise and narrow east and west-wise. Therefore, it was called Jiaocheng, meaning a place shaped like a banana leaf. On November 14, 1999, Ningde Prefecture administration was promoted to Ningde Municipal Administration with its government located in Jiaocheng District which came into official use.

(二)霞浦县

据《霞浦县志》,清置霞浦县,县境西南有霞浦江,东流入海。又有霞浦山,海中有青、黑、元、黄四屿,日出照映,江水如霞彩,这是山以江名,县以江名。

2.1.2.2 Xiapu County

It was recorded in *The Annals of Xiapu* that "When the Government of the Qing Dynasty established Xiapu County, it got its name from the Xiapu River flowing along its southeast into the East Sea. Besides, there was Xiapu Mountain there by the sea with four islets of Qing, Hei, Yuan and Huang scattering around. When the sun rose, the river looked sun-setting colors on its surface with radiations. That was how a mountain was named after a river and the county named after a river."

(三)福安市

公元1245年,乡人殿中御史郑采献诗理宗:"韩阳风景世间无,堪与王维作画图,四顾罗山朝虎井,一条带水绕龟湖。形如丹凤飞衔印,势似苍龙卧吐珠,此处不堪为县治,更于何处拜皇都"县治因而议定。理宗御批"敷赐五福,以安一县。"析长溪县西北二乡、九里建福安县,福安因而得名。

2.1.2.3 Fu'an City

In 1245 AD, Zheng Cai, a local scholar and a royal historian in the imperial court, wrote a poem to Emperor Li Zong suggesting Fu'an County Administration should be established: "The scenes in Hanyang(Fu'an now) are rare in the world and can be compared to the paintings by Wang Wei. Looking around the Chaohu Well in Luoshan Mount, one can see the river like a ribbon surrounding the Tortoise Lake as if a flying phoenix carrying a royal seal in its mouth and a lying dragon bursting out pearls (all very auspicious scenes). If such a place cannot be a county, where can one find a place to bow to the emperor? As a result, the county establishment was settled, so Emperor Li Zong replied with "Five Blessings(Fu) and Safety(An) For Thy County". Therefore, two villages in the northeast of Changxi County and Jiuli area were rezoned together to be Fu'an County and its name was coined with Fu and An on the reply of the emperor. That was how Fu'an came into being.

（四）福鼎市

据《福鼎通志》中记载:福鼎山,在县东,县命名以此。另外,福鼎山是为闽浙界山,按上北下南的方位惯例,福鼎县位于闽之上,亦为福建之"顶",取福鼎之名,一为福气之鼎,二为福建之顶,即祥瑞,又明示方位与闽地属性。

2.1.2.4 Fuding City

According to *The Chronicles of Fuding*, "There is Fuding Mountain in the east of the county so Fuding County was named after the mountain." Another explanation goes, Fuding Mountain is a boundary mountain between Fujian and Zhejiang provinces. Based on the common geographical divisions that the upper part is the north and the lower the south, Fuding is located in the upper area and the top(Ding) of Fujian Province. Therefore, Fu from Fujian and Ding (top) were coined together for its county name, firstly for being the happiest place and secondly for being the upper part of Fujian, both auspicious and indicative of geographical locations in Fujian.

（五）古田县

古田历史悠久,早在殷周时代,境内已有先民繁衍生息。唐以前为峒豪所据,开元二十九年(741)置县,因谢能等人在此垦辟古田定居而得名。

2.1.2.5 Gutian County

Gutian boasts a long history. As early as in the dynasties of Yin and Zhou, there were people living here. Before the Tang Dynasty, the area was occupied by Tonghao folks. In the 29th year (741AD) of the Kaiyuan period of the Tang Dynasty, county administration was established, and Xie Neng and his folks "explored the ancient plowed fields(Gu Tian) and settled down there." That was how it got the name, Gutian.

(六)屏南县

据《屏南县志》,清置屏南县,以位于古屏山之南而得名。

2.1.2.6 Pingnan County

Based on *The Annals of Pingnan*, the Government of the Qing Dynasty established county administration here. They named it after its location. It happens that the county is located in the south of Mount Gu Ping so it was named Ping Nan, referring to the south of Mount Gu Ping.

(七)寿宁县

明景泰六年(1455)析福安县西北地、政和县东北地置寿宁县,据《今县释名》,因歼平矿贼置县,取安宁之义。

2.1.2.7 Shouning County

In the 6th year (1455AD) of the reign of Emperor Jingtai of the Ming Dynasty, the northwest of Fu'an County and the northeast of Zhenghe County were rezoned for establishing Shouning County. Based on *The Notes on the Names of the Counties*, the county was established after many mine bandits there had been wiped out so the name of the county Shou Ning (longevity and security) indicates happiness and peace.

(八)周宁县

明嘉靖三十五年(1556)于宁德县境建周墩城。清雍正十三年(1735)设县丞驻治。1935年析宁德县西北地置周墩特种区。1945年设周宁县,取周墩、宁德首字为县名。1945年设周宁县,取宁德县之"宁"字,周墩特种区的"周"字为县名。

2.1.2.8 Zhouning County

In the 35th year (1556AD) of Emperor Jiajing of the Ming Dynasty, Zhoudun (Town) was established in Ningde area. In the 13th year (1735AD) of Emperor Yongzheng of the Qing Dynasty, magistrate administration was established in Zhoudun. In 1935, the northeast of Ningde County was rezoned for establishing Zhoudun Special District. In 1945, Zhouning County was set up with the first character of Zhoudun and Ningde as its county name of Zhouning.

（九）柘荣县

原名柘洋，因在东狮山下的一大片山间小平洋上，生长大量柘树（在南方极为罕见的北方树种）而得名。1945 年 10 月 1 日撤销柘洋特种区建制，设柘荣县，取木石尔雅，欣欣向荣之意，是福建所有县城中，唯一以树命名、与树共荣的县城。

2.1.2.9 Zherong County

Its former name was Zheyang(Cudrania Wide Area). Because there was a wide area of cudrania trees(which is a northern tree and rare in the south) at the foot of the Dongshi Mountain and that was how the county got its name. Zherong County was established on October 1,1945 after Zheyang Special Zone was abolished. Zhe Rong means the trees and the rocks there are beautiful and the cudranias grow vigorously and prosperously indicating prosperity of the place. Zherong County is the only county in Fujian Province that was named after a tree and seeks to be as prosperous as trees.

三、宁德历史大事记

2.1.3 Historical Events in Ningde

（一）温麻船屯与温麻县的设立

三国时期，约公元 3 世纪中叶，孙吴政权在今霞浦沿海开设了造船工场“温麻船屯”，建造了许多海船，支持吴国壮大水上力量和发展海运。

温麻船屯，是孙吴官办的造船工场，它的创办为开发闽东沿海集聚了一大批精干劳动力和技术人才，开通了沿海航线。辽阔的福宁湾成了闽东人走向海洋的第一站，闽东便揭开了有志可考的历史。

晋太康三年(282)，在温麻船屯基础上设置温麻县，辖区包括现宁德市大部及政和、连江、罗源的部分。辖区多属山区，但县治却设于海滨，即今霞浦沙江。

温麻县是闽东历史上第一个县级政区，也是福建省内较早设立的县之一。福建历史上最早设置的县是汉代公元前 85 年设立的冶县（后改称侯官，今福州地）。此后过了一百多年，至 282 年时福建共设有 15 个县，温麻乃其中之一。

2.1.3.1 Establishment of Wenma Shipyard and Wenma County

During the Three Kingdoms Period, about the mid third century AD, Kingdom Wu set up shipyards called “Wenma Shipyards” in today's coastal Xiapu County. Many ships were built there and helped Kingdom Wu strengthen its marine forces and provided great support for its shipping business.

Wenma Shipyard, a state-owned yard run by Kingdom Wu, helped gather many capable labor forces and technological talents along the coast of Mindong. The opening of the coastal navigation routes made the wide Funing Bay the first stop for the people in Mindong to go overseas. With the march towards the ocean, the recorded history of Mindong came into being.

In the third year (282AD) of the Taikang period of the Jin Dynasty, on the base of the Wenma Shipyard, Wenma County was established administering most of Ningde today and also some parts of Zhenghe County, Lianjiang County and Luoyuan County. Wenma County administered mostly mountainous areas, but its county proper remained ever by the coast, i.e. Shajiang, Xiapu today.

Wenma County was the first county-level administrative zone in the history of Mindong, and also was one of the few counties that were established early in Fujian. The earliest county set up in the history of Fujian was called Ye County in 85AD of the Han Dynasty. Later, Ye County was changed to Houguan, now Fuzhou. After more than 100 years till 282AD, there were in total 15 counties established in Fujian and Wenma County was one of them.

(二)霍童山被列为道教"三十六洞天"之首

据史书、方志记载,自三国起,左慈、葛玄、邓伯元、王玄甫、褚伯玉、陶弘景、司马承祯、白玉蟾等著名道士均曾在此修道或仙逝,故被列为道教"三十六洞天"之首。

唐代以前将华夏大地的名山列为"十大洞天""三十六小洞天"等。"三十六洞天中之第一霍桐(即霍童山),又名霍林洞天"。明代《闽都记》:闽境之山,西则武夷,东则霍童。有"不到霍童不为仙"之说。

2.1.3.2 Huotong Mountain on the Top of the List of "36 Taoist Mountains" by Taoists in China

According to the historical books and the local annals, since the Three Kingdoms Period, famous Taoists like Zuo Ci, Ge Xuan, Deng Boyuan, Wang Xuanfu, Zhu Boyu, Tao Hongjing, Sima Chengzhen, Bai Yuchan, etc., practiced Taoism in Huotong Mountain or passed away there. Therefore, Huotong Mountain was listed on the top of the 36 Taoist Mountains in China. Before the Tang Dynasty, all the famous mountains were classified into "10 Most Famous Mountains" and "36 Less Famous Mountains" in China. Among the 36 less famous mountains in China, Huotong Mountain stood out on the top of the list, and was also called Huolin Mountain. According to *The Historical Records of Capital Fuzhou of Fujian*, "Among all the mountains in Fujian, Wuyi Mountain is the most famous in its west while Huotong Mountain is in its east". Therefore, there is a saying "Whoever has not been to Huotong Mountain fails to be a Taoist".

（三）王审知开辟黄岐港

唐末五代时期，王审知（"闽王"）从898—925年统治福建近30年，为促进福建的繁荣做出重大贡献。王审知治闽的主要举措之一就是大力发展福建的对外联系与对外贸易，为此他十分重视海港与航道建设。黄岐港的开辟就是王审知的一个大手笔。黄岐港当年属长溪县管辖，是闽国北部最大的港口，但因有礁石当道，航路不畅。王审知上任伊始，就致力于黄岐港的开凿、疏浚，历时6年，904年竣工。唐昭宗赐名"甘棠港"。甘棠港的开辟，有利于加强福建与中原的联系，改善了福建尤其是闽东地区的交通条件，促进了福建海外贸易的发展，从而推动了福建，特别是闽东的开发。甘棠港开通后，海运蒸蒸日上，对外贸易盛况空前，黄岐一跃而成福建名镇，其经济繁荣持续了200多年。明代时改称下白石。

2.1.3.3 Wang Shenzhi Opened Huangqi Port

At the end of the Tang Dynasty and the Five-Dynasties period, Wang Shenzhi (King of Fujian), reigned Fujian about 30 years from 898 AD to 925 AD and made great contribution to the prosperity of Fujian. His main measure of governance of Fujian was sparing no efforts in developing outbound relations and foreign trade. Therefore, he attached great importance to the construction of ports and navigation routes. The opening of Huangqi Port was one of his great projects. Huangqi Port was under the jurisdiction of Changxi County that time and was the largest port in the north of Kingdom Min (Fujian). Because there were lots of reefs in the sea area, the navigation routes were not so smooth. When Wang Shenzhi took office, he was committed to the development of Huangqi Port. After 6 years, the port was open in 904 AD. Emperor Zhaozong of the Tang Dynasty named it "Gantang Port". With its opening, connection between Fujian and Central China was greatly boosted so that the traffic condition of Fujian, especially East Fujian was improved and foreign trade of Fujian also grew strongly. As a result, the development of East Fujian was greatly pushed forward. After the opening up of Gantang Port, the shipping business boomed and foreign trade prospered. Huangqi also became a famous town in Fujian. Its economic prosperity lasted for over 200 years.

During the Ming Dynasty, its name was changed to Xiabaishi.

(四)三都澳的开埠

1898年清廷将三都澳辟为福建的三个商埠之一(前两个是福州、厦门)。1899年,清廷在三都成立福海关,三都澳正式开放为对外贸易港口,与英、美、德、日、俄、葡萄牙、西班牙、荷兰、瑞典等十三个国家的21家公司建立贸易关系,在此开办洋行或分公司,英国修建杂货泊位、石油泊位各一个,美国建油泊位一个、油库两个。三都澳由此繁荣起来,光绪三十三年(1907)英国海军上将阿塞·摩理乘"阿拉克里提"号舰到三都澳访问。光绪三十四年(1908)多国集资在福鼎县七星岛修航海指示灯塔,1万支光,每10秒钟闪亮两次,民国十四年三月二十二日,英国海军上将阿塞·摩理乘"阿拉克里提"号舰到三都澳访问。同年,福鼎沙埕与台湾、香港、澳门等地区,以及日本、英国、新加坡等国相继通航通商,成为闽东又一重要外贸港口。顶峰是20世纪30年代初。抗战期间,日军飞机数次轰炸,其海军陆战队又登岛纵火,岛上建筑大多被毁,从此衰落。福海关于1949年关闭。当年三都港输出的货物中以茶叶为最大宗,占其总输出货值的90%以上,其茶叶出口量居福建首位,占全省一半至60%,在全国名列前茅。

2.1.3.4 Opening up of Sandu Bay

In 1898, the Qing Government opened Sandu Bay as one of the three trading ports(the other two were Fuzhou and Xiamen). In 1899, the Qing Government set up Fuhai Customs, indicating the formal opening of Sandu Bay for foreign trade with 21 companies of the above 13 countries. They set up their banks or branches. UK built one cargo berth and one oil berth. USA built one oil berth and one oil tank After that Sandu Bay gradually prospered. During the 33rd year of Emperor Guangxu's reign of the Qing Dynasty, British Admiral Arthur Mori in his ship Alan Kriti visited Sandu Bay. In the 34th year (1907 AD) of the reign of Emperor Guangxu, many countries raised money in Fuding County to build a beacon tower on Qixing Island with 10,000 light radiations and flashed twice every 10 seconds. On March 22nd, 1914, British Admiral Arthur Mori in his ship visited Sandu Bay again. In the same year, Shacheng Port of Fuding opened its shipping route with regions such as Taiwan, Hong Kong, and Macau, and countries such as Japan, the UK, and Singapore so that it became an important port in East Fujian. Its heydays were in the 30's of the 20th century. During the Counter-Japanese War period, the Japanese planes carried out several bombings on the island and the Japanese coast guards stepped on the island and set fires so most of the buildings on the island were destroyed. Ever since Sandu Bay had declined. Fuhai Customs were shut down in 1949. Those years Sandu Bay Port mainly exported tea, taking up 90% of the total exported value of goods. The amount of the exported tea topped that of Fujian province and took up at least a half or 60% and stood at the top in the country.

(五)沙埕港与郑成功

明清时沙埕港曾是东南沿海的重要经济贸易口岸,后成为郑成功抗清部队的重要物资补给地。郑成功于清初在东南沿海抗清,为解决士卒众多、地方狭窄、粮饷不足等困难,遂依托港口,积极推行海内外贸易,首先同日本通好,接着与菲律宾、泰国、越南等交易。这是郑成功以海外弹丸之地养兵十余万,而用财不匮的根本原因。对此,沙埕港发挥了巨大作用。此外,张煌言(1620—1664,号苍水,浙江鄞县人)于1645年起兵,奉鲁王朱以海监国,在浙东组织抗清多年,曾经"三渡闽关",在沙埕设立过战时指挥部。从1649年底到1651年,舟山群岛成为朱以海浙东抗清武装活动的中心,牵制了东南地区的大量清军,这就为郑成功在福建沿海的扩展,创造了有利的条件。

2.1.3.5 Shacheng Port and Zheng Chenggong

During the Ming and Qing dynasties, Shacheng Port was an important economic and trade port in the southeast of China. Later it became a key material supplier for the anti-Qing government forces led by Zheng Chenggong. He at the beginning of the Qing Dynasty carried out fights against the Qing Dynasty. In order to solve the problems of many soldiers, small areas, short supply of grains and so on, he relied on the ports and took active measures to boost trade at home and abroad. Firstly he conducted friendly relations with Japan, and then carried out trade with the Philippines, Thailand, and Vietnam and so on. That was why Zheng Chenggong sustained with a small coastal place to keep going his tens of thousands of soldiers without being broken. In addition, Zhang Huangyan(1620-1664AD), with Changshui as his alternative name, a native of Yin County of Zhejiang Province, uprose in 1645 and under the leadership of Acting Emperor Zhu Yihai of Kingdom Lu, carried out many battles against the Qing Government for many years. And he for three times came to Fujian and set up his headquarters in Shacheng Port. From 1649 to 1651, the Zhoushan Islands became the central battle fields for Zhu Yihai to fight against the Qing forces so that a large amount of the Qing armies were pinned down, which created a favorable condition for Zheng Chenggong to expand his forces in Fujian.

(六)余仁椿创办古田县蓝田书院

闽东最早的书院可以追溯到南唐晚期古田县的蓝田书院。蓝田书院旧址在今杉洋乡北门外,是当地人余仁椿于955年前后创办的。据说南宋著名理学家朱熹晚年在闽东讲学授徒约五年时间,直接推动了理学在闽东的传播。据史料记载,全国朱子门人共511人,其中福建省171人,闽东籍的有17人,形成"闽东理学群贤",使闽东在理学发展史上占有一定地位。

2.1.3.6 Yu Renchun Established Lantian Private College of Gutian County

The earliest private college in Mingdong dated back to Liantian Private College of Gutian County during the final period of the South Tang Dynasty. Its site is located in Beimenwai in Shayang Village today. Mr. Yu, a local, helped set up the college in 955 AD. It is said that Zhu Xi, the most famous Neo-Confucian scholar in his final life taught here for five years, which directly boosted the spread of Confucianism in East Fujian. According to the historical records, there were about 511 students of Zhu Xi, of whom 171 came from whole Fujian and 17 from Ningde so that an elite group of Neo-Confucian scholars in Ningde came into being. As a result Ningde plays a relatively important role in the development of Confucianism in history.

(七)黄鞠兴修水利工程

隋代黄鞠所修隧道水利工程,是闽东现存年代最早、规模最大、最富特色的一个水利工程。黄鞠组织民众在南岸挖断山岩,凿石渠引水,利用落差安装多级水碓;开日、月、星三湖蓄水,水先环绕村中民房再流入田里,既便于村民洗涤、防火,又提高了水的养分,有利于肥田。水渠回转九曲,每曲都镇一块石蛤蟆,用来缓阻急流,提高水位。工程设计相当巧妙。

在霍童溪北岸,则从十五里外的堵坪湖引水灌溉,沿途有几处山岩阻隔,必须开凿隧道,也由黄鞠主持,灌溉受益面积达数百顷。现在,位于湖头村岩角以西仙莱岩下的溪边,还保存一条长千余米的古代灌溉水渠,由明渠和七段涵洞连接而成。黄鞠所修水利工程,代表了闽东乃至整个福建隋代水利工程的最高成就,也集中反映了当时闽东地区在北方移民和先进技术影响下农业生产的快速进步。

2.1.3.7 Huang Ju Built an Irrigation Project

In the Sui Dynasty, the irrigation project built by Huang Ju still is the earliest, the largest and the most characteristic in Ningde. He led the folks to cut the rocks for a ditch for water. He made use of the falls to build many water receptors and three reservoirs named of the sun, the moon and the star. He then made the water go around the folk houses and then into the fields, which made it convenient for the folks to wash and firefight. Meanwhile, the practice raised the water nutrient to benefit farming land. The water turned nine twists and at each twist there was a rock frog to soothe the flow of water and to raise the water level. The designs are rather smart.

In the northern bank of the Huotongxi River, water is introduced for irrigation from the Zhuping Lake 7.5 kilometers away. There were several cliffs that needed tunnels to go through, which was also chaired by Huang Qu. As a result, several hundreds of hectares of farming land were irrigated. Nowadays, by the riverside under the Xixianlaiyan Rock Conner in Hutoucun Village, there still remains an ancient irrigation ditch over a thousand meter long. It is connected with open ditches and 7 sections of tunnels. The irrigation project by Huang Qu indicated the highest achievement of the irrigation engineering in Ningde or even in Fujian and also highlighted the rapid progress of agriculture in Ningde under the impact of the coming of the northern immigrants and their advanced technology.

(八)戚继光入闽“第一奇捷”

戚继光——明代抗倭名将、军事家,对练兵、治械、阵图等均有创见,于明嘉靖四十一年(1562)和嘉靖四十二年(1563)率部先后于宁德横屿、小石岭全歼所在倭寇,为平息闽东倭患立下头功。

明嘉靖三十九年(1560),一股在浙江受到当地抗倭军民有力打击的倭寇突然流窜并占领了此地,烧杀抢掠无恶不作,致使横屿百姓民不聊生。而朝廷派出的抗倭军队已屡次失败。两年后,戚继光率领他的戚家军前来,不负众望收复了被倭寇占据了三年之久的横屿岛。这次歼倭大捷被后人称之为明代抗倭第一奇捷。

明代的抗倭斗争距今已400多年,但闽东各地不少抗倭遗址依然存在。福鼎有秦屿古堡和冷城古堡,霞浦有大京古堡和传胪古堡,宁德县城有“继光街”,漳湾镇有“戚公祠”,戚继光“辕门斩子”的传说至今仍在流行。

2.1.3.8 General Qi Jiguang Came to Fujian and His First Surprising Victory

Qi Jiguang, a famous general against the Japanese pirates and a military strategist, was creative and smart at training soldiers, managing weapons and battle formations.

In the 41st year (1562AD) of Emperor Jiajing of the Ming Dynasty and the following year, he respectively led his army to Hengyu Island and Xiaoshiling to wipe out all the pirates and won the first merit in ridding the pirates in Mindong.

In the 39th year (1560AD) of Emperor Jiajing of the Ming Dynasty, a group of pirates who were under forceful attack by the army and the folks in Zhejiang ran away and suddenly came to occupy Hengyu Island. They burned down houses, killed people and looted properties without mercy so that the folks there suffered to death. What was more, the army sent by the government lost again and again to the pirates. Two years later, Qi Jiguang led his army here and lived up to the folk expectation and also realized his own promise that he wanted to overcome the whole island in one day and took back Hengyu Island that had been occupied by the pirates for three years. This victory is remembered by the coming generations as the first surprise victory against the Japanese pirates.

The fights against the pirates already are 400 years away from today, but the fighting sites against the pirates in Mindong remain for his memory. In Fuding City, there are Qinyu Ancient Fort and Lengcheng Ancient Fort; in Xiapu County, there is Dajing Ancient Fort and Chuanlu Ancient Fort; in Ningde proper, there is Jiguang Street; in Zhangwan there is Temple to Lord Qi and the story that he killed his son to discipline still goes around.

(九)明清畲族入迁

在明清两代,畲族人大批移居闽东特别是在明清之交的150年间,迁入的主要是雷、钟、蓝三姓,合占总数的95%左右,此外还有李、吴、杨以及其他姓氏。有人根据闽东畲村现存宗谱资料统计,在74支畲族移民中,明代迁入30支,清代前期迁入42支,约占总数的97%。

由于明清畲族大量迁入,闽东成为全国畲族分布最多的地区。清代中叶以后,部分山区畲民向沿海地区延伸,加上早期的沿海畲民,今天沿海畲族村数和人口数均占总数的44%左右,终于形成了闽东畲族村镇的现实分布格局。

2.1.3.9 Immigration of the She Ethnic People to Mindong in the Ming and Qing Dynasties

Their immigration of the She ethnic people in large quantity took place in the Ming and Qing dynasties, especially in the interval period between the two dynasties. Those immigrated were mainly the folks with surnames of Lei,

Zhong and Lan, taking up 95% of the total. Besides, there were other folks with surnames of Li, Wu, Yang and others. Someone used the remaining clan chronicles of the She Ethnic Villages to calculate that there were 74 immigration groups. 30 of them came in the Ming Dynasty and 42 of them arrived at the beginning of the Qing Dynasty, taking up 97% of the total.

Their coming in the Ming and Qing dynasties made Mindong the largest area for the She ethnic people in China. After the mid period of the Qing Dynasty, some mountainous She ethnic people moved to the coastal area. Plus the earlier coastal She ethnic people, the population of the She villages in the coastal area takes up 44% of that of the country so finally the actual distribution and layout of the She villages and town appear as what they are.

(十)中国工农红军闽东独立师的独特贡献

在闽东这块红色土地上,早在1927年就建立了闽东地区第一个中国共产党基层组织——中共古田县特别支部,书记陈炳。该支部在中共福州地委领导下开展革命活动,燃起了革命烈火。1931年后,老一辈无产阶级革命家邓子恢、陶铸、叶飞、曾志等来到闽东,与当地党的领导人马立峰、詹如柏、阮英平、范式人等一道,开展了轰轰烈烈的农民运动和武装斗争。1934年成立了中共闽东临时特委、闽东苏维埃政府、中国工农红军闽东独立师,创建了近万平方千米的闽东苏区,成为福建省重要的革命老根据地,以及中国共产党领导的全国八大主要革命根据地之一。中央红军长征后,闽东红军独立师进行了艰苦卓绝的闽东三年游击战争。抗日战争爆发后,闽东红军独立师改编为新四军第三支队第六团,开赴苏皖抗日前线。闽东红军独立师和由该师发展壮大起来的老部队,为民族的独立和人民的解放,为保卫社会主义建设事业,做出了重要贡献。

2.1.3.10 The Unique Contributions of the Independent Division of the Red Army of Workers and Peasants in Mindong of China

On the red land of Mindong, as early as in 1927(the 16th of the Republic of China), the special branch of Gutian County was established, which was the first CPC grassroots organization in Mindong. The Party Secretary was Chen Bing. The branch was under the leadership of Fuzhou Prefectural Committee of the CPC and carried out revolutionary activities and lit up the revolutionary fire. After 1931, the senior revolutionaries came to Mindong like Deng Zihui, Tao Zhu, Ye Fei, Zeng Zhi, etc. and worked together with the local Party leaders like Ma Lifeng, Zhan Rubai, Ruan Yingping, Fan Shiren, etc., and carried out vigorous peasants movement and armed struggles. In 1934, the Temporary Special Committee of the CPC of Mindong and the Soviet-style government of Mindong as well as the Independent Division of the Red Army of Workers and Peasants of Mindong of China were established. They created about 10 000 square kilometers of areas under the Soviet-style governance so Ningde became an important revolutionary base in Fujian and one of the eight major revolutionary bases under the leadership of the CPC. After the Central Red Army started their long march, the Independent Division carried out unprecedented guerrilla warfare. After the breakout of the anti-Japanese war, the Independent Division of Mindong was regrouped to be the sixth regiment of the third branch of the new fourth army and then they went to the anti-Japanese battle front in Jiangshu and Anhui provinces. The Independent Division of the Red Army of Mindong and the senior army growing up there made great contributions to the independence of the nation and the libration of the people as well as to safeguarding the socialist construction causes.

(十一)宁德县人民民主政府成立

1949 年 8 月 13 日,宁德三都岛解放,8 月 15 日,宁德全境解放,并成立宁德县人民民主政府筹备委员会,9 月 19 日正式成立宁德县人民民主政府。

1949 年 10 月 1 日,中华人民共和国成立,各县(除屏南县外)召开庆祝大会,并将县人民民主政府统一改称县人民政府。同日中国人民银行发行的人民币成为区内唯一合法货币,一切公私款项、物价计算、契约债务均以人民币为计算单位。

2.1.3.11 Establishment of the People's Democratic Government of Ningde County

On August 13, 1949, Sandu Island of Ningde County was liberated. On August 15, the whole Ningde County was liberated and the preparatory committee of the People's Democratic Government was set up. On September 19, the People's Democratic Government of Ningde County was established formally.

On October 1, 1949, the People's Republic of China was founded. Each county(except Pingnan County) held a celebration and changed the People's Democratic Government of Certain County to People's Government of Certain County. On the same day, the Prefectural Government stipulated that the Renminbi(RMB) issued by the People's Bank of China was the sole legal currency. All public or private funds, pricing calculations of goods, deeds and debts all were settled in RMB.

四、宁德历史名人

2.1.4 Historical Figures in Ningde

(一)开闽第一进士——薛令之

薛令之,字君珍,号明月先生,唐福建道长溪廉村(今福安市溪潭镇廉村高岑)人,永淳二年(683)八月十五日生。福建第一个进士,官至太子侍讲。唐神龙二年(706),24岁的薛令之赴京应试,一举登科,成为福建历史上第一位进士。薛令之留任在长安约30年时间,以清正廉洁而著世,晚年两袖清风告老还乡。在他死后,唐肃宗为薛令之的清廉所感动,赐封他的故乡为"廉村",村前小河为"廉水",村后山岭为"廉岭",从此"三廉"名扬远近。薛令之生前所著《明月先生集》和《补阙集》,今已无存。《全唐诗》仅录其《自悼》和《灵岩寺》二诗。

2.1.4.1 Xue Lingzhi—The First Jinshi in Fujian Province

Xue Lingzhi, with Junzhen(cherishing gentleman) as his courtesy name and Mr. Bright Moon as his art name, was from Liancun Village, Changxi, Fujian province in the Tang Dynasty, which is now Gaocen, Liancun Village, Xitang Township, Fu'an City. He was born on August 15 in the 2nd year (683AD) of the Yongchun period. He became the first Jinshi—a successful candidate in the highest imperial exams and was appointed a teacher of the prince. During the 2nd year (706AD) of the Shenlong period of the Tang Dynasty, he went to Chang'an for the imperial exam at the age of 24 and was succeeded in the exam and became the first Jinshi in the history of Fujian province. Xue had been working in Chang'an for over 30 years and became known for his honesty and uprightness. At his old age he retired back home with nothing. After his death, Emperor Xiaozong of the Tang Dynasty was touched by his honesty and uprightness and conferred his hometown a title "Honest and Upright Village, the river in front of his village as honest and upright River; the back range in his hometown "Honest and Upright Range". Since then the "three honest and upright places" became well-known near and far. The two books he wrote, *Collections of Mr. Bright Moon* and *Collections of the Supplements*, did not survive. *The Complete Poems of the Tang Dynasty* collects two of his poems: "Self Mourning" and "The Lingyan Temple".

(二)佛教五大禅师之一——灵佑禅师

灵祐(771—853),俗姓赵,唐代长溪县(今霞浦县)人,大历六年(771)出生,中国佛教禅宗五宗之一的沩仰宗的创始人。14岁时,灵祐依法常律师出家于长溪县建善寺(在今霞浦),后在浙江杭州龙兴寺剃发受戒,并在寺中广究大小乘经律。贞元九年(793),他云游江西,参谒高僧百丈怀海,怀海见他生性颖悟,学佛心专,允其留在身边。从此,灵祐成为参加学佛者的首领,后来又被选为所居洪州(今江西南昌市)百丈山寺的典座。唐元和十五年(820),灵祐遵怀海之嘱到沩山(今湖南省宁乡县西)开法。

灵祐敷扬宗教凡四十余年,于大中七年(853)圆寂,敕谥"大圆禅师"。著有《沩山警策》《潭州沩山灵祐禅师语录》各一卷。

2.1.4.2 Lingyou—One of the Five Zen Masters in the Buddhist Circle

Lingyou (771-853AD), having a worldly surname of Zhao, was from Changxi County (Now Xiapu County) in the Tang Dynasty. He was born in the 6th year (771AD) of the Dali period. He was the founder of the Weiyangzong Denomination, one of the Five Buddhists of Zen. At the age of 14, he became a monk in Jianshen Temple (now in Xiapu). Later he tonsured in the Longxing Temple in Hangzhou, Zhejiang to accept Buddhist doctrines and studied hard the Buddhism scriptures there. In the 9th year (793AD) of the Zhenyuan period, he travelled to Jiangxi and visited Baizhanhuaihai, a famous monk, who discovered that he was bright and devoted to Buddhism and kept him in the temple. Since then, Lingyou became a leader in studying Buddhism. Later he was chosen as the director of the Baizhanshan Temple in Hongzhou (now in Nanchang City, Jiangxi). During the 15th year (820AD) of the Yuanhe period, he followed his teacher's entrust and went to Weishan (now Ningxiang County, Hunan) to promote Buddhism.

Lingyou had promoted Buddhism over 40 years. He passed away in the 7th year (853AD) of the Dazhong period and was honored a title of "Great Zen Master". He also published *Alert Countermeasures in Weishan* and *Quotations of Zen Master Lingyou in Weishan, Tangzhou*. Both remain.

(三)开凿隧道水利第一人——黄菊

黄鞠(569—657),字玄甫,河南光州固始县人氏,是一位杰出的农田水利专家,曾任隋朝谏议大夫,以敢言不避权贵而著称于当世。失意庙堂后,他花费几十年的时间在霍童凿出了南北岸两条引水隧道，南岸的隧道宽 1 米、深数米、长 100 多米，北岸的隧道高 2.5 米、宽 1 米、长 400 多米。霍童引水隧道与闽南洛阳桥相媲美，堪称当时福建的三大工程之一，至今仍有效益。

2.1.4.3 Huang Ju—The First Person in Fujian to Have Irrigation Tunnels Built

Huang Ju (569-657AD), with Xuanpu as his courtesy name, was from Gushi County, Guangzhou, Henan Province. He was an outstanding irrigation expert. Once he worked as an imperial remonstrator for the emperors in the Sui Dynasty. He was well-known for his bold remonstration in front of the influential officials. When he lost favor, he spent tens of years in Huotong, Ningde digging two irrigation tunnels in the northern and the southern banks of a river. The tunnel in the southern bank is one meter wide, several meters deep, and over 100 meters long. And the tunnel in the northern bank is 2.5 meters high, 1 meter wide, and over 400 meters long. The irrigation project could match with the Luoyang Bridge in South Fujian in its importance. It was one of the three huge projects in Fujian at that time. It is still in use.

(四)南宋教育家、理学家——陈普

陈普，字尚德，号惧齐，世称石堂先生，宋淳祐四年(1244)生于宁德二十都石堂(今虎贝乡文峰村)，南宋著名教育家、理学家，其铸刻漏壶为世界最早钟表之雏形。他饱学理学，精通经史，著述颇丰，名闻闽浙。陈普一生著作甚丰，著有《四书句解铃键》《学庸指要》《孟子纂图》《周易解》《尚书补微》《四书五经讲义》《浑天仪论》《咏史诗断》《字义》凡数百卷，大多散失。传世之作今可查者有《石堂先生遗集》二十二卷，《石堂先生遗稿》一卷，《武夷棹歌》一卷(朱熹撰，陈普注)。

2.1.4.5 Chen Pu—An Educationist and Neo-Confucian of the Southern Song Dynasty

Chen Pu, with Shangde (revere virtue) as his courtesy name and Juqi as his art name and Shitang as his folk name (name of his hometown), was born in the 4th year (1244AD) of the Chunyou period of the Song Dynasty in Ershidu Shitang, Ningde (now Wenfeng Village, Hubei, Ningde). He was a famous educationist and Neo-Confucian scholar in the southern Song dynasty. The water clock he cast was the rudiment of the earliest horologe in the world. He was well learned in Neo-Confucianism and good at scriptures and history. He wrote many books and was famous in Fujian and Zhejiang. In his life he wrote *Interpreting the Four Books*, *The Essentials of Confucianism*, *Mencius Thoughts in Pictures*, *Interpreting the Book of Changes*, *the Minor Supplement to the Book of History*, *Lectures on the Four Books and the Five Classics* , *A Study on the Celestial Globe*, *Poems on History* and *The Meaning of Words*. In total he wrote hundreds of volumes but most of them were lost. His surviving works include 22 volumes of *The Remaining Collections of Mr. Shitang*, one volume of *The Remaining Scripts of Mr. Shitang* and one volume of *The Fishermen's Songs of Mount Wuyi*(Written by Zhuxi and annotated by Chen Pu).

(五)南宋诗人——谢翱

谢翱(1249—1295),字皋羽,号晞发子,生于宋淳祐九年(1249),福建路福安县樟南坂(今福安市晓阳镇)人,后徙浦城。南宋著名爱国诗人,为宋元之交最具代表性的文学家。咸淳元年(1265),谢翱赴临安(今杭州)考进士,不第,落魄于漳、泉二州。1276年,遂变卖家产,募乡勇数百前往投效,并且担任"咨议参军"等职务。他一生辛勤笔耕,被誉为"南宋翘楚""宋末诗人之冠"。谢翱生前著书殆百卷,有《晞髪遗集》《晞髪遗集补》一卷及《天地间集》。其中最著名的篇章有《西台哭所思》《登西台恸哭记》《许剑录》《晞发集》。

2.1.4.5 Xie Ao—A Famous Poet of the Southern Song Dynasty

Xie Ao(1249-1295AD), with Gao Yu as his courtesy name and Xi Fa Zi as his art name, was born in the 9th year(1249AD) of the Chunyou period of the Song Dynasty. He was from Zhangnanban (now Xiaoyang township), Fu'an, Fujian province. Later he migrated to Pu Cheng. He was a patriotic poet of the Southern Song Dynasty as well as the most representative writer at the turning of the Song and the Yuan Dynasties. In the first year (1265AD) of the Xuanchun period, Xie Ao went to Lin'an(now Hangzhou) to sit on the exam to be a successful candidate in the imperial exams, but he failed and became down and out in Zhangzhou and Quanzhou. In 1276, he sold all his property and gathered hundreds of folks to join the army and shouldered a consultant position. In all his life he toiled with his pens and created many works. He was praised to be an outstanding poet in the Southern Song Dynasty as well as the champion of the poets at the end of the Song Dynasty. He wrote over 100 volumes of books. His works include *The Remaining Collections of Poet Xixu*, *The Supplement to the Collections of Xixu* as well as one volume of *Between the Heaven and the World*. His most famous works include "Thoughts of Crying at Xitai", "Records of Crying at Climbing Xitai"and so on.

(六)余复——闽东科举史上第一位状元

余复(生卒年不详),字子叔,蕉城城关人。闽东科举史上第一位状元(宋绍熙元年,即公元1190年),初任洪州(今江西南昌)佥判,在任上体恤民情,办事认真,爱民如子,兴农田水利,修名胜古迹。宋庆元元年(1195)被诏入史馆,参与编纂实录。对儒学经典有一定造诣,著有《礼经类说》《左氏纂类》《祭礼》和诗文集子,多未传世。现存清乾隆李拔纂修的《福宁府志》载有余复中状元之时的两篇谢表。

2.1.4.6 Yu Fu—The First "Zhuangyuan" in the History of Mindong(East Fujian)

Yu Fu(natal and obituary year unknown), with Zishu as his courtesy name, was the first Zhuangyuan—Top 1 Candidate in the Highest Imperial Exams in the first year (1190AD) of the Shaoxi period of the Song Dynasty. His first official assignment was a judge in Hongzhou(now Nanchang, Jiangxi). During his term there, he sympathized with folks, judged earnestly, treated his folks like his family members, built irrigation projects and repaired historical relics. In the first year (1195AD) of the Qingyuan period of the Song Dynasty, he was called on to work in the national museum, participating in compiling historical facts. He made quite some attainments in Confucianism Classics and wrote many works such as *On the Varieties of Etiquettes Classics*, *Compilations of the Zuo's Clan*, *Sacrificial Rites*, and other poems collections, but most of which were lost. What survive are the two gratitude articles he wrote when he succeeded being the Top 1 Successful Candidate collected in *Funing Annals* compiled by Li Bo during Emperor Qianlong's reign of the Qing Dynasty.

(七)一代忠将——郑虎臣

郑虎臣(1219—1276),字廷翰,又字景兆,南宋嘉定十二年(1219)生于福建路长溪县柏柱南山(今福安市溪柄南山洋头村)。父郑埙,宋理宗时任越州同知,遭贾似道陷害,流放至死。郑虎臣受株连,被充军边疆,后遇赦放归。后郑虎臣在押解贾似道途中将其诛杀,为天下除奸。该事迹被载入《闽都别记》。翌年,贾似道的同伙陈宜中逃至福州,拥立赵昰,捕杀郑虎臣。郑虎臣遭害后,葬于南山村的馆园旁,乡人及其后裔在村前建祠纪念他。明朝抗倭名将俞大猷在木棉庵前的石亭中立下石碑,并亲书"宋郑虎臣诛贾似道于此"。明代王紫衡也就郑虎臣诛贾一事写诗赞扬他。郑虎臣曾编《吴都文粹》一书,今犹存。

2.1.4.7 Zheng Huchen—A Loyal General in His Life

Zheng Huchen (1219-1276AD), with Tinghan and Jingzhao as his courtesy names, was born in the 12th year (1219AD) of the Jiading period of the Southern Song Dynasty in Nanshan Village, Baizhu, Changxi, Fujian (now Yangtou Village, Nanshan, Xibing, Fu'an City). His father Zhen Yun was an official in Yuezhou during Emperor Lizong's reign of the Song Dynasty, and was set up by Jia Sidao, a minister, and was sent into exile till death. Zheng Huchen was associated with the frame-up by Jia Sidao and was sent to a distant place for penal servitude. Later he was pardoned and allowed to go home. When Jia Sidao was sent away somewhere under armed guard by Zheng Huchen, he killed the traitor on the way and got rid of the wicked for the country. His deeds were recorded in *The Expository Notes of Fuzhou*. In the following year, Chen Yizhong, a gang of Jia Sidao, escaped to Fuzhou and supported Zhao Shi. They arrested Zheng Huzhen and killed him. After Zheng's death, he was buried by a pavilion in Nanshan Village. His folks and younger generations also built a memorial hall by the gate of the village in his memory. Yu Dayou, a famous general against Japanese pirates in the Ming Dynasty set up a tablet in the stone pavilion in front of the Mumian Temple and wrote himself: Zheng Huchen Killed Jia Shidao here in the Song Dynasty. Mr. Wang Ziheng of the Ming Dynasty also wrote a poem to praise him. Zheng Hucheng also compiled a book *Literary Highlights of Wudu Capital*, which still survives.

(八)元末明初著名文学家——张以宁

张以宁,字志道,元大德四年(1300)生于古田县官宦之家,是闽东继谢翱之后又一位有全国性影响的诗人,代表了境内元明两代文学创作的最高成就。元泰定四年(1327),张以宁考中进士,任浙江黄岩县判官,后升江苏六合县尹,因执法不阿,触犯豪门,上任不久便被罢官。此后他流落江淮、扬州一带达十年。元至元四年(1338),元惠宗召其为国子监助教,后累迁翰林侍讲学士,知制诰兼修国史。洪武三年(1370)秋,张以宁奉旨持节出使安南(时为中国藩属,即今越南),封安南之主陈日煃为国王。洪武四年(1371)五月,封王礼毕,张以宁回朝复命,因年老体衰,不胜劳瘁,途中于临清病卒。张以宁生前著述颇丰,可惜大多散佚。1990 年出版的《全明诗》第一集收录其不少佚诗。

2.1.4.8 Zhang Yining—A Famous Litterateur of the Yuan and Ming Dynasty

Zhang Yining, with Zhi Dao as his courtesy name, was born in an official family in Gutian County in the 4th year (1300AD) of the Dade period of the Yuan Dynasty. He was another nationally influential poet after Xie Ao, both from Mindong. They represented the highest level of literature in this region. During the 4th year (1327AD) of Emperor Taiding's reign of the Yuan Dynasty, Zhang was enrolled as "Jinshi" in the highest imperial exams and was appointed a magistrate judge in Huangyan County, Zhejiang. Later he was promoted to magistrate of Liuhe County, Jiangsu. Because of his just execution of laws, he offended the rich and was dismissed from office shortly after a while. He was sent in exile in Jianghuai and Yangzhou over 10 years. In the 4th year (1338AD) of the Zhiyuan period, he was summoned to be a royal assistant. Later he was promoted to be a teacher in the Imperial Academy, worked as a drafter of documents and concurrently compiled national histories. In the autumn of 1370, he was called upon to be an ambassador to Annan (now Vietnam) to confer Kingship to Chen Rikui, head of Annan then. In May of 1371, he returned from Vietnam after the ceremony. Because of his old age, poor health and fatigue, he died on the way in Linqing. He wrote many books, and unfortunately most of them got lost. The first volume of *The Complete Poems of the Ming Dynasty* published in 1990 collected quite a few of his poems.

（九）首创了"秋后决"朝审制刑法改革——林聪

林聪(1417—1482)，字季聪，号见庵，宁德七都浦源人，生于明永乐十三年(1415)，于正统五年(1440)中进士，正统八年(1443)拜刑科给事中上任伊始。天顺元年(1457)，英宗复辟，擢拜林聪为左佥都御史，1447 年 1453 年两次上疏恳请免除宁德不应承受的银课，终为朝廷采纳，解除了闽东、闽北人民繁重的税课负担。天顺二年(1458)，林聪看到在当时的苛刑峻法之下冤狱屡有发生，遂上《乞缓重狱疏》，专题提出"秋后决"的主张：实行春判冬决制度，以延缓死刑执行期来进行死刑复核，使案中属以矜疑者得免死，以减少错杀。英宗纳其言，下诏曰："每岁霜降后，三法司会同廷臣审录重囚，谓之朝审，遂为永制"。成化二年(1466)，擢升右都御史。成化十三年(1477)，林聪升任刑部尚书加太子太保，成化十八年(1482)病逝于任上。林聪卒后，明廷诰授其荣禄大夫太子太保，谥"庄敏"。其灵柩归乡后葬于宁德八都铜镜山。林聪著有《奏议》八卷、《见庵文集》十四卷，今民间仍流传其手抄本。

2.1.4.9 Lin Cong—The First Reformer of Qiuhoujue in the Imperial Criminal Law

Lin Cong(1417-1482AD), with Ji Cong as his courtesy name and Jian An as his art name, was from Puyuan, Qidu, Ningde. He was born in the 13th year (1415AD) of Emperor Yongle's reign of the Ming Dynasty. In the 5th year

(1440AD) of the Zhengtong period, he succeeded in being a "Jinshi" in the highest imperial exams. In the 8th year (1443AD) of the same period, he became in charge of the criminal affairs. In the first year (1457AD) of Emperor Tianshun's reign, ousted Emperor Yingzong staged a comeback and promoted him to an investigating censor. From 1447 to 1453 he twice submitted reports to the emperor to waive the taxes on the people in Ningde, which were finally adopted by the emperor so he helped reduce the heavy taxation burdens on the people in the north and the east of Fujian.

In the 2nd year (1458AD) of Emperor Tianshun's reign, Lin Cong found out wronged cases often occurred under the severe judicial system. Therefore he submitted a report "Request for Postponing the Executions of the Death Penalties" (*Qiuhoujue*). He raised the idea of executing the death penalties in fall after sentencing them in spring. The purpose of postponing the execution was to check the death penalties so that the wronged cases could be corrected to reduce wronged killings. Emperor Yingzong accepted his suggestion and ordered: "Each year after Frost's Descent (in October), the three departments of the judicial administration recheck the cases of the death penalties, and it is called the imperial check and will become an everlasting practice". In the 2nd year (1466AD) of Emperor Chenghua's reign, he was promoted to be a royal censor. In the 13th year (1477AD) of Emperor Chenghua's reign, he was appointed to be a judicial minister and in charge of the security for the princes. In the 18th year (1482AD) of Emperor Chenghua's reign, he died at his post. After his death, the imperial government conferred him honorable titles. He was buried in the Tongjing Mountain in Badu, Ningde. He wrote 8 volumes of *Reports to the Emperors*, and 14 volumes of *Collections of Mr. Jian An*. Nowadays, his manuscripts still circulate among folks.

(十)一代廉吏——游朴

游朴(1526—1599),字太初,号少涧,柘荣县黄柏乡人。隆庆元年(1567)中举人,万历二年(1574)中进士后步入仕途,曾供职于吏部、刑部及四川、广东、湖广等地,政声卓著,在二十余载的为官生涯中,他清理冤狱、惩奸除恶、厉行改革、赈灾济困、兴修水利、清正爱民、政绩卓著,深受百姓敬重和当朝赞许,《福建省志》称赞其为"三主法司,无一冤狱"。

游朴为官刚直不阿、不畏权势。任广东按察司副使时,总兵李栋勾结城社势力,鱼肉人民,官吏士民敢怒不敢言。他挺身而出,呈文举报,挫其气焰。

万历二十七年(1599)游朴去世。为了纪念游朴,颂扬游朴一生为人"智、仁、勇"和为官"清、勤、慎"的高尚品德,在游朴出生地柘荣县黄柏乡上黄柏村建立了富有特色的福建历史名人游朴纪念馆。

游朴著有《藏山集》《岭南稿》《满山社草》《石仓诗选》《武经七书解》《浙江恤刑谳书》《游太初乐府》等,但大多数散佚。后人整理其遗文,编成《游参知文集》二卷传世。目前,发现了新的游朴著作《诸夷考》三卷,这是目前发现唯一的游朴存本专著。

2.1.4.10 You Pu—An Honest and Upright Official of His Generation

You Pu(1526-1599AD), with Taichu as his courtesy name and Shaojian as his art name, was from Huangbai Village, Zherong County. In the first year (1567AD) of Emperor Longqing's reign of the Ming Dynasty, he became a Juren (a successful candidate in the imperial exams at the provincial level). In the 2nd year (1574AD) of Emperor Wanli's reign, he succeeded in being a Jinshi (a successful candidate in the highest imperial exams at the national level). After that he took up government positions and worked in the National Personnel Ministry, the Judicial Ministry as well as in places like Sichuan, Guangdong, Hunan, Hubei, etc. He was outstanding for his political fame. In his official life over 20 years, he corrected wronged cases, punished the wicked, carried out courageous reforms, relieved the people from disasters, built irrigation projects and so on. He was clean and caring for the people with prominent achievements and was greatly respected by them and the imperial government. In *The Fujian Provincial Annals*, he was highly praised "to be in charge of the judicial departments for three times without a single wronged case".

You Pu was upright and outspoken in his post and was not afraid of the influential and powerful officials. When he was a deputy prosecutor in Guangdong, Li Dong, an army chief, colluded with the gangs of the society and cruelly victimized the people. The officials and the people just dared to feel angry, but dared not sue him. You Pu came out boldly, sued him in a report to subdue his arrogance.

In the 27th year (1599AD) of Emperor Wanli's reign, You Pu passed away. In order to memorize him and praise him for his "wisdom, kindness, bravery" and "cleanness, diligence and caution" as an official, people in his hometown Huangbai Village built distinctively You Pu Memorial Hall of the Famed

Historical Figures of Fujian.

You Pu wrote many works such as *Collections of the Mountain Hermit*, *Manuscripts in Lingnan Ranges*, *Poem Collections of Shicang*, *Interpreting the Seven Books on the Martial Arts*, *Merciful Judgments of the Criminals in Zhejiang*, *Songs and Poems of the You's* and so on, but most of the books were lost. His later generations sorted out his remaining works and compiled two volumes of *Collections of Consultant You Pu*, which still survive. At present, three volumes of his works *Explorations into Different Foreign Nations* were discovered and they are the only survived works of You Pu.

(十一)中国第一任华籍主教——罗文藻

罗文藻,明万历四十年生于福安县罗江罗家巷里巷村,为中国第一任华籍主教。乳名罗才,字汝鼎,福安赛岐罗江人,崇祯六年(1633)秋由方济各会会士、意大利神甫利安当领洗入教,以"额我略"为洗名,入教后以传道员身份,随利安当到南京传教。顺治七年(1650),在藤头加入多明我会,成为中国第一位多明我会会士。康熙十二年(1673),罗马教皇格肋孟多十世颁通谕,命罗文藻为南京主教。康熙二十九年(1690),罗马教皇宣布在中国成立北京和南京两个主教区与澳门分立,罗文藻为南京教区主教。同年十月间突患重病,康熙三十年(1691)病逝,葬于南京雨花台。他被捕过,出过国,足遍10省,为中国天主教的第一位中国籍神甫和第一位中国籍主教。

2.1.4.11 Luo Wenzhao—The First Chinese Bishop in China

Luo Wenzhao(1616-1691AD) was born in Lixiang Village, Luojiaxiang, Luojiang, Fu'an County. He was the first bishop in China. His birth name was Luo Cai(meaning talented) and his courtesy name Ruding. He came from Luojiang, Saiqi Town. In the fall of the 6th year (1633AD) of Emperor Congzhen's reign of the Ming Dynasty, he was baptized by the Italian priest Antonio de Santa Maria Caballero of the Dominican Denomination with Gregorio Lopez his baptism name. After his conversion, Luo Wenzhao worked as a missionary in Nanjing area. In the 7th year (1650AD) of Emperor Shunzhi's reign, he joined the Dominican Denomination in Tengtou and became the first Dominic in China. In the 12th year (1673AD) of Emperor Kangxi's reign of the Qing Dynasty, the Pope of Rome Clemente issued an order and appointed him bishop of Nanjing. In the 29th year (1690AD) of Emperor Kangxi's reign of the Qing Dynasty, the Pope of Rome announced the establishment of two parishes in Beijing and Nanjing, and they be independent from Macau. Luo became bishop of the Nanjing Parish. In October of the same year, Luo suddenly fell ill and passed away in the 30th year (1691AD) of Emperor Kangxi's reign and was buried in Yuhuatai, Nanjing.

(十二)清朝著名虎将——甘国宝

甘国宝,字继赵,号和庵,祖居古田县二十二都(今屏南漈下村),清康熙四十八年(1709)生于勤田县二十六都(今小梨洋村)。康熙五十四年(1715),迁居古田县长岭村。雍正四年(1727),复迁福州文儒坊。曾官至福建陆路提督,兼闽阅操大臣,为清代名将。

雍正七年,中武举。雍正十一年,殿试中二甲八名进士,授御前侍卫。乾隆三年(1738),领侍卫内大臣。旋任广东右翼镇标中军游击、参将。乾隆十六年,授湖广洞庭协副将。乾隆二十年至二十四年,相继出任贵州威宁、江南苏松、浙江温州、闽粤、南粤等地总兵。乾隆二十四年(1759)十月,任台湾挂印总兵,就职后,严疆界,谨斥侯,制总巡、时刻防范来犯之敌;同时深入民间,熟悉风土民情,教台民明礼义,勤耕种,搞好民族团结,从而稳定台湾局势,使"兵安其伍,民安其业"。乾隆二十六年(1761),擢升为福建水师提督。乾隆三十二年(1767),升任广东提督。乾隆三十四年(1769),任福建陆路提督,兼闽阅操大臣。甘国宝致力海防,热心公益,先后倡修古田汤寿桥、朝天桥,厦门天后宫,泉州元庙观。乾隆四十一年,出巡福建八府,途经泉州府邸,忽染重病,医治无效而逝。葬于福州北关外猫头山。六营十郡将校思慕其恩,台湾百姓敬仰其政绩,均建祠设祀。

2.1.4.12 Gan Guobao—A Famous and Brave General of the Qing Dynasty

Cian Guobao, with Jizhao as his courtesy name and He'an as his art name, was born at No. 26 Village of Gutian County (now Xiaoliyang Village, Pingnan) in the 48th year (1709AD) of Emperor Kangxi's reign of the Qing Dynasty. In the 54th year (1715AD) of Emperor Kangxi's reign, his family moved to Changling Village of Gutian County. In the 4th year (1727AD) of Emperor Yongzheng's reign, he removed to the Wenlufang Lane of Fuzhou City. He was appointed chief army general of Fujian and minister in charge of the training of the army. He was a famous general in the Qing Dynasty.

In the 7th year of Emperor Yongzheng's reign, he was a successful candidate in the imperial military exams. In the 11th year of the same period, he became one of the 8 successful candidates in the highest imperial exams of Class II and was awarded by the emperor to be an emperor's bodyguard. In the 3rd year (1738AD) he was in charge of the imperial bodyguard army. He was once a frontier military commander of a battalion in Guangdong. In the 16th year of Emperor Qianlong's reign, he was appointed deputy general in charge of Hubei, Guangdong and Dongting areas. From the 20th to 24th year of the same period, he consecutively was appointed general commander in Weining of Guizhou, Susong of Jiangsu, Wenzhou of Zhejiang, Fujian, Guangdong, and Macau, etc.

During October of the 24th year (1759AD) of Emperor Qianlong's reign of the Qing Dynasty, Gan Guobao was appointed army chief of Taiwan. He strengthened the boundary check, frequently reconnoitered and patrolled to be instantly alert against any invasion of the enemies. Meanwhile he mingled with the folks to be familiar with the situations, taught them good manners and emphasized farming as well as harmonized the ethnic relations in order to stabilize Taiwan's situation so that the solders would serve voluntarily and the folks were satisfied with their business and life.

During the 26th year (1761AD) of Emperor Qianlong's reign of the Qing Dynasty, Gan Guobao was promoted to the provincial commander-in-chief of the navy of Fujian province. In the 32nd year (1767AD) of the same period, he was promoted to be commander in chief of Guangdong Province. During the 34th year (1769AD) of the same period, he was appointed commander in chief of the army and concurrently minister in charge of the military training in Fujian Province. He spared no efforts in strengthening the coastal defense and was zealous in promoting public welfare. He suggested successively building Tanshou and Chaotian bridges in Gutian County; Tianhou Palace in Xiamen, and Yuanmiao Temple in Quanzhou. In the 41st year of the same period, he toured through the eight prefectures of Fujian province. When inspecting Quanzhou Prefecture, he suddenly fell ill seriously and passed away after some vain medical treatment. He was buried in the Maotou Mountain in the northern gate of Fuzhou City. All the army and the generals in the 6 battalions and ten prefectures missed him and the folks in Taiwan also revered his administrative merits so they all built temples to honor him.

(十三)佛教领袖——圆瑛

圆瑛,俗名吴亨春,法名宏悟,别号韬光。光绪四年(1878)生于古田县平湖乡端上村农家。中华人民共和国成立后为中国佛教协会首任会长。圆瑛6岁时父母双亡,自幼聪颖,诗文过目成诵,乡人视之为“神童”。18岁时考中秀才,萌生出家之念。翌年,决意皈依佛门,遂至福州鼓山涌泉寺拜增西上人为师,后转至雪峰寺为僧。民国三年被选为中华佛教总会参议长。民国十七年,他被推为刚成立的中国佛教会主席,并连任七届,成为中国佛教界的领袖人物。民国三十四年(1945),在上海创立"圆明楞严专宗学院",自任院长以来培养大批高级佛学人才。1953年5月,圆瑛被推选为中国佛教协会首任会长,为当代爱国名僧、佛教领袖。圆瑛不仅佛学造诣精湛,且擅长诗文、书法,国内主要禅林都留有他的墨迹。1992年,古田人民在古田极乐寺内修建了圆瑛纪念馆。

2.1.4.13 Yuan Ying—A Leader of the Buddhist Circle

Yuan Ying, with Wu Xiangchun as his secular name, Hongwu as his Buddhist name and Taoguang as his art name, was born to a peasant's family in Ruishang Village, Pinghu Township, Gutian County. He became the first director of China Buddhism Association after the founding of the People's Republic of China. When he was only 6 years old, both of his parents died. He was very smart since childhood and could remember all the poems and prose he read once. He was regarded as a genius child by his folks. When he was 18, he succeeded in becoming a successful candidate in the imperial exams at the county level. However, the thought to become a Buddhist struck him. The following year, he decided to be converted to Buddhism. Therefore, he went to the Yongquan Temple in Mount Gushan in Fuzhou to be a student of Monk Zeng Xi Shang Ren. Later he was assigned to be a monk at the Xiefeng Temple.

During the 3rd year of the Republic of China, he was selected chief consultant for the General Association of China Buddhism. In the 17th year of the ROC, he was appointed chairman of the newly founded China Buddhism Association. What was more, he was reelected 7 times and became the leader of Buddhism in China. In the 34th year of the ROC, he established in Shanghai Yuanming Lengyanzhuan Denomination Institute, acted president himself there and cultivated many high-caliber Buddhism talents. In May 1953, he was recommended to be the first chairman of China Buddhism Association. He was a renowned patriotic Buddhist monk at modern times and a leader of Buddhism. He was not only an expert at Buddhism, but was also good at poems and calligraphy. The main temples in China keep his calligraphy. In 1992, Yuanying Memorial Hall was built in the Jile Temple for him.

(十四)中国世界语第一人——林振翰

林振翰,字永修,号蔚文,清光绪十年(1884)生于宁德蕉城士绅家庭。民国时期著名盐政专家，中国第一部世界语教材翻译者。

光绪二十三年(1897)，林振翰入福州格致书院，1902 年以优异成绩被选送到北京"京师大学堂译学馆"深造。他利用课余时间研读波兰柴门霍夫的《世界语》，并逐一翻译成汉语，编著成《汉译世界语》一书，经英国学者乌克那博士审校后于 1911 年正式出版。

林振翰除荐介世界语到中国为世所珍外，在盐政改革上亦业绩卓著。在近代盐政史上他与盐政专家左司勤齐名。其著述百余万言，在当时曾被盐政人员奉为圭臬。其著作今仍行世者有《中国盐政史》《盐政辞典》《精盐调查录》《川盐纪要》《淮盐纪要》《汉译世界语》《英文正字》等。

2.1.4.14 Lin Zhenhan—The First Person to Introduce Esperanto to China

Lin Zhenhan, with Yongxiu as his courtesy name and Weiwen as his art name was born into a gentry's family in Jiaocheng District of Ningde. He was a well known expert on salt administration and a translator of the first Esperanto textbook.

During the 23rd year (1897AD) of Emperor Guangxu's reign of the Qing Dynasty, he was enrolled by Fuzhou Gezhi College. In 1902, he was sent to Translation Department of Beijing Imperial School to receive further education. He made use of his spare time to study *Esperanto* compiled by Zamenhof of Poland, translated it into Chinese sentence by sentence and compiled into *Chinese Version of Esperanto*. In 1911, it was formally published after proofreading by Wu Kena, a British scholar.

Mr. Lin Zhenhan was highly thought of for his introduction of Esperanto to China. In addition, he was well achieved in the reforms of the salt administration and was as famous as Mr. Zuo Siqin, an expert in the same field in the modern history. He had published over millions of words which were regarded as masterpieces by the salt administrators. His works in circulation are: *The History of the Salt Administration in China*, *The Dictionary of the Salt Administration*, *The Investigation of the Refined Salt*, *The Memoir of the Salt Business in Sichuan*, *The Memoir of the Salt Business in the Huai River Areas*, *Esperanto in Chinese Version*, and *English-Chinese Dictionary*, etc.

(十五)著名易学专家——黄寿祺

黄寿祺，字之六，号六庵，一度自号巢孙，霞浦县盐田人。民国元年生于清末秀才家庭。曾任福建师范大学教授、副校长，著名易学专家。

民国十七年，黄寿祺考入省立福州第一高级中学。翌年，赴北平考入私立中国大学文科预科。两年后升入本科国学系。又四年毕业，获文学士学位。民国二十六年，撰写《易》类提要 30 篇，《礼》类提要 60 篇，并整理《易类提要目录》1 册。民国二十九年，著有《汉易条例》《六庵易话》《六庵读礼录》《历代易学目录考》《尚氏易要义》《丧服浅说》《宋儒学说讲稿》《明儒学说讲稿》等计 42 卷，以及《六庵读书札记》100 余册。

民国三十年冬，他先在福建省立师范专科学校（下称师专）、继在国立海疆学校任副教授，后又重返师专任教授兼国文科主任，直至 1949 年 8 月福州解放。

1972 年秋，任福建师范大学教授兼中文系主任。1979 年，升任副校长。兼任硕士研究生导师。1981 年，加入中国共产党。著有《六庵诗选》《易学群书平议》《楚辞全译》《周易译注》《周易研究论文集》（1—4 辑）（后三书系与人合著或合编）等专著和《从易传看孔子的教育思想》《论易学之门庭》等专稿。

2.1.4.15 Huang Shouqi—A Famous Expert on *The Book of Changes*

Huang Shouqi, with Zhiliu as his courtesy name and Liu'an as his art name and Caosun as his self-calling name, was from Yantian, Xiapu County and was born in the first year of the ROC to a scholar family from the Late Qing Dynasty. He was a professor, and an associate president of Fujian Normal University as well as a well-known expert on *The Book of Changes*.

During the 17th year of the ROC, he was admitted to Fuzhou No. 1 High School of Fujian Province. The next year, he went to Peking for the entrance exams and was admitted to the preparatory class of social arts of China Private University. Two years later, he was enrolled into the National Classical Studies Department at the undergraduate level. Four years later, he graduated and received a bachelor degree. In the 26th year of the ROC, he wrote 30 summaries on *The Book of Changes* and 60 summaries on *The Book of Courtesy* and compiled and edited one volume of *the Catalog of the Main Ideas on The Book of Changes*. In the 29th year of the ROC, he wrote *The Ordinances of the Book of Changes*, *Thoughts on the Book of Changes by Liu An*, *Notes on Reading The Book of Courtesy by Liu An*, *A Survey of the Catalogs of the Studies on The Book of Changes over Generations*, *The Summaries of the Studies on The Book of Changes by Mr. Shang*, *A Brief Talk on the Funeral Uniforms*, *Lectures on Confucianism in the Song Dynasty*, *Lectures on Confucianism in the Ming Dynasty*, in total 42 volumes; in addition, he also published over 100 issues of *Reading Notes by Liu An*.

In the winter of the 30th year of the ROC, he worked as an associate professor in Fujian Provincial Teachers College and National Haijiang College respectively. Later he returned to work in the teachers college as a professor and director of the Social Arts Department till the liberation of Fuzhou in August 1949.

In the fall of 1972, he became a professor and dean of the Chinese Department of Fujian Normal University. In 1979, he was promoted to be vice president and a mentor to the postgraduates there and in 1981, he joined the Communist Party of China. In his life he wrote many books like *Poem Collections of Liu An*, *Comments on the Different Books on the Book of Changes*, *The Complete Translation of the Ci Prose of the Chu State*, *Notes on the Book of Change* and *Essay Collections of the Researches on the Book of Changes*(*Vol*.1-4), as well as articles such as "A Glimpse at the Educational Ideas of Confucius on the Book of Changes" and "The Research on the Book of the Changes".

(十六)医学寄生虫学家,医学教育家——陈心陶

陈心陶,清光绪三十年(1904)生于古田县松吉乡曹阳村。1925年毕业于福建协和大学生物学系。1928—1931年在美国明尼苏达大学攻读寄生虫学,获理学硕士学位,在哈佛大学医学院进修比较病理学,获哲学博士学位。他曾任岭南大学医学院和江西省中正医学院寄生虫学及细菌学教授,福建厦门大学生物学教授,广东省血吸虫病研究所所长,广东省热带病研究所所长,广东省生物学会理事长,广东省寄生虫学会理事长。

陈心陶还曾担任中共广东省委委员,第三、四届全国人民代表大会代表,中共广州中山医科大学委员会委员、中山医科大学教研室主任,并参加过最高国务会议和政协全国会议,多次受到毛泽东和周恩来的接见。

2.1.4.16 Chen Xintao—A Medical Expert on Medical Parasitology and Medical Education

Chen Xintao was born in Caoyang Village, Songji Town, Gutian County in the 30th year (1904AD) of Emperor Guangxu's reign of the Qing Dynasty. In 1925 he graduated from the Biology Department of Fukien Christian University. From 1928-1931, he was doing his master studies in Minnesota University and received his master degree. Then he studied comparative pathology and obtained his doctor degree.

He had been a professor of Lingnan University of Guangdong, Zhongzheng Medical University in Jiangxi, Lingnan Medical University in

Guangzhou, Xiamen University of Fujian, etc. He was also a director of many institutes such as of Schistosoma Research School of Guangdong, Tropical Diseases Research Institute of Guangdong, Guangdong Provincial Biology Association, and Guangdong Provincial Schistosoma Research Association.

He was also a member of the Party Committee of Guangdong Province, a representative of the third and fourth National People's Congress, a member of the administrative committee of Zhongshan Medical College of Guangzhou, as well as the director of the Teaching and Research Division of Zhongshan Medical College. He also attended the highest State Council meetings and political consultative conferences of the country and was received many times by Chairman Mao Zedong and Premier Zhou Enlai.

(十七)开国少将 闽东第一位将军——陈挺

陈挺出生于福建福安白石乡山头仔村,两岁随母(改嫁)迁至潭头乡后洋村。少年于福安潭头镇长大。1930 年加入中国共产党,1932 年参加中国工农红军,曾任队长、连长、营长、支队长、团长、副师长、师长,福建军区司令部参谋长、副司令员,福州军区司令部副参谋长,闽北指挥部副司令员,江西生产建设兵团副司令员,江西省军区副司令员、顾问,福建省军区副司令员、福建省军区顾问(副兵团职待遇)等职。陈挺 1961 年被授予少将军衔,成为中华人民共和国成立后闽东最早的一位将军。2005 年 2 月 18 日,陈挺因病在江苏省苏州市逝世,享年 94 岁。

2.1.4.17 Chen Ting—A Major General of PRC and the First General in Mindong (East Fujian)

General Chen Ting was born in Shantouzi Village, Baishi Township, Fu'an. When he was two years old, he followed his mother who was remarried and moved to Houyang Village, Tantou Township and grew up there. In 1930 he joined the Communist Party and was a member of the Red Army of the Workers and Peasants in 1932 and consecutively became a team leader, a commander of a company, a battalion, a branch, a regimental, and a deputy commander and commander of a division, a commander of Fujian Military Region, chief of staff, deputy commander, commander, deputy chief staff of Fuzhou Military Region, deputy commander of Northern Fujian Headquarters, deputy commander of the production and construction region, deputy commander and consultant of Jiangxi Provincial Military Region, as well as deputy commander and consultant of Fujian Provincial Military Region. In 1961 he was appointed major general and became the first general in Mindong.

On February 18, 2005, he passed away because of illness at the age of 94 in Suzhou City, Jiangsu Province.

第二节 时 政

2.2 The Present Ningde: Facts and Figures

一、宁德城市性质与发展目标

宁德市人民政府在《宁德市城市总体规划(2009—2030)》中提出,宁德城市性质为“海峡西岸经济区东北翼中心城市,沿海重要港口枢纽,能源和临港产业基地,绿色宜居海湾新城”。

城市发展目标是建设成为海西东北翼中心城市,对接长三角前沿区域、对台交流合作重要平台、临港先进制造业基地、东南沿海重要港口枢纽、海西特色文化和生态旅游基地、绿色宜居海湾新城。

宁德作为“海峡西岸经济区东北翼中心城市”,除了具有得天独厚的港口资源优势外,还具有良好的区域优势。如今宁德肩负着改革开放的历史使命,发扬“滴水穿石”的闽东精神,人一我十、力求先行,坚定不移地建设“海峡西岸经济区东北翼中心城市”。

2.2.1 Characteristics of Ningde and Its Goals for Development

Ningde Municipal Government in its *General Urban Planning of Ningde City* (2009-2030) proposes that the nature of Ningde City is “a central city in the northeast of the Western Taiwan Strait Economic Development Zone, a key coastal port pivot, an energy and coastal industrial base, a green and livable new city.

Its goals for developments are: to build itself into a central city in the northeast of the Western Taiwan Strait Economic Development Zone, to be a front area connected with the Yangtze River Delta Regions, an important platform for exchanges with Taiwan, an advanced coastal manufacturing base, a key coastal port pivot in the southeast of China, a cultural and tourism base with features of the Western Taiwan Economic Development Zone as well as a new coastal and livable city.

Ningde City, as a central city in the northeast of the Western Taiwan Strait Economic Development Zone, enjoys advantageous locations and unique port resources. Nowadays Ningde City is shouldering a historical mission of opening up and reforms and striving hard and steadily to construct "a central city in the northeast of the Western Taiwan Strait Economic Development Zone" with the spirit cultivated Mindong like "Dripping Water Wears down Rocks", "Working Ten Times Harder than Others", "Strive to Take Earlier Action" and so on.

二、宁德的城市精神

"滴水穿石"是习近平主席在闽东工作期间提出并倡导的工作作风和精神品格。

1988年10月,习近平同志在接受《经济日报》记者采访时指出,中华人民共和国成立以来,闽东发生的变化,是"滴水穿石"般的变化,是不简单的。这是他首次提出"滴水穿石"的理念。他指出:"闽东的落后状况是历史形成的,改变闽东的落后面貌不能靠一朝一夕之功,而需要有一股韧劲。没有锲而不舍的毅力,不愿付出艰辛于他人数倍的努力,不靠一点一滴量的积累,涓滴成流,聚沙成塔,是不能做成事业的。"

二十多年来,在"滴水穿石"的闽东精神引领和激励下,经过多年来坚持不懈地打基础、强配套,闽东人民终于初步实现了"三大梦想"。2000年11月实现撤地设市,现在宁德中心城区已经初具规模,功能逐步完善,建成区面积是建市之初的三倍。2007年,宁德市委提出环三都澳区域发展构想,2008年上升为省委、省政府决策,2009年进入国家规划,促进了宁德发展向海洋拓展、向新型工业化转型,使宁德由全省边缘地区向对接长三角和对台合作的战略前沿转变。2009年9月温福铁路投入运营,以沈海高速、温福铁路、宁武高速为标志的现代化交通基础设施建成使用,使宁德实现了从山区到沿海的"华丽转身"。这些发展变化就是闽东人民发扬"滴水穿石"精神的结果。

二十多年来,"滴水穿石"的闽东精神始终在宁德得到传承、弘扬和发展,始终是振兴闽东的力量源泉和动力。今天,面对"承载新梦想、实现新跨越"的新任务、新要求,我们坚信"滴水穿石"精神也必将继续鞭策和鼓舞闽东人民实现科学发展、跨越发展,为打造"机制活、产业优、百姓富、生态美"的新福建做出更大贡献。

2.2.2 The City Spirit of Ningde

The spirit of "Dripping Water Wears down Rocks" or the spirit of perseverance and a type of working style, was proposed, advocated by President Xi when he worked in Eastern Fujian. In October 1988, when having an interview with *Economics Journal*, President Xi pointed out, since the founding of PRC, great changes had taken place in Eastern Fujian. The changes were achieved difficultly as the results of "Dripping Water Wears down Rocks". That was the first time he proposed the concept of "Dripping Water Wears down Rocks". He pointed out, "The backward situation in Mindong was a result of history. To change the backwardness was not easy and could not be done overnight, yet requires perseverance. Without it, or unwilling to work much harder than others, or without accumulation bit by bit like a small brook turning into a river, or like some small amount sand gathering into a tower, nothing can be achieved."

For over 20 years, driven and inspired by the Mindong Spirit of "Dripping Water Wears down Rocks", and after many years of perseverance to lay a solid foundation and strengthen the relevant development, the people in Mindong finally realized their three major dreams: in November, 2000, the prefectural administration was replaced by municipal administration in Ningde City. Now the central urban area of Ningde City is in quite a shape and its functions improve steadily and its size triples that of Ningde when the municipal administration was established. In 2007, Ningde Municipal Party Committee put forward the development ideas for the Sandu Bay regions. In 2008, those ideas were adopted and became the strategies of Fujian Provincial Party Committee and Government. In 2009, the strategies became the national plan which boosted Ningde's expansion towards the sea, as well as transformed the industrial growth to a new type so that Ningde became a strategic zone which was a mountainous area and now is connected with the Delta and Taiwan regions. In September, 2009, Wenzhou-Fuzhou Railway was put into operation in addition to the completion of Shenyang-Hainan Expressway and Ningde-Wuyishan Expressway, which made Ningde have a beautiful transform from a mountainous city to a coastal city. All these changes were the results achieved by the people of Mindong with the spirit of "Dripping Water Wears down Rocks".

Over 20 years, the spirit of "Dripping Water Wears down Rocks" has been passed on, promoted and expanded in Ningde. The spirit has become a power source and momentum for Ningde to rejuvenate. Today, with the new task and new requirement of bearing new dreams and realizing new leaps in mind, we firmly believe that the spirit will encourage the people in Ningde to carry out balanced and leaping development so as to make greater contribution to building a new Fujian of "Flexible Mechanism, Excellent Industries, Prosperous Citizens and Beautiful Environment".

三、宁德市政府工作重点

2009年5月6日,国务院以国发〔2009〕24号印发《关于支持福建省加快建设海峡西岸经济区的若干意见》。为贯彻落实国务院《意见》,省委八届六次全会审议通过了《福建省贯彻落实国务院〈意见〉的实施意见》,讨论并通过了《福建省建设海峡西岸经济区纲要(修编)》。国务院《意见》和我省的这两份重要文件的出台,为宁德市发展提供了千载难逢的历史性机遇。为认真贯彻国务院《意见》和我省这两份重要文件,2009年9月4日,宁德市委、市政府制定了市政府的工作重点:加快建设海西东北翼中心城市,全力推进环三都澳区域发展。

2.2.3 Work Focus of Ningde Municipal Government

On May 6, 2009, the State Council issued the 24th Document 〔2009〕of *Decisions on Supporting Fujian to Speed up the Building of the Western Taiwan Straits Economic Zone*. In order to implement *The Decisions*, Fujian Provincial Committee in its 6th Session of the 8th Congress Meeting passed *Implementing Decisions of Fujian Province Carrying out the Decisions of the State Council*. Meanwhile *Revisions of the Outlines of Fujian Province on How to Build the Western Taiwan Straits Economic Zone* were passed in principle. *The Decisions* of the State Council and the two important documents of Fujian Province provide an unprecedented opportunity for Ningde to integrate itself into the comprehensive building of the Western Taiwan Straits Economic Zone and speeding up the development of the regions around Sandu Bay. Therefore, Ningde Municipal Party Committee and Government on September 4, 2009 mapped out the work focuses: to speed up the building of the central city in the northeast of Fujian Province and to go all out boosting the regional development around Sandu Bay.

(一)加快建设海西东北翼中心城市

2009年5月6日,国务院以国发〔2009〕24号印发《关于支持福建省加快建设海峡西岸经济区的若干意见》,表明福建省已成为国家重点发展海峡西岸经济区建设的主体,发展战略已从区域战略上升为国家战略。这标志着海峡西岸经济区建设站在了一个新的起点上,极大地提升了福建在全国格局中的地位,也凸显了宁德的区位、港口、资源和后发优势,为承接国内外产业转移,调整优化经济结构,在更高层次上加速发展创造了条件,今日的宁德已经进入了一个蓄势待发、加快发展的新阶段。

2.2.3.1 Speed up Building the Central City in the Northeast of the Western Taiwan Straits Economic Development Zone

On May 6,2009, the State Council issued its 24th Document 〔2009〕 of *Decisions on Supporting Fujian to Speed up the Building of the Western Taiwan Straits Economic Zone*, which indicates that Fujian Province have become a major area for construction in the Western Taiwan Straits Economic Zone. Fujian's development strategy has been upgraded to a national strategy. It also shows that the building of the Western Taiwan Straits Economic Zone was at a new start and that Fujian had upgraded itself to a more important place, which also highlighted the potential advantages of the locations, ports and resources in Ningde. Now there are conditions for Ningde to receive transfer of domestic and foreign industries, to restructure its economies and to develop at a higher level. Ningde today is gaining momentum and at a new stage to speed up its growth.

(二)全力推进环三都澳区域发展

环三都澳区域,是指以三都澳为中心,以宁德沿海 1 046 千米岸线为主轴,立足宁德、融入海西,面向台湾、背靠内陆,北承温州、南接福州,具有独特优势和巨大潜力的经济发展区域。宁德作为海峡西岸经济区东北翼的重要增长极,应结合区位、资源、环境、产业、人文等优势,重点明确六个方面发展定位:其一是海西对接长三角前沿区域。充分发挥区位优势,增强与长三角区域的互动融合,大力推进金融、物流服务、商贸流通、旅游开发、基础设施及招商平台建设等领域的双向对接,重点加强与温州、丽水、衢州等浙南地区和上饶等赣东北地区的区域合作,主动承接其产业、资金、技术及人才转移,增强要素虹吸效应,加快建成海峡西岸对接长三角的前沿区域。其二是对台交流合作重要平台。发挥对台前沿优势,实施先行先试政策,加快对台直航口岸、台湾水产品集散中心和万亩台湾工业园等建设,争取设立两岸合作的海关特殊监管区,推动与基隆市经济文化交流合作向更广领域、更大规模、更高层次迈进,努力把环三都澳区域建设成为两岸交流合作的重要平台。其三是临港先进制造业基地。科学规划,加快开发深水港湾资源,主动对接台湾制造业,大力发展能源、冶金、机械、船舶、石化、风电设备等产业,努力打造技术先进、支撑有力、竞争力强的海峡西岸先进制造业基地。其四是东南沿海重要港口枢纽。大力推进高等级公路、大运力铁路、深水泊位等交通通道建设,加快完善港口集疏运体系，构建便捷的“北承南联，西进东出”的现代化综合交通网络，形成海峡西岸服务内陆省份和拓展对台合作的出海大通道，打造我国东南沿海的重要港口交通枢纽。其五是海西特色文化和生态旅游胜地。发挥宁德“山海川岛湖林洞”等自然资源与人文景观交融的独特优势，精心打造一批国家级、省级重点风景区，拓展与弘扬畲族文化、民俗文化、宗教文化、红色文化、海洋文化、茗茶文化等特色文化内涵，大力发展生态旅游休闲度假产业，将宁德打造成为海西重要的自然和文化旅游中心，和国内一流、世界知名的旅游度假胜地。其六是绿色宜居海湾新城。按照“临海、跨海、环海”三步跃升的城市发展战略，走产业、城市、港口与生态相协调的发展道路，优化城市空间布局，完善城市基础设施和公共服务体系，提升城市功能，增强辐射带动能力。大力推动环三都澳城市群发展，建设布局合理、结构协调、功能明确、特色鲜明、环境优美、绿色宜居的城镇体系。

2.2.3.2 Efforts on the Development of Circum-Sandu Bay Region

That refers to these places with unique advantages and huge potential for development that are centered around Sandu Bay, with the 1 046-kilometer coastline of Ningde as the main axis, facing Taiwan in the east and connecting with the hinterland provinces in the west, Wenzhou in the north and Fuzhou in the south of the Western Taiwan Straits Economic Zone.

Ningde, as an important growth pole in the northeast of the Zone, and combined with its locations, resources, environment, industries and cultures and so on, has decided the six aspects for development:

First, to become a close place that is connected with the Yangze River Delta regions in the Western Taiwan Straits Economic Zone. Ningde is making full use of its location advantage and strengthens its interaction with the Delta regions to push forward its mutual integrations of financing, logistics, trade, tourism, infrastructure, and investment promotion, etc. The focus is to enhance the cooperation with Wenzhou City, Lishui City and Quzhou City in the south of Zhejiang Province and Shangrao City in the northeast of Jiangxi Province. Initial steps are taken to receive their transfer of industries, capital, technology and talents. The power to receive the factors must be strengthened so as to speed up the building of Ningde of the Western Taiwan Straits Economic Zone.

Second, to turn Ningde into an important exchange platform with Taiwan. Make full use of the close advantage with Taiwan and implement the Trial and Piloting Policies. Speed up the process of the direct shipping route with Taiwan, and the construction of the Distribution Center of Taiwan Aquatic

Products as well as of the 10 000-Mu Taiwan Industrial Park and so on. Efforts are made to set up the special supervision zone of the customs between the Strait. Push forward the economic and cultural cooperation between Ningde and Keelung (Jilong) to a wider scope, greater scale and higher level so as to build the Saudu Bay areas into an important exchange platform with Taiwan.

Third, to turn Ningde into an advanced coastal manufacturing base. Carry out scientific planning and speed up the development of the deep-harbor resources. Take initial steps to be connected with the Taiwan industries and strive to develop the industries of energy, metallurgy, machinery, ships, petro-chemicals, and wind and electricity, etc. Work hard to turn Ningde into an advanced manufacturing industrial base with Hi-tech, solid foundation and competitiveness.

Fourth, turn Ningde into an important port hub in the southeast coast of China. Great efforts are made to build the traffic channels of high-class expressways, high-capacity railways, and deep-water berths so as to better the transportation systems and build up the modern and comprehensive communication networks that link the four directions of the north, south, east and west. As a result, a grand maritime exit will be built in the Western Taiwan Straits Economic Zone for the inland provinces in the west and will also extend cooperation with Taiwan so that an important port hub will be turned into reality in the southeast coast of China.

Fifth, turn Ningde into a resort of unique cultures and eco-tourism. Make good use of the unique advantages of the natural resources of "mountains, seas, rivers, islands, lakes, forests, and caves" that are integrated with the cultures. Great efforts are made to build a bunch of national and provincial scenic spots. Expand and promote the unique cultural connotations of the local She Ethnic culture, folk culture, religion culture, "Red" culture, maritime culture, and famous tea culture, etc. Strive to develop eco-tourism and leisure holidaying. Turn Ningde into a natural and cultural tourism center in the Western Taiwan Straits Economic Zone as well as a well-known holiday resort at home and abroad.

Sixth, to turn Ningde into a green and livable coastal city. Based on the urban development strategy of the three phases of "by the sea, cross the sea, and round the sea", it is planned to adopt the coordinated development path of linking industries, cities, ports and eco systems together so that the layout of the urban areas can be improved. The urban infrastructural facilities and public service system will be bettered. The functions of the urban areas will be upgraded and their radiating influence will be strengthened. Great efforts are made to push forward the development of urban area so as to build cities that are well planned for construction, well-coordinated in structures, clearly defined in functions, uniquely highlighted with features, environmentally beautiful and the most livable.

(三)开发建设环三都澳区域的目标

努力将环三都澳区域建设成新兴临港先进制造业基地、东南沿海重要港口枢纽,对台交流合作的重要平台,海峡西岸东北翼重要经济增长极,经济快速发展、文化更加繁荣、综合实力不断增强、社会和谐、生态良好、人民安居乐业和绿色宜居海湾新城。

2.2.3.3 Goals for Developing Circum-Sandu Bay Region

We aim to turn the areas into advanced coastal manufacturing bases, important port pivots in the southeast of China, a key exchange platform with Taiwan, a new growth pole in the northeast of Fujian Province and a new coastal city that is fast-paced with its development, more prosperous with its culture, increasingly stronger with its comprehensive power, harmonious with its society, beautiful with its environment, and that the people are happy with their life and work as well as a green and livable city.

四、宁德市委主要党政机关

2.2.4 Major Municipal Party and Government Departments

宁德市党委 Ningde Municipal Party Committee

宁德市政府 Ningde Municipal Government

宁德市金融工作办公室 Ningde Municipal Working Office of Finance

宁德市海防委员会办公室 Ningde Municipal Office of Sea Disaster Prevention Committee

宁德市机关效能建设领导小组办公室 Ningde Municipal Leading Group of Efficiency of the Government Organizations

宁德市发展和改革委 Ningde Municipal Development and Reform Commission

宁德市经济贸易委员会 Ningde Municipal Commission of Economy and Trade

宁德市教育局 Ningde Municipal Education Bureau

宁德市科学技术局 Ningde Municipal Bureau of Science and Technology
宁德市民族与宗教事务局 Ningde Municipal Bureau of Ethnic and Religion Affairs
宁德市公安局 Ningde Municipal Public Security Bureau
宁德市监察局 Ningde Municipal Supervising Bureau
宁德市民政局 Ningde Civil Affairs Bureau
宁德市司法局 Ningde Municipal Justice Bureau
宁德市财政局 Ningde Municipal Finance Bureau
宁德市公务员局 Ningde Municipal Public Servants Bureau
宁德市人力资源和社会保障局 Ningde Municipal Human Resources and Social Security Bureau
宁德市国土资源局 Ningde Municipal Land Resources Bureau
宁德市住房和城乡建设局 Ningde Municipal Housing and Urban Construction Bureau
宁德市交通运输局 Ningde Municipal Transport Bureau
宁德市水利局 Ningde Municipal Bureau of Water Conservancy
宁德市农业局 Ningde Municipal Agricultural Bureau
宁德市对外贸易经济合作局 Ningde Municipal Cooperation Bureau of Foreign Trade and Economy
宁德市文化广电新闻出版局 Ningde Municipal Publishing Bureau of News, Culture and Television
宁德市卫生局 Ningde Municipal Bureau of Healthcare
宁德市人口和计划生育委员会 Ningde Municipal Bureau of Population and Family Planning
宁德市审计局 Ningde Municipal Bureau of Auditing
宁德市林业局 Ningde Municipal Bureau of Forestry
宁德市外事侨务办公室 Ningde Municipal Office of Foreign and Overseas Chinese Affairs
宁德市城乡规划局 Ningde Municipal Bureau of Urban and Rural Planning
宁德市环境保护局 Ningde Municipal Bureau of Environmental Protection
宁德市体育局 Ningde Municipal Bureau of Sports
宁德市统计局 Ningde Municipal Bureau of Statistics
宁德市海洋与渔业局 Ningde Municipal Bureau of Ocean and Fishery
宁德市旅游局 Ningde Municipal Bureau of Tourism
宁德市粮食局 Ningde Municipal Bureau of Grains

宁德市无线电管理局 Ningde Municipal Bureau of Wireless Communication
宁德市地方税务局 Ningde Municipal Bureau of Local Taxation
宁德市工商行政管理局 Ningde Municipal Bureau of Industrial and Administrative Affairs
宁德市质量技术监督局 Ningde Municipal Supervising Bureau of Quality and Technology
宁德市食品药品监督管理局 Ningde Municipal Supervising Bureau of Foods and Medicines
宁德市国家税务局 Ningde Branch of the National Taxation Bureau
宁德市物价局 Ningde Municipal Price Bureau
宁德市房地产管理局 Ningde Municipal Bureau of Real Estate
宁德市乡镇企业局 Ningde Municipal Bureau of Urban and Township Enterprises
宁德市国有资产监督管理委员会 Ningde Municipal Supervising Commission of the National Assets

五、中央、省驻宁德机构

2.2.5 Branches of the Central and Provincial Organs Stationing in Ningde

宁德市国家安全局 Ningde Branch of the National Security Bureau
宁德市国家税务局 Ningde Branch of the State Administration of Taxation
福建省宁德市地方税务局 Ningde Local Taxation Branch of Fujian Provincial Administration Taxation
中华人民共和国宁德海关 Ningde Customs of PRC
中华人民共和国宁德海关缉私分局 Ningde Customs Anti-Smuggling Branch of PRC
中华人民共和国宁德出入境检验检疫局 Ningde Exit and Entry Inspection and Quarantine Bureau of PRC
宁德市工商行政管理局 Ningde Industrial and Commercial Administration of PRC
宁德市质量技术监督局 Ningde Quality and Technology Inspection Bureau of PRC
宁德市食品药品监督管理局 Ningde Foods and Medicine Supervision Bureau of PRC

宁德海事局 Ningde Maritime Affairs Bureau of PRC

中国人民银行宁德中心支行 Ningde Central Branch of the People's Bank of China

中国人民银行监督管理委员会宁德监管分局 Ningde Supervision Bureau of the Supervision Administration of the People's Bank of China

国网福建省电力有限公司宁德供电公司 Ningde Branch of the Electric Power Co., Ltd of Fujian Province of PRC

福建省宁德市无线电管理局 Ningde Radio Management Bureau of Fujian Province

国家统计局宁德调查队 Ningde Investigation Team of the National Statistics Bureau

福建省宁德市烟草专卖局 Ningde Tobacco Monopoly Bureau of Fujian Province

福建省烟草公司宁德市公司 Ningde Branch of Fujian Tobacco Company

宁德市交通综合行政执法支队 Ningde Executive Branch of the Traffic Regulations of Fujian Province

福建省宁德市邮政管理局 Ningde Postal Administration of Fujian Province

福建省盐业公司宁德分公司(宁德盐务局) Ningde Branch of Fujian Salt Company

福建省宁德市气象局 Ningde Municipal Meteorological Bureau of Fujian Province

宁德水文资源勘测分局 Ningde Municipal Branch of the Water Resources Surveying Department of Fujian Province

福建省地震局宁德地震台 Ningde Municipal Seismological Branch of Fujian Provincial Seismological Department

福建省农业科学院茶叶研究所 Tea Research Institute of the Agricultural Academy of Fujian Province

福建省第四地质大队 The Fourth Geological Surveying Team of Fujian Province

福建省闽东海洋环境监测中心站 The Supervising and Surveying Center of the Ocean and Fisheries of Fujian Province

福建省海洋与渔业执法总队直属一支队 Affiliated Branch No.1 of the General Executive Team of the Ocean and Fisheries of Fujian Province

福建省宁德市海洋与渔业执法支队 Ningde Branch of the Executive Department of the Ocean and Fisheries of Fujian Province

福建省宁德市文化市场综合执法支队 Ningde Municipal Branch of the Executive Department of the Cultural Markets of Fujian Province

六、宁德市新闻媒体

2.2.6 News Media in Ningde

闽东日报 *Mindong Daily*

宁德晚报 *Ningde Evening News*

三都澳侨乡报 *Sandu'ao Overseas Chinese Newspaper*

宁德广播电视报 *Ningde Broadcasting and Television Newspaper*

福建日报报业集团东南网宁德站 Ningde Branch of the Southeast Web of *Fujian Daily* Newspaper Group

福建日报驻宁德记者站 Reporters Station of *Fujian Daily* in Ningde

宁德市人民政府公报 Ningde Municipal Government Gazette

书法报社宁德工作站 Ningde Branch of *Calligraphy Newspaper*

海峡摄影时报宁德记者站 Ningde Branch of *TIMES*

海峡教育报宁德办事处 Ningde Branch of *Strait Education Newspaper*

宁德市电视转播台 Ningde Municipal Television Relay Station

宁德市电视微波站 Ningde Municipal Television Microwave Station

宁德市文化广电新闻出版局 The Department of Culture, Radio, Film, TV, Press and Publication of Ningde

宁德市广播电视网络传输中心 Ningde Municipal Television and Broadcasting Networks Transmission Center

宁德市广电中心 Ningde Municipal Broadcasting and Television Center

宁德电视台 Ningde Municipal Television Station

宁德新闻综合频道 Ningde Municipal Comprehensive News Chanel

宁德公共影视频道 Ningde Municipal Public Film Chanel

宁德传媒网 Ningde Municipal Media Networks

宁德广播网 Ningde Municipal Broadcasting Networks

宁德新闻网 Ningde News Networks

福建广播电视台记者站 Ningde Correspondent Station of Fujian Broadcasting and Television Station

第三章 宁德经济

Chapter 3 Economy in Ningde

第一节 经济概况

3.1 Overview

一、综合实力

改革开放以来,宁德取得了辉煌的成就。国民经济快速健康发展、综合实力显著增强,基础环境不断完善、城乡面貌深刻变化,人民群众安居乐业。面对国际金融危机的冲击,宁德人民发扬"滴水穿石"的闽东精神,人一我十、力求先行,抓住福建省已成为国家重点发展海峡西岸经济区建设战略的主体这一历史机遇,坚定不移地加快建设海西东北翼中心城市,全力推进环三都澳区域发展。

2014 年全年实现地区生产总值 1 377.65 亿元,比增 10.8%。公共财政总收入(不含基金收入)140.37 亿元,比增 11.6%;国税总收入 59.06 亿元,比增 12.1%;地税总收入 96.57 亿元,增长 8.2%,固定资产投资 1 157.99 亿元,比增 23.9%,年末城镇登记失业率 1.58%,比省控制目标低 2.42 个百分点。全年进出口总额 40.16 亿美元,比增 23.3%,新签外商直接投资合同项目 21 个,比增 5.0%,实际利用外商直接投资 1.75 亿美元,比增 21.0%。全市居民人均可支配收入 17 560 元,比增 10.1%,实际增长 8.0%。其中,农民人均可支配收入 11 302 元,比增 11.7%,实际增长 9.6%;城镇居民人均可支配收入 23 956 元,比增 9.1%,实际增长 7.1%。全市居民人均生活消费支出 13 128 元,比增 8.9%,实际增长 6.9%。农村居民食品消费支出占消费总支出的比重为 41.0%,城镇居民为

37.4%。人口自然增长率7.0‰。

县域经济发展呈现不断发展壮大的良好发展势头。宁德本市2008年就荣膺“中国商业地产投资环境最佳城市奖”,宁德本市及所辖的福鼎市、福安市,柘荣县、古田县入选2014年“县域经济发展十佳”。此外,宁德霍童荣膺“中国十佳生态养生旅游名镇”,宁德本市级和福鼎市、霞浦县、古田县、蕉城区被授予“2012—2014年度省级文明城市(县城、城区)”荣誉称号,还有蕉城区霍童镇邑坂村等27个村镇被授予“省级文明村镇”称号,实现历史性突破。2015年宁德市被正式命名为“国家园林城市”,福鼎市被正式命名为“省级园林城市”。此前,柘荣县于2007年被命名为“省级园林县城”等称号。

目前,全市拥有省政府批准设立的开发区有5个,分别是宁德东侨经济开发区、闽东赛岐经济开发区、福安畲族经济开发区、宁德三都澳经济开发区、周宁县工业扶贫开发区。

宁德市政府批准设立的开发区有6个,分别是福鼎星火工业园区、屏南溪坪工业小区、闽浙边界寿宁工业小区、古田玉田工业小区、闽东工业园区、福安秦溪洋工业园区。一个经济快速健康发展、综合实力显著增强的新宁德正在崛起;一个基础环境不断完善、城乡面貌深刻变化的新宁德正在崛起;一个民生民利同步提升、人民群众安居乐业的新宁德正在崛起。

3.1.1 Comprehensive Strength

After the reform and opening up to the outside world, Ningde has achieved splendid success. Its national economy has been growing both rapidly and healthily with significantly improved comprehensive strength. Its infrastructural environment has been better and better and its urban and village images have taken on a great look. People are enjoying their life and work. In front of the international financial crisis, people in Ningde, bearing in mind the Mindong Spirit of "Dripping Water Wears down Rocks" and "Working Ten Times Harder than Others" as well as "Strive to Take Earlier Action", firmly speed up the building of the Western Taiwan Straits Economic Zone and push forward with all efforts the development of the Sandu Bay regions by seizing the golden opportunity that the development plans of the Western Taiwan Straits Economic Zone has been upgraded from a local government plan to a national one.

Its GDP in 2014 reached 137.765 billion yuan, up 10.8% over the same period of the previous year. Its total public financial revenue (excluding fund revenue) netted 14.037 billion yuan, up 11.6%. Its national tax income was 5.906 billion yuan, up 12.1%. The total local tax revenue was added up to

9.657 billion yuan, up 8.2%. The investment of fixed assets totaled 11.5799 billion yuan, up 23.9%. The registered unemployment rate was controlled within 1.58%, and it was 2.42% lower than the required goal by the province. The total value of the imports and exports reached 4.016 billion dollars, up 23.3%. The newly signed FDI contract was 21, up by 5.0%. The actual use of FDI was 175 million dollars, up by 21.0%. The per-capital income of the urban residents was up to 17 560 yuan, up by 10.1% and an actual growth of 8.0%, of which the farmers' disposable income was 11 302 yuan, up 11.7% and with an actual growth of 9.6%; the urban residents' disposable income was 23 956 yuan, up 9.1% and with an actual growth of 7.1%. The average spending per capital annually was 13 128 yuan, up 8.9% and with an actual growth of 6.9%. The percentage of spending on food in the villages took up 41% while it was 37.4% in the cities. The natural population growth rate was at 7.0‰.

The economic development in the local county regions has been showing vigorous and strong momentums. Ningde Municipality was awarded in 2008 the honorable title "Best Investment Environment City For Real Estate Business in China". Fu'an City, Fuding City, Zherong County and Gutian County under jurisdiction of Ningde Municipality were enrolled in 2014 as "Ten Best Counties/Regions for Economic Development". Besides, Huotong Town of Ningde received an honor to be one of "Ten Best Eco-Tourism Townships in China". And Ningde Municipality and its Fuding City, Xiapu County, Gutian County, Jiaocheng District were awarded an honorable title "2012-2014 Provincial Model Cities (County/District) of Civilization". In addition, Yibang Village and 27 other villages locally were awarded "Provincial Model Villages/Townships of Civilization so that there was a historic breakthrough in this regard. In 2015 Ningde City was awarded formally "National Garden City" while Fuding City was awarded "Provincial Garden City". Before this, Zherong County in 2007 was already awarded "Provincial Garden County".

So far, there are five economic development zones in Ningde approved by the Provincial Government. They are Dongqiao Economic Development Zone of Ningde City, the Saiqi Economic Development Zone of Ningde City, the She Ethnic Development Zone of Fu'an City, Ningde Sandu'ao Economic Development Zone, and Poverty-Relief Industrial Development Zone of Zhouning County.

Ningde Municipal Government also approved 6 development zones. They are Fuding Spark Industrial Zone, Xiping Industrial Zone of Pingnan County, Shouning Industrial Park Between Fujian and Zhejiang Provinces, Yutian Industrial Zone of Gutian County, Mindong Industrial Zone, and Qinyangxi Industrial Zone of Fu'an City. A new Ningde is emerging with fast and healthy economic development and obviously strengthened comprehensive capacity; A new Ningde is emerging with ever improved infrastructural environment and fundamentally changed outlooks; A new Ningde is emerging with co-improvement of the wellbeing and benefit of the residents as well as of the happy residence and employment for the local people.

二、经济结构

经济发展由传统经济向现代化技术经济加速转变,产业结构加快调整,由1978年的45.1∶28.4∶26.5,调整为2008年的19.8∶40.4∶39.8,到2010年的18.5∶43.4∶38.1,再到2015年调整为10∶51∶39。经济实现跨越式发展,形成电机电器、船舶修造、新能源、冶金等一批产值超百亿、拥有自主知识产权和知名品牌、竞争力较强的优势重点企业和特色产业集群。优势产品逐步向高附加值发展,产业链不断延伸拓展。

加快推进传统优势产业转型升级,培育发展一批战略性新兴产业,为宁德实现跨越发展增添新动力,大力培育和发展市场前景广、资源消耗低、带动系数大的新能源、新材料、生物医药三大战略性新兴产业,并积极向节能环保、IT、物联网、电子元器件、地质勘探仪器等领域拓展,加快发展现代服务业,包括现代物流、商贸流通、房地产、金融保险拓展服务业发展领域,加快培育旅游产业,打造世界知名旅游品牌,加快海洋经济开发,做大做强海洋经济,着力强化海洋科技创新,切实加强海洋开发保护。

围绕建设"六新大宁德"(高质高效新产业的大宁德、宜业宜居新城镇的大宁德、畅通便捷新交通的大宁德、丰富多彩新文化的大宁德、幸福和谐新民生的大宁德、优质优美新环境的大宁德)的总任务,深入实施"工业立市、海洋强市、科教兴市、生态美市、创新活市"战略,更加注重转变经济发展方式,更加注重发展实体经济,更加注重保障和改善民生,更加注重统筹城乡建设发展,更加注重深化改革开放,更加注重社会管理创新,加快形成"五位一体"的建设格局,努力走出新型工业化、信息化、城镇化、农业现代化的发展新路,把宁德打造成为福建新增长极,跻身全省第二方阵,到2017年与全省同步全面建成小康社会。

3.1.2 Economic Structure

Economic development speeds up its shift from the traditional economy to modern technological economy with industrial structure adjustment ratio of 45. 1 : 28. 4 : 26. 5 in 1978 to 19. 8 : 40. 4 : 39. 8 in 2008, and then to 18. 5 : 43. 4 : 38. 1 in 2010, and 10 : 51 : 39 in 2015. Economy here saw striding development and witnessed many key and feature industrial groups of electric motors and appliances, ship repairing and building, new energy, and metallurgy, etc. Each group is worth over 10 billion yuan and has its own intellectual property and famous brands as well as competitive advantages. The advantageous products become more value-added and their industrial chains are expanding.

The transformation and upgrading of traditional advantageous industries have been accelerated. And some new strategic industries have been cultivated and developed so that new momentum has been added to the striding development of Ningde. Great efforts are made to cultivate and develop three new strategic industries that enjoy broad prospects with markets, energy-friendly and bigger driving coefficient such as new energy, new material and biomedicines. Meanwhile great efforts are made also to expand to energy saving and environment friendly industries, IT, objects-networking, electronic components, geological surveying devices. And the development has been sped up for modern logistics, commercial circulation, real estate, finance and insurance and the like. Efforts are made to speed up the cultivation of tourism in order to create the world famous brands. Ocean economic development is sped up so that ocean economy can get stronger and bigger. Efforts are made to innovate ocean technology so as to strengthen ocean development and protection.

Centered around the construction of "Mega Ningde in Six New Aspects" (Mega Ningde with High-Quality and High-Efficient New Industries; Mega Ningde with Business-Friendly and Livable Towns; Mega Ningde with Convenient Traffic and Transportation; Mega Ningde with Colorful and New Culture; Mega Ningde with Happy and Harmonious New Wellbeing; Mega Ningde with Excellent Quality and New Environment), Ningde Municipality further implements new strategies that "Industries become the cornerstone for the city; the ocean helps strengthen the city, science and technology prosper the city; the ecological environment beautifies the city; and the innovation activates the city. More attention will be paid respectively to the shift of the economic development modes; the development of actual economies; the social guarantee and improvement of the wellbeing; the mutual development of the urban and countryside areas; the further reforms and opening up; the innovation of the social management of "five aspects getting integrated". Efforts are made to find new paths for new types of industrialization, information, urbanization and agricultural modernization so that Ningde will be built into a new growth pole in Fujian Province and will join the second tier cities in the province so as to build a moderately prosperous society in 2017 with other parts of the Province.

第二节　现代农业

3.2 Modern Agriculture

一、新农村建设

宁德市在加快推进新型工业化进程中，加快推进农业现代化，坚持"三农"重中之重地位不动摇，大力推进社会主义新农村建设，加快转变农业发展方式，完善强农惠农投入稳定增长机制，夯实农业农村发展基础，落实各项强农惠农政策，及时兑现农资综合补贴、农作物良种补贴、粮食直补、农机具购置补贴等补贴政策，确保赋予农民的实惠不缩水等，农村各项改革成效明显。新农村建设，围绕"百姓富、生态美"的主题，启动"农村普惠金融"工程建设，大力提高农村金融服务覆盖面，实现农村金融服务均等化、便捷化、全面化、现代化的目的，让农业更强、农民更富、农村更美。加快农村水利、道路、电网、沼气、渔港，城乡公路网建设和村村通客车工程等基础设施建设。2015 年，又将实施新一轮"千村整治、百村示范"工程，整治改善 134 个村庄人居环境，创建 13 个美丽宜居村庄(美丽乡村示范村)，深入开展"新农村试点示范"建设和"创绿色家园、建富裕新村"行动，农村饮水安全工程，(28.4 万农村居民饮水安全问题得到解决)。继续实施"造福工程"搬迁。广泛开展"家园清洁行动"，推广普及农村沼气开发应用，加强垃圾、污水等污染物处理，改善农村生产生活条件。

实施科普惠农工程，整合培训资源，组织实施农业生产技术培训，培育新型现代农民。抓好农村劳动力转移就业培训，提高进城务工技能，增加工资收入。完善利益补偿和风险补助措施，建立农业生态环境补偿机制，加大农村政策性保险体系建设。健全农村社会保障体系，实现新型农村社会养老保险制度全覆盖。

至此，宁德市已有国家级农业标准化示范区 9 个、省级农业标准化示范区 12

个。2015年市政府以农标示范为平台，促进农业品牌建设，服务地方经济增长。指导企业积极开展有机食品、绿色农产品、无公害等各类农业品牌认证和商标创建活动实现新增产值60亿元，年增长23.3%，带动农户年均增收800多万元，有效促进了地方经济发展。

3.2.1 A New Countryside Construction

In the process of pushing forward the new types of industrialization, Ningde Municipality is speeding up its agricultural modernization, sticking to its prioritization, striving to build up a new socialist countryside, fastening the shift of the agricultural development mode, improving the growth mechanism of strengthening and favoring farmers so as to lay a solid foundation for the countryside development and implement all the related favorable policies for farmers and realize the subsidies for agricultural resources, seeds, grain and machinery in time in order to guarantee all the complete and obvious implementation of the favorable agricultural policies. In the building of new countryside, the project of "the Financial Inclusive System in the Countryside" was launched to center on the theme of making sure "the farmers are rich and the environment remains beautiful" so as to enlarge the financial service scopes in the countryside, realize the balance, convenience, inclusiveness and modernization of the financial service so that agriculture is to get stronger, farmers to be richer and countryside to become more beautiful. It is sped up to construct in the countryside regions the irrigation projects, roads, electric networks, methane projects, fishing ports and connected roads between urban and countryside areas as well as the infrastructural projects of connecting each village by public bus.

In 2015, a new round of "Project of Tidying Up 1000 Villages and Setting Up 100 Model Villages" was carried out again to have helped tidy up residential areas for 134 villages and set up 13 beautiful demonstration villages. Construction of "New Countryside Models", "Green Homeland and Prosperous New Countryside" went on further. The Safe Water-Drinking Project helped solve the water drinking problem for 284 000 villages. Actions of the "Blessing Projects" were further taken to relocate the farmers from dangerous areas to safe areas, and "Project of Cleaning up Homelands" was widely conducted. Use and application of methane were popularized and treatment of rubbish and sewage was strengthened so the living conditions in the countryside were improved.

Project of Benefitting Farmers with Science and Technology was conducted to integrate training resources. Training of agricultural production technology was also carried out to cultivate new and modern farmers. Training of the migrant farmers was implemented so as to improve the working skills of the migrant farmers and raise their income. Mechanisms of benefiting subsidizing and risk insurance were improved. And the subsidizing system for agricultural environment was established. More investment went to the construction of the insurance system of favorable policies in the countryside. The social security systems in the countryside were bettered and the inclusive systems of the new social welfare mechanisms in the countryside established.

So far Ningde Municipality had established 9 national-level agricultural demonstration zones and 12 provincial-level agricultural demonstration zones. In 2015, Ningde Municipal Government with the agricultural demonstration zones as platforms boosted the construction of agricultural brands to serve the local economic growth. Meanwhile, Ningde Municipal Government took active approaches to certify all sorts of agricultural brands and set up trademarks of organic food, green and harmless agricultural products and realized a new growth value of 6 billion yuan with an annual growth of 23.3%, which helped increase an average income of 8 million yuan for the farmers and pushed forward the local economic growth.

二、农业和农村经济

围绕农业农村工作“三个三化”方针，以促进农民收入持续较快增长为核心，用先进科学技术提升农业，用现代经营方式拓展农业，加强农业物质装备条件建设，加快农业科技创新推广及经营体制机制创新，推进“一村一品、一乡一业、一县一特”形成特色区域板块经济，改造提升传统优势产业、粮食生产、林业、畜牧业、蔬菜产业、水果业。巩固发展特色产业、茶业、海洋渔业、食用菌业、药材种植业。重点培育新兴产业、生物质能源产业、生物种业、生物有机肥产业、中药制药产业。大力发展高效农业，扩大特色产业规模，提升优势特色产业，积极发展乡村旅游与休闲观光农业等多举措施，实现农业增产、农民增收、农村发展等多举措施，推进农业农村经济保持平稳、健康发展。各县(市、区)均创建了省级农业标准示范区、农民创业园。11 个市级千亩高优农业示范园区，30 个现代山地农业开发示范基地加快建设，农民专业合作社总量居全省设区市首位，新增国家级农民合作社示范社 13 家。涌现出“中国最有魅力休闲乡村”、“全国生态文化村”、“海西十佳魅力乡村”、寿宁县犀溪镇西浦村和"中国十佳生态养生旅游名镇"霍童镇等一批发展亮点，成为农村经济新的增长点。

2013年全市农林牧渔业总产值386亿元、增长5.9%，粮食总产量稳定在66万吨。农业产值174.71亿元，增长4.7%；林业产值23.86亿元，增长5.2%；牧业产值24.08亿元，增长12.5%；渔业产值156.38亿元，增长6.2%；农林牧渔服务业产值7.00亿元，增长7.6%。茶叶产量8.09万吨，增长6.7%。食用菌产量16.66万吨，增长6.3%。水产品产量77.87万吨，增长6.4%。海水产品73.69万吨，增长6.3%；淡水产品4.18万吨，增长7.8%。肉蛋奶总产量11.98万吨，增长8.6%；水果产量35.97万吨，比增9.1%；蔬菜产量121.26万吨，比增2.2%；中药材产量4.03万吨，比增63.16%；油料产量0.58万吨，增长5.5%，截至2013年，全市现有省级以上农业产业化龙头企业57家(含国家级2家)，市级254家。全市229家市级以上龙头企业实现总产值340.14亿元，比上年增长17.7%；带动农户72.17万户，农户从龙头企业得到的收入达94.98亿元，实现销售收入331.29亿元，比上年增长18.1%；实现增加值73.42亿元，比上年增长14.3%；农民人均纯收入突破万元(10 065元)，增长14%，高于全省平均增幅1.5个百分点，增幅居全省首位。

3.2.2 Agriculture and Rural Economy

The work of the agricultural and rural economy of Ningde Municipality focuses on boosting the continuous increase of income of the farmers, improving agriculture with advanced science and technology as well as with modern management methods to expand agriculture, strengthen the construction of agricultural facilities and fasten the popularization of agricultural hi-tech and management innovation.

We will carry out the feature development of local regional economies like "one village grows one kind of fruits, one village majors in one business, and one county deals in one special trade". We will fransform and upgrade the traditionally advantageous industries, grain production, forestry, animal husbandry, vegetable production and fruit industry. Characteristic industries, tea, fishing, edible fungi and medicinal herbs will be further consolidated and developed. Focus on cultivating new industries, biological new energies and seeds, biological organic industries, traditional medicine manufacturing. We will strive to develop the high efficient agriculture, expand and upgrade the unique industries. Each county has established provincial-level agricultural model zones, entrepreneurship gardens of farmers, 11 municipal-level 1,000-

mu agricultural model zones, and the construction of 30 modern mountainous agricultural model zones has been speeded up. Some towns and villages have emerged such as Xipu Village of Xixi Township of Shouning County dubbed as "the most attractive leisure village in China" and also Huotong Township dubbed as one of the "Ten Most Attractive Villages in the Western Taiwan Straits Economic Development Zone in China" as well as one of the "Ten Most Eco-friendly Regimen and Tourism Townships in China".

In 2013, the total value of the agriculture, forestry, husbandry and fishery of Ningde City was 38.6 billion yuan with an increase of 5.9%. The total grain output stabilized at an output of 660 thousand tons. The total production value of agriculture was 17.471 billion yuan with an increase of 4.7%; the total value of forestry was 2.386 billion yuan with an increase of 5.2%; the value of husbandry was 2.408 billion yuan with an increase of 12.5%; the total value of fishery was 15.638 billion yuan with an increase of 6.2%, the service industry of agriculture, forestry, fishery and husbandry was 700 million yuan with an increase of 7.6%. The output of tea was 8.09 million tons with an increase of 6.7%; the output of the edible fungi was 166 600 tons with an increase of 6.3%; the output of aquatic products was 778 700 tons with an increase of 6.4%; the total output of meat, eggs and milk was 119 800 tons with an increase of 8.6%; the output of fruits was 359 700 tons with an increase of 9.1%; the output of vegetables was 121 260 tons with an increase of 2.2%; the output of Chinese herbs was 40 300 tons with an increase of 63.16%; the output of oils was 5 800 tons with an increase of 5.5%. As of 2013, there were 57 leading agricultural enterprises at provincial levels (including two national level enterprises) and 254 municipal level enterprises in the city. At this round there were newly increased 22 enterprises at the provincial level and 59 enterprises at the municipal level. Of them, 229 enterprises realized a total production value of 34.014 billion yuan with an increase of 17.7% and involving 721 700 farmers. They received 9.498 billion yuan from the leading enterprises which also netted a sale income of 33.129 billion yuan with an increase of 18.1%, and an added value of 7.342 billion yuan with an increase of 14.3%. The per capita income of the farmers broke the 10 000 yuan limit and reached 10 065 yuan with an increase of 14%, and 1.5 percentage higher than the average of the province and topping Fujian.

三、粮食生产

粮食作物主要有水稻、甘薯、马铃薯、大麦、小麦、大豆、杂粮等。其中播种面积最大的是水稻，其次是甘薯，再次是马铃薯、大、小麦、大豆、杂粮。

改革开放后，党中央高度重视"三农"工作，在耕地面积逐年减少，人口数量不断增加的情况下，一是推出以联产承包责任制为主的一系列农村改革政策。二是提升种粮科技水平。将提高粮食单产作为主攻方向，鼓励引导社会资本参与粮食生产科技创新与推广运用，努力提高科技对粮食生产的贡献率，扶持一批"育繁推"一体化粮食种子企业，培育和推广"高产、优质、多抗"粮油品种，组织开展绿色增产模式攻关，推进标准化的高产高效、绿色环保技术模式。三是实施粮食高产创建示范区和产能区建设为抓手，集成技术、集约项目、集中力量进一步提高粮食单产和品质。"大力发展马铃薯、甘薯、玉米、大豆等旱粮作物，同时，加强农田基础设施建设，实施抛荒山垅田复耕项目，鼓励新型经营主体对适宜种粮的抛荒山垅田进行复垦。四是大力实施"五新"示范，为农业发展夯实基础，推广水稻工厂化育秧、机械化插秧、测土配方施肥、病虫害专业化统防统治等增产增效关键技术，带动大面积均衡增产，确保粮食稳产。五是推动粮食产业升级。培育壮大粮食类农业产业化龙头企业，促进生产要素向优势企业集聚。支持骨干粮食企业技术升级和技术创新，依托"6·18"平台对接粮食科技项目，提高粮食企业创新能力，对符合条件的优先给予安排"6·18"对接项目资金。

3.2.3 Grain Production

The main crops are rice, sweet potato, potato, barley, wheat, soybean, grain, etc., of which the largest planting area is of rice, followed by sweet potato, potato, and large and small wheat and soybeans as well as grains.

Since the reform and opening up, the Central Committee of the CPC attaches great importance to the work of "agriculture, countryside and farmers". In a situation where the area of arable land decreases year by year while the population increases each year, the government firstly introduces a series of rural reform polices of the household contract responsibility system with remuneration linked to the output; and secondly raises the scientific and technological level of grain seeds and highlights the increases of per unit yield of grain for main research direction, and encourages and guides social capital to improve food production technology and innovation, so as to raise the contribution rate of science and technology to food production by supporting a group of grain seeds enterprises in hopes that they cultivate and promote various grain and oil products of "high yield, high quality and multiple resistances against diseases" as well as by organizing research on green production modes and promoting the standardized production modes of high yield and high efficiency and green environmental protection. Thirdly, the government is sparing no efforts to raise grain yield and quality through the construction of a high-yielding demonstration area and production area with intensive integration of technology, projects and strength. It also spares no efforts to grow potatoes, sweet potatoes, corns, soybeans and other crops, and at the same time strengthens the agricultural infrastructure construction, implements rehabilitation projects of the barren mountains and fields, and encourages new farm managers to reclaim the barren mountain ridges and fields. Fourthly, the government spares no efforts implementing five new demonstration projects, to help lay a solid foundation for the development of the agriculture and promote factory-style cultivation of rice seedling, mechanized planting, soil testing and fertilizer, specialized treatment of pest harm so as to have a greater harvesting to guarantee stabilized grain production. Fifthly, the government encourages the food industry to upgrade and cultivate and strengthen the leading enterprises in the agricultural industrialization, and promote the production factors to go to the leading enterprises. The government supports the backbone grain enterprises with their technical upgrading and technological innovation. Based on the investment fair platform on June 18th, the government is trying to match food technological projects, and improve food industrial innovation. For those enterprises that are up to the conditions, priority was given to help match the enterprises and the funds at the fair on June 18th.

四、副业生产

3.2.4 Subsidiary Production

(一)种植业

全市农业实施“五新”应用,即新品种、新技术、新肥料、新农药、新机具。按照“两带一区”(沿海蓝色产业带、山区绿色经济带和城郊高优农业示范区)的农业区域布局,积极调整和优化农业产业结构,加快发展山区绿色经济带,立足发挥山区特色资源优势,充分发挥屏南、周宁、寿宁等县的高山生态优势,加快发展茶叶、食用菌、竹木、果蔬、中药材、花卉等绿色产业，大面积推广种植伏季和反季节蔬菜，重点支持绿色食品开发和生态种植模式项目，鼓励开发和种植高效益蔬菜品种。建立种球花卉育种，鲜花生产基地，马铃薯、槟榔芋等球根、茎作物无毒苗繁育基地。建立柘荣、周宁、屏南等县组成的高山中药材生产集中区，重点支持中药材种植企业、合作社以及以中药材生产种植加工为主的技术创新企业。提升食用菌生产水平和科技含量，重点支持菌用林培育与食用菌产业化、食用菌栽培与资源循环利用、食用菌新品种选育与栽培推广项目，提高出口创汇能力。科学有序发展太子参、金银花、黄栀子和珍稀中药材，培育一批区域性中药材品牌，城郊平原突出高优农业示范区建设，以设施园艺业作为重点，大力发展设施蔬菜、设施瓜果，率先建立设施农业示范基地，发展立体综合性农业，带动现代绿色(生态)农业全面发展，使宁德市成为海峡西岸特色突出的绿色农产品生产、加工和购销中心之一。目前，全市农业类地理标志证明商标已达 23 件，6 个农产品(穆阳水蜜桃、福安巨峰葡萄、福鼎桐江鲈鱼、福鼎槟榔芋、霞浦榨菜、霞浦晚熟荔枝)获得国家农产品地理标志登记证书，获证产品数量居全省前列。42 件地理标志商标，其中柘荣太子参、古田银耳、坦洋工夫、福鼎白茶、福鼎槟榔芋和宁德大黄鱼等先后被认定为中国驰名商标，古田县被誉为“中国食用菌之都”，福安市被誉为“中国茶叶之乡”和“南方葡萄之乡”，福鼎市被誉为“中国名茶之乡”和“中国白茶之乡”。柘荣县被誉为“中国太子参之乡”。

3.2.4.1 Crop Farming

The city has carried out the “Five New” Program, i.e., new varieties, new techniques, new fertilizers, new pesticides, and new farm tools. According to the agricultural regional layout of “two belts and one zone” (coastal blue industrial belt and mountainous green economic belt as well as outskirt hi-tech and excellent agricultural demonstration zone), agricultural structures were vigorously adjusted and optimized so that the development of the mountainous green economic belts was fastened. Based on the advantage of the mountainous green resources in Pingnan, Zhouning and Shouning, the development of tea, mushrooms, bamboos, fruits, vegetables, traditional Chinese herbs and flowers was speeded up. In and out of season vegetables were planted in large scales. Key support went to the growth of green food and eco-friendly planting projects. Development and planting of high efficient vegetables were encouraged.

Production bases of bulb flowers breeding and fresh flowers were established as well as breeding bases for potatoes, Binglang taros and other stem crops free of nuisance. Concentrated production zones of mountainous

Chinese herbs were set up in Zherong, Zhouning and Pingnan. Key support went to the planting enterprises of Chinese herbs, coops and those innovative enterprises that mainly engaged in herbal planting and production. Production level and hi-tech content of edible mushrooms were upgraded. Key supports went to the nurture of the forest for mushroom growth and its industrialization, planting and recycle of resources, as well as the selections of new mushroom varieties and promotion projects so as to improve the earning ability of foreign exchange through export. Balanced measures were taken to grow Taizi ginsengs, honeysuckles, gardenias and other rare herbs and great efforts were taken to nurture a batch of famous brands of Chinese herbs in the region. By the outskirt plains the focus went to establish the hi-tech and excellent demonstration zones of agriculture with protected horticulture as a key area, and great efforts were made to develop protected vegetables and fruits. Some protected agriculture model bases were established to develop comprehensive and multi-dimension agriculture to promote the modern and green agriculture so that Ningde became one of the centers that produce, process and sell the unique and green agricultural products in the Western Taiwan Strait Economic Zone.

At present, Ningde City has 23 certified and registered geographic trademarks of agricultural products. Six of them received national certificates and tops in Fujian Province. The six are Honey Peaches in Muyang, Fu'an; Mega Grapes in Fu'an; Perches in the Tongjiang River, Fuding; Binglang Taros in Fuding; hot pickled mustard tuber in Xiapu; late-in-season Lychees. There are also 42 registered geographic trademarks, of which the following are listed as well-known trade marks in China: Taizi Ginsengs in Zherong; Edible Fungi in Gutian; Tangyan Kunfu Tea in Fu'an; Binglang Taros in Fuding; and Yellow Croakers in Jiaocheng. In addition, Gutian County has been named "Capital of Edible Fungi in China"; Fu'an City—Hometown of Teas in China" and "Hometown of Mega Grapes in South China"; Fuding City—Hometown of Famous Teas in China" as well as "Hometown of White Tea in China"; Zherong County—"Hometown of Taizi Ginsengs in China", etc.

（二）畜牧业

宁德市政府，大力发展特色、绿色养殖业，推进生态型、规模型、标准化畜牧业，切实转变畜牧业发展方式，加强畜禽产品绿色品牌建设，生产由过去农户单一养猪转向猪、牛、羊、禽、兔等全面发展，稳定发展生猪及禽蛋生产，重点建设畜禽标准化养殖场，良种繁育场建设，地方优良畜禽品种资源保护与开发，生态种养生产基地建设，畜禽配合饲料生产建设。强化畜禽防疫、饲养生产监管和技术推广体系建设，重点扶持畜牧业龙头企业和规模化养殖场开展农产品质量安全认证，带动和辐射规模养殖农户按标准化组织生产。

突出抓好草食节粮型畜禽生产和畜禽良种繁育体系建设，环境保护和循环经济建设，逐步建立优质、生态、高效，具有一定竞争能力的现代畜牧业生产体系。切实落实养殖环境保护管理措施；加快构建现代生态畜牧业产业体系；加强协作，依法严把审批关；加大对畜牧业发展的扶持力度。例如南阳实业先后被认定为福建省著名品牌、农业产业化国家级重点龙头企业、国家扶贫重点龙头企业、国家生猪活体储备基地、国家农产品加工示范企业、福建省品牌农业企业金奖、福建省农业产业化十强龙头企业、福建省高新技术企业。

3.2.4.2 Animal Husbandry

Ningde Municipal Government spares no efforts in developing the unique and green animal husbandry; makes it eco-friendly, large scale and standardized; earnestly changes its development mode and enhances the establishment of the green brands of livestock and poultry products from a single raising mode of hogs in the past shifting to multi cultivations such as of hogs, cattle, sheep, poultry, rabbit and so on. Meanwhile raising of hogs and poultry, and production of eggs have been stabilized. Much importance has been attached to construction of standardized cultivation farms of animal husbandry, construction of farms for fine breeds, protection and development of local fine species of animal husbandry, construction of the eco-friendly planting and breeding bases as well as production of the auxiliary feeds for animal husbandry. Much emphasis has been paid to the epidemic prevention mechanism, production supervision and technological promotion systems. The leading husbandry enterprises and the large-scale cultivation farms to carry out quality and safety certification of their products were supported by the government so as to lead and influence the large scale raisers to carry out production according to the standards.

Prominence has been given to the production of grass-and-grain saving animal husbandry and construction of the breeding systems of fine species as well as environmental protection and recycling economy. Gradual steps have been taken to establish a modern animal husbandry system that is ecological, efficient and competitive.

The government earnestly implements the environmental protection measures of cultivation, accelerates the construction of a modern ecological animal husbandry system, strengthens cooperation, strictly examines the approval of production and enhances support for the development of animal husbandry. In this regard, Nanyang Industrial Co., Ltd. of Ningde City has been awarded many provincial and national titles.

(三)渔业

宁德市所辖海域面积和海岸线长均居全省之首,原生态岸线滩涂资源丰富,生物种类多样,海域水质良好,是福建省乃至全国最大规模的大黄鱼人工育苗、养殖和加工出口基地,也是我国八大优势出口养殖水产品——大黄鱼优势养殖区域的核心区,养殖网箱12万口,年产量2万吨以上,占福建省年产量的40%,海带、紫菜等水产养殖名列全省、全国前列。目前,全市水产品加工企业达300多家,其中省级农业产业化龙头企业4家、省级水产产业化龙头企业21家。全国年产量30%以上,在我国大黄鱼产业中具有举足轻重的地位和显著的影响力。全市拥有5个全国驰名商标、4个国家注册地理标志商标、1个国家农产品地理标志、17个福建省名牌及27个省著名商标,蕉城区、福鼎市、霞浦县分别被授予"中国大黄鱼之乡""中国鲈鱼之乡""中国海带之乡"和"中国紫菜之乡"称号。

发展健康生态养殖,是宁德市现代海洋渔业发展的一大方向。充分利用内陆水域建设"海上田园",大力发展名特优水产品养殖,同时调整优化养殖布局,规范湾内养殖,加快湾外增养殖品种与模式研究,推进湾外深水大网箱养殖和陆上工厂化循环水养殖,鼓励发展湾外"海洋牧场"市级政府予以项目资金扶持。加快水产品园区及市场建设,培育壮大龙头企业也是扶持渔业发展重点。重点培育壮大宁德大黄鱼、霞浦海带、霞浦海参等区域公共品牌,支持企业产品通过无公害、绿色、有机食品认证;支持加工企业进行技术改造和产业升级,发展精深加工,鼓励水产加工企业开发具有自主知识产权、高技术含量、高附加值的水产加工产品;兑现落实有关培育、扶持和奖励上市企业、品牌奖励的各项政策。在远洋渔业方面,加大远洋渔业扶持力度,扩大交流合作。积极扩大水产品对外贸易,引导渔业企业从"立足国内"向"两种资源、两个市场"并重方向转变,提升渔业国际竞争力。通过鼓励申请地理标志产品保护,注册地理标志证明商标、集体商标,发展了一批具有宁德市产业特色,集生产、加工、销售、服务于一体的海洋渔业品牌,大大提高了宁德市水产产业的竞争力。加强标准化池塘养殖、浅海设施养殖、工厂化养殖、渔业种业、休闲渔业、水产品加工、海洋生物制品等七大类现代渔业产业园区建设,培育一批大型水产养殖、种业、加工龙头企业,加大品牌创建力度,提高精深加工水平。扶持霞浦顺来发、正冠等远洋渔业企业发展,完成14艘远洋渔船建造并投入生产,实现远洋渔业新突破。

3.2.4.3 Fishery

The sea area and the coastline of Ningde City both rank first in Fujian province. There are abundant primitive shore and mudflat resources with various biodiversities and high-quality marine waters. Ningde is the largest breeding, sea-farming and processing export base of yellow croakers in Fujian Province and even nationwide. It's also a core sea-farming area of the yellow croaker, one of eight main export aquatic products in our country, and there are 12 000 sea farming cages in the local area with an annual output of more than 20 000 tons which accounts for 40% of the total annual output in Fujian Province. Besides the output of other aquatic products like kelp and seaweed also rank the top in the province. At present, there are more than 300 enterprises engaged in aquatic products processing, four of which are the provincial leading enterprises in agricultural industrialization and twenty one of which are provincial leading enterprises in aquatic industry. They take up more than 30% of annual output of aquatic products in our country and play a decisive role and cast significant influence on large yellow croaker industry in China. Ningde has five national well-known trademarks, four nationally registered geographical trademarks, one geographical trademark of national agricultural products, 17 famous brands of Fujian Province and 27 provincial famous trademarks. Three places in Ningde: Jiaocheng District; Fuding City; Xiapu County were respectively awarded the titles of "Homeland of Large Yellow Croakers in China", "Homeland of Perches in China", "Homeland of Kelps in China" and "Homeland of Lavers in China".

The healthy and eco-friendly sea farming is the major trend of modern marine fishery in Ningde. The inland waters are made full use of for establishing "A Garden at Sea" and efforts are made to vigorously cultivate well-known, special and high-quality aquatic products, and meanwhile the layout of sea farming has been adjusted and optimized. The norm of sea farming in the bays has been regulated and the research on marine culture of various species and models outside the bays fastened. The deep-water sea farming in cages outside the bays as well as industrialized water recycle of aquaculture on land have been pushed forward, and the funding support has been provided by the municipal government to encourage the development of the "ocean ranch" outside the bays. Measures have been taken to focus on accelerating the construction of aquatic product centers and markets, and fostering and expanding the leading enterprises of sea farming. The dominance has been given to foster the growth of large yellow croakers in Jiaocheng as well as kelps and sea cucumber in Xiapu and other regional public brands of products. The government also encourages the enterprises to apply for the certifications of pollution-free, green and organic foods; supports them to engage in technological transformation and industrial upgrading for deep processing, encourages them to develop high value-added products with independent intellectual property rights and high technology. The government realizes the relevant incentive policies on training, supporting and rewarding the enterprises to be listed on the stock market. Besides the government also supports the development of the pelagic fishery, expands its exchanges and co-operation and the foreign trade of aquatic products, and ensures the fishery shifts from relying on a single resource and market based at home to relying on two resources and two markets based at home and abroad so that the international competitiveness of the fishery is enhanced. A bunch of fishery brands have been created that integrate local industrial features, production, processing, sales and service together through protection of the products of the registered geographical marks, and the certification of the registered geographical marks as well as collective trademarks so that the competitiveness of the aquatic industry in Ningde has been greatly enhanced. The government also strengthens the standardized construction of seven types of modern industrial fishery parks of aquaculture ponds, shallow coastal breeding facilities, factory sea farming, fish seeds industry, leisure fishery, aquatic products processing and marine biological products so that quite a few leading enterprises in aquatic farming, fish seeds and processing have been nurtured with their brand construction strengthened and their refined processing improved. New breakthroughs in ocean fishery have been achieved with the construction and launches of 14 ocean fishing vessels through support to Shunfa Ocean Fishing Enterprise and Zhengguan Ocean Fishing Enterprise in Xiapu County.

(四)林业

全市有林地面积 1 296.63 万亩,活立木总蓄积量 4 157.94 万立方米,重点生态公益林 510.8 万亩,森林覆盖率 66.3%,居全省第四,林地绿化率 89.6%。简要概括为沿海最绿、生态优良,发展最快、特色明显。拥有国家级森林公园 2 个,省级森林公园 13 个，森林人家授牌经营单位 16 户，省级自然保护区 2 个，国家林业重点龙头企业 1 家，省级林业龙头企业 12 家，市级农业产业化龙头企业 49 家。林业系统有 9 个县(市、区)林业局、1 个森林公安局、9 个森林公安分局、114 个林业工作站、11 个林业检查站、12 个省属国有林场和 10 个国有苗圃。

突出抓好四大工程实施:生态优化工程，抓好造林绿化任务，突出三沿一环、森林生态景观园和小憩园建设等四绿工程建设，巩固森林通道建设后期管护和沿海防护林基干林带断带补齐加厚等工作。森林养护工程，强化森林抚育管理和森林防火、林业有害生物防治、林业执法等资源保护工作，确保森林资源双增目标实现。产业提升工程。制定出台扶持花卉苗木产业发展的具体措施和花卉产业发展规划。改革创新工程，积极推进林权抵押贷款和森林保险工作，力争林权抵押贷款和林业小额贷款新突破，持续推动林业合作经济组织健康发展。

3.2.4.4 Forestry

The area of forests in Ningde covers 12.9663 million Mu, with a total live forest reserve of 41.5794 million cubic meters and a key eco forest of 5.108 million Mu. The total forest coverage is 66.3%, ranking the 4th in Fujian and the greening rate reaches 89.6%. In summary, Ningde is the greenest along the coast with excellent ecology. Its forestry develops the fastest with obvious features. Ningde has 2 national forest parks, 13 provincial forest parks, 16 authorized units dealing in forests, 2 provincial natural reserves, 1 national leading forestry enterprise, 12 provincial leading forestry enterprises, 49 leading enterprises of agricultural industrialization, etc. The forestry sector has 9 county (city/district) forestry bureaus, 1 forestry public security bureau, 9 forestry public security branches, 114 forestry work stations, 11 forestry inspection stations, 12 provincial state-owned forest farms and 10 state-owned forest nurseries.

Four forestry projects are being carried out earnestly: beatifying project of ecological forest, forestation and landscaping are well taken care of with attention paying to the greening of the roadsides, riversides, sea-sides and around mountains, as well as to the construction of the ecological forest sightseeing scenes and parks for leisure. Meanwhile, the follow-up management of the forests pathways and the make-up and enforcement of the broken parts of the coastal forest belts are being strengthened. Caring Project for Forests: forestry work related to its care, nurture and management, fire prevention, diseases treatment, law-enforcement and protection, etc. was strengthened so as to ensure the double increase of forest resources. Forestry Upgrading

Project: specific measures are being stipulated to support the growth of horticultures and seedlings and the forestry development blueprint is being mapped out. Innovation Project: Work related to forests rights for loans and forest insurance has been pushed forward. New breakthroughs have been sought for forest rights for loan as well as small loans for forestry so that the cooperative economy of forestry can grow healthily.

(五)水利

通过实施“六千”水利工程(千万农民饮水工程、千座水库保安工程已动工加固、千万亩农田节水灌溉工程、千万方山地水利工程、千千米河道清水工程、千万亩水土流失治理工程)建设和农田水利建设,改善农民生产生活条件。加大力度综合整治重点流域饮用水源环境污染,确保饮用水源安全。此外,通过加强水土保持管理也取得初步成效。一是认真把好水土保持方案审批关,把水土保持方案审批作为发改、环保等立项审批、环评的前置条件;二是加大水土保持执法检查力度,联合县级水土保持监督部门加强对省、市重点项目的执法检查,督促整改落实;三是积极提升水土保持监督管理能力,市政府出台了《宁德市人民政府办公室关于进一步加强全市水土保持监督管理工作的通知》,进一步规范水土保持监督管理工作;四是及时协调水土流失纠纷,使水土流失治理的过程成为群众增收致富的过程。努力为环三都澳区域发展和海西东北翼中心城市建设营造更加良好的生态环境。

3.2.4.5 Water Conservancy

Ningde continues to improve the construction of water conservancy and the livelihood of the farmers through the implementations of six major water conservancy projects: one to ensure that 10 million farmers have access to clean drinking water, one to ensure the security and consolidation of 1 000 reservoirs, one to irrigate 10 million Mu (about 666.667 hectares) of farm lands, one to irrigate 10 million Mu of barren hills, one to clean up 1 000 kilometers of rivers and one to conserve soil and water in 10 million mu of land. Greater efforts were taken to treat the key reaches of the rivers so that drinking water sources are safe and free from pollution. Besides, initial effectiveness has been achieved through strengthening water conservancy. Firstly, the approval procedures for the water conservancy have been checked properly and have become the precondition for approving and checking of the projects of development, reforms and environmental protection. Secondly, legal inspection has been strengthened for water conservancy. The relevant departments of water conservancy at the county level are coordinated to carry out legal check of the provincial and municipal projects and to ensure the implementation of the changes of the water conservancy projects. Thirdly, active approaches are taken to improve the supervision of the water conservancy. Ningde Municipal Government issued a circular by Ningde Municipal People's Government Office on *Further Improving the Supervision of the Water Conservancy in the Whole City*, so that the supervision of water conservancy has been more regulated. Fourthly, the conflicts derived from water and erosions are dealt with and coordinated timely so that the process of treating water and soil erosions becomes a process for the farmers to become prosperous. Great efforts are taken to create a better ecological environment for the development of the Pan-Sandu Bay regions as well as for the construction of the central city in the northeast of Fujian.

五、重点企业

3.2.5 Key Enterprises

(一)宁德市南阳实业有限公司

宁德南阳实业有限公司，是一家集种猪育种、商品猪养殖、饲料加工、生猪屠宰、放心肉连锁专卖、肉食品加工、大米加工、生物有机肥生产、现代码头物流等于一体的现代农业综合开发企业。公司紧密围绕养猪产业发展，已建立了13个经营实体，形成产业规模效益。实现了猪肉产品从基地到餐桌质量安全保障一条龙生产目标和福建省唯一特色生猪产业集群发展的企业。公司的质量管理体系通过了ISO9001:2009国际质量标准认证，产品通过农业部质量安全中心认证。先后被认定为农业产业化国家级重点龙头企业、国家扶贫重点龙头企业、国家生猪活体储备基地、国家农产品加工示范企业、福建省农业产业化十强龙头企业、福建省高新技术企业等。

3.2.5.1 Nanyang Industrial Co., Ltd. of Ningde City

It is a modern comprehensive agricultural enterprise that integrates breeding boars, raising of commercial hogs, feeds processing, butchering of hogs, franchised meat chain shops, meet product processing, rice processing, bio-fertilizer production and modern port logistics. The company, centering on the industry of log rising, has established 13 managing companies and achieved certain scale effectiveness. One-stop production goal from meat production at the bases to the safe food on the table has been achieved and was awarded the only intensive hog enterprise group in Fujian. The management system of the company has passed the ISO9001：2009 international certification with its products checked and approved by the National Agricultural Ministry. One after another, the company has been appointed "National Leading Enterprise of Agricultural Industrialization"," National Leading Enterprise with Poverty Relief", "National Reserve Base of Hogs", "National Processing Model Enterprise of Agricultural Products", one of "Ten Strong Leading Enterprises of Agricultural Industrialization", and "New and Hi-tech Enterprise of Fujian Province".

(二)福建福鼎海鸥水产食品有限公司

福鼎海鸥水产食品有限公司，是农业产业化国家重点龙头企业，拥有3家全资子公司。

目前已发展为集海珍品繁育、养殖、捕捞、加工、贸易于一体的大型综合性渔业集团企业。公司拥有中国唯一的国家级大黄鱼原种场，国内最大的海水生态养殖网箱，标准化厂房和2万吨冷库，形成以大宗海水养殖和海捕品种为主要产品的完整产业链。通过了ISO9001、ISO14000、ISO22000、HACCP和美国、欧盟水产品注册等认证审核，坚持以HACCP、GAP标准检验，并始终贯彻无公害养殖和水产品可追溯体系，保障了食品从原产地到餐桌的安全；"九洋"商标被评为"福建省著名商标""中国驰名商标"，"九洋"牌虾皮被评为"中国国际农业博览会名牌产品"。先后被国家农业部评为"农业产业化国家重点龙头企业""全国农产品加工示范企业""全国乡镇企业创名牌重点企业""国家扶贫龙头企业"等。

3.2.5.2 Fuding Seagull Aquatic Products Co., Ltd. of Fujian Province

It is a national leading enterprise of agricultural industrialization with 3 whole-owned branches. It is now grown into a large scale comprehensive group of holdings that integrate breeding of precious aquatic products, sea farming, fishing, processing and trade. It has the only largest breeding farm of yellow croakers in China as well as the largest sea water farming cages and standard industrial shops and 20 000-ton freezing storages. It has a whole industrial chain of main sea water farming and fishing and passed ISO9001, ISO14000, ISO22000, HACCP and other certifications of the USA and EU. The company sticks to the HACCP and GAP standards and ever implements the pollution-free sea farming and the tracing systems of their aquatic products to ensure the food safety from the original production to the dining table. Its "Nine Oceans

Brand" was awarded "Famous Brand in Fujian Province" as well as "Well-known Brand in China". Its shrimp skins of "Nine Oceans Brand" was awarded "Famous Brand of the International Agricultural Products Expo of China". The company was honored one after another to be a national leading enterprise of agricultural industrialization in China by Ministry of Agriculture of China, "Model Enterprises of Agricultural Products Processing in China", "Key Enterprise of Brand Building of National Township Enterprises" and "National Leading Poverty-Reduction Enterprise" and so on.

(三)福建坦洋工夫集团股份有限公司

该公司是全国茶叶行业百强和目前国内最具规模的"坦洋工夫"红茶专业生产企业,集茶叶种植、加工、科研、销售为一体,是福安市人民政府首家授权"坦洋工夫"品牌特许经营和唯一参与起草、制定"坦洋工夫"国家标准的企业。公司已通过ISO9000、ISO14000、ISO18000、ISO22000 和 HACCP 等国际体系认证和有机转换产品、绿色食品认证。公司先后自主研制出了以"茗红"为品牌的"英伦""坦洋""茗红""世博"等四大系列产品。主打品牌"茗红"及其产品分别被认定为福建省著名商标、福建名牌产品公司产品先后获得中国鼎尖名茶,福建省名茶,第五、六、七届"闽茶杯"金奖茶王,中国十大红茶品牌奖,金芽奖和福建二十强茶企等殊荣。目前公司已在北京、上海、广东、江苏、浙江等 20 多个省、区、市开设了 100 多家连锁经营网点。还与台湾瑞穗有机生态农场联手打造精品红茶"两岸红",共同拓展海内外市场。

3.2.5.3 Tanyang Kungfu Black Tea Group Co., Ltd of Fujian Province

It is one of the Top 100 tea producers and the largest black tea enterprise of Tangyang Kunfu brand at home. It integrates tea planting, processing, research and sales together. It is the sole brand of Tangyan Kunfu Black Tea authorized by Fu'an Municipal Government and is also the sole enterprise that participated in drafting and designing the national standard for the brand "Tangyang Kunfu Black Tea". It has been checked and authorized by ISO9000, ISO14000, ISO18000, ISO22000 as well as by HACCP and other international organic transferred and green food authorities. It has one after another researched and made black teas of different brands of "Minghong" series like "Yinglun", "Tangyang", "Minghong" and "Shibo". The main brand "Minghong" and its products were designated famous brands of Fujian Province as well as famous brand products of Fujian Province. Its products one after another were awarded many honors like Outstanding Tea in China, Famous Tea in Fujian, Gold Award of the 5th, 6th and 7th Fujian Tea Cup Competitions as well as One of Ten Most Influential Black Teas in China, Gold Sprout Award and One of the Twenty Strongest Tea Enterprises in Fujian. At the moment, it has opened 100 branches in Beijing, Shanghai, Guangdong, and provinces like Jiangsu, Zhejiang etc, in total over 20 provinces and cities. It also works together with Taiwan's Ruihui Organic Farm to produce fine black tea of "Lianganhong" to explore international markets together.

(四)古田县金松食品有限公司

福建省古田县金松食品有限公司,主要经营香菇、银耳等各类食用菌产品以及全国各地土特产品粗、深加工、贸易等业务。现有产品近百种,产品质量均能达到国家标准,并符合国际市场要求。与沃尔玛、家乐福、万客隆、迪亚等以及日本、韩国为主的东亚、东南亚国家的客户建立了广泛的贸易合作关系。已通过了ISO9001质量管理体系认证,连续数年被当地政府评为"纳税大户""诚信纳税户""重合同、守信用"企业和"质量放心工程"示范单位,先后被评为省级农业产业化重点龙头企业和农产品加工龙头企业,"金松"牌(香菇、银耳)获省名牌产品称号,跻身福建省百强农产品加工企业行列。

3.2.5.4 Jinsong Foods Co., Ltd. of Gutian County

It mainly deals in various fungi like mushrooms, etc., as well as rough and deep processing and trade of all kinds of local specialties. Now there are over 100 kinds of products. All the quality is up to the national standard and meets the international demand. Long term trade relationship has been established with Wal-Mart, Carrefour, Makro, Concordia and countries like Japan, South Korea and ASEAN. It has passed ISO9001 quality management system and was awarded many honors by the local government for many years like "Big Taxpayer", "Honest Taxpaying Unit", "Enterprise Honoring the Contract and Integrity", a model unit of "Quality Free From Care". One after another, the company has been awarded honors like "Provincial Leading Enterprise of Agricultural Industrialization" and "Provincial Leading Processing Enterprise". The mushrooms and fungi of "Jinsong Brand" won the honor of the provincial famous brand and the company becomes one of 100 powerful enterprises of agricultural processing in Fujian.

六、宁台农业合作

霞浦三沙港与台湾基隆隔海相望,相距仅126海里,是宁德对台工作的窗口,也是福建最早开放的对台贸易口岸,历史上就是福建省最早开放的对台小额贸易点、对台短期渔工劳务输出点、台轮停泊点和海上台货快运试点之一。1979 年,省政府在三沙镇设立全省首个台胞接待站,率先开展对台小额贸易和渔工劳务输出业务。2006 年,国务院台湾事务办公室批准在三沙镇建设“台湾水产品集散中心”并开辟台湾水产品“零关税”进口先行先试区和对台小额交易先行先试区,八种台湾水产品实施进口“零关税”措施由此进入大陆市场。这是继厦门台湾水果集散中心之后,福建省成立的又一个涉台集散中心,也是大陆地区批准建设的唯一涉及台湾水产品生产、销售、加工的项目。大大推动了宁台两地渔业交流合作,为两岸水产品互通拓展了渠道。据了解宁德通过已开辟的台湾水产品“零关税”进口先行先试区和对台小额贸易先行先试区,进境台湾水产品总量上万吨。

近年来,宁德市通过加强对台农业合作,引导台商投资宁德市农业综合开发、农产品精深加工等产业,实现宁台农业合作不断提升、产业对接加速,取得了一定成效。在第九届中国·海峡项目成功交易会宁德市项目签约仪式上,台湾明道大学与福建宁德津田农业发展有限公司签订合作协议,引进台湾先进农业管理技术建设闽台农业生产示范园项目及农业“五新技术”(包括台湾灯照设施早收葡萄种植技术)设立台湾、大陆地区和日本水果新品种育苗种植技术研训基地。

2013 年全市引进台湾优良果蔬、茶叶、食用菌等品种 48 个,利用宁德投洽会、“9·8”投洽会等平台签约农牧业外资项目 14 个。完成“6·18”现代农业科技成果对接 146 项,成功举办第五届“海峡论坛两岸特色乡村对接暨农民合作组织发展交流会”宁德分会场活动,与台湾农民合作社成功对接,并签订合作协议。同时加大与台商台农及专家学者的合作力度,加强投资环境建设,吸引台商在宁德市直接投资和合作生产经营。此外,《宁德(霞浦)台湾渔民创业园总体发展规划(2012—2020)》已完成编制并通过专家评审。根据规划,宁德(霞浦)台湾渔民创业园将构建“三区一圈一中心”发展格局,即建设现代渔业加工产业集聚区、海峡两岸渔业物流贸易区、低碳渔业生产作业区以及海峡休闲渔业文化旅游圈、综合服务与管理中心,推动其集约化、产业化发展。

3.2.6 Agricultural Cooperation Between Taiwan and Ningde

Sansha Port of Xiapu County of Ningde and Keelung Port of Taiwan face each other across the sea with only a distance of 126 nautical miles. It was a window that reflected Ningde's relations with Taiwan and was also the earliest opening port to trade with Taiwan in Fujian. Besides, in the history of Fujian it was the earliest port opened to Taiwan for small scale trade, an export place of short-term fishermen labor to Taiwan, a berthing port of Taiwan ships as well as one of the experimental zones for the express delivery of Taiwan goods by sea to the mainland. In 1979, the first reception center for Taiwan compatriots was set up in Sansha by the provincial government and led the development of the small scale trade with Taiwan and the export of the fishermen labor there. In 2006, approved by the Taiwan Affairs Office of the State Council, Taiwan Aquatic Products Distribution Center was set up in Sansha, and the establishment of the "tariff free" trial import zone of aquatic products from Taiwan as well as the experimental zone of small scale trade with Taiwan kicked off and eight types of Taiwanese aquatic products were imported to the mainland market "tariff-free". This center was the other distribution center that was related to Taiwan in addition to the Taiwan Fruits Distribution Center established in Xiamen earlier. It was also the only authorized project which included the production, sale and processing of Taiwan aquatic products. It greatly promoted the exchange and cooperation of fishery between Taiwan and Ningde, and expanded the exchange channels for aquatic products across the Strait. According to some information, the total import quantity of the Taiwanese aquatic products reached more than ten thousand tons through the pioneering "tariff free" import experiment zone of Taiwanese aquatic products and the pioneering experimental zone of small scale trade with Taiwan.

In recent years, Ningde has strengthened agricultural cooperation with Taiwan and guided Taiwan businessmen to invest in the integrated agricultural development projects and refined and deep processing of agricultural products. Some obvious results were achieved in the promotion of agricultural cooperation between Taiwan and Ningde as well as in the agricultural connectivity. At the signing ceremony of Ningde-related projects during the 9th China Cross-Strait Technology Projects Fair, Mingdao University of Taiwan signed a cooperation agreement with Ningde Jintian Agricultural Development Co., Ltd so as to introduce Taiwan's advanced agricultural management technology for setting up an agricultural production demonstration garden and promoting the "Five New Technologies" of agriculture. This included the planting technology of the earlier harvested grape by the use of light facilities, and the establishment of a research and training base for sharing planting technologies of growing new fruits from Taiwan, China, the Chinese mainland, and countries such as Japan.

In 2013, Ningde introduced from Taiwan 48 varieties of excellent fruits and vegetables, tea, edible mushrooms, etc. There were 14 foreign funded projects of agriculture and animal husbandry signed at the June 18th Ningde Investment Fair and the September 8th Investment Fair of China in Xiamen. 146 modern agricultural and technological achievements were matched up at the Investment Fair on June 18th. The parallel sessions of the 5th Cross-Strait Forum and the Seminar on the Connectivity of the Distinctive Villages & Seminar on the Development of the Farmers Cooperation Organizations across the Strait were successfully held in Ningde. As a result Taiwanese Farmers Cooperation Organization was successfully connected and a cooperation agreement was signed. Meanwhile, cooperation was intensified with Taiwan businessmen, farmers, experts, scholars as well as the building of the investment environment so that more Taiwanese businessmen were attracted to directly invest in, produce and do businesses in Ningde. Besides, 2012-2020 General Development Plan of the Innovation Park for Ningde(Xiapu)-Taiwan Fishermen had been compiled, appraised and checked by the experts. According to the Plan, this innovation park would be built on a development pattern of "Three Zones, One Circle, One Center", namely, a modern and intensive fishery processing industrial zone, a cross-Strait fishery industrial logistics trade zone, a low carbon fishery production zone, a cultural tourism circle of leisure fishery across the Strait and a comprehensive service and management center so that their intensified and industrialized development would be promoted.

第三节 现代工业

3.3 Modern Industry

一、工业招商

宁德现代工业基于产业发展情况，积极应对新常态经济形势，以转变经济发展方式为主线，充分发挥区位、资源优势，高起点发展临港重化产业，积极培育战略性新兴产业，改造提升传统优势产业，建设新型特色工业园区取得了显著成效，为全市经济社会发展做出了突出贡献。近年来，宁德加大工业招商力度，新型特色工业园区蓬勃发展，经济社会实现了跨越式发展。

1978 年工业总产值 3.64 亿，发展到 1995 年过 100 亿，2005 年突破 200 亿，2010 年过 1 000 亿，2013 突破 2 000 亿，是 1978 年的 692 倍。宁德市现有工业单

位 7 467 家(不含个体),规模以上工业覆盖 35 个大类行业,主要行业有电机电器、冶金新材料、新能源、船舶修造、食品加工、生物医药、建筑建材、汽摩配件,皮塑工业产业等九个。

宁德工业招商引资与招才引智并重,坚持多措并举,紧紧围绕宁德现代工业产业发展重点,着力引进、培养、留住一批掌握电机电器,农业产品深加工、生物制药、新能源、新材料等重点产业核心技术,能够带动产业升级,实现科技成果转化的技术研发人才,并重点扶持和发展了一批主业突出,竞争力强的大企业、大集团。

3.3.1 Industrial Investment Promotion

Based on its industrial development, Ningde's modern industry copes with the new normal economic situation actively. With the transformation of the economic development mode as the main line, the government gives full play to regional and resource advantage, develops the heavy chemical industry in the harbor at a higher starting point, positively cultivates new strategic industries, transforms and upgrades the traditional advantageous industries. As a result, it has not only made remarkable achievements in constructing industrial zones with new characteristics, but also has made predominant contributions to the economic and social development of the entire city. In recent years, Ningde has highlighted the industrial investment, and the industrial zones with new characteristics have flourished and society and the economy have achieved leapfrog developments.

The gross industrial output value in 1978 was 364 million yuan and 10 billion yuan in 1995. It exceeded 200 billion yuan in 2005 and 100 billion yuan in 2010 and it surpassed 200 billion yuan in 2013, which was more than 692 times that of 1978. Now, there are 7 467 industrial units in Ningde (not including individual industry). Scale industrial enterprises have covered 35 industrial sectors, which mainly include the following nine industries: electric motors and appliances, new metallurgic materials, new energy, ship repair and building, food processing, biological medicine, building materials, automobile components and leather plastic industry.

Both industrial investment and personnel recruitment are equally focused on Ningde where various measures have been taken to tightly center on the modern industry growth, and emphasize on introducing, cultivating and retaining a galaxy of talents who are proficient at key industries and core technology on electric motor and appliances, intensive processing of agricultural products, biomedicines, new energy and new material, and who can promote the industrial upgrading and realize the transformation from technological achievements into technological development. Besides, focuses are on the support and development of a batch of large businesses and enterprises which have strong competitive edge.

二、产业集群

宁德市已逐步形成了电机电器、食品加工、新能源、船舶修造、建材、生物医药、化工、冶金、皮塑、新材料等10多个产业集群优势。2014年,市政府还提出加快产业结构调整,推进电机电器、船舶修造、汽摩配件、食品加工等传统产业转型升级,做大做强传统产业集群,全力打造冶金新材料、新能源、电机电器三大千亿产业集群。

重点培育主营业务收入超10亿元企业25家以上,产值超100亿元产业集群6个、产值超500亿元产业集群2个,并对宁德市有一定产业基础的冶金、化工、汽车、船舶、水泥等五大行业及重点区域产业发展布局进行了对接梳理,端出了9大工业区打造特色产业集群的发展大盘。

漳湾临港工业区:重点发展冶金新材料、机械装备、战略性新兴产业,主要布局东侨工业集中区、三屿、漳湾。

赛甘湾下工业区:重点发展冶金新材料、机械装备、建材,主要布局湾坞片区、白马港和赛江两岸。

海西宁德工业区:重点发展装备制造、清洁能源、精细化工、海洋高新技术产业,主要布局溪南半岛。

环沙埕湾工业区:重点发展机械电子、船舶修造、合成革及深加工产业,主要布局沙埕港两岸。

古田工业园区:重点发展冶金新材料、机械制造、医药产业。

屏南工业园区:重点发展精细化工、新材料产业。

寿宁工业园区:重点发展工业新材料、机械制造、食品加工业。

周宁工业园区:重点发展机械制造、轻工业。

柘荣工业园区:重点发展生物医药、刀剪产业。

3.3.2 Industrial Clusters

Ningde has gradually developed into competitive advantageous clusters of more than ten industries, which include motors and appliances, food processing, new energy, ship repair and shipbuilding, building materials, biomedical, chemical engineering, metallurgy, leather plastic industry, new energy and new material and so on. In 2014, the municipal government advocated the speeding up of trans-formation and upgrading of traditional industries, which referred to the adjustment of industrial structure, and further developed industries of motor and electrical appliances, ship repair and shipbuilding, motorcycle accessories and food processing. What's more, the municipal government has also spared no efforts to make the traditional industrial cluster larger and stronger and build three 100-billion-yuan-plus industrial clusters of new materials for metallurgy, new energy and motor and electrical appliances with all might.

Ningde focuses on cultivating more than 25 enterprises whose individual avenue of major business exceeds 1 billion; and 6 industrial clusters whose individual output value exceeds over 10 billion; and 2 industrial clusters whose individual output value exceeds 50 billion. Meanwhile, the government has sorted out 5 main industries of metallurgy, chemical industry, automobile industry, ships building and cement, which Ningde has a certain industrial foundation and ultimately put forward 9 main industrial zones for building the industrial clusters with characteristics.

Zhangwan Harbor Industrial Zone: focusing on development of new metallurgic materials, mechanical equipments, emerging strategic industry and mainly located in Dongqiao industrial concentration zone, Sanyu, and Zhangwan areas.

Saiganwanxia Industrial Zone: focusing on new metallurgic materials, mechanical equipments, building materials, and mainly located in Wanwu, Baima Harbor and both shores of the Saijiang River.

Ningde Industrial Zone of the Western Taiwan Straits Economic Development Zone: focusing on equipment manufacturing, clean energy, fine chemical industry, marine Hi-tech industry, and mainly located in Xinan Peninsula.

Circular Shacheng Bay Industrial Zone: Focusing on machinery and electronics, ship building, synthetic leather and intensive processing industry and is mainly located on both sides of Shacheng Harbor.

Gutian Industrial Zone: Focusing on new metallurgic material, mechanical manufacturing and pharmaceutical industry.

Pingnan Industrial Zone: Focusing on fine chemical and new material industry.

Shouning Industrial Zone: Focusing on new material, mechanical manufacturing and food processing industry.

Zhouning Industrial Zone: Focusing on mechanical manufacturing and light industry.

Zherong Industrial Zone: Focusing on biomedicines and the knife-scissor industry.

三、以港兴市

宁德充分发挥区位、港口和资源优势，实施海洋强市、以港兴市的经济发展战略，着力规划和培育五大临海产业集群：以冶金、火电、核电、精细化工、建材为主的能源、原材料产业集群；以电机电器、船舶修造、汽摩配件为主的机械制造产业集群；以医药制造、海洋生物工程、电子信息、环保产业为主的高技术产业集群；以精细农业、绿色食品、农特产品及水产品精加工和竹木加工为主的农产品产业集群；以现代物流、商贸、物资储备为主的第三产业集群，努力形成城澳、漳湾片区、赛江两岸、溪南半岛和沙埕湾五大临海工业板块，使临海产业成为推动宁德经济快速发展的重要突破口。

宁德港是福建省沿海港口的重要组成部分，分为三都澳、赛江、三沙、沙埕 4 个港区、16 个作业区。现有一类口岸 1 个(城澳、白马作业区及三沙港区)，二类口岸 6 个(沙埕、姚家屿、三沙、赛岐、三都、漳湾)，拥有港口码头泊位 98 个，其中万吨级以上泊位 8 个，港口吞吐能力达 2 002.8 万吨。今后几年，还将有一批“重量级”的港口开工或建成，例如白马港区湾坞作业区 8＃泊位工程，新建 5 万吨级散杂货泊位 1 个，年设计吞吐量 200 万吨，15＃泊位工程，新建 1 个 7 万吨级通用泊位(码头水工结构按照靠泊 10 万吨级船设计)及配套设施，年计划货物吞吐量为 320 万吨，设计通过能力 345 万吨。

此外还有连接“出海口”的功能建设。按照“大港口、大交通、大腹地、大循环、大发展”的要求，加快交通网络建设，使宁德成为海峡西岸经济区连接内陆与沿海乃至国际经济联系的重要港口枢纽。

宁德港为国家一类口岸，可利用岸线 222.9 千米，其中工业岸线 80.3 千米。四个港区可建泊位 221 个，其中万吨级以上泊位 151 个，年吞吐能力可达 4 亿吨以上，届时宁德港将跨入亿吨港之列，发展为对台“三通”的重要口岸，连接内陆与沿海乃至国际经济联系的枢纽港口。

3.3.3 City Development Through Port Construction

Ningde fully utilizes its priorities of location, harbor and natural resources, carries out the economic development strategy with its marine and harbor resources in the city, and focuses on planning and cultivating the five costal industrial clusters, i.e., energy and raw materials industrial clusters focusing on metallurgy, thermal power, nuclear power, fine chemical industry and building materials; mechanical manufacturing industrial clusters focusing on electrical machinery and appliances, ship repair and shipbuilding and automobile parts; and high-tech industrial clusters focusing on biomedicines, marine biotechnology, electronic information and environmental protection industry; the agricultural products industrial clusters focus on precision agriculture, green food, agricultural special products and aquatic products and bamboo processing; the tertiary service industry cluster based on modern logistics, trade, material reserves with efforts to build five coastal industrial zones in Cheng'ao, Zhangwan, both shores of the Saijiang River, Xinan Peninsula and Shacheng Bay. As a result, the coastal industries made an important breakthrough for Ningde's economy to develop rapidly.

Ningde Port which is an important part of Fujian costal ports can be divided into 4 zones (Sandu Bay, the Saijiang River, Sansha Bay and Sancheng Bay) and 16 operational sites. At present, Ningde has first-class ports in Cheng'ao, Baima and Sansha) and 6 second class ports in Shacheng, Yaojiayu, Sansha, Saiqi, Sandu and Zhangwan. There are 98 berths, of which 8 are of the 10 000 category and has a handling capacity of 20 028 000 tons. In the next few years, there will be "heavyweight" ports for construction or completion, such as, No.8 Berth Project at Baima Port where a new 50 000-ton bulk cargo berth is to be built with a handling capacity of 2 million tons. And No. 15 Berth Project, of which a new general berth of 70 000 tons (hydraulic structure is designed according to the needs for berthing 100 000-ton ships) and its auxiliary facilities are under construction with a planned annual handling capacity of 3.2 million tons and a designed channeling capacity of 3.45 million tons.

And more importantly it is the construction of the functions of the export ports. In accordance with the demands of "large ports, big traffic hub, vast hinterland, huge circulation, and extensive development", Ningde will speed up the building of the traffic networks, and make itself an important port hub that connects the Western Taiwan Strait Economic Development Zone with hinterland and coastal regions as well as with international economies.

Ningde Port belongs to the national first-class ports with 222. 9-km shoreline available including 80.3-km of industrial shoreline. 221 berths can be built in the four port zones, among which there will be 151 berths each at the 10 000-tons level with an annual handling capacity of more than 400 million tons. At that time Ningde Port will become a 100 million-ton port and an important port of "Three Direct Links with Taiwan (link of trade, travel and post)" as well as a hub port that connects the inland with the coastal areas and even with the international economies.

四、重点产业

3.3.4 Key Industries

(一)电机电器制造产业

宁德电机电器产业系福建省首批重点培育的产业集群之一,也是宁德市首个百亿产业集群。目前,全市共有电机电器整机及配套企业1 000多家,全行业从业人员近20万人。其中,电机、水泵整机企业逾200家,化油器生产企业约100家,电子保健器械企业40家,配件及贸易企业近700家。

2013年全市电机电器产业规模以上工业总产值566亿元,外贸出口13.15亿美元,电机电器全行业规模以上企业306家,高新技术企业达14家,创新型(试点)企业达35家;全行业共25家企业被认定为福建省战略性新兴产业企业,拥有中国驰名商标8件、福建省著名商标42件、福建省名牌产品31件。现已有10多个种类、200多个系列、2 000多个规格。280多家企业通过ISO9001、ISO9002质量体系认证,上百家企业通过欧共体国家CE、GS、TUV认证,30多家企业通过美国UL认证,先后获得中国中小电机出口基地,全国百佳产业集群,中国中小电机之都,和中国按摩器具生产/出口基地等称号。2013年全市电机电器产业规模以上工业总产值566亿元。

3.3.4.1 Manufacturing Industry of Electric Motors and Appliances

Manufacturing Industry of Electric Motors and Appliances in Ningde is not only one of the first key nurtured industrial clusters in Fujian Province, but also the first industrial cluster worth over 10-billion yuan. At present, there are more than 1 thousand electric motor and appliances related companies in the whole city with 200,000 people involved. Among these industries, there are more than 200 motor and pump companies, including 100 carburetor production/enterprises, 40 electronic healthcare equipment enterprises and nearly 700 auxiliary companies and trade enterprises.

In 2013, the total value of output of the city's motor and electrical appliance industries was 56.6 billion yuan, and the export was $1.315 billion. There were 306 scale electrical appliance enterprises, 14 Hi-Tech enterprises, and 35 innovative (pilot) enterprises. 25 enterprises have been appraised as emerging strategic industrial enterprises in Fujian province, of which eight are well-known trademarks in China, 42 are famous brands in Fujian, and 31 are brand-name products in Fujian.

At present, there are more than ten categories of products in more than two hundred series and over two thousand specifications. More than 280 enterprises have passed the ISO 9001, ISO 9002 quality system certification, and hundreds of enterprises have been certified by CE, GS and TUV of European Union countries, and more than 30 enterprises have passed American UL certification. Successively, those enterprises have won the names of "China's small and medium-sized motor export base", "the national top industry cluster", "the Chinese small and medium-sized motor", and "production/export base of massagers in China" and so on. In 2013, the gross industrial output of the scale motor and electric appliances industry in Ningde reached 56.6 billion yuan.

(二)冶金产业

冶金新材料产业是宁德市目前的主导优势产业,产值占全市规模以上工业近三分之一,以福安、蕉城、福鼎、霞浦、寿宁、柘荣、古田为主要集聚区,产品涵盖不锈钢、铁合金等。2014 年全行业规模以上企业 108 家,从业人员 2.07 万人,产值亿元以上企业 57 家,50 亿元以上企业 3 家,100 亿元以上企业 2 家。

实现产值 799.7 亿元,对全市规模以上工业增长贡献率达 55.1%,已成为宁德市发展速度最快、产值最大的产业。当前,青拓集团正在推进不锈钢新材料项目,总投资 210 亿元,年产 400 系列、300 系列、取向硅钢、优质特钢结构板 650 万吨。如全面建成,可新增工业产值 550 亿元,吸纳 7 000 多个就业人员。

届时,全国乃至全球重要的不锈钢基地将在宁德建成,力争在 2020 年实现不锈钢下游深加工产业年产值 1 000 亿元,到 2025 年形成集研发设计、生产加工、物流仓储、贸易服务等于一体的冶金新材料全产业链体系的冶金新材料全产业链体系的发展目标。

3.3.4.2 Metallurgical Industry

Currently, metallurgic new materials industry is the dominant industry in Ningde City with an output value accounting nearly for a third of all the citywide industries. Fu'an, Jiaocheng, Fuding, Xiapu, Shouning, Zherong and Gutian are the main concentrated areas, where products cover stainless steel, iron alloy and so on. In 2014, there were 108 scale enterprises of the industry with more than 20 700 workers. There were 57 enterprises, whose output value was over one hundred million yuan. There were 3 enterprises with a value each over five billion yuan and 2 with a value over ten billion yuan. They realized an output value of 79.97 billion yuan which contributed 55.1% to the scale industrial growth in the city and became the fastest growing industry with the largest output value in Ningde City. The Qingtuo Group is promoting the new stainless steel materials project with a total investment of 21 billion yuan. The annual output of Series 400, Series 300, high-quality steel plates and oriented silicon steel reached 6.5 million tons. If the whole project is completed, the total output value for the new emerging industry will increase to 55 billion yuan with more than 7 000 employees.

By that time, a significant stainless steel base at the national and even the global levels will be built in Ningde. By 2020, more than 100 billion yuan of annual output of the intensive processing of the stainless steel industry has been worked on. By 2025, a set of design, production, processing and services of the new metallurgical material industrial chain system will be formed.

（三）能源产业

宁德市充分利用山海兼备的资源优势，合理布局发展核电、风电、太阳能光伏和新型动力电池等多种形式的新能源产业，构建稳定、清洁、安全的能源保障体系，其目标是力争到 2017 年形成新能源千亿元产业集群。

2013 年全市电源装机总容量 578.9 万千瓦时，发电量 276.27 亿千瓦时，全市能源行业（发电供电）实现工业产值 167 亿元，其中规上工业产值 164.69 亿元，核电全年发电量 75.19 亿千瓦时，实现产值 21.57 亿元；火电全年发电量 128.26 亿千瓦时，实现产值 46.17 亿元；水电全年发电量 71.89 亿千瓦时，实现产值约为 21.14 亿元。霞浦大京风电场已建成投产，总装机容量 0.9 万千瓦的宁德漳湾垃圾焚烧发电厂已经投产，中聚天冠一期已经开工，总装机量为 10 兆瓦的东侨光伏发电示范项目也已投产并网发电，被列入国家“金太阳”示范工程。此外还有拥有全球第四大锂电池供应商和全球最大的聚合物锂电池供应商宁德新能源科技公司、年产 7 000 万安时锂离子动力电池的福安博瑞特公司、年产 1.2 亿 Ah 高性能磷酸铁锂动力电池的福鼎华正新能源公司。海峡西岸一个新能源基地初具雏形。

3.3.4.3 Energy Industry

Ningde makes good use of the advantages of mountains and seas, and develops rationally a variety of new energy industries like nuclear power, wind electricity, solar photovoltaic and new-typed power battery, etc. to establish a stable, clean and secure energy security system at the same time aiming at forming a hundred million yuan industry cluster of the new energy by 2017.

In 2013, the installed capacity of electric power in the city was 5.789 million kilowatt-hours with a generation amount of 27.627 billion kilowatt-hours. The whole city's energy industry (power supply) realized an industrial output value of 16.7 billion yuan, of which the scale industrial output value reached 16.469 billion yuan. The annual nuclear capacity was 7.519 billion kilowatt-hours with an output value of 2.157 billion yuan. The thermal power generating capacity was 12.826 billion KWH throughout the year with an output value of 4.617 billion yuan. The annual capacity of hydro power was 7.189 billion kilowatt-hours with an output value of about 2.114 billion yuan. In addition, Dajing Wind Farm in Xiapu County had been completed and put into operation. The total installed capacity of Zhangwan Garbage Incineration Power Plant with an capacity of 9 thousand kilowatts was under operation. The first stage of Zhongju Tian'guan Energy Company of 300 thousand tons of fuel ethanol was finished. The total installed capacity for 10 MW Dongqiao photovoltaic power generation demonstration project had been put into production in grid generation, and it was included in the national "golden sun" demonstration project. Ningde has the fourth largest lithium battery supplier in the world and the world's largest lithium polymer battery supplier named Amperex Technology Limited (ATL Ningde) and another company named Fu'an Boruite Company with an output of 70 million-Ah lithium ion power battery annually, as well as Fuding Huazheng New Energy Company with an annual output of 120 million-Ah high performance iron phosphate lithium battery. A new energy base has been in shape in the West Coast of the Taiwan Strait.

（四）船舶修造产业

宁德市是福建省拥有民营船舶企业、船台、船坞数量最多的船舶修造基地，外轮修理基地，出口成品油轮建造基地，海洋工程船建造出口基地，和福建省唯一民办的服务船舶行业的高级技师培训基地，也是国内第三大民间船舶修造基地。产业主要分布在蕉城区、福安市、福鼎市、霞浦县等4个沿海县(市、区)。全市从事船舶修、造、拆的企业有50多家,船舶上下游关联企业800多家,拥有10万吨级干船坞2座(福建新远造船有限公司、闽东丛贸船舶实业有限公司),船坞、船台总容量分别占全省80%左右,具备承修12万吨级、承造8.5万吨级普通船舶的修造能力,产品涉及海洋工程船、驳船、拖轮、油轮、货轮、游艇等众多领域,还拥有船舶设计、研发、制造、检验、交易、金融等服务平台。

3.3.4.4 Ships Building and Repairing Industries

Ningde City boasts in Fujian many bases of shipbuilding enterprises with the most ship docks and yards, and bases of foreign ships-repairing, and of the oil vessels for export as well as the base for building marine engineering vessels for export and the only private base for senior vocational engineer training of the vessels business service, and Ningde is also the third largest private base of civic shipbuilding and ship-repairing. The industry distributes mainly in four coastal counties (county-level cities or districts)—Fu'an, Jiaocheng, Fuding and Xiapu. There are more than 50 enterprises engaged in repairing, building, and disassembling of ships in the entire Ningde City and 800 affiliated shipping industries in the upper and lower chains. There are two 100 000-ton dockyards (Fujian Xinyuan Ship Co., Ltd. and Mindong Congmao Ship Industrial Co., Ltd.). The capacity of its docks and its shipways had accounted for about 80% of that in the entire province. And it had the capability of repairing common vessels of 120 000-ton ships and building common vessels of 85 000 tons. Its products involve various fields of off-shore vessels, barges, tugboats, oil tankers, cargo boats and yachts. It also owns a service platform for ship's design, development, building, checking, trade and finance.

(五)食品加工产业

宁德市农产品资源丰富,是全国最大的大黄鱼人工养殖基地、茶叶种植基地,也是银耳、香菇、太子参的主产区,有着发展资源转化型产业和农产品加工业的良好基础。2013年,全行业规模以上企业277家(其中蕉城51家,霞浦44家,福安44家,福鼎56家,寿宁14家,屏南5家),实现规模以上产值370亿元。水产品加工业以蕉城、霞浦、福鼎为主要集中区,主要加工大黄鱼、紫菜、海带、海蜇和虾类等。制茶业以福安、福鼎、寿宁、周宁为主要集中区,产品以绿茶、红茶为主,也有乌龙茶、白茶等,茶企星罗棋布,品牌众多;食用菌加工业以古田、屏南、寿宁为主要集中区,产业已朝精深加工、珍稀菌种开发方向发展。全行业拥有"柘荣太子参""海旸""古田银耳""福鼎白茶""坦洋工夫""岳海""海名威""三都港"等中国驰名商标。

3.3.4.5 Food Processing Industry

Ningde is rich in agricultural products resources. It is the biggest base of yellow croaker sea farming and tea planting in China as well as major producing area of tremalla, mushrooms and Taizi ginseng, which lay a favorable foundation for developing a resource-transforming industry and agricultural processing. In 2013, scale enterprises were added up to 277(including 51 in Jiaocheng, 44 in Xiapu, 44 in Fu'an, 56 in Fuding, 14 in Shouning, 5 in Pingnan), achieving a scale output value of 37 billion yuan. The main concentrated areas of seafood processing are Jiaocheng, Xiapu and Fuding, where yellow croakers, porphyra, kelps, jellyfish, and shrimps are mainly processed. Tea processing industries are concentrated in Fu'an, Fuding, Shouning and Zhouning. The main products are green tea and black tea, Oolong and white tea, etc. Tea enterprises are sporadic everywhere, and there are many brands. The edible fungi processing industries are dotted in Gutian, Pingnan and Shouning, and the industries have developed with elaborate processing and rare species development. The industry possess many famous brands in China, like Zherong Taizi Ginsengs, Hai Yi Pork, Gutian Tremella, Fuding White Tea, Tanyang Kungfu Black Tea, Yue Hai Seafood, Hemingway Seafood and Sandu Bay Seafood.

（六）生物医药制造产业

宁德市生物医药制造业形成了以柘荣海西药城为重点，古田、福鼎各具特色的“一城两基地”发展格局，即以开发生产新药与中成药为重点的柘荣药城，以开发生产化学原料药与化学制剂为重点的古田药业基地和以发展生物制药为重点的福鼎药业基地。随着安发（福建）生物科技园一期在东侨工业区建成，标志着宁德生物医药产业发展又迈上了一个新台阶。

目前，已拥有粉针剂、冻干粉针剂、片剂、胶囊剂、颗粒剂及无菌注射用原料药等9条现代化生产线的闽东力捷迅药业有限公司，福建省规模最大、品种最齐的中药饮片专业生产企业福建天人药业有限公司，以及福建广生堂药业有限公司，安发（福建）生物科技有限公司，今古通生物科技有限公司，青岛澳柯玛等。产品涵盖生物技术药物、化学新药和新型制剂、现代中药，先进医疗器械和海洋药物等系列数百种产品。

2013年，全市生物医药规模以上企业10家，实现规模以上工业产值20.18亿元，其中产值亿元以上企业4家，实现产值17.07亿元，产值5亿元以上企业1家（力捷迅），实现产值9.7亿元，产业规模居全省第三。

3.3.4.6 Biomedicine Manufacturing Industry

The biomedicine industry in Ningde City has formed a growth pattern of "one town and two bases" which refer to Medicine Town that focuses on new medicine production and traditional Chinese medicines in East Fujian as well as the medicine base in Gutian that focuses on new chemical material medicines and chemical doses, and the medicine base in Fuding that focuses on biomedicines.

The first stage of the construction of Alpha (Fujian) Group Holdings Ltd. in Dongqiao Industrial Zone marks a new era for the biomedicine industry in Ningde City.

At present, Ningde boasts Lijiexun Pharmaceutical Co., Ltd. in East Fujian that has about 9 modern production lines of powder injection, freeze-dried powder injection, tablets, capsules, granules, sterile and injection APIs as well as Fujian Tianren Pharmaceutical Co., Ltd. which has the largest scale and most varieties of Chinese herbal pills in Fujian province. Also, there are some other companies in Ningde, such as the Gosunter Pharmaceutical Company Limited, the Alpha Biotechnology Science and Technology Company Ltd., Goldentone Biotechnology Science and Technology Company Limited, Qingdao Aucma Medical Instrument Company that produce hundreds of products covering several series like biotechnology drugs, chemical drugs and pharmaceutical preparation, advanced medical device and marine drugs.

In 2013, there were 10 biological medicine scale enterprises in Ningde, and the industrial output value 2.018 billion yuan was achieved. Among them, there were 4 enterprises, whose output value reached above one hundred million yuan, and the output value of 1.707 billion yuan was achieved. There was one enterprise (Lijiexun Pharmaceutical Ltd.), whose output value reached 500 million yuan), and an output value of 970 million yuan had been achieved. And it is the third highest scale industry in the province.

(七)汽摩配件产业

宁德市汽摩配件产业主要分布在福鼎市和霞浦县,形成福鼎化油器和霞浦汽摩配件两个集群。福鼎是全国最大的化油器生产基,化油器类型从摩托车化油器发展到通用机化油器、舷外机化油器,产品从五六个品种发展到 152 个。

截至 2013 年全市 228 家企业获 135 项专利、生产 1.4 亿台化油器、化油器配件 16 000 多万套,销往全国 18 个省 37 个城市、20 多个国家,总产值达 103 亿元,产品市场占有率居全国第一，被中国机械工业联合会授予“中国化油器名城”称号。

霞浦县制动材料总厂是国内汽车摩托车刹车片生产的重点企业，也是福建省汽车工公司定点生产制动器衬片的专业厂，年生产摩托车刹车片 1 500 万片，制动器衬片 2 800 吨的能力。主要产品有石棉、无石棉摩托车刹车片、汽车盘式刹车片、汽车鼓式刹车片、汽车鼓式刹车蹄快等，摩托车刹车片荣获福建省优质产品称号。

在发展汽车产业上，宁德市将依托宁德时代新能源科技有限公司等龙头企业，充分利用现有储能电池技术领先的优势，大力研发高性能纯电动汽车储能电池及系统集成设计、制造，同时加快研发拥有自主知识产权的新能源汽车，努力打造漳湾新能源汽车产业基地，促进新能源汽车产业集群发展。

3.3.4.7 Industry of Automobile and Motorcycle Parts

Automobile and motorcycle parts industry are mainly located in Fuding and Xiapu counties, forming two clusters of carburetors and automobile & motorcycle accessories respectively. Fuding is one of the country's largest production bases of carburetors ranging from motorcycle carburetors and general machine carburetors, outboard machine carburetors, and the products varieties started from 5 or 6 to 152.

By the end of 2013,228 companies from the city had won 135 patents,and produced 140 million carburetors and more than 160 million carburetor sets. The products had been sold to 18 provinces, 37 cities, and more than 20 countries. The output values reached 10.3 billion yuan. The market occupying rate of the products had been the first in China. And the honorable title "China Carburetor City" had been awarded by China Machinery Industry Federation to Fuding City.

The General Factory of Braking Materials in Xiapu County is not only the key enterprise in China which specializes in the production of the brake linings of autos and motorcycles, but also a professional factory which produces the brake linings designated by Fujian province Automotive Industry Corporation. Every year the factory produces 15 million pieces of motorcycle brake blocks and 2 800-ton brake linings.

The main products are asbestos, non-asbestos motorcycle brake pads, auto brake pads, drum brake pads and drum brake blocks, etc. And motorcycle brake pads had won the title of high quality products in Fujian province.

As far as the development of automobile industry is concerned, Ningde will rely on Amperex Technology Ltd. and other leading enterprises, making full use of existing energy enterprise of batteries with leading advantages in technology, and vigorously develop the pure electric vehicle energy storage battery of high performance, as well as their system integration design and manufacture. At the same time, accelerate the research and development with independent intellectual property rights of new energy vehicles have been accelerated and a new energy automotive industry base has been built so that the development of a new energy automobile industry cluster has been furthered.

(八)建筑建材工业产业

宁德市建材产业主要以石材加工为主,以福鼎白琳、古田鹤塘为主要集中区。花岗岩是宁德市内非金属矿中最有优势的矿种,蕴藏量达数亿立方米,主要品种有花岗石、闪长石、玄武岩、辉绿岩等,福鼎白琳“福鼎黑”玄武岩、古田鹤塘“桃花红”花岗石等比较有代表的5个品种被纳入“天然石材首批国家标准”。2013年,全市建材行业规模以上企业133家,完成规模以上工业产值101.79亿元,其中亿元以上企业21家,实现产值40.51亿元,产值5亿元以上企业数2家。全社会建筑业增加值112.95亿元,全市具有资质等级的总承包和专业承包建筑企业完成建筑业总产值182.37亿元,房屋建筑施工面积1 527.63万平方米,房屋建筑竣工面积452.01万平方米。全社会建筑业增加值112.95亿元,全市具有资质等级的总承包和专业承包建筑企业完成建筑业总产值182.37亿元,房屋建筑施工面积1 527.63万平方米,房屋建筑竣工面积452.01万平方米。

3.3.4.8 Building Materials Industry

The building materials industry in Ningde is mainly in stone processing, which is centered in Bailin Village in Fuding and Hetang Township in Gutian. Granite is the most advantageous nonmetallic mineral in Ningde, whose reserves amount to hundreds of millions of cubic meters. The main varieties include granite, diorite stone, basalt, diabase, etc. “Fuding Black Basalt”, Hetang Basalt in Gutian with a nickname of “red peach blossom” and other three varieties had been listed as the national standard of “natural stones and rocks”. In 2013, the scale building materials industry enterprises in the city were added up to 133, with an industrial output value of 10. 179 billion yuan, and among them, there were 21 enterprises whose industrial output value was up to one hundred million yuan, scoring the output value of 4. 051 billion yuan. And there were 2 companies whose industrial output value reached 500 million yuan. The whole society constructed added value scored 11. 295 billion yuan.

The constructed output value of 18. 237 billion yuan had been achieved with the enterprises with qualification of general contracting and professional contracting in the entire city for constructing a housing floor area of 15. 2763 million square meters, and a finished housing area of 4. 5201 million square meters.

(九)皮塑工业产业

宁德皮塑工业形成了以 PU 革为主的皮塑工业,产品主要有湿式 PU、干式 PU、压延革、超细纤维和干法 PVC 合成革四大系列数千个品种。产业集聚度逐步显现,形成了以树脂、革基布、无纺布、置绒和制鞋等上下游产业组成的产业链,产业主要分布在福鼎市和霞浦县。2013 全行业拥有规模以上企业数 73 家,完成工业总产值 258. 38 亿元。其中产值亿元以上企业 55 家,实现产值 249. 49 亿元,产值 5 亿元以上企业 31 家。

3.3.4.9 Leather Industry

Leather industry in Ningde has developed the PU leather as main products, which primarily include wet and dry PU leather, pressed leather, superfine fiber and dry process PVC. The four series synthetic leather products have thousands of varieties. The industrial agglomeration gradually highlighted, and formed an industry with the upper and lower chains, ranging from resin, leather fabric, non-woven fabric, and cashmere set and footwear, etc., chiefly in Fuding and Xiapu Counties. There were 73 scale companies in 2013, with a gross industrial output value of 25. 838 billion yuan achieved. There were 55 scale enterprises with output value of 24. 949 billion yuan. Besides there were 31 companies with an industrial output value of 500 million yuan.

五、高新技术产业

3.3.5 High-Tech Technologies

(一)产业简况

大力推进产学研相结合,鼓励企业建立与高校、科研院所有机结合的知识创新体系,提高企业的科技水平和竞争力,促进高新技术成果的产业化。

全市共有 610 家高新技术产业,主要形成六大高新科技产业:以福安的泰格、安波、亚南等为主的电机高新技术产业,以宁德新能源科技有限公司等为主的新能源工业高新技术产业,以青拓集团、鼎信实业有限公司等为主的冶金新材料产业,以长兴船舶重工有限公司、立新船舶工程有限公司、恒生船舶重工有限公司等为主的船舶高新技术产业，以安发(福建)生物科技有限公司、福鼎药业、柘荣药城、古田药业等为主的生物医药高新技术产业，以福鼎化油器霞浦县制动材料总厂等为主的汽摩配高新技术产业。

从高新技术产业区域分布情况看，主要集中在蕉城、福安、福鼎等三个县市区。从行业分布来看，主要分布在高新技术改造传统产业、高新技术制造业中的电子及通信设备制造业、医药制造业、医疗器械及仪器仪表制造业以及高技术服务业中的信息服务行业。

3.3.5.1 Brief Introduction

Great efforts have been devoted to promoting the integration of production, teaching and research, encouraging the enterprise to build knowledge innovation system with universities and scientific research institutions, enhancing the technologies and competitiveness of enterprises, and promoting the industrialization of high-tech achievements.

There are 610 new hi-tech industrial enterprises in the city, forming 6 new hi-tech industries mainly of motors of Taige, Able, Yanan of Fu'an; New energy industry of Amperex Technology Ltd. Ningde; new materials of metallurgy of Tsingshan Holdings Group Co., Ltd. and Dingxin Industrial Limited Company; Hi-tech industries of shipbuilding industries of Changxin Shipbuilding Heavy industry Limited Company, Lixin Ship Engineering Limited Company and Hengsheng Shipbuilding Heavy Industry Limited Company; biomedicine high-tech industries of Alpha Group Holdings and pharmaceutical industries of Fuding, Zherong and Gutian; automobile and motorcycle hi-tech industries of carburetors in Fuding and the General Factory of the Braking Materials in Xiapu County.

As to the regional distribution of the new hi-tech industries, most are located in Jiaocheng, Fu'an and Fuding. From the distribution of businesses, most industries are mainly engaged in traditional industrial upgrading, as well as in the hi-tech industries of electronics, communications equipment manufacturing industry, pharmaceutical manufacturing industry, medical equipment and instrument manufacturing industry and information service industry in high-tech services sector.

（二）产业基地

3.3.5.2 Major Industrial Bases

宁德国家农业科技园

宁德国家农业科技园是宁德首个国家级科技园区，由核心区、示范区和辐射区构成，涉及县（市、区）包括蕉城区、福安市、福鼎市和霞浦县沿海连片集中区。目前园区已进驻30多家龙头企业，拥有农业部健康养殖示范场12个；国家级原良种场2家，国家大黄鱼遗传育种中心1家；中国驰名商标4个，省著名商标20个，无公害产品58个，并配套完善了垂钓、游艇、游泳、餐饮、娱乐、休闲等设施。

科技园带动科技示范户280家，为当地农渔民提供了3 000多个就业岗位，示范带动了周边十几万名育苗户、养殖户、加工户等农渔民开展优质苗种培育、健康养殖和产品精深加工。

根据规划，到2020年科技园将新增自主创新和引进国内外优良品种20～30个，国内外领先技术120项以上，名牌产品和驰名商标20个以上，培育和壮大一批水产科技型企业和出口型水产品加工基地，引进和培育年销售收入超亿元的水产龙头企业40家以上，生产总值达1 000亿元，利税150亿元，出口创汇60亿美元。

3.3.5.2.1 Ningde National Agriculture Hi-Tech Park

As the first national agriculture hi-tech park in Ningde, it consists of a core zone, a demonstration plot and a radiating area, including Jiaocheng, Fu'an, Fuding countries and Xiapu coastal contiguous clusters. By far, more than 30 leading enterprises have located in the industrial park. The park possess 12 eco-friendly sea-farming demonstration spots by Ministry of Agriculture, 2 national original breeding farms, 1 national genetic breeding center of larimichthy crocea, 4 China famous brand trademarks, 20 provincial famous trademarks and 58 nuisance-free products. Besides there are some auxiliary facilities for fishing, yachting, swimming, catering, entertainment and relaxation. The park also guides 280 scientific and technological model households, provides over 3 000 jobs for the local farmers and fishers, and sets the examples for the farmers and fishermen of hundreds of thousands of households in quality seeding, cultivating, healthy raising and deep processing of the products.

As planned, the park will increase or introduce 20-30 newly self-innovated brands, introduced domestic and overseas excellent varieties, over 120 domestic and overseas leading technologies, and over 20 famous-brand products and well-known trademarks by 2020.

And a batch of aquatic product technology firms will be fostered and strengthened, and 40 enterprises with an annual sales income exceeding 100 million will be introduced and cultivated with a total output value of 100 billion yuan, and a taxation profit of about 15 billion yuan, as well as a foreign exchange earnings through export of about 6 billion U.S. dollars.

宁德欲建五大高新产业基地

根据《"十二五"科学技术发展专项规划》,未来宁德市将依托国家创新基金闽东中小电机产业集群项目,建立闽东电机、新能源、新材料、生物医药、船舶、汽摩配件工业高新技术产业化基地。同时,构建五大高新科技园区,使之成为推动宁德市高新技术产业发展的强大引擎。具体包括中科院宁德海西高新技术产业示范园、海西生物医药园区、宁德软件科技园区、宁德光伏产业科技园区、三都澳水产科技园区。

未来宁德市将依托国家创新基金闽东中小电机产业集群项目,建立闽东电机高新技术产业化基地,从管理创新、技术升级、成果转化、市场开拓等环节实现转型目标,做大做强宁德电机电器产业集群。

建立闽东新能源工业高新技术产业化基地,对接国家新能源产业政策,引导有实力的企业进入新能源领域,形成新能源产业链和产业集群。

建立闽东新材料高新技术产业化基地,依托龙头企业,强化产学研结合,延伸产业价值链,做大做强新材料产业。闽东生物医药高新技术产业化基地建立,促进宁德市特色中药材产业化发展。

闽东船舶高新技术产业化基地建立,重点发展高技术含量、高附加值的全新产品领域,建造广泛使用于海上油田等领域的海洋工程船、驳船、拖轮等新船型。闽东汽摩配高新技术产业化基地等建立。

同时,构建五大高新科技园区。发挥园区的产业集群效应,使之成为推动宁德市高新技术产业发展的强大引擎。具体包括中科院宁德海西高新技术产业示范园、海西生物医药园区、宁德软件科技园区、宁德光伏产业科技园区、三都澳水产科技园区。

3.3.5.2.2 Five High and New Industrial Bases to be Built in Ningde

According to the *Special Program of the Development of Science and Technology for the* 12th *Five-Year Program*, by relying on the group projects of the country's innovative foundation for small and medium motor industry in Eastern Fujian, Ningde will build a Hi-tech industrialized base, including motors, new energy, new materials, biomedicine, ship and motorcycle accessories. Meanwhile, it will also construct five advanced and new scientific parks, and become a powerful engine, which will push forward the development of the high-tech industry in Ningde.

Specifically, it includes the Hi-tech Industrial Demonstration Park of the Western Taiwan Strait Economic Zone of Chinese Academy of Science, the Biomedicine Park of Western Taiwan Strait Economic Zone, Ningde Software Park, Ningde PV Science Park and Sandu Bay Aquatic Science Park.

In the future, Ningde will rely on the national innovation fund of the small and medium-sized motor industry cluster projects to establish Eastern Fujian Electric Hi-tech Industrial Base. Links with the management innovation, technological upgrading, transformation, marketing and others to achieve the transformation goals must be enhanced, and Ningde's electrical appliance industry cluster will be built into a stronger and larger group.

We can carry out high-tech industrialization of a new energy industry base in eastern Fujian by keeping up with the national policies on new industry, and guide the strong enterprises into the new energy sectors, and form new energy industrial chains and clusters.

We can establish a new materials hi-tech industrial base in eastern Fujian by relying on pilot enterprises, strengthen the unity of production, teaching and research, and stretch industrial value chains so as to build a bigger and stronger material industry. We can establish a biological medicine and new technology industrial base to promote the development of distinctive medicine industry in Ningde.

We can establish eastern Fujian marine high-tech industrial base, focusing on the hi-tech content and high value-added new products. We can build the ocean engineering ships, barges, tugs and others widely used in the marine oil fields and build up hi-tech industrialized base in eastern Fujian.

At the same time, we will establish the five hi-tech parks, and bring into play the cluster effect in the park, making it the powerful engine for pushing the development of hi-tech industry in Ningde.

Priority has been given to the specific areas. They are the Hi-tech Industrial Demonstration Park of the Western Taiwan Strait Economic Zone of Chinese Academy of Science, the Biomedicine Park of Western Taiwan Strait Economic Zone, Ningde Photovoltaic Industry Science and Technology Park, Sandu Bay Aquatic Science Park.

六、重点企业

3.3.6 Key Enterprises

(一)宁德新能源科技有限公司

新能源科技有限公司,简称 ATL,位于宁德市东侨经济开发区,是国家火炬计划重点高新技术企业,全球最大锂离子电池生产基地,主要生产高端消费类产品电池、电动汽车电池与储能电站。

该公司是一家致力于可充电锂离子电池的电芯、封装和系统整合的研发、生产和营销的国家高新科技企业,产品获得国家科技进步二等奖,广泛应用于手机、蓝牙耳机、MP3、PMP、移动 DVD、笔记本电脑、电动工具、电动汽车、储能电站等各种移动设备。

在全球十大锂离子电池供应商中,其技术、产能与销量始终处于领先地位,向全球消费电子顶级品牌供货,与清华大学、香港大学主导开发的"汽车用动力型锂离子电池系统的开发和产业化"项目,技术水平达到世界先进水平。公司研发生产的全球最薄日用消费类电池,被多家世界顶级手机、平板电脑和笔记本电脑厂商所采用。

3.3.6.1 Amperex Technology LTD Ningde (ATL)

Amperex Technology LTD Ningde (ATL) located in Dongqiao Economic and Technological Development Zone, Ningde City, is the National Torch Plan's key high-tech enterprise, as well as the world's largest production base for lithium-ion batteries. It mainly produces the high-end consumer products, such as the electric vehicle battery and energy storage power stations. It's a national hi-tech enterprise, which concentrates on the cells and packaging of rechargeable Li-ion, and the development, production, and marketing of system integrations. The products have won the second prize of National Scientific and Technological Progress Award and have found a wide application in mobile devices including mobile phones, blue-tooth headsets, MP3, PMP, portable DVDs, laptops, electronic instruments, electric vehicles, energy storage, etc.

Among the ten largest lithium-ion battery suppliers in the world, ATL has always been in a leading position in its technology, capacity and sales, supplying the top electronics brands consumed around the globe, and it takes an active exploitation into the projects together with Tsinghua University and

Hong Kong University as a result the development and industrialization of the lithium-ion battery system in automobile use, and technology has reached the world's top level. The company has researched and developed the most thin consumer batteries, which is adopted by many world-renown telephones, tablet personal computers and laptop producers.

(二)安发(福建)生物科技有限公司

安发(福建)生物科技有限公司,总部位于福建省宁德市东侨经济开发区,是国家火炬计划重点高新技术企业,是新西兰安发国际控股集团投资创办的。公司集全球一流的专业研究,开发推广药用真菌、天然植物和海洋生物,生产制造纯天然、高效能、无毒、无副作用的高科技天然药品、保健食品和健康食品,主要产品有甘诺宝天然药物、功能性保健品、功能性饮品、新西兰原装奶制品、护肤品等系列 50 款,有 20 预科产品填补了国内外市场空白。产品销往国内 28 个省市,在国外市场网络已分布缅甸、泰国、印尼等东南亚国家,专卖店达 200 多家,2014 年实现工业化产值 30 多亿。同时安发也正在进行生物科技产品转型和升级,目前部分产品已通过审核。

3.3.6.2 Alpha Group Holdings (Fujian) of Biological Technology

The group with its headquarters in Dongqiao Economic and Technological Development Zone, Ningde, Fujian, is a leading enterprise of the National Torch Program and is invested by New Zealand Alpha International Group Holding. Endowed with professional studies of the first class in the world, the group is engaged in the development and promotion of medicinal fungus, natural plants and marine lives, as well as manufacturing of natural, high-effect, non-poisonous and no side effect hi-tech natural medicines. The main products of the group are Gannuobao natural medicines, functional health care products, functional drinks, New Zealand original dairy products, skin care products and so on. Besides 20 of its preparatory products have filled market vacancies at home and abroad. The products have been sold to 28 provinces and cities in China and the overseas sales net has already extended in some Southeast Asian countries, such as Myanmar, Thailand, Indonesia, etc., and over 200 exclusive shops have opened there, and the production value of the industry reached more than 3 billion in 2014. At the same time, the products of Alpha biological technology are under transferring and upgrading, and some have already passed the appraisal and examination.

(三)福安市闽东安波电器有限公司

福安闽东安波电器有限公司是集生产、贸易、科研为一体的有限责任公司。公司主要产品为电动机、水泵及发电机组,产品销往东南亚、欧美、中东、澳洲等五十多个国家和地区,深受客户青睐,成为美国滨特尔(Pentair)、德国威乐(Wilo)、意大利阿特拉斯(Atlas)、芬兰科尼(Konecrane)等世界500强企业的战略合作伙伴。公司已通过了CCC、CSA、UL、CE/GS、ISO9000、ISO14000等认证,并荣获中国首家电机出口免验企业、中国驰名商标、福建省名牌产品、福建出口名牌企业、福建省创新型示范企业、中国机电行业AAA信用企业等诸多荣誉。

3.3.6.3 Able Motor Co., Ltd of Fu'an City

Able Motor Co., Ltd of Fu'an City, is a limited liability company devoted to production, trade, and scientific research. Its main products are motors, water pumps and generators and they are exported to more than 50 countries and regions, such as Southeast Asia, Europe, America, the Middle East, Australia etc., and won much favor from customers. It has become a strategic partner with top 500 enterprises in the world, such as Pentair(the USA), Wilo (Germany), Atlas (Italy), Konecrane (Finland). The company has passed the CCC, CSA, UL, CE/GS, ISO 9000 and ISO 14000 certifications, and has been awarded honors like "China's First Motor Export Inspection-free Enterprise", "Chinese Famous Export Trademark", "Brand-name Product in Fujian Province", "Fujian Famous Brand Enterprise", "Innovative Demonstration Enterprise in Fujian", "AAA Credit Enterprise in Electrical Industry in China", and many others.

(四)福建华龙化油器有限公司

福建华龙化油器有限公司是福建省第一家专业研制生产摩托车、通用汽油机化油器的福建省外资重点企业之一,先后被省政府评为"省百家重点企业""省先进技术企业""省中外合资先进企业",产品多次荣获"省优质产品""省消费者信得过产品""创名牌产品"等称号,被誉为"福建省高新技术企业"称号。公司已通过ISO9001和ISO14001认证,主营产品有摩托车化油器、通用化油器、MC13C3化油器、MC13E1化油器、MC13H1化油器、MC14C1化油器。公司拥有大型的实验室和生产厂房,具备数控车床、加工中心、磨刀机、大型清洗机等大批生产检测设备,以及CMM分析能力和完善的材料与品质分析仪器,年生产能力在500万台/套以上。

3.3.6.4 Fujian HuaLong Carburetor Co., Ltd.

It is the first specializing company in the development and production of carburetors for motorcycles and vehicles in Fujian. It is one of the most important foreign-funded enterprises in Fujian. Besides, the company was awarded honors by the governmental departments at various levels like "Fujian Provincial Key Enterprises", "Fujian Provincial Advanced Technology Enterprise" and "Fujian Provincial Advanced Enterprise of Sino-Foreign Joint Venture". What is more, the product has won the tiles of "Fujian Provincial Quality Product", "Fujian Provincial Consumer Trustworthy Product" and "Famous Brand Product" many times. It is also honored as "Hi-tech Enterprise" in Fujian province. The company has passed ISO9001 and ISO14001 authentication. The main products of the company are motorcycle carburetors, general carburetors, MC13C3 carburetors, MC13E1 carburetors, MC13H1 carburetors, and MC14C1 carburetors. It is equipped with large laboratories and production workshops, CNC lathes, machine centers, grinding machines, large washing machines, and a large number of production testing equipment, with strong analysis capacity of CMM and analysis instruments for better material and quality. Its annual production capacity reaches over 5 million sets.

（五）大唐宁德火电厂

大唐宁德火电厂是闽东第一个大型火电厂。公司规划总装机容量 452 万千瓦，分三期建设。目前公司投产总装机容量 252 万千瓦，是福建省已投产机组单机容量最大、总装机容量第二大的发电公司。2013 年，该公司全年利润总额累计完成数亿元，超出年初预算近 3 亿元。2014 年 1 月，电厂完成发电量 10.7 亿千瓦时，实现利润数千万元。

3.3.6.5 Datang Ningde Power Plant

Datang Ningde Power Plant, one of the key power projects sponsored by the state in the Western Taiwan Straits Economic Development Zone, is located in Wanwu, Fu'an City. It is the first large thermal plant and the biggest project in history of Ningde. The total installed capacity reaches 4.52 million kilowatts and is divided for three stages for construction. At present, the production of the total installed capacity of 2.52 million kilowatts has been put into operation in Fujian Province, becoming the largest power company with the individual unit capacity, and the second power generation company with its total installed capacity; 2 sets of 1 million mw ultra supercritical units the third stage are under preparation. In 2013, the company profits totaled at hundreds of millions of yuan exceeding nearly 300 million yuan of the budget at the beginning of the year. In January, 1.07 billion kilowatt-hours of electricity was produced with a profit of tens of millions of dollars in 2014.

七、品牌战略

宁德市大力推进实施品牌战略，加快经济发展方式转变，提升企业的品牌形象和核心竞争力，带动产业集群更好更快发展，实现跨越崛起取得了显著成效。截至2014年底共有宁德市知名商标463件，福建著名商标225件，福建名牌产品73件，地理标志证明商标的总数49件，位居全国各区市前列。其中，既是地理标志又是驰名商标的有6件，居全国各区市首位，中国驰名商标34件，稳居全省第4位，实现9县(市、区)、东侨全覆盖。其中，“霞浦海带”的成功认定，不仅使霞浦县实现了驰名商标“零”的突破，而且使宁德市10个县(市、区)的驰名商标实现“满堂红”“全覆盖”。每个县(市、区)至少拥有一枚驰名商标。“甘诺宝力”的成功认定，也实现了宁德市食品加工(保健品)行业的驰名商标“零”的突破，这将为地方经济发展增添新的发展动力。

3.3.7 Brand Strategies

Ningde is promoting the implementation of brand strategy, accelerating the transformation of the economic development pattern, developing the industry brand image and core competence, furthering the development of the industry better, and achieving significant results in realizing a leapfrog success. By the end of 2014, well-known trademarks reached a total of 463 in Ningde; and the famous trademarks in Fujian province were added up to 225, and the famous products in Fujian province reached 73, and the number of geographical certification trademarks of origin hit 49, and these quantities of trademarks stood at the front rank of all the prefectural-level cities in China. Among them, trademarks that are both of geographical origin indication and well-known reached 6 pieces, and outstood at the first place of among all prefectural-level cities, and the number of the Chinese well-known trademarks were 34, taking the fourth place comfortably in the province, and distributed evenly among 9 counties (city, district). Among them, the kelp in Xiapu was successfully certified so that it not only made Xiapu County realize a breakthrough with its zero well-known trademarks but also made Ningde realize its every county or city has one well-known trademark. At least, there was one famous trademark in each area. And Gannuobaoli Brand was also certified, which made Ningde realize a break-through with the zero well-known trademarks of the food processing industry in the city, and added a new momentum to local economic development.

第四节 现代服务业

3.4 Modern Service Industries

一、社会服务业

现代服务业方面：一是发展现代物流业。加快构建以物流园区、物流中心和配送中心为主体的三级物流体系，打造福建重要的地区性物流节点城市。推进物流公共信息平台建设，大力发展第三方物流，开展跨区域物流合作。二是壮大商贸流通业。创新商贸经营业态、流通方式、组织形式，积极培育大型商贸企业集团，着力提升商贸服务业等级和业态水平。加快建设和改造提升电机电器、茶叶、食用菌、水产品、药材等专业批发市场，建成一批特色鲜明、功能完善的新型商贸集聚区。三是提升特色旅游业。注重旅游与文化的融合发展，提升旅游智能化信息技术，延伸旅游服务产业链。四是培育科技和信息服务业。加快推动中国·声立方产业综合体项目建设，打造海峡两岸最高品质的呼叫中心；开发建设具有宁德特色的信息技术软件园，大力发展第三方电子商务。五是发展金融保险业。加快发展金融中介服务业，大力引进银行业金融机构到宁德设立分支机构、营业网点和拓展业务，提升小微企业、农村金融服务水平，加快村镇银行发展，拓展特色保险产品和政策性农业保险业务。

3.4.1 Community Service

The aspects of modern service industry are: firstly, developing modern logistics industry, which includes quickly building Logistics Park (LP), Logistics Center (LC) and Distribution Center (DC) as the main body of the three level logistics system in order to build an important regional logistics node city of Fujian Province, promoting the construction of logistics public information platform, vigorously developing the third party logistics, and launching cross-regional logistics cooperation; secondly, expanding trade circulation industry, which includes innovating business operation forms, circulation patterns and organizational forms, actively cultivating large business enterprise groups, improving business levels of service and professions, speeding up the construction and improvement of wholesale markets of electrical machines and equipment, tea, edible mushrooms, sea food, medicinal materials and so on, and building a batch of new types of trade concentrated areas with distinctive characteristics and convenient functions; thirdly, promoting tourism with special characteristics, which includes focusing on the integration of tourism and cultural development, promoting intelligent information technology of tourism, and extending tourism service industry chain; fourthly, cultivating the science, technology and information service industry, which includes promoting the construction of complex projects of China Sound Cubic Industry, creating the calling center with the highest quality on both sides of the Taiwan Strait, developing and building the Information Technology Software Park with local characteristics of Ningde City, and developing the third party electronic commerce; finally, developing the finance and insurance industry, which includes speeding up the development of financial intermediation services, actively introducing the banking financial institutions to Ningde City to expand business and set up the branches of banks and business-net spots, promoting the service levels of small and micro enterprises and rural finance industry, speeding up the development of village banks, and developing distinctive insurance products and policy-oriented agricultural insurance business.

二、商贸物流业

宁德现代物流随着产业壮大,企业内部管理的完善和先进管理理念的引入,多数企业对物流服务的需求迅速增加。同时宁德物流发展还具有"对台"优势。两地协同发展物流业有着现实的可能性。因此,具有建设大商场、发展大商贸、搞活大流通的优势。沃尔玛、万达等众多的精品名店商店纷纷入驻,目前营业面积超过0.5万平方米的商超有20家,其中超过1万平方米有6家,大型商超逐步成为宁德市的商贸形态。

随着大唐火电、宁德核电等一批重大工业项目相继建成投产,为现代物流业发展提供了广阔空间。截至2013年底,全市共有物流企业263家(工商登记数),全市物流行业法人单位6 090家(统计数),含铁路、道路、水上、航空、装卸搬运、仓储业、邮政业、批发业、零售业,还涌现出一批机制灵活、经营规范的第三方物流企业,如盛辉物流、顺丰速递等入驻宁德开展经营业务。福鼎晖达物流和宁德烟草物流有限公司被中国物流与采购联合会评定为“3A”和“2A”级物流企业，实现宁德市A级物流企业“零”的突破。

目前，宁德三都澳港物流园区、白马门煤炭综合物流、宁德豪迈粮食物流、宁德三都澳水产品冷链物流中心、宝信城市广场、天润国际城市综合体等重点物流项目正在加快建设进度，福建万成港口码头仓储、蕉城漳湾物流园也在加快项目前期，力争在“十二五”期间建设形成一批现代物流商贸产业基地。

3.4.2 Trade Logistics

With the development of modern logistics industry, the improvement of enterprise internal management and the introduction of advanced management concepts, the demand for logistics services of most enterprises in Ningde City increases rapidly. Meanwhile, the development of logistics industry in Ningde City also has the advantage of cooperating with Taiwan, and these two places have the possibility to develop logistics industry in reality. Therefore, there are advantages of building big shopping malls, developing big commerce and enlivening great circulation. Many famous stores with high-quality products have opened here, such as Wal-Mart, and Wanda Plaza. At present, there are 20 stores opened whose business area is over 5 000 square meters, 6 stores over 10 000 square meters, so large business stores gradually become the business forms in Ningde City.

With the construction and operation of a batch of major industrial projects, such as Datang Thermal Power Station, and Ningde Nuclear Power Plant, which have provided a broad space of development for modern logistics industry. By the end of 2013, there were 263 logistics enterprises which had registered in the Industrial and Commercial Administrative Department, and also there were 6 090 legal entities of logistics industry, including railway, roads, maritime, aviation, loading and moving, warehousing, post industry, wholesale business and retail business. A group of third party logistics enterprises also spring out, which are operated by flexible management mechanism and business regulations. Chenghui Logistics, Shunfeng Express and others had carried out business in Ningde city. Huida Logistics in Fuding City had been evaluated as the logistics company of AAA level and Ningde Tobacco Logistics Co., LTD as the logistics of AA level, which gives the breakthrough of logistics enterprises of A level.

At present, The Logistics of Ningde Sandu Bay Port, Baimamen Comprehensive Coal Logistics, Ningde Haomai Grain Logistics, Ningde Sandu Bay Cold Chain Logistics Center of Aquatic Products, Baoxin City Plaza, Tianrun International City Complex and other major logistics projects are speeding up their construction progress, Fujian Wancheng Port Storage and Zangwan Logistics Park in Jiaocheng District are speeding up their preliminary engineering project so that a batch of industrial bases of modern logistics business can be built during the Twelfth Five-Year Plan.

三、文化创意产业

融合闽东传统优秀文化,结合与时俱进先进文化理念的闽东文化产业发展进入了快车道,成为宁德市经济发展中最具发展潜力的支柱产业之一。在演艺界,畲族歌舞团富有民族特色的畲族歌舞节目成为文化交流的经典特色节目。寿宁北路戏、屏南四平戏、平讲戏和蕉城霍童线狮等先后被列为国家级非物质文化遗产名录。寿宁县梦龙陶艺有限公司、霞浦县长溪盆景发展有限公司跻身省级文化产业示范基地。全市现有工艺美术企业 300 多家,生产工艺品共 10 大类 31 个品种。福安市珍华工艺品有限公司成为宁德市首个国家文化产业示范基地。“盈盛号”是我省唯一一家“全国民族特需商品定点生产企业”,年销售额达 1 亿元以上。“畲族民俗银饰制造技艺”被列入福建省非物质文化遗产项目。

2015 年实施文化产业“七个一”工程,加快建设宁德工艺博览城、霞浦国际滨海影视文化创意产业园,扶持畲族银器、柘荣剪纸、霞浦木石盆景、蕉城仿古家具、寿宁乌金陶艺、古田双坑油画等特色文化产业示范基地做大做优,培育一批文化产业龙头企业。推进文化与旅游深度融合发展,加快建设一批重点文化旅游项目。

3.4.3 Culture and Ideas

Mindong culture industry, which combined Mindong's excellent traditional culture and the latest advanced cultural ideas, has entered rapid growth, and it becomes one of the pillar industries that have the most potential for development in the economic development in Ningde city. In artistic performances, Singing and Dancing Troupe of the She Ethnic Group with rich national characteristics, which was created by Singing and Dancing Troupe of the She Ethnic People, becomes a classical program in cultural communication. Shouning North-Road Drama, Pingnan Siping Drama, Pingjiang Drama, the Roll-Controlled Lines Lions Dances and others have been listed one after another as Intangible Cultural Heritage of National-Level. Shouning's

Menglong Potter Co., Ltd. and Xiapu's Changxi Penjing Development Co., Ltd. are among the provincial cultural industry demonstration bases. There are more than 300 arts and crafts enterprises in the city, which can produce arts and crafts of 10 categories of 31 kinds of products. Zhenhua Arts and Crafts Co., Ltd. of Fu'an City becomes the first national cultural industry demonstration base in Ningde city. Yingsheng Brand is the only National Ethnic Special Commodity Fixed-point Production Enterprise, whose annual sale is above 100 million yuan. Shezu's folk silver manufacturing skills have been listed as Intangible Cultural Heritage in Fujian province.

In 2015, the "Seven One-Project of Cultural Industry" will be implemented, Ningde Arts and Technology Expo Center and Xiapu's International Coastal Film and Television Cultural Creative Park will be rapidly built, the cultural industry demonstration bases with special characteristics, support for silverware of the She Ethnic People, Zherong's Paper-cuts, Xiapu's Wood and Stone Miniature Garden, Jiaocheng's Antique Reproduction Furniture, Shouning's Ironware Pottery, Shuangkeng's Oil Painting and others will be greatly improved, and a batch of cultural industrial leading enterprises will be developed. The development of the integration of culture and tourism will be advanced, and a batch of key cultural tourism projects will be rapidly constructed.

四、金融保险证券业

宁德市现拥较为齐全的银行金融机构，有各类银行网点 390 个，可以办理取款，贷款、外汇通兑、外汇调剂，国际结算，拆借与债券、信托与代理等业务，已建立较为完善的金融监管体制以防范和化解金融风险。2013 年全市年末金融机构本外币各项存款余额 1 032.81 亿元，金融机构本外币各项贷款余额 1 171.76 亿元。

宁德市保险行业共有产、寿险公司 24 家，保险业已渗透各个领域，相继开办了财产保险、人身保险、责任保险等业务，2013 年各类保险公司保费收入 25.18 亿元。从 2015 年 6 月 17 日保险业即将全面上线使用“投保人记录系统”，该系统是由福建省保险行业协会自主研发，用于记录保险销售关键环节中投保人亲笔签名等影像和基本信息的系统。

证券期货市场运行总体平稳有序。现有广发华福、兴业、东兴 3 家证券公司，主要从事证券经纪业务，包括证券代理买卖、代理还本付息、分红派息、证券代保管、代理登记开户等。营业部为投资者代理股东账户开户，提供交易通道和服务，投资者可采取网上交易、电话委托、自助委托、柜台委托等多种委托方式，还可以进行 A 股、基金、权证、债券以及进行新股申购和开放式基金认、申购等。2013 年年末全市股民资金开户数为 10.15 万户，股票、权证、基金交易量达 554.52 亿元，华福证券宁德营业部。

3.4.4 Finance, Insurance and Securities

There are comparatively completed banking and financial institutions, containing 390 different bank branches, which can run businesses of withdrawal, loan, foreign exchange deposits, foreign exchange swap, international settlements, lending and bond, assets under trust, agency and others, and a comparatively complete financial supervision system has been constructed to address financial risks. In 2013, the foreign currency outstanding of deposits of financial institutions in the city was 103.281 billion yuan, and the foreign currency outstanding loan of financial institutions was 117.176 billion yuan.

There are 24 Property and Life Insurance companies in Ningde city, whose insurance businesses get access to every field and successively opened its businesses, such as property insurance, personal insurance and liability insurance. In 2013, the premium income of all kinds of insurance companies was 2.518 billion yuan. On June 17, 2015, Insurance Applicants Recording System, which was studied and developed dependently by Fujian Insurance Association as first in China, was used comprehensively to record the image and other basic information about the activity of signing the name of insurance applicants in the process of buying insurance projects.

Securities and futures market are developing smoothly and orderly. There are three securities companies named Guangfa Huafu, Xingye and Dongxing, which are engaged in securities brokerage services, including acting sale of securities, acting servicing, dividend payout, securities generation custody and agent registration accounts and other business. Sales departments help set up accounts for the investors, and provide trading channels and services. Investors can take many means of entrustment, such as online trading, telephone commission, self-help commission, commission with the counter, and they can also subscribe the A-share, funds, warrant, bond, new shares and open-ended fund. In the end of 2013, the number of city's shareholder capital accounts was 10 150 000, and the volume of business of stock, warrant and funds was 55.452 billion yuan, Huafu Securities Sales Department in Ningde provided the above information.

五、邮电通信业

全市现有邮政普遍服务营业网点133个，建设邮政信报箱21 673个；取得快递经营许可证的快递服务企业18家，服务网点43个，从业人员877人；取得邮政用品用具生产许可证的企业5家。主要业务有特快专递、邮政快件、电子信函、包件、邮政储蓄、报刊发行、集邮等。

宁德邮电通信产业迅速发展。电信业务从单纯的电话电报发展到移动电话、可视电话、无线寻呼、电子信箱、INTERNET数据通信等。传统业务与新兴业务相互促进和互补，在"十二五"期间，已完成TD五期工程建设，"数字福建·智慧宁德"信息化应用项目，已渗透应用进政务、民生、经济三大领域在内的近20个行业当中，同时加快建设"数字宁德·宽带工程"，重点实施"城市光网""农村宽带入乡进村""无线宽带局域网络""宽带城域网、骨干网""宽带推广应用"六大工程。2013年全年完成邮电业务收入29.69亿元，年末固定电话用户53.53万户，移动电话用户306.48万户，全市固定电话交换机容量88.97万门，移动电话交换机容量444.9万户，光缆线路长度4.98万千米。城区光纤覆盖率均已达到98%以上。农村8M宽带覆盖率达90%。6M和12M高带宽占比均为全省第一。

3.4.5 Postal and Telecommunication Services

The number of the city's existing convenient postal service outlets was 133, and 21 673 postal boxes had been built. There were 18 express service companies that had been awarded an Express Delivery Business License with 43 service network stations opened, and 877 employees hired. And there were also 5 postal service companies that had received the production license, whose businesses include express mail service, express mail, electronic mail, postal parcel, postal savings, newspapers and magazines distribution, stamp collecting and so on.

The post and telecommunication industry in Ningde city developed quickly. Telecommunication service businesses had developed from simple telephone and telegraph to mobile telephone, video telephone, wireless paging, E-mail, INTERNET data communication, etc. Traditional business and emerging business promote and complement each other, during the Twelfth Five-Year Plan, the Fifth-Stage Engineering Project of TD and the Information-applying Project of Smart Ningde of Digital Fujian had been completed, whose application can be found in nearly 20 industries of government affairs, people's livelihood and economy. Meanwhile, the Broadband Project of Digital Ningde was under rapid construction so that Six Great Engineering Projects including MONET, Broadband into Village and Countryside, Broadband Wireless Local Network, BMAN, Backbone Network, Broadband Application had been implemented. In 2013, posts and telecommunications business income of the whole year was 2.969 billion yuan, and the number of fixed telephone subscribers was 535.3 thousand, and the number of mobile phone subscribers was 3.0648 million. In addition the capacity of telephone exchanges in the city reached 889 700, and the mobile capacity of telephone exchanges was 4 449 000, and the length of optical fiber cable was 49 800 kilometers. The coverage rate of urban optical fiber was over 98%, and the coverage rate of broadband of 8M in rural areas was up to 90%, and the proportion of higher broadband of 8M and 12M was on top of the province.

六、交通运输业

宁德公路、铁路、水路交通便利，基本形成四通八达的现代交通体系。机场正在建设中，位于霞浦县，属于支线机场。2013 年底有公路通车里程 10 652 千米，其中等级公路 9 466 千米，高速公路 278 千米。全市交通运输总周转量达 103 亿吨/千米，对 GDP 的贡献率 5%。

公路：已建成通车的沈海高速公路、宁武高速公路宁德段构成“T”形交通网络。“十二五”期间，重点推进“三纵四横三联”高速公路网建设，里程 840 千米，到 2015 年，全市高速公路通车里程将突破 600 千米，实现“县县通高速”。国省干线通车里程 955 千米，各县(市)都有一条二级以上的公路连接宁德市中心城区。农村公路里程达到 9 420.5 千米，建制村通村公路硬化率达 100%。

铁路：衢宁铁路与温福铁路形成“一横一纵”的格局。“十二五”期间，推进“三纵五横”铁路网建设，里程 783 千米。[“三纵”即温福铁路宁德段、宁德至漳州高速铁路宁德段、沿海货运铁路宁德段；“五横”即浙江衢州至宁德铁路宁德段、合肥至福州高速铁路宁德段、宁德至古田(南平)铁路宁德段、宁德至浙江丽水铁路宁德段、宁德至江西上饶铁路宁德]

水路：1992 年已有内河通航里程 418 千米，并已开通直达香港、上海、广州、青岛等 9 条不定期的海上航线。“十二五”期间，港航规划建设码头项目 16 个、航道项目 3 个，新增港口通过能力 5 000 万吨，货物吞吐量突破 5 000 万吨。重点突破溪南、白马、漳湾、城澳四大作业区和沙埕港区，推进现代化、集约化港口群建设，形成海峡西岸服务内陆省份和拓展对台合作的出海大通道。

届时将建成以港口为取向的立体交通网络和“三纵四横四联”高速公路网主骨架，以及完成“三纵五横”国省道干线升级改造和农村公路建设，实现县县通高速公路,村村通客车的目标。

3.4.6 Transportation

The highway, railway and waterway are very convenient in Ningde city, which forms a modern transportation system extended in all directions. The airport being built locates in Xiapu County, which is a feeder route airport. By the end of 2013, the length of existing highways in operation was 10 652 kilometers, among which classified highway was 9 466 kilometers and expressway was 278 kilometers. The total turnover of transportation was up to 10.3 billion ton/kilometer, which contributed 5% to the GDP growth.

Highway: The Ningde section of the Shenyang-Haikou Expressway and that of the Ningde-Wuyishan Expressway form the traffic network of a T-shape. During the Twelfth Five-year Plan, the expressway network of "three verticals, three horizontals and three links" had been be built with a mileage of 840 kilometers. By 2015, the city's highway traffic mileage had reached 600 kilometers so that highway can reach every county of the city. The provincial trunk mileage was 955 kilometers, and every county or city will have one highway above Grade-Ⅱ connected to central urban Ningde City. Rural road mileage was up to 9 420.5 kilometers, and the rate of highways connecting different villages was 100%.

Railway: Quzhou-Ningde Railway and Wenzhou-Fuzhou Railway form the shape of one vertical and one horizontal line. During the Twelfth Five-year Plan, the railway network of "three vertical and 5 horizontal lines" which is 783 kilometers will be carried out for construction. The three vertical lines are Ningde section of Wenzhou-Fuzhou Railway, High Speed Railway from Ningde to Zhanghzou and Coastal Freight Railway; Five horizontal lines are Ningde Section of the Railway from Quzhou of Zhejiang province to Ningde, High Speed Railway from Hefei to Fuzhou, the Railway from Ningde to Gutian(to Nanping), the Railway from Ningde to Lishui of Zhejiang province and the Railway from Ningde to Shangrao of Jiangxi province.

Waterway: In 1992, the length of navigable inland waterways was 418 kilometers, and there were nine lines of aperiodic sea lanes opened which directly reach Hong Kong, Shanghai, Guangzhou, and Qingdao. During the Twelfth Five-Year Plan, 16 wharf construction projects and 3 waterway projects had been completed, which increased port handling capacity by 50 million tons and cargo handling capacity by 50 million tons. More focus was put on the four operational zones of Xinan, Baima, Zhangwan and Cheng'ao and Shacheng Port so that construction of modern and intensive port groups was pushed forward and intensified, and the passages to sea along the west coast of the Taiwan Straits and the inland provinces were expanded.

At that time, the dimensional traffic network focusing on port connection and the highway networks of "three vertical and four horizontal lines" will be built, and the national and provincial main lines of "three vertical and five horizontal lines" will be upgraded. The rural highways will be constructed, which will be helpful to realizing the aim that every county has highways and every village has a concrete way for public buses.

七、会展业

这是一座现代都市必不可少的建筑，一条让宁德经济与外部经济更加紧密联系的纽带，一个让宁德了解外部世界和让外部世界了解宁德的窗口——宁德会展中心 2008 年 6 月 13 日正式投入使用。目前会展中心已成功举办了"宁德投资洽谈会"、"海峡两岸茶业博览会"、"海峡两岸电机电器博览会"、"闽台名优特商品交易会"等多个全国性展会。一直以来，宁德是对台小额贸易的前沿阵地，宁德会展中心以此为"突破口"，设立宁德台货购物中心，以台货为媒，促进两岸经贸交流。同时也推进了宁德与其他区域、省市，及境外企业的交流与合作。展会已经成为宁德市乃至福建省对外开放和招商引资的重要平台和推动宁德经济的又一引擎。

3.4.7 Convention and Exhibition

June 13th, 2008, Ningde Exhibition Center was officially put into use, which is an indispensable modern building, a connection closely linking the economy of Ningde with the external economy as well as a window for Ningde and the outside world to know each other. Many national exhibitions have been held successfully, such as Ningde Investment Fair, Tea Expo of the Both Sides of the Taiwan Straits, Motor Electric Appliance Exposition of the Both Sides of the Taiwan Strait, Unique and Branded Commodities Fair between Fujian and Taiwan. For a long time, Ningde has been the forefront city that had petty trade with Taiwan. Ningde Exhibition Center, as an important platform, has established a shopping center for Taiwanese goods to promote cross-strait economic and trade exchanges with Taiwan, which can also promote exchanges and cooperation between Ningde and other provinces and cities, overseas enterprises and groups. Conventions and exhibitions have been an important engine and platform for Ningde and even Fujian Province to open up and to attract foreign businesses and investments.

八、旅游业

宁德大力推动高铁旅游业的跨越发展。随着合福高铁的开通，将串联起沿线包括太姥山、白云山、白水洋等风景名胜区，成为闽赣皖三省最具发展潜力的旅游黄金走廊，这将极大地拉动宁德旅游产业，迎来又一次里程碑式的跨越发展：一块闪耀世界的金字招牌——宁德世界地质公园、一条久享盛誉的度假线路——闽东北亲水游、一道魅力无限的人文风景——闽东乡村清新游。抢抓机遇，借路发力，宁德旅游将从更高站位谋篇布局，树立"大旅游、大产业"发展理念，深入挖掘"山、海、川、岛、湖、林、洞"潜力，进一步打造滨海休闲度假旅游目的地，融入合福高铁旅游黄金走廊。目前宁德已进入全省旅游竞争城市"到达人气城市"(不含本省)中居第 5 名，"过夜人气城市"(不含本省)中均居第 6 名。2013 年全市共接待游客1 130 万人次，旅游收入 86 亿元。

3.4.8 Tourism

Ningde is pushing forward the striding development of tourism with the help of high-speed railways. Hefei-Fuzhou High-speed Railway will connect many tourist scenic spots along the road, such as Taimu Mountain, Baiyun Mountain and Baishuiyang River Square in Ningde, which will become the Tourist Golden Corridor with the largest development potential for Fujian, Jiangxi and Anhui provinces, and will give a great pull for the tourism industry of Ningde that will welcome a surpassing development that has a landmark significance again. Ningde Global Geopark is a shining brand in the world. And the Waterside Tourist Route in Northeast Fujian is a resort line with a high reputation, and the Fresh Countryside Tourist Route of East Fujian is a charming humanistic landscape. With the help of opportunities and high-speed railway, Ningde will plan the development structure of tourism on a higher ground, and keep in mind the development ideas of "Grand Tourism and Great Industry", trying to develop the tourism potential of mountains, sea, rivers, inlands, lakes, forests and caves, furthering to build coastal leisure vacation travel destinations, and link with the Tourist Golden Corridor of Hefei-Fuzhou High-speed Railway. At present, Ningde city has become one of provincial tourism competitive cities, and ranked 5th as "A Popular City to Visit by the Visitors outside Fujian", and was awarded at Number 6 as an "Overnight Popular City outside of Fujian Province". In 2013, 11.3 million tourists came to Ningde, bringing an tourist income of 8.6 billion yuan.

九、房地产业

宁德房地产业总体平稳健康发展。宁德城区已初步建立起廉租房、经济适用住房、经济租赁房和限价房为主的住房保障体系。近年来,宁德根据《宁德市城市总体规划(2011—2030)》规划中的城市总体发展目标,积极拓展中心城市、不断构筑、建设、海西东北翼中心城市。2013全年房地产开发投资221.05亿元,增长60.1%,其中商品住宅投资153.30亿元,增长64.3%。商品房销售面积183.62万平方米,增长22.4%,其中商品住宅166.97万平方米,增长22.8%。商品房销售额131.99亿元,增长17.4%。

3.4.9 Real Estate

The overall real estate industry of Ningde city has developed stably and healthily. Ningde has established the housing security system initially, which consisted mainly of low-rent housing, the practical economical housing, practical rent housing and price-limited housing. In recent years, according to the development target of *Ningde's Overall Development Plan* (2011-2030), Ningde actively expands the central city, continuously builds and constructs the central city in the northeast of the west coast of Taiwan Strais. In 2013, the total development investment of the real estate, which grew by 60.1%, was 22.105 billion yuan, of which commercial housing investment was 15.33 billion yuan with an increase of 64.3%. The sales of commercial residential buildings, which grew by 22.4%, was 1.8362 million square meters, in which commercial housing was 1.6697 million square meters. The sale of commercial housing, which grew by 17.4%, was 13.199 billion yuan.

第五节 对外经济合作

3.5 Foreign Economic Cooperation

一、对外经济贸易

宁德的对外贸易始于1988年，当年贸易自营出口总额352万美元，揭开了闽东对外贸易的新篇章，走上了国际贸易的大舞台。伴随着外贸体制改革的深化，促进宁德市产业结构由低级向高级发展，改变宁德市原材料加工、进料加工为主的低附加值贸易方式，宁德的对外贸易发展迅猛，社会经济发展硕果累累，呈现对外贸易数额迅猛增长，经营主体范围明显扩大，出口商品不断优化，出口市场日趋多元等繁荣景象。2013年全年进出口总额32.57亿美元，进出口差额（出口减进口）24.19亿美元，对东盟、欧盟等主要贸易伙伴的贸易额保持较快增长。中誉开发、顺天祥实业、金达盛电机等多个项目投资额均超亿美元，投资领域不断拓宽，涉及旅游开发、城市环保、休闲养生、商贸物流等第三产业项目。同时宁德市政府鼓励外贸厂商积极联合协作，通过建立产业园区等方式形成集群效应与规模效应，增强宁德市在国际贸易中的竞争力，多措并举以拓宽市场，促进对外经贸稳步发展，主要措施有壮大重点出口行业、加大出口金融支持、支持开展出口信用保险、支持开拓国际市场、优化退税服务、改善通关环境等方面缓解宁德市外贸进出口企业压力，进一步增强宁德市外经贸发展后劲。

3.5.1 Foreign Trade

Foreign trade in Ningde began in 1988 when the total import and export trade amounted to ＄3.52 million, paving a way for further international foreign trade. Owing to the economic reform and a demand for a more advanced industrial structure, low value-added trade had been altered, mainly in the field of processing of raw materials and imported materials. Ningde witnessed a fruitful development in foreign trade and social economy, such as the rapid increase and expansion in business scopes, the significant optimization in products, and the remarkable diversity of the export market. In addition, the export volume totaled ＄3.257 billion in 2013; the trade balance (exports minus imports) ＄2.419 billion; trades with the ASEAN, EU and other major partners were in rapid growth. Investment in Zhongyu Development Co., Ltd., Shuntianxiang Industrial Co., Ltd., Jindasheng Motors Co., Ltd. and other projects exceeded over $100 million. Besides, Ningde was making more investments in the tertiary industry, such as tourism, urban environmental protection, leisure and health, trade logistics, and at the same time motivating foreign trade companies to seek collaboration in forms of industrial parks so as to achieve cluster effects and intensify international competitiveness. Other equally effective measures were also taken to ensure market prosperity and alleviate on companies of foreign trade pressure giving, like expanding key export industries, finding more financial support for export, more support for export credit insurance and the expansion of international market, optimizing of tax services, and improving of the customs clearance.

二、利用外资

中外合资经营企业、中外合作经营企业、外商独资企业是外商投资最主要的几种形式。近年来,市政府大力提升对外开放水平:支持企业参加国内外重要展会,鼓励企业到境外设立营销服务网点;引导企业创建自主出口品牌,提高产品附加值和竞争力,推进外贸转型升级;拓宽利用外资领域,鼓励外资企业增资扩股,引导外商投资商贸物流、融资租赁、育幼养老等服务业;深化宁港澳侨合作,拓展友城合作领域。2013年全年新签外商直接投资合同项目20个,比上年增长11.1%。按验资口径统计,合同外资金额3.1亿美元,增长9.0%;实际利用外商直接投资1.44亿美元,增长20.2%。2014年按验资口径统计,合同外资金额3.76亿美元,增长21.1%;实际利用外商直接投资1.75亿美元,增长21.0%。

3.5.2 Utilization of Foreign Capital

Sino-foreign joint ventures, cooperative ventures and foreign-owned enterprises constitute the major forms of foreign investment. In recent years, the municipal government has been fully engaged in the enhancement of the city's opening-up, by encouraging enterprises to participate in domestic and foreign exhibitions and to set up overseas marketing service networks, together with guiding them to create their own export brands so as to improve product value and competitiveness, and promote the transformation and upgrading of foreign trade. Furthermore, the government is embarking on the expansion of foreign investment, and guidance of foreign investment flowing into trade and logistics, financial leasing, pension and other nursery and nursing services. The cooperation among Ningde, Hongkong and Macao has been enhanced and the cooperation between sister cities also expanded. In 2013, twenty foreign direct investment projects were contracted, 11.1% higher than the previous year. According to fund examination, contracted foreign investment totaled $ 310 million in 2013 and $ 376 million in 2014, an increase of 9.0% and 21.1% respectively; the actual use of foreign direct investment was $ 144 million in 2013 and $ 175 million in 2014, with an increase of 20.2% and 21.0% respectively.

三、国际经济技术合作

宁德国际经济技术合作范围逐步扩大。在注重招商引资的同时,坚持内外协调,推动一批龙头企业与境外同行业优势企业对接,加强技术交流合作,促进良性互动。主要形式有向境外派遣工程、生产及服务行业的劳务人员,境外投资等业务。主要单位和劳务经营企业有宁德市对外贸易经济合作局、中国宁德外轮代理有限公司、宁德国际经济技术合作公司等。

3.5.3 International Economic and Technological Cooperation

International economic and technological cooperation has been gradually expanded. The city, while attaching importance to investment, persists in domestic and foreign coordination, and promotes a number of leading enterprises to technologically interact with renowned overseas counterparts, in forms of, e.g., dispatching workers for engineering, production and service overseas, and making foreign investments, too. Major organizations and enterprises involved in such programs include Foreign Trade and Economic Cooperation Bureau of Ningde, Ocean Shipping Co., Ltd. of Ningde (China), and Ningde International Economic and Technological Cooperation Company.

四、宁台经贸交流与合作

通过举办海峡两岸茶博览会、海峡两岸渔博会和电机电器博览会、设立“台湾水产品集散中心”“零关税”进口先行先试区、对台小额交易先行先试区,恢复开展输台渔工劳务派遣工作,设立宁德台货购物中心等,进一步拓宽两岸经贸交流与合作领域,吸引台商投资。主要涉及冶金、电机、石材、食品加工、农业、保险、金融等产业,并已有东元、义联、康师傅、润泰、国产实业等七家台湾百大、百强企业落地宁德。此外,三沙对台小额贸易口岸通过国家审批,台湾科技产业园、福安赛岐“海峡两岸葡萄科技合作示范基地”、屏南“台湾名贵兰花种植培育基地”、柘荣“京林生物科技现代大棚种植珍贵药用花卉——铁皮石斛和名贵树种大苗培育基地”、台湾国泰人寿、富邦参股的厦门银行宁德分行、台湾建筑服务企业聂子文(宁德)建筑设计顾问公司入驻宁德。联德镍合金项目加快建设。2013 年全年台资项目总投资达 6 284万美元，占外资总额的 43.5%。截至 2015 年 9 月，宁德有台资企业 56 家，总投资额 9.5 亿美元。

3.5.4 Economic Exchange and Cooperation Between Ningde and Taiwan

The Tea Fair, Fishery Fair and Electric Motor and Appliance Exposition by the two sides of the Taiwan Straits are held to enhance the economic exchange and cooperation between Ningde and Taiwan so as to attract Taiwanese investment, as is the case of the establishment of Distribution Center of Taiwan Aquatic Products in Xiapu, and the "Zero Tariff" Import Pilot Zone, Micro-Transaction Pilot Zone, and Taiwan Goods Shopping Centers, as well as the restoration of dispatching fishermen to work in Taiwan. A number of industries are involved, including metallurgy, motors, stone, food processing, agriculture, insurance, and finances, etc., and seven of the Top 100 Taiwan companies such as TECO, E United Group, Master Kong, Ruentex Group, Goldsun Group have landed in Ningde. In addition, Sansha-Taiwan Micro-Transaction Port received the national authority's approval to be set up in Ningde, so did Taiwan Science and Technology Industrial Park, Cross-strait Grape Technology Demonstration Base in Saiqi, Fu'an, Taiwan Rare Orchid Cultivation Base in Pingnan, Dendrobium and Valuable Large Seedlings Cultivation Base—precious medicinal flowers growing in modern greenhouses of Jinglin Biotechnology Co., Ltd. in Zherong. Taiwan's Cathay Life Insurance, Xiamen Bank Ningde Branch shared with Fubon, Nie Ziwen (Ningde) Architectural Consultant Co., a leading architectural service company from Taiwan, were all settled in Ningde. Liande Group is accelerating the pace of its nickel alloy industry. In 2013 annual Taiwan-funded investments totaled $ 62.84 million, accounting for 43.5% of total foreign investment. Up to September 2015, Ningde had attracted 56 Taiwan-funded enterprises, with a total investment of $ 950 million.

五、贸易合作平台

3.5.5 Major Trade Cooperation Platforms

(一)海峡两岸电机电器博览会

“电博会”作为宁德市第一个由国务院正式批准的高规格、高水平、全方位的海峡两岸经贸交流合作盛会,也是中国唯一专业的中小电机产业展会。每年 6 月在宁德市举行的电博会、投洽会对于海内外客商来说都是一次不容错过的寻找商机之旅,正因如此,这个“宁德制造”的“电博会”成功举办六年来,投资结构更趋合理、展会规模越来越大、层次越来越高、效果越来越好,已成为宁德市对外扩大开放和招商引资的重要平台。历届“电博会”参展企业总数已达 2 800 多家(次),共签约项目六百多项,其中外资项目一百多项,利用外资近七十亿美元,吸引了来自港、澳、台等地区,美国、英国、德国、日本、伊拉克、尼日利亚、埃及、埃塞俄比亚、约旦、叙利亚、土耳其等国家的客商,以及商务部、中国贸促会等组织。连续五年电博会、投洽会的成功举办,成就了宁德市首个百亿产业集群,有利于发挥宁德的产业优势,推进国际和区域经济贸易投资合作,对推进闽东电机电器千亿产业集群发展起到了极其重要的作用。

3.5.5.1 Cross-Straits Electric Motor and Appliance Exposition

The Cross-Straits Electric Motor and Appliance Exposition (CEMAE), as the only professional fair for small and medium electric motors in China, is the first high-level, full-range economic exchange pomp in Ningde with official approval from the State Council. The CEAME and CIFIT are held annually in Ningde in June. It is regarded as a golden opportunity for domestic and foreign businessmen. The investment structure tends to be more reasonable, and the exposition to be more influential and effective, enabling the city of Ningde to be a pivotal platform for opening-up and investment. Previous CEMAEs attracted more than 2 800 exhibiting enterprises, some of whom were from areas including Hong Kong, Macao, Taiwan, countries like the US, the UK, Germany, Japan, Iraq, Nigeria, Egypt, Ethiopia, Jordan, Syria, Turkey as well as organizations such as the Ministry of Commerce, China, and the CCPIT, etc. They signed more than 600 contracts, of which over 100 were foreign-invested projects totaling nearly $7 billion. The success of the CEMAE and CIFIT for 5 years contributes to the advent of the first billion-yuan industrial cluster conducive to showing Ningde's industrial advantage, promoting international and regional economy and investment, and facilitating the development of East Fujian's 10-billion-yuan Electric Motor and Appliance industrial cluster.

(二)海峡两岸茶业博览会

为进一步构建福建茶产业的发展平台,打响闽茶品牌,建设福建茶叶强省,促进海峡西岸经济区建设和海峡两岸农业合作与交流,福建省决定从2007年起举办海峡两岸茶业博览会。宁德市成功举办了第三届海峡两岸茶业博览会,提升了闽东茶叶的国内外知名度和市场竞争力。该届茶博会共有来自海峡两岸主要产茶区及欧盟、日本、俄罗斯、东南亚等600多家茶叶企业、近千名经销商赴会参展,共有45个项目(投资项目28个、购销合同17个)在现场签约,签约总金额9.95亿元。其中,宁德市签约项目21个(投资项目11个、合作项目1个、购销合同9个),总金额近6亿元。签约项目中既有种、养、加的项目,又有产供销、贸工农的项目,反映了福建省、宁德市农业产业集约化的发展趋势,此外,还有来自斯里兰卡、加拿大、美国等客商,充分体现了福建省、宁德市农业已走上国际化、市场化的发展路子。

3.5.5.2 Cross-Straits Tea Fair

In 2007, it was decided by Fujian Provincial Government to host the Cross-Straits Tea Fair, to build a platform for further development of the tea industry and tea brands, to promote Fujian as a leading province of tea, and to boost the West Taiwan Straits Economic Development Zone and strengthen cross-straits agricultural cooperation and exchange. The City of Ningde has successfully hosted the 3rd Cross-Straits Tea Fair, enhancing domestic and foreign reputation and competitiveness of tea from East Fujian. Over 600 tea enterprises and nearly 1 000 retailers from the Chinese Mainland, Taiwan, and the European Union, Japan, Russia, Southeast Asia came to the fair. In all 45 projects (including 28 investment projects, and 17 purchase & sales contracts) were signed on the spot, totaling 995 million yuan. Among them, 21 projects totaling 600 million yuan were in Ningde (including 11 investment projects, 1 cooperation project, and 9 purchase & sales contracts). These projects include planting and processing as well as producing, supplying and selling. It shows that Fujian Province and the city of Ningde have a great demand in intensive agriculture. In addition, merchants from Sri Lanka, Canada and the United States connected Fujian and Ningde with the international market.

（三）涉外机构

宁德市人民政府外事侨务办公室、中共宁德市委外事工作领导小组办公室、宁德市人民政府港澳事务办公室、宁德市对外交流服务中心、宁德市人民对外友好协会秘书处、宁德市公安局出入境管理处、宁德进出口商品检验局、宁德市民政局婚姻登记处、国家外汇管理局宁德市中心支局、中国国际贸易促进委员会宁德市支会、宁德市商务局、宁德市外经贸局、宁德海关、宁德市旅游局、宁德市工商局等。

3.5.5.3 Major Foreign Service Agencies

The Foreign and Overseas Chinese Affairs Office of Ningde Municipal People's Government, Foreign Affairs Leading Group of Ningde Municipal Committee of the CPC, Hong Kong and Macao Affairs Office of Ningde Municipal People's Government, Ningde Foreign Exchange Service Center, the Secretariat Office of the People's Association for Friendship with Foreign Countries of Ningde, Ningde Public Security Bureau, Ningde Import and Export Commodity Inspection Bureau, Ningde Marriage Registry of Civil Affairs Bureau, the State Administration of Foreign Exchange Ningde branch, China Council for the Promotion of International Trade (Ningde Branch), Ningde Municipal Bureau of Commerce, Ningde Municipal Bureau of Foreign Trade, Ningde Municipal Customs Office, Ningde Municipal Tourism Bureau, and Ningde Municipal Industrial and Commercial Bureau.

六、宁德国家级、省级对外开放产业基地

3.5.6 National and Provincial-Level Foreign-Invested Industrial Bases in Ningde

（一）东侨经济开发区

宁德东侨经济开发区工业集中区，是经国家发改委审核成立的国家级经济开发区，是宁德市委、市政府推进市本级工业发展的重要载体，位于宁德市域东部。

东侨工业集中区总规划面积 24 平方千米，由塔南园区与漳湾园区组成，已开发建设面积约 5 平方千米，目前落户企业 93 家，其中工业生产性企业 72 家，已投产 41 家，产值上亿元 22 家，以电机电器、食品加工等传统产业为主导，初步形成了电机电器、食品加工、生物科技、新型制造业、新能源新材料五大支柱产业的产业集群。东侨工业集中区将实行现行国家级经济技术开发区政策，充分发挥独特地理优势和政策优势，积极参与发达地区产业的分工和协作，注重对接现有园区产业集

群上下游配套项目,有效推动宁德市工业经济的发展。

3.5.6.1 Dongqiao Economic Development Zone

Dongqiao Economic Development Zone, Ningde, is a state-level zone set up by the National Development and Reform Commission, an important carrier of local industry promoted by the Ningde Municipal Committee and Government. It is located in the eastern region of Ningde City, with a planning area of 24 square kilometers, consisting of Tanan Zone and Zhangwan Zone. So far, the government has developed about five square kilometers, home to 93 enterprises, including 72 industrial enterprises, 41 of which have been put into operation and 22 of which yield more than 100 million yuan each. It centers on traditional industries such as electric motor and appliances, and food processing. Apart from these two pillar industries, biotechnology, new manufacturing, new energy and new materials play an equally important role in this industrial cluster.

The Development Zone continues to implement the current national economic and technological policies, makes full use of its unique geographical and policy advantages, actively participates in the division of labor and cooperation with developed areas, and focuses on the supporting projects, so as to promote the industrial development of Ningde.

(二)宁德三都澳经济开发区

三都澳经济开发区于1992年经宁德地区行署批准设立。1998年经省政府批准列入省级开发区。开发区规划的主导产业为临港工业、港口运输业、加工业、毛角石开采业、养殖业和旅游业。可供开发1万至30万吨级码头泊位20个。目前已建成万吨级多用途码头1个,8 000吨级石料专用码头4个,已通过省级有关部门核准和预审,进行前期工作的码头9个,分别为1至10万吨级的集装箱码头,通用码头和油品码头。2006年,经国台办牵头国家九部委对城澳直航点进行验收检查,宁德城澳港正式成为对台湾地区金门、马祖、澎湖直航货运口岸,被省政府列为全省建设的四大港口之一。

3.5.6.2 Sandu Bay Economic Development Zone of Ningde

Sandu Bay Economic Development Zone was, with the approval from the Administrative Office of Ningde Prefecture, established in 1992 and in 1998, thanks to the provincial government, upgraded as a provincial development zone. It was led by port industry, port transportation, processing industry, stone mining industry, aquaculture and tourism. Twenty 10 000 to 300 000-

tonnage wharves remain to be developed. A 10 000-ton multi-functional wharf, and four 8 000-ton docks specialized in stone mining have been completed. Besides, another 9 wharves, including 10 000 to 100 000-ton container terminal, general terminal and oil terminal, have got provincial authoritative approval for their preliminary work. As early as in 2006, nine national ministries, with the coordination of the Taiwan Affairs Office of the State Council, came to inspect Cheng'ao Direct Shipping Port to Taiwan. After that, the port became an official shipping port conducting shipping business with Kinmen, Matsu, Penghu islands, and was listed as one of the four major ports supported by the province.

(三)福建福鼎工业园区

福建福鼎工业园区(省级开发区)创办于1998年9月,总体规划面积15平方千米。下辖三个项目区(星火项目区、双岳项目区和文渡项目区),目前已入园企业169家,其中已投产企业92家,动工建设26家,还有51家正在办理前期手续和待供地。目前园区规模以上工业年产值达200多亿元,力争"十二五"后期实现工业产值300亿元,打造成闽浙边界最具活力、最具竞争力的工业园区。

文渡项目区:创办于2004年4月,以生产泵阀、特钢、服装革为主。双岳项目区:创办于2005年12月,以光伏电子、通用机械、服装产业为主,星火项目区:创办于1998年9月,以食品、医药、轻工机械为主。

3.5.6.3 Fuding Industrial Park (Provincial Development Zone)

The park was established in September 1998, with an overall planning area of 15 square kilometers. It consists of three zones, Xinghuo Zone, Shuangyue Zone, and Wendu Zone, home to 169 enterprises, among which 92 have been put into operation, 26 remain to be completed, and 51 are under preparation. The current annual turnover of the park exceeds 20 billion yuan. During the 12th Five-Year Plan, it was planned to have a turnover of 30 billion yuan, and to be one of the most dynamic and competitive industrial parks in the border areas of Fujian and Zhejiang.

Wendu Zone: set up in April 2004, mainly producing valves, steel, clothing and leather. Shuangyue Zone: founded in December 2005, mainly dealing with photo-voltaic electronics, general machinery, and garments. Xinghuo Zone: established in September 1998, mainly specialized in foods, medicines, light industrial machinery.

(四) 霞浦经济开发区

2014年1月,省政府批准霞浦经济开发区纳入省级经济开发区管理。一期规划产业定位为:服装鞋业、金属制品、电子电器等;二期规划产业定位为:新材料、新能源、机械设备制造等高新技术产业。开发区现已引进投资千万元以上的实体项目共59个(其中亿元以上8个),总投资38.5亿元。目前已投产21家,开工建设22家,正在开展前期工作16家。2013年工业产值30亿元,外贸出口总额达8 000多万美元。

霞浦台湾水产品集散中心是2006年6月22日国台办批准建设的大陆地区首家台湾水产品加工、贸易基地,位处福建省霞浦县三沙镇陇头湾,其功能定位是建设海峡西岸具有影响力的台湾水产品集散基地、蓝色海洋经济及台湾渔民创业园,以水产品(食品)加工、冷藏、中转为主,兼有生活居住、商业贸易、休闲度假等综合性功能的工业园区。目前,园区已落户企业18家,主营水产品加工、冷藏、冷链物流等产业,完成《宁德(霞浦)台湾渔民创业园产业发展规划》编制和专家评审,获准列入我省第一批省级海洋产业示范园区。

3.5.6.4 Xiapu Economic Development Zone

Xiapu Economic Development Zone was, with the approval of the provincial government in January 2014, managed as a provincial zone. The primary phrase was oriented by industries such as clothing and footwear, metal products, electrical and electronic appliances, and the second phrase for planning: new materials, new energy, machinery, equipment manufacturing, and other high-tech industries. It has attracted 59 ten-million-yuan project entities (including 8 over one hundred-million-yuan projects) with a total investment of 3.85 billion yuan. So far, 21 have been put into operation, 22 are under construction, and 16 are under preparation. In 2013 the industrial output reached 3 billion yuan, and total exports amounted for over $80 million.

Xiapu-Taiwan Aquatic Products Distributing Center is the first base in the Chinese mainland approved by Taiwan Affairs Office of the State Council on June 22, 2006, and specializes in Taiwan aquatic products processing and trade. Located at Longtou Bay, Sansha, Xiapu County of Fujian Province, it aims at being an influential distribution base, a blue ocean economy and an entrepreneurship park for Taiwanese fishermen, with its priority to fish (food) processing, cold storage, and transit, and in the meantime functions as a residential, commercial and entertaining Industrial Park. Currently, the park has settled 18 enterprises dealing with aquatic products processing, cold storage, cold chain logistics and other industries. The Industrial Development Plan for the Entrepreneurship Park for Taiwanese Fishermen in Xiapu (Ningde) has been edited and assessed by experts, and the park also has been listed as the first batch of the provincial marine demonstration zones for development.

(五)福安经济开发区

福安经济开发区(原闽东赛岐经济开发区)成立于1988年,是宁德地区(市)设立的省级开发区。近年来,开发区开放开发势态良好,基础设施逐步完善,投资环境更加优化。开发区成立以来就致力于基础设施建设,50万伏大唐火电厂、22万伏输变电站、4万吨自来水厂先后建成投入使用。赛岐港已建成300～3 000吨级码头泊位20座,4座3 000～10 000吨船坞已投入使用。区内邮电通讯便捷,金融、税务、工商、医院、学校、宾馆等机构配套齐全,是目前宁德市基础设施较为完善的投资区域。目前,开发区拥有规模以上企业59家,初步形成冶金铸造、有色金属、电机电器、能源机械、食品包装等行业为主的工业体系。

3.5.6.5 Fu'an Economic Development Zone

Fu'an Economic Development Zone (formerly known as Saiqi Economic Development Zone of East Fujian) was established in 1988 by Ningde Prefecture (City). In recent years, it has been in promising momentums with the infrastructure gradually improved, and investment environment more optimized. Since the establishment, it has been committed to building up the infrastructure. The 500 000-volt Datang Thermal Power Plant, a 220 000-volt power transmission station, and a 40,000-ton water plant have been built and put into use. Twenty 300 to 3 000-ton berths have been completed and four shipyards with 3 000 to 10 000 tonnage have been put into use. It is a relatively sound investment center in Ningde owing to its friendly postal communications, financial and taxation institutions, industrial and commercial centers, hospitals, schools, hotels and so on. At present, 59 enterprises have settled in the zone, and an initial industrial system of metallurgical casting, non-ferrous metals, electrical appliances, energy, machinery, food packaging and other industries have been completed.

(六)福建屏南工业园区

屏南工业园区,总规划面积9 300亩,由溪坪工业小区、际头工业小区和溪角洋工业小区三个部分组成。溪坪工业小区主要以化工、冶金和竹木加工为主。际头工业小区，现已落户的有海西大青实业有限公司、福建健神生物工程有限公司、福建乡下厨房食品有限公司、福建毅达电子有限公司等企业，已初具规模。溪角洋工业小区着力发展以下几个产业。一是绿色食品加工园。发展具有地方特色绿色食品、旅游食品和旅游工业加工区。二是生物制品产业园。发展灵芝、无患子等特色农林产品深加工及生物医药保健业。三是机械制造园。重点发展与汽车工业、船舶、电器二次配套型机械产业等产品加工制造。四是竹木家具制造园。发展竹木加工、家具制造和工艺品制造，促进现有竹木工艺产业提升。五是电子产业园：重点发展与电子元器件、节能灯具等相关产业。六是物流配送园。利用溪角溪工业区交通优势，发展集产品加工、堆放和销售于一体物流配送中心。

3.5.6.6 Pingnan Industrial Park of Fujian

Pingnan Industrial Park, with a total planned area of 9 300 mu, consists of three zones, namely Xiping Industrial Zone, Jitou Industrial Zone and Xijiaoyang Industrial Zone. Xiping Industrial Zone mainly specializes in chemical, metallurgical and wood processing. Jitou Industrial Zone is home to West Coast Daqing Industrial Co., Ltd., Fujian Jianshen Biological Co., Ltd. Fujian Countryside Kitchen Foods Co., Ltd. and Fujian Yida Electronic Co., Ltd., and is in its preliminary shape. Xijiaoyang Industrial Zone focuses on the following industries: the first focus is green food processing, that is, to develop local green food, tourism food and tourism processing industry. Secondly, it is oriented to biological products, such as ganoderma lucidum, soapberry and other special agricultural and forestry products, and the nutrition and health industry. Thirdly, it focuses on the development of a machinery manufacturing park, including the automobile industry, shipbuilding, electronics and secondary supporting mechanical manufacturing products. The fourth orientation is wooden furniture manufacturing, to develop wood processing, furniture manufacturing and handicraft manufacturing, so as to upgrade the existing bamboo craft. Fifthly, it centers on electronic industry, i.e. the development of electronic components, energy-saving lamps and other related industries. The sixth is a logistics park, which makes use of the advantageous transportation of the zone and develops a logistic distribution center of processing, stacking and selling.

(七)柘荣经济开发区

柘荣经济开发区创建于 19 世纪 80 年代，2013 年获省政府批准为省级开发区。目前，入驻园区企业已达 93 家，其中投产 80 家，在建 13 家。2013 年实现产值 106 亿元。园区建设形成了“富源综合区”、“生物医药循环经济产业园”和“砚山洋山海协作示范园”的“一区两园”格局。富源综合区：定位为新能源、新材料、电子信息、环保产业等，现已入驻广生堂药业、国泰医药包装、久鑫手套等企业 24 家。生物医药循环经济产业园：定位为中药材种植供应基地、药品加工制造基地和药品区域物流中心目前已入驻力捷迅药业、三本高科、天人药业等药业相关联企业 9 家，拥有“准字号”产品达 258 个，“食健号”23 个，兽药品种 26 个，剂型覆盖了化学原料、中成药六大领域。该园区还是福建首个县级生物医药产业园。砚山洋山海协作示范园以轻工业为主，污染较小的重工业为辅，是一个发展机电加工等综合加工产业的劳动密集型技术产业园。

3.5.6.7 Zherong Economic Development Zone

Zherong Economic Development Zone, founded in the 1980s, was listed as a provincial zone in 2013 by the provincial government. At present, 93 enterprises have settled in the zone, among which 80 have been put into operation and 13 under construction. The output value in 2013 totaled 10.6 billion yuan. It has 1 zone and 2 parks, namely Fuyuan Comprehensive Zone, Biomedical Circular Economy Park and Yanshanyang Cooperation Demonstration Park of the Coastal and Mountainous Regions. Fuyuan Comprehensive Zone is positioned towards new energy, new materials, electronic information, and environmental protection industry. 24 companies have settled there, including Gosunter Pharmaceutical Co., Ltd., Cuotai Pharmaceutical Packaging Co., Ltd., and Jiuxin Gloves Co., Ltd. Biomedical Circular Economy Park specializes in planting and supplying Chinese medicine, pharmaceutical processing and manufacturing, as well as regional pharmaceutical logistics. Nine companies including Rejuvenation Pharmaceutical Co., Ltd., Sanben Agricultural High-Tehnology Co., Ltd. and Tianren Pharmaceutical Co., Ltd. have settled in this park. Besides, it has got 258 certified famous products, 23 products of healthy-food brands, and 26 varieties of veterinary drugs, varying from chemical materials and six other areas of Chinese traditional medicines. It was the first county-level biomedical industry park in Fujian.

Yanshanyang Cooperation Demonstration Park of the Coastal and Mountainous Regions mainly specializes in light industry supplemented by less polluting heavy industries. It has become a labor-intensive processing and technological park with emphasis on electrical and mechanical processing.

第四章 社会事业

Chapter 4 Public Welfare

第一节 教 育

4.1 Education

一、历代大事记

据史料记载，宁德市是福建文化开发较早的地区之一。早在唐代就建有灵谷草堂、林降神草堂，闽东籍进士共5人，其中唐神龙二年(706)及第的薛令之，是福建省第一位进士、第一个到中央王朝任职的闽人，对闽东教育具有开创性意义。南唐时，古田余仁椿创建杉洋蓝田书院，是区内当时最具规模的书院。

南宋时期，区内的书院教育盛极一时，宋代共创办书院25所。长溪、古田、宁德、福安4县先后创办县学，私塾遍布各大村落，教育事业空前发展，闽东进士及第者达422人。

元代社会动荡，书院教育受到限制，逐渐转为官办，城乡虽有社学和义学，但整个教育事业衰微，到了明清两代，闽东教育有了新的发展，寿宁、霞浦、屏南、福鼎相继创办县学，书院、私塾、社学不断增加。全区除府(县)学外，有书院30余所、私塾800余所。光绪十年(1884)英国教会在古田创办女子私塾，后改称精英女子教堂，为闽东创办最早的教会学校。光绪二十四年(1898)五月，清廷命各地书院改办学堂，区内福安穆阳兴办第一所新式学堂。清末，区内共有小学55所、中学1所。光绪三十三年(1907)改福宁中学校，为闽东近代第一所中学。

民国时期，除中小学外，师范、职业教育开始受到重视。民国三十四年(1945)

全区共有中等学校 11 所,其中完全中学 1 所、初级中学 7 所、师范 2 所、农校 1 所,共 76 个教学班,学生 2 593 人。小学校 372 所,其中中心国民学校 80 所、国民学校 282 所、私立小学 10 所,在校小学生 28 416 人,适龄儿童入学率为 22.6%。

1949 年 10 月,宁德市人民政府接管区内中等学校 9 所,共 67 个教学班,学生 1 606 人,教员 177 人;小学 233 所,学生 16 726 人,教员 759 人。此后在人民政府的领导下,废除旧教育制度,停用旧教材,整顿教师队伍,在教师中开展思想改造学习,教育工作不断发展。

1998 年宁德与全省同步实现了"两基"(基本普及九年义务教育,基本扫除青壮年文盲)目标。2010 年宁德电大和业余大学合并,保留宁德电大,该校成为目前我市唯一的成人高校。闽东高级技工学校和工业学校整合重组为宁德理工职业技术学院。同年 3 月 18 日,宁德师专升格为宁德师范学院。截至 2013 年,全市有高等学校 2 所,中等职业学校 12 所,完全中学 36 所、高级中学 14 所、初级中学 114 所,小学 279 所(含独立设置少数民族学校 9 所),幼儿园 416 所,特殊教育学校 6 所。

4.1.1 Major Events

According to the historical records, Ningde is one of the regions that were culturally developed in Fujian in the earlier period. As early as in the Tang Dynasty, there was Lingu Academy and Linxiangshen Academy. There were five natives from Ningde who succeeded in the highest imperial exams, of whom Xue Lingzhi who made it in the second year (706AD) of Emperor Shenlong's reign, was the first Jinshi (a successful candidate in the national imperial exams) in Fujian and also the first Fujianese who was enrolled to work in the imperial central government, which ushered in a new beginning for the education in Ningde. During the South Tang Dynasty, Yu Renchun, a native of Gutian established Lantian Academy, which was the largest in Ningde.

In the South Song Dynasty, the academy education in this region prospered quite a while. In the Song Dynasty 25 academies were set up. County-level schools were set up in counties of Changxi, Gutian, Ningde and Fu'an. Private schools were everywhere and the educational causes boomed than ever. Those succeeded in the imperial exams from Ningde reached 422 persons.

In the Yuan Dynasty, the society was in chaos and the academy education was limited and gradually turned public education. Though there were public and voluntary education, the whole education declined. But in the Ming and Qing Dynasties, the education in Mindong had new development. Shouning,

Xiapu, Pingnan and Fuding one after another ran county-level schools. Private academies, private schools, and social schools increased constantly. In Mindong except the prefectural and county-level schools, there were 30 private academies, and 800 private schools. In the tenth year (1884AD) of Emperor Guangxu's reign of the Qing Dynasty, a British Missionary Church established a private girls' school in Gutian and later the school was changed to Elite Girls' School which was the earliest missionary school in Mindong. In May of the 24th year (1898AD) of Emperor Guangxu's reign, the Qing government ordered that all the local private academies be changed to public schools. In Mindong, the first new style school was set up in Muyang, Fu'an. At the end of the Qing Dynasty, there were 55 primary schools, 1 middle school. In the 33rd year (1907AD), the middle school was changed to Funing Middle School, which was the first middle school in modern times.

During the governance of the Republic of China (ROC), besides primary school and secondary education, teacher education and vocational education began to be put emphasis. In the 34th year (1945AD) of the ROC, there were 11 middle schools, of which there was one complete school that ran both senior and junior education, 7 junior middle schools, 2 teachers schools, 1 agriculture school. In total there were 76 classes with 2 593 students. Moreover, there were 372 primary schools, of which 80 were central national primary schools, 282 national primary schools, 10 private primary schools. In total there were 28 416 pupils at school with an enrollment rate at 22.6%.

In October, 1949, the local government took over 9 middle schools with 67 classes, 1 606 students and 177 teachers. 233 primary schools were also taken over with 16 726 pupils and 759 teachers. Since then, under the leadership of the government, former education systems were abolished and their textbooks were cancelled with the teaching teams reassigned. Ideological education was conducted among teachers and the local education went on constantly.

In 1988, Ningde simultaneously realize its educational goals of "Two Basically"(to basically popularize the nine-year compulsory education and to basically eliminate illiteracy among the young labor forces) with other regions of Fujian. In 2010 Ningde Television University and Ningde Part-time University were joined together and became Ningde Television University which is the sole higher learning institute for the adults in the city. Mindong Senior Technicians School and Mindong Industrial School were joined together to become Ningde Technological College. On March 18 of the same year Ningde Teachers College was upgraded to Ningde Normal University. As of 2013, there were 2 higher learning institutes, 12 middle vocational schools, 36 complete middle schools (both senior and junior schools together), 14 senior middle schools, 114 junior middle schools, 279 primary schools (including 9 ethnic ones), 416 kindergartens and 6 special educational schools.

二、书院及教会学校简介

4.1.2 Academies and Missionary Schools

(一)唐代

唐代区内书院3所,分别为薛令之就读的长溪灵谷草堂(在今福安市溪潭镇城山村后)、林嵩就读的林降神草堂(在今福鼎市太姥山西脉的灵山中)和南唐余仁椿创办的古田县蓝田书院(今古田县杉洋村)。这3所书院均为私人所办,规模亦小,就学仅数人至数十人。唐代境内尚无县学,却脱颖而出5名进士(福安薛令之于唐神龙二年及第、霞浦林嵩于唐乾符二年及第、曹愚于景福二年及第、卓文于乾宁四年及第、福鼎黄洗于乾宁二年及第)。

4.1.2.1 The Tang Dynasty

During the Tang Dynasty there were 3 academies in Mindong, namely Linggu Academy of Changxi County (now in Chengshan Village, Xitang Township of Fu'an City) where Xue Lingzhi received his education, Linxiangshen Academy (now in Lingshan Mountain of the west side of Mount Taimu of Fuding City) where Lin Song obtained his education, Lantian Academy (now in Shanyang, Gutian County) run by Yu Renchun in the South Tang Dynasty. All the three academies were run by the local people and were small in scale with only a few to dozens of students. During the Tang Dynasty, though there was no county-level school yet, the academies fostered 5 Jinshi (the successful candidates in the highest imperial exams). They were Xue Lingzhi from Fu'an in the second year of the Shenlong period of the Tang Dynasty, Lin Song from Xiapu in the second year of the Qianfu period of the Tang Dynasty, Cao Yu in the second year of the Jingfu period, Zhuo Wen in the fourth year of the Qianning period and Huang Xi from Fuding in the second year of the Qianning period.

（二）宋代

宋代庆元年间朱熹又到闽东讲学，闽东的书院教育盛极一时，长溪、古田、宁德、福安4县共创办书院24所。其中古田有蓝田、溪山、螺峰、洗溪、魁龙书院、东华精舍、兴贤斋和西斋等8所；长溪县有蓝溪、乡校等9所，宁德县有六经讲堂、五经讲社、来青、仁丰、晦庵书院等5所；福安有北山、晦翁、考亭书院3所。古田、长溪所办书院之多，当时在省内仅次于闽北的建阳和崇安县。宋代书院比唐代多，宋代及第进士达423人。

4.1.2.2 The Song Dynasty

During the period of Qingyuan of the Song Dynasty, Zhu Xi, the great Confucian philosopher came to give lectures in Mindong so the education of the academies here bloomed a while. 24 academies in Changxi, Gutian, Ningde and Fu'an were established, of which there were 8 academies of Lantian, Xishan, Luofeng, Xianxi, Kuilong, Donghua Jingshe, Xingxianzai and Xizai were established. In Changxi County there were Lanxi Academy and other 8 village schools altogether. In Ningde there were five academies, namely Six Classics Academy, Five Classics Academy, Laiqing Academy, Renfeng Academy, Hui'an Academy. In Fu'an there were three academies, namely Beishan, Huiweng, and Kaoting. At that time the number of academies in Ningde was only fewer than that of Jianyang and Cong'an counties in the North Fujian. And the number of academies in the Song Dynasty was bigger than that of the Tang Dynasty. In the Song Dynasty 423 candidates succeeded in the highest imperial exams.

（三）元代

元代农民起义频繁，书院教育受严重破坏，故元代境内新办书院仅1所。闽东及第进士仅古田张以宁等6人。

4.1.2.3 The Yuan Dynasty

During the Yuan Dynasty, there were frequent peasants uprisings. As a result, the education of the academies was affected greatly. There was only one new academy and the number of the folks who succeeded in the imperial exams was just 6 including the famous native Zhang Yining from Gutian.

（四）明代

明代区内书院有20所之多。古田有崇正、正学、翠屏、桑山、溪山、青山、鹤鸣、明德等书院 8 所；福安有斗南、景台、环溪、兴文、苏江等书院 5 所；福宁本州有正学书院、李汝延师古斋、守约斋、敬义书屋、德业书屋等 5 所。

4.1.2.4 The Ming Dynasty

During the Ming Dynasty, there were 20 academies in Mindong. In Gutian there were eight, i.e. Chongzheng, Zhengxue, Cuiping, Sangshan, Xishan, Qingshan, Heming, Mingde; in Fu'an there were five, respectively Dounang, Jingtai, Huanxi, Xingwen, Sujiang; in Funing there were five, respectively Zhengxue, Li Ruyan Shigu Zhai, Shouyue Zhai, Jingyi Shuwu, Deye Shuwu.

（五）清代

清代新设书院 15 所：福鼎有龙门、桐山书院两所；古田有奎光、屏山、玉泉书院 3 所；宁德有白云、鹤峰、莲峰书院 3 所；福安有笔峰、紫阳、仰山书院 3 所；寿宁有鳌阳、紫阳书院两所；周宁有初晴书院 1 所，屏南有双溪书院 1 所。此外，清雍正六年（1728），朝廷令闽中各府、县学传习官话（普通话），古田、宁德、福安、福鼎、寿宁 5 县均于雍正七年创办正音书院，场所利用宫庙或其他书院斋堂，有的干脆在其他书院内再挂出一块书院的牌子。雍正十二年，屏南、霞浦亦开设正音书院，后因师资之争（用本地或外地）、经费不足、当局不重视等原因，不久停办。

据史料记载唐至清代的 1 200 多年中，闽东见之文字记载的书院有 66 所。元代以前书院以民办为主，元明两代官方加强对书院的控制，同时出现官办书院。清代书院以官办为主。

4.1.2.5 The Qing Dynasty

During the Qing Dynasty, 15 new academies were established: in Fuding there were two, Longmen and Tongshan; in Gutian there were three, Kuiguang, Pingshan and Yuquan; in Ningde there were three, Baiyun, Hefeng and Lianfeng; in Fu'an there were three, Bifeng, Ziyang and Yangshan; in Shouning there were two, Aoyang and Ziyang; in Zhouning there was one, Chuqing; in Pingnan there was one, Shuangxi. Besides, in the 6th year (1728AD) of Emperor Yongzheng's reign of the Qing Dynasty, the imperial government ordered all the counties learn mandarin. In the 7th year of Emperor Yongzheng's reign, counties like Gutian, Ningde, Fu'an, Fuding and Shouning established "Improving-Pronunciation Schools". Palaces, temples, and other academies were made use of for the purpose, or in some academies a sign of "Improving-Pronunciation School" was directly put up. In the 12th year of Emperor Yongzheng's reign, Pingnan and Xiapu also set up improving-pronunciation schools. Later because of the quarrels about whether using or not local teachers, shortage of fund, as well as indifference of the government, all the improving-pronunciation schools stopped running soon after.

According to the historical records, over the 1 200 years from the Tang Dynasty to the Qing Dynasty, there were 66 academies recorded in files in Mindong. The academies were mainly run privately before the Yuan Dynasty. During the Yuan Dynasty and the Ming Dynasty, the central government strengthened their control over academies. Meanwhile there appeared some state-run academies. In the Qing Dynasty, the academies were normally run by the government.

(六)教会学校

女子私塾:光绪十年(1884)英国教会在古田创办女子私塾,后改称精英女子教堂,为闽东最早创办的教会学校。

传道师范班:清光绪三十二年(1906)天主教福宁教区在福安罗江创办女子传道师范班,学生都是各地教堂保送来的贞女,学习后回原地传教。该女子传道师范班于民国二十七年停办。民国十年,福安顶头教堂神甫创办顶头女子传道师范班,又名公教女学,除招收当地天主教徒中的青少年女子入学外,也培训各地教堂神甫保送来的贞女。该班于民国十六年中断,二十六年复办,1950 年停办。

读经班:民国期间,有天主教堂开设男、女读经班,学习时间不限。

修院:天主教专门培养神职人员的学校。修院有男女之分,男修院是培养司铎以上的神职人员,女修院培养修道女和女传教士。福宁教区所办的修院都不连续招生,福安教区创办的修院有 8 所。

4.1.2.6 Missionary Schools

Private Girls' School: in the tenth year (1884AD) of Emperor Guangxu's reign of the Qing Dynasty, a British church set up a private girls' school in Gutian. Later it was changed to Elite Girls' School, which was the earliest missionary school in Mindong.

Preachers' School: in the 32nd year (1906AD) of Emperor Guangxu's reign of the Qing Dynasty, Funing Parish of Catholics ran a girl preachers' school in Luojiang, Fu'an. All the students were virgins chosen from different churches in the local. After training, they returned to their original places. The school stopped running in the 27th year of the ROC. In the 10th year of the ROC, the priest of Dingtou Church of Fu'an ran another girls preachers' school, which had another name of Public Girls' School. Besides enrolling the young girls in the local churches, they also trained the virgins sent by the local priest. That school was stopped in the 16th year of the ROC. In 26th year of the ROC, the school was resumed, and in 1950 it was closed.

Bible Study School: in the period of the ROC, most Catholic churches ran Bible study classes. Their study time was not fixed.

Converts: there were the specialized schools for training priests of Catholics. The converts were of men and women. The converts of men mainly trained priests while the converts of women trained nuns or female missionaries. The converts in Funing Parish did not enroll each year. Fu'an Parish of Catholic ran 8 converts.

三、基础教育

(一)重点幼儿园

宁德市有省示范性幼儿园6所：
宁德市机关幼儿园
福安市实验幼儿园
福安市第二实验幼儿园
蕉城区机关幼儿园
福鼎市实验幼儿园
霞浦县实验幼儿园
市示范性幼儿园18所：
蕉城区实验幼儿园
蕉城区儿童学园
古田县实验幼儿园
周宁县实验幼儿园
屏南县实验幼儿园
寿宁县实验幼儿园
柘荣县实验幼儿园
柘荣县机关幼儿园
福安市直属机关儿童学园
福鼎市童星艺术幼儿园(私立)
福安市溪柄中心幼儿园
屏南县光明幼儿园

周宁县机关幼儿园
霞浦县机关幼儿园
福安市甘棠中心幼儿园
霞浦县第一幼儿园
福安市赛岐中心幼儿园
福安市坂中中心幼儿园

4.1.3 Elementary Education

4.1.3.1 Leading Kindergartens

There are 6 provincial model kindergartens in Ningde:

The Kindergarten Attached to the Ningde Municipal Departments

Fu'an Experimental Kindergarten

The Second Experimental Kindergarten of Fu'an City

The Kindergarten Attached to the Departments of Jiaocheng District Government

The Experimental Kindergarten of Fuding City

The Experimental Kindergarten of Xiapu County

There are 18 municipal model kindergartens in Ningde City:

The Experimental Kindergarten of Jiaocheng District

The Nursery School of Jiaocheng District

The Experimental Kindergarten of Gutian County

The Experimental Kindergarten of Zhouning County

The Experimental Kindergarten of Pingnan County

The Experimental Kindergarten of Shouning County

The Experimental Kindergarten of Zherong County

The Kindergarten Attached to the Departments of Zherong Government

The Nursery School Attached to the Departments of Fu'an City

The Child Star Art Kindergarten of Fuding City (Private-owned)

Xibing Central Kindergarten of Fu'an City

Guangming Kindergarten of Pingnan County

The Kindergarten Attached to the Departments of Zhouning Government

The Kindergarten Attached to the Departments of Xiapu Government

Gantang Central Kindergarten of Fu'an City

The First Kindergarten of Xiapu County

Saiqi Central Kindergarten of Fu'an City

Banzhong Central Kindergarten of Fu'an City

(二)重点小学

宁德师范附属小学
蕉城区实验小学
东侨实验小学
福安师范附属小学
霞浦县实验小学
寿宁县鳌阳小学
4.1.3.2 Leading Primary Schools
The Affiliated Primary School of Ningde Normal University
The Experimental Primary School of Jiaocheng District
Dongqiao Experimental Primary School
The Affiliated Primary School of Fu'an Teachers School
The Experimental Primary School of Xiapu County
Aoyang Primary School of Shouning County

(三)重点小学简介

宁德师范附属小学

宁德师范附属小学创办于 1970 年,1999 年被确认为福建省示范小学,1979 年被确定为福建省首批十六所重点小学之一。学校现有教职工 145 人,49 个教学班,学生 2 700 多人,校园占地 10.37 亩,旧校区有建筑面积 12 234 平方米。学校有全市第一个编播能力较强的校园电视台和第一个完整的校园网;400 多台计算机,实物展示台,网络中心,教学资源库,多媒体教学设施,还有少先队活动室、电脑室、语音室、音乐室、美术室、阶梯教室、电子备课室、实验室、标本室、劳技室、图书馆、师生阅览室、多功能活动厅、排练厅、器材室等专用室 20 多间。各种教学设备均按一类标准配备,能满足各科教学活动需要。

宁德师范学院附属小学新校区位于东侨经济开发区,占地面积 50 亩,规划建筑面积 20 010 平方米,规划办学容量 48 个班级,建成后将增加 2 160 个学位。宁德师范学院附属小学新校区于 2015 年秋季开始招生。

蕉城区实验小学

蕉城区实验小学是一所省级示范小学,始建于 1958 年。现有 54 个教学班,4 500多名学生,在编教职工 195 人。校园占地面积 13 公顷,有一个 200 米环形塑胶跑道的操场,拥有计算机 400 多台。学校建成了校园闭路电视系统、广播系统、校园网络。校园环境优美,教学设施先进。

福安师范附属小学

福安师范附属小学是省级示范小学，福建省三届文明学校。这是一所百年名校，学校始创于1902年，前身是福安县官立紫阳高等小学堂，是福安最早开办的一所官立小学。

现有42个教学班，在校生2 562名，教职员工134人。学校教学设施先进、能满足各科教学活动需要。为了丰富校园文化内涵，创设深厚校园精神文明建设氛围，并根据学生乐于接受的内容和方式，开设的微型课程有德育栏目、生活小常识、我的生活故事、快乐英语角、每周一歌等深受学生喜爱。

4.1.3.3 Profiles of the Leading Primary Schools

The Affiliated Primary School of Ningde Normal University

It was established in 1970 and designated to be a provincial model primary school in 1999 by Fujian Province. In 1979 it was listed to be one of the 16 key primary schools that would be given priority support in Fujian Province. Now there are 145 teachers and other staff, 49 classes with more than 2 700 students in the school. The old campus covers an area of 10.37 Mu of land with a constructed area of 12 234 square meters. It has the first campus television station that is good for editing and broadcasting and the first complete campus network. There are over 400 computers, teaching aid showcases, network center, teaching resources rooms, and multi-media facilities, etc. Besides there are over 20 places like activity rooms for the young pioneers, computer rooms, language labs, music rooms, art rooms, step teaching halls, digital preparatory rooms, experiment rooms, species rooms, hands-on rooms, library, reading rooms, multi-function rooms, rehearsal rooms, kits rooms and so on. All the teaching facilities are equipped according to Class-Ⅰ standards and can meet all the teaching needs.

It has a new campus in Dongqiao Economic and Technological Development Zone covering an area of 50 Mu with a planned constructed area of 20 010 square meters. Its planned number of classes is 48. After its completion, it is to increase to 2 160 seats. It started enrollment of pupils in the fall of 2015.

The Jiaocheng Experimental Primary School of Jiaocheng District

It is a provincial model primary school and was established in 1958. Now it has 54 teaching classes, 500 computers, 4 500 pupils and 195 teaching staff. It covers an area of 13 hectares and has a playground with a 200-meter track of synthetic rubber. The school is equipped with campus closed circuit television system, broadcasting system, and campus network. The whole school is beautiful and enjoys advanced facilities.

The Affiliated Primary School of Fu'an Teachers School

It is a provincial model primary school and the school has been honoured as civilization schools for 3 times in Fujian province. It is also a famous school over 100 years old and was first established in 1902. Its predecessor was the government-run Ziyang Senior Primary School of Fu'an County and is also the first government-run primary school in Fu'an. There are now 42 classes with 2 562 pupils and 134 staffs in the school. It enjoys advanced teaching facilities which can meet the teaching needs of different subjects. In order to create a cultural atmosphere and deep ideological cultivation of the school and based on the accepted contents and methods, the school offers some popular micro courses like "Virtue Education", "Daily Life Knowledge", "My Life Story", "Happy English Corner" and "Weekly Songs", etc.

四、中等教育

4.1.4 Secondary Education

(一)重点中学：

宁德市共有 8 所省一级达标高中，分别为：

宁德一中

古田一中

福安一中

福安二中

霞浦一中

柘荣一中

宁德市民族中学

福鼎一中

4.1.4.1 Leading Senior Middle Schools

There are 8 senior middle schools that meet the Class-I Standard of Fujian Province. They are:

No.1 Senior Middle School of Ningde City

No.1 Senior Middle School of Gutian County

No.1 Senior Middle School of Fu'an City

No.2 Senior Middle School of Fu'an City
No.1 Senior Middle School of Xiapu County
No.1 Senior Middle School of Zherong County
The Ethnic Senior Middle School of Ningde City
No.1 Senior Middle School of Fuding City

(二)部分重点中学简介

宁德一中

福建省宁德第一中学创办于 1940 年 2 月,初名宁德县立初级中学,择址莲峰书院,校园面积 1 248 平方米。1978 年 4 月,学校被福建省教育厅确定为全省首批办好的 17 所重点中学之一,并定名为"福建省宁德第一中学",2006 年 4 月被评为省一级达标学校。目前正向着国家级示范高中的目标挺进。学校占地面积为 5.3 万平方米。现有教职工 193 名,专任教师 170 名,其中高级教师 95 人,比率为 56%;特级教师 8 位。2014 年培养高中毕业生 765 人,高中按时毕业率 98%,2014 届高中会考及格率 100%,优良率 99%,中学生体质健康标准合格率 99%,高考本科上线率 98.7%。2015 年有 40 个教学班,在校生 2 047 人。2014 年 3 月 4 日晚,宁德一中代表队在第二季中国谜语大会总决赛上力挫群雄,获得冠军。

古田一中

古田县第一中学,是福建省宁德市一所重点中学。创办于 1943 年,建校 70 来,成为有资格向全国高等院校保送新生的全省 40 所重点中学之一,被列入全省第 22 所、全区首所办学水平一级达标和免予参加全省高中会考的学校;连续 10 年高考上线数居全市第一位,1997 年通过省办学水平一级达标学校验收,2003 年入选中国名校 600 家。校园总面积达 103 亩,目前仅有高中部,现有三个年段,42 个教学班,在校学生 2 200 人。学校建成了校园宽带网,接通了信息高速公路,开通了福建省古田一中校园网站和电视演播中心,学校图书馆藏书达 11 万余册,先后培养了 4 万多名高、初中和师范毕业生。

福安一中

福安一中是福建省办学历史最悠久的省重点中学之一,由 1902 年创立的宁郡中学堂和 1924 年创立的福安县立初级中学合并而成,1954 年正式定名为福建省福安第一中学,并被福建省确定为首批 14 所省重点中学之一。

校园占地 69 000 多平方米,图书馆拥有 13 多万册藏书,是福建省第十届文明学校。2010 年 3 月 4 日被确认为福建省一级达标高中。目前在校生 3 166 人,57 个教学班,工作人员 245 名。学校有教学大楼、科技实验楼、图书馆、体育馆、综合楼、多媒体教室、计算机房、闭路电视系统等现代教育技术设施,设备配置达到省达标学校标准。

霞浦一中

霞浦第一中学即创建于1902年(清光绪二十八年)的“宁郡中学堂”。中华人民共和国成立后,改称霞浦县中学,1958年被定为省重点中学,定名为“福建省霞浦第一中学”,2008年搬迁至霞浦城关新城区,占地面积214亩,建筑面积48 200平方米,包括教学楼、图书馆、办公楼、科技楼、专家楼、体育馆、学生公寓等七幢主要建筑物及各类先进的附属配套设施,校内有千兆主干网和百兆局域网、数字化教学系统。学校实现了班班多媒体,硬件设施名列全省前茅。2014年通过省一级达标高中验收并确认。目前学校共有教职工249人,教学班57个,学生2 970人。学校拥有高级职称教师101人,中级职称教师85人,国家级骨干教师3人,省级学科带头人3人,省级骨干教师5人,连续四届被授予“福建省文明学校”称号。

宁德市民族中学

宁德市民族中学创办于1958年,原名“福建省福安民族中学”,2001年更名为“福建省宁德市民族中学”。学校目前为福建省一级达标学校,全省唯一的少数民族重点中学。学校占地面积28 479平方米,拥有实验楼、图书馆、多功能办公大楼及先进的教学设备,有计算机网络中心、校园网和演播教学子网,图书馆藏书7.9万册。学校现有44个班级,学生2 422名:其中初中部12个班级,学生662名,均为少数民族学生,向全区招生;高中部32个班级,学生1 760名,其中少数民族生1 024名,占58.2%。教职员工191名,其中专任教师160名,特级教师4名,高级教师64名,国家级骨干教师4名,省级骨干教师10名,省级学科带头人4名,市学科带头人10名,教师学历达标率100%。办学以来,学校确立以培养少数民族人才为主的指导思想,形成了以少数民族为主体的生源结构体系,根据少数民族地区经济、文化发展的需要,成立畲族经济研究小组、畲族传统文化、体育研究小组等等。连续九次被中共福建省委、省人民政府授予“文明学校”称号。2013年高考再创历史新高,本科上线率达89%。

福鼎市第一中学

福鼎一中的前身是1938年秋成立的“私立北岭初级中学”。该校于1956年开办了高中教育,1957年更名为“福建省福鼎市第一中学”。福鼎一中是福建省重点中学和省级一级达标学校,有资格将毕业生直接保送至各高等学校。学校占地83亩,建筑面积26 828平方米。全校有45个班级,高中部有学生数2 686人,初中部1 950人,在编教职工有330人,其中高级教师30人,中级教师66人。福鼎一中是一所拥有现代化教学设施的高中新课程实验示范学校,国家课程改革和基础教育资源的研究学校,同时也是“全国教育特色单位”。2002年,该校成为福建省知识产权教育实验学校和“环境友好学校”,被国家教育部指定为教育信息化的实验学校。2013年,学校一本大学的入学率达到67.5%,本专科院校的入学率达到98%。福鼎一中力争在不久的将来建设成为“闽东领先、海西一流、中国知名”的全国模范高中。

4.2.4.2 Profiles of Some Leading Senior Middle Schools

No.1 Senior Middle School of Ningde City

It was established in February 1940 with its school name as Ningde County-Run Junior Middle School. It was located in Lianfeng Academy with an area of 1 248 square meters. In April 1978, it was included in the first 17 leading middle schools by Fujian Educational Bureau to be given priority for construction and named "No.1 Senior Middle School of Ningde". In April 2006 it was appraised to be a "Provincial Class-Ⅰ School" by Fujian Education Bureau. At the moment it is striving toward the goal of constructing a national model senior middle school. It covers an area of 53 000 square meters. There are 193 teachers and clerks, of whom 170 are specialized teachers, 95 are senior teachers who account for 56% of the all the teachers, and 8 are special-class teachers. In 2014, 765 students graduated, who represented a 98% graduation rate. In 2014 its passing rate of the national senior middle school exams was 100% and 99% of the students were up to grades A or B. The passing rate of health test of middle school students was 99% and the rate of admission to universities and colleges was up to 98%. In 2015, there were 40 classes with 2 047 students. On March 4, 2015, the contestants of No. 1 Middle School of Ningde City overcame all the powerful rivals and obtained the championship in the "Final Competition of Guessing Riddles in China".

No.1 Senior Middle School of Gutian County

It is a leading senior middle school of Ningde City of Fujian Province and was established in 1943. Over 70 years since its establishment, it has become one of the 40 leading middle schools that are qualified to recommend its graduates to national colleges and universities. It has been included in the 22 schools in Fujian province and become the first one in Ningde to be up to the National Class-Ⅰ Standard of Education and exempt from the unified provincial achievement tests. It has been for over 10 years that its number of students that were enrolled into universities topped all schools of Ningde City. In 1997, it passed the appraisal check of the Provincial Educational Class-Ⅰ Standard. In 2003, it was enrolled into the famous 600 middle schools in China. Its area covers 103 Mu of land and at the moment there runs only senior high school education with 42 classes and 2 200 students. On-campus wide-band network has been constructed with high speed information circulation. There is

"Campus Network Center of No.1 Senior Middle School of Gutian County" and the campus television center has been on. Now the school library stores over 110 000 books. Since the establishment of the school, it has cultivated about 40 000 graduates of senior, junior middle school students and also some teachers-to-be.

No.1 Senior Middle School of Fu'an City

No.1 Senior Middle School of Fu'an City is one of the leading middle schools that have been running for long in Fujian Province. It was joined by Ningjun Middle School established in 1902 and Junior Middle School of Fu'an County founded in 1924. In 1954, its name was fixed to be "No. 1 Middle School of Fu'an of Fujian Province" and was designated to be one of the 14 leading middle schools by Fujian Province.

The School covers an area of 69 000 square meters of land and has over 130 000 books in its library. It is one of the tenth batch of civilization schools of Fujian province. In March 4, 2010, it was appraised to be a middle school up to Class-Ⅰ Standard of Education in Fujian Province. There are now 3 166 students, 57 classes and 245 teachers and clerks in the school. It is a complete system with teaching buildings, science labs, library, gym, complex building, multi-media rooms, computer rooms and close-circuit television rooms etc, and its modern educational facilities are up to the provincial level school standard。

No.1 Senior Middle School of Xiapu County

It was established in 1902(the 28th year of Emperor Guangxu's reign of the Qing Dynasty) in the name of "Ningjun Middle School". After the People's Republic of China was founded in 1949, its name was changed to Middle School of Xiapu County. In 1958, it was designated to be a leading middle school in Fujian province with its name as "No. 1 Middle School of Xiapu County of Fujian Province. In 2008, it was moved to the new town area of Xiapu County, covering an area of 214 mu of land with a constructed area of 48 200 square meters including a teaching building, an library, a office building, a science labs building, a scholar's building, a gym, a dorm and their accessory facilities. The school has a 1 000 MG main network and 100 MG local domain digital teaching system so that each classroom is connected with multi medias and its hardware topped schools of Fujian province. 2014 saw the school pass the appraisal check of Fujian province and confirmed. At the moment the school has a staff of 249 persons, 57 classes, and 2970 students. It also has 101 teachers with senior academic titles, 85 teachers with intermediate academic titles, 3 national backbone teachers, 3 provincial leaders with subject studies and 5 provincial backbone teachers. The school was awarded four times in a row the honorable title of "Civilization School of Fujian Province".

The Ethnic Middle School of Ningde City

It was established in 1958. Its former name was "Fu'an Ethnic Middle School of Fujian Province". In 2001 its name was changed to "Ningde Municipal Ethnic Middle School of Fujian Province". It is now one of the schools that are up to Class-Ⅰ Standard of Education in Fujian Province and also the only leading ethnic middle school in Fujian. It covers an area of 28 479 square meters and has labs building, library, multi-function office building and advanced teaching facilities. There are computer centers, campus networks and teaching broadcasting mini websites and 79 000 books in its library. The school has 44 classes of 2 422 students, of which there are 12 classes of 662 students in its junior middle school, which takes up 58.2% of all students. Its number of staff is 191, of whom there are 160 specialized teachers, of whom there are 4 special-class teachers, 64 senior teachers, 4 national backbone teachers, 10 provincial backbone teachers, 4 provincial leading teachers with their subjects, 10 municipal leading teachers with their subjects etc. All the academic degrees of the teachers 100% met with the requirement. Since its establishment, the school, keeping in mind its education orientation for nurturing the ethnic minorities, enrolls mainly the ethnic students, sets up research groups on the economy of the She ethnic people, their culture and their sports. It has been awarded "Civilization School" by the Fujian Provincial Party Committee and Provincial Government for nine times in a row. In 2013 it achieved a new record with its national entrance exams. 89% of its students were enrolled by the national colleges and universities.

No.1 Middle School of Fuding City

Its predecessor was "Private Bailing Junior Middle School" established in the fall of 1938. In 1956 it ran senior middle school education. In 1957 its name was "No.1 Middle School of Fuding City of Fujian Province". It is a leading middle school and a provincial Class-Ⅰ Standard school in Fujian Province, which is qualified to send its graduates directly to national colleges and universities. The school covers an area of 83 mu of land with a constructed area of 26 828 square meters. It has 45 classes with respectively 2 686 and 1 950 students in its senior and junior middle school. The number of its staff is 330, of whom 30 are senior teachers and 66 are intermediate teachers. It is an experimental school with modern teaching facilities, and an experimental model school with the new curriculums of the senior middle school as well as a research school of national curriculum reforms and elementary educational resources. It is also a "National Unique Education Unit". In 2002 it became an experimental school with the education of intellectual rights in Fujian Province as well as an "Environment-Friendly School". It was also designated by the National Ministry of Education to be an experimental school with education information. In 2013 its enrollment rate by the Class-Ⅰ universities reached 67.5% and what is more, its enrollment rate by undergraduate colleges and universities was up to 98%, so both the top students in Ningde City in the exams of the social arts or sciences were graduates from No. 1 Middle School of Fuding City. It is striving to build itself into a national model senior middle school, "leading in Mindong, and the first class in the Western Taiwan Straits Economic Development Zone and well-known in China" in the near future.

（三）主要中职学校

宁德市目前有中职学校 13 所，其中国家级 7 所，省级 5 所，一般校 1 所，分别为：

国家级中职学校：
闽东卫生学校
宁德职业中专学校
宁德财经学校
宁德技师学院
霞浦职业中专学校
福鼎职业中专学校
福安职业技术学校
省级中职学校：
寿宁职业技术学校
周宁职业中专学校
屏南职业中专学校
古田职业中专学校
柘荣职业技术学校
一般中职学校：

福安市成人中专学校

4.1.4.3 Major Vocational Schools

Ningde City has 13 vocational schools, of which 7 are national, 5 are provincial and 1 common.

National Secondary Vocational Schools:

Mindong Medical School

Ningde Vocational School

Ningde Financial School

Ningde Technicians College

Xiapu Vocational School

Fuding Vocational School

Fu'an Vocational School

Provincial Vocational Schools:

Shouning Vocational Technicians School

Zhouning Vocational School

Pingnan Vocational School

Gutian Vocational School

Zherong Vocational Technicians School

Common Vocational School:

Adults Vocational School of Fu'an City

(四)部分主要中职学校简介

闽东卫生学校

闽东卫生学校是一所国家级重点中专,省级文明学校。学校创办于 1958 年,占地面积 86 亩。现有教职工 136 人,其中专任教师 118 人,博士研究生 1 人,硕士研究生 12 人,高、中级职称 70 人,有全日制在校生 3 000 多人。设有护理、助产、农村医学、药剂、医学检验技术等八个专业,仪器设备总值达 2 000 多万元,图书馆藏书 10 万余册。并确定闽东医院、宁德市医院等 15 所二甲以上医院为教学医院。2013 年被评为全省卫生系统先进集体,2015 年被评为省示范学校。截至本书完稿时,学校正在申报更名为“宁德卫生职业学院”。

宁德职业中专学校

宁德职业中专学校,前身为 1983 年设立的蕉城十中职高部,2000 年被评为首批国家级重点职业中学,是当时闽东唯一的一所国家级重点中专学校。校园占地 51 亩,现设有十大类共 20 多个专业,58 个教学班,3 067 名学生,有 187 名教职员工,其中专任教师 159 名,国家级骨干教师 8 名,省级骨干教师 25 名,具有硕士研究生学历的有 9 名。

学校图书馆拥有 10 多万册的藏书，建有各类专业的模拟实验室和众多的校外实训基地，拥有计算机中心和教学楼、综合楼、学生公寓楼、教工宿舍楼、学生生活服务楼、田径场等完善的现代化教学设施，能满足 3 000 多名学生学习生活需要。目前学校正朝着全国示范性中等职业学校的目标奋进。

宁德财经学校

宁德财经学校，为国家级重点中专学校，创建于 1981 年，是经省人民政府批准设立的全日制普通中等职业学校。校园占地面积 144 亩；现有教职工 139 人，其中中高级职称 75 人，双师型教师 55 人；图书馆藏书 10.173 万册，在校生 4 000 多人，设有 20 个专业，其中会计电算化为省级重点专业，财务会计、计算机应用等 7 个专业为市级重点专业。

宁德技师学院

宁德技师学院创办于 1980 年，位于宁德市区蕉城南路 56 号，是一所公办综合性国家级重点学校。学院占地面积 158 亩，实习试验场地建筑总面积达 16 161 平方米。学院现有在校生 3 265 人，专任教师中高级职称教师 68 人，“双师型”教师 183 人，其中具有高级工、技师、高级技师职业资格证书的实习指导教师 78 人。学院实行院系两级管理，按专业分为电气工程、机械工程、信息工程、汽车工程、经贸管理五个教学系部，开设有电气自动化设备安装与维修、数控加工、模具制造、汽车维修、时装设计、会计、计算机应用、烹饪、酒店服务等各级各类专业 26 个。建有电子装配、变流与调速、可编程控制器、机床电器维修、电力拖动、钳工、数控加工中心、模具加工中心、汽车维修、电气焊接、影视制作中心等 93 个实习实训场所、1 300多台教学电脑，所有专用教室、多功能阶梯教室全部配备多媒体投影设备，学院已成为闽东地区综合实力最强的职业技术院校。

福鼎职业中专学校

福鼎职业中专学校创办于 1983 年，2010 年为国家级重点中等职业学校，2013 年为福建省中小学中等职业学校信息化试点学校，2015 年为福建省中等职业教育改革发展建设示范学校。学校占地面积 104 144.63平方米，现有在校生 3 948人，专任教师 146 人，从企业聘任专兼职教师 23 人，双师型教师 74 人，国家级骨干教师 12 人，省级骨干教师 57 人，市级骨干教师 17 人。学校有稳定的校内和校外实训基地，烹饪专业实训基地为省级技能型紧缺人才培养基地、中央财政支持的中等职业教育实训基地、福建省烹饪专业公共实训基地。校内有中餐烹饪、电子商务、学前教育、茶叶、美容美发、机电等专业实训基地，实训设备总值达 2 260.28 万元，在宁德市中等职业学校中起引领示范作用。

福安职业技术学校

福安职业技术学校系省级重点中等职业学校，目前占地面积 100 亩，建筑面积

25 000平方米，是宁德市中职类学校中的第一所百亩花园式校园。学校教育教学设施完备，拥有几十家省内外实训实习基地及校内多功能实训大楼。学校开设有机电技术应用、电子技术应用、数控技术应用、计算机应用、会计电算化、学前教育、旅游等十几个专业，设有职业中专、函授大专、短期培训等多层次、多形式的学历教育和非学历教育，每年均有 200 多名优秀学子从这里升入高等院校继续深造，连续几年高职单招升学率居宁德市同类学校前茅，毕业生就业率高达 95%以上。

4.1.4.4 Profiles of Some Major Vocational Schools

Mindong Medical School

It is a national leading secondary vocational school, and also a provincial "civilization school". It was established in 1958 and covers 86 Mu of land and has a staff of 136 people, of whom 118 are specialized teachers, 1 is PhD postgraduate, and 12 are BA postgraduates, and 70 are either senior or intermediate teachers. There are 3 000 full time students in the school which offers eight majors like nursing, midwifery, rural medicine, pharmacy, medical lab technology, etc. The total value of the school equipment is over 20 million yuan, and its library stores over 100 000 books. It has been designated as a teaching hospital by 15 Class-Ⅱ hospitals like Mindong Hospital and Ningde Municipal Hospital. In 2013, it was awarded as an advanced unit by the provincial medical circle and in 2015 it was appraised to be a provincial model school. When the book is being written, it is applying to be "Mindong Medical Vocational College".

Ningde Vocational School

Its predecessor was the Vocational Branch of Jiaocheng No. 10 Middle School established in 1983. In 2000, it was appraised to be one of the first batch of national leading secondary vocational schools, the only secondary national leading school in Mindong then. It covers an area of 51 Mu and offers more than 20 majors in 10 categories and has 58 classes of 3067 students. Its staff number is 187, of whom 159 are specialized teachers, 8 are national backbone teachers, and 25 are provincial backbone teachers, 9 are postgraduates, which top those of all the secondary vocational schools in Ningde.

The School library stores over 100 thousand books and has built all kinds of modulation rooms of different majors and many off-campus internship bases. It has modern teaching facilities like computer centers, teaching buildings, complexes, dorms, teacher's apartment buildings, playground, etc., which can meet the demand of life and the study of students. At the moment the school is striving to become a national model vocational school of secondary education.

Ningde Financial School

It is one of national leading secondary vocational schools and was established in 1981 after approval of the Fujian Provincial Government to be a full-time secondary vocational school. It covers an area of 144 Mu of land with a staff of 139 members, of whom 75 are senior teachers and 55 are dual-track teachers. Its library keeps 101 730 books. There are more than 4 000 students in the school. It offers more than 20 majors, of which Accounting Computerization is a provincial leading major. Besides there are seven municipal leading majors like Financial Accounting and Computer Application, etc.

Ningde Technicians College

It dates back to 1980 and is located at No. 56, Jiaocheng South Road, Ningde City. It is a public comprehensive national leading school which covers an area of 158 mu with an experimental area of 16 161 square meters. At the moment the school has 3 265 students. Among the teachers 68 have senior academic titles and 183 are dual teachers who can both teach and apply what they teach in real life. There are 78 teachers who have obtained their senior workers certificates or senior technician certificates or technician certificates. The school carries out two-level management at college and department and based on the classifications of majors there are five departments of electrical engineering, mechanical engineering, information engineering, automobile engineering and economic and trade management. 26 majors have been offered like electrical automatic equipment installation and maintenance, digital control processing, module manufacturing, automobile maintenance, fashion design, accounting, computer application, cooking, hotel service, etc. 93 internship places have been constructed for the practice of electrical assembling, converting and adjusting; programming controller, machine tool electric maintenance, electric dragging, welding, digital processing center, mould processing center, auto repair, electric welding, film and television making center, etc. Besides, there are over 1 300 computers, and special-purpose rooms, and multi-functional rooms. They are all equipped with multimedia facilities. It has become the strongest technician college in Mindong comprehensively speaking.

Fuding Vocational School

It was first established in 1983. In 2010 it became one of the national leading secondary vocational schools and in 2013 was a pilot school of the informatization of the secondary vocational schools of Fujian Province and in 2015 became a model school of the educational reform and development of the secondary vocational schools of Fujian Province. The school covers an area of 104 144.63 square meters. There are 3 948 students, 146 specialized teachers, 23 part-time teachers hired from enterprises and companies. Among the teachers, 74 are dual teachers, 12 are national backbone teachers, 57 are provincial backbone teachers, 17 are municipal backbone teachers. The school has fixed campus and off-campus internship bases. Its cookery internship base is a provincial scarce-talent training base in Fujian Province. It is also an internship base of the secondary vocational schools that was built with the financial support from the central government. It is also a public internship base for the cookery majors of Fujian Province. On campus there are internship bases of Chinese cookery, electronic commercial business, pre-school education, teas, hair beautifying, electrical motors and so on. The school has a total value of 22.6028 million yuan of facilities and is a leading and model secondary vocational school in Ningde City.

Fu'an Vocational School

It is a leading secondary vocational school in Fujian Province. It covers an area of 100 Mu of land and a constructed area of 25 000 square meters. It is the first over 100-Mu and garden-like secondary vocational school in Ningde. It possesses complete teaching facilities and has dozens of internship bases in and out of Fujian province and a multi-functional internship building on campus. It offers over ten majors like applied electric motor technology, applied electronics, applied digital control technology, applied computerization, accounting digitalization, pre-schooling education, tourism and so on. There are 128 specialized teachers in the school and it offers full-time and part-time education ranging from secondary vocational education, correspondence college, and short-term training, etc. Each year more than 200 graduates from the school leave for further studies in the higher learning institutes. For many years its enrollment rate among the students from vocation schools to higher learning institutes topped that of the similar schools in Ningde City and its employment rate reached more than 95%.

五、高等教育

宁德现有高校 2 所。其中本科 1 所，高职高专 1 所。

宁德师范学院

宁德师范学院是经教育部批准设立的公办全日制本科层次的普通高等学校。学院地处福建省东部滨海城市宁德市，学院的前身是建于 1958 年的福安师范专科学校，1978 年复办时更名为“宁德师范高等专科学校”，2010 年 3 月 18 日教育部批准升格为本科层次的宁德师范学院。2014 年获得学士学位授予权。校园占地面积1 210亩，建筑面积 28 万平方米，教学仪器设备总值 7 330 多万元，图书馆藏书 134 多万册（含电子图书），建有畲族文献数据库、闽东名人数据库。全日制在校学生7 000多人，现有 14 个教学系（部），各类专业 32 个，其中应用型专业 17 个，师范类专业 15 个。学院拥有一支数量适当、结构合理、素质优良的师资队伍。有中央组织部直接联系的优秀专家、享受国务院特殊津贴、入选百千万人才工程、省优秀专家、省级教学名师等一批优秀人才。现有专任教师 426 人，教授 45 名，副教授 132 名，高级职称教师占专任教师比例为 41.5%，博士 36 人，硕士 247 人，硕博士教师比重为 66.4%。学院坚持开放办学方针，同国内外 50 多家知名大学、科研机构和企事业单位建立了良好的合作关系，努力构建多形式、多层次、多样化的合作办学格局。

宁德职业技术学院

宁德职业技术学院是经福建省人民政府批准、教育部备案，由宁德农业学校和福安师范学校合并升格的闽东唯一一所具有高等教育招生资格的高等职业技术院校。前身校是创办于 1934 年的省立福安农业职业学校和 1939 年的省立霞浦师范学校，1993 年学院坐落于福安市区，占地面积 520 亩。现设有机电工程系、生物技术系、信息技术与工程系、文化传媒系、财经管理系、公共基础部和成人教育部等 7 个教学单位，37 个高职专业以及 19 个成人教育专业。学院拥有一支结构合理、素质优良的师资队伍。现有教职工近 300 人，其中专任教师中教授 1 人、博士生导师 1 人，享受国务院政府特殊津贴专家 1 人，福建省高等学校教学名师 2 人，福建省高等职业院校百名优秀专业带头人 3 人，副高及以上职称占专任教师 29%，具有博士、硕士学位教师占专任教师 39%；双师素质教师比例达 78%。还大量聘请行业企业生产一线的专业技术人才担任兼职教师或实践教学指导教师，已建成一支具有专业理论水平较高、教学和实践经验较丰富的“双师型”教师队伍。校内实验实训设施完善、设备先进。国家级、省级、校级实训基地共 56 个，教科研仪器设备总值 2 700 多万元。目前与 80 多家企业开展校企合作，建立了 80 多个校外实训基地，为学生提供顶岗实习平台，从而促进校企深度融合，办学条件不断改善，教学质量不断提高。

4.1.5 Higher Education

There are two institutions of higher learning in Ningde: one university and one vocational college

Ningde Normal University

It is a full-time public undergraduate higher learning institution approved to be established by National Ministry of Education with its location in coastal Ningde City in the east of Fujian Province. Its predecessor was Fu'an Teachers College set up in 1958. In 1978 it was resumed and its name was changed to Ningde Teachers College. On March 18, 2010 approved by the National Ministry of Education, it was upgraded to Ningde Normal University, a undergraduate higher learning institution. In 2014 it was authorized the qualification to confer bachelor degrees. The university covers an area of 1 210 Mu of land with a constructed area of 280 000 square meters. Its total value of teaching facilities reached 73.30 million yuan and its library keeps over 1.34 million books(including digital ones). It has built Cultural Database of the She Ethnic People and Database of the Famous People in Mindong. There are over 7 000 students in the University of 14 departments with 32 majors, of which 17 are applied majors and 15 educational ones. The University has fostered a fine-quality teaching team that is fit with its number and suitable with its structure, of whom there are some excellent experts who are directly affiliated to the National Central Organization Ministry and who enjoy special allowances from the State Council. There are also some experts who have been selected onto the "National 100/1000/10 000 Talents Project" and there are some teachers chosen to be "Provincial Excellent Experts and Provincial Famous Teachers". Now there are 426 specialized teachers, of whom 45 are professors and 132 are associate professors. The teachers who have senior academic titles account for 41.5%. There are also 36 PhD holders and 247 masters, all taking up 66.4% of the total teachers. The university sticks to the educational orientations of opening up and keeps good cooperation relations with more than 50 domestic and international famous universities, scientific research institutes as well as some enterprises and national organs. It is striving to construct a cooperative educational pattern that is various, multi-tiered and diversified.

Ningde Vocational College

It was approved the Fujian People's Government, and filed by the National

Ministry of Education and joint by Ningde Agriculture School and Fu'an Teachers School and was upgraded to be the only vocational school that is qualified for education of higher learning in Mindong. Its predecessors were Provincial Agricultural Vocational School of Fu'an County founded in 1933 and Provincial Teachers School of Xiapu County founded in 1939. In 1993 the college was located in the downtown of Fu'an and covered an area of 520 Mu. There are 7 departments of electrical engineering, biotechnology, information technology and engineering, culture and media, financial management, selective courses, and adult education etc., with 37 vocational majors and 19 adult educational majors. The college has fostered a fine-quality teaching team that is reasonably structured and well qualified. It has over 300 staff members, of whom one is professor; one is PhD mentor, one enjoys the allowances by the State Council; two are famous teachers of Fujian province, and 3 are of 100 leading leaders with their subjects in the vocational colleges of Fujian Province. Those teachers who have associate professorship or above account for 29% and those who have PhD degrees and master degrees take up 39% and those who are dual teachers reach 78%. The college also hired lots of professionals from relevant enterprises and companies to be part-time teachers or advisers to the internship students so that a "dual teacher team" has been fostered that are good at theory of education and teaching practice.

There are complete and advanced internship facilities on campus with 56 national, provincial and university-level practice bases with a total value of over 27 million yuan of teaching and research equipment and facilities. At the moment it is conducting cooperation with more than 80 enterprises and has built over 80 internship bases off campus so as to provide internship platforms for students. As a result, the cooperation between the college and the enterprises have been further strengthened and deepened with ever-improving educational condition and quality.

六、民办教育

宁德市民办教育覆盖小学、中学等各层次。

4.1.6 Private Education

Private education in Ningde covers primary and secondary education levels.

(一)民办小学(不完全统计)

宁德实验小学
宁德侨兴小学
宁德兴旺小学
福鼎茂华学校小学部
福安市德艺学校小学部

4.1.6.1 Private Primary Schools(Incomplete)

Ningde Experimental Primary School
Ningde Qiaoxing Primary School
Ningde Xingwang Primary School
Maohua Primary School of Fuding City
Deyi Primary School of Fu'an City

(二)民办中学(不完全统计)

福鼎市金桥学校
福鼎茂华中学
霞浦福宁中学
宁德树德学校
福安市德艺学校中学部
福鼎太姥山中学
福安扆山中学
古田溪山中学
柘荣双城中学
宏翔高级中学
鹤峰中学

4.1.6.2 Private Middle Schools(Incomplete)

Jinqiao Middle School of Fuding City
Maohua Middle School of Fuding City
Funing Middle School of Xiapu County
Shude Middle School of Ningde City
Deyi Middle School of Fu'an City
Taimushan Middle School of Fuding City
Yishan Middle School of Fu'an City
Xishan Middle School of Gutian County

Shuangcheng Middle School of Zherong County
Hongxiang Senior Middle School of Xiapu County
Hefeng Middle School of Ningde City

（三）主要民办学校简介

宁德市实验学校

宁德市实验学校的前身是宁德市东侨实验学校，2003 年由宁德一中、宁德师范附小联合创办。2004 年经宁德市教育局批准变更为非公有制学校。2009 年，并入浙江红绿蓝教育集团，升级更名为“宁德市实验学校”，总投资一亿多元创办的一所集小学、初中、高中、精英部、国际部为一体的现代化学校，地处宁德市新城区兴宁路 8 号（新市政府后面）成为宁德市教育局直属民办学校。

福鼎市金桥学校

福鼎市金桥学校是一所民办普通完全中学，前身是福鼎求新中学和万春中学，学校位于福鼎市区凤架山上。2015 年 1 月，由市政府、市教育局决定与福鼎一中合作办学，由福鼎一中派出管理人员管理学校，派出教师任教。校园面积 130 亩，建筑面积 12 000多平方米。现有教学班 24 个，学生 1 200多人，教职工 106 人。其中高级职称 18 人，中级职称 29 人，学校自创办以来成绩显著，有 50 多名学生在全国、省市各种竞赛中获奖，历年高考本科上线率和中考综合比率均居市各中学前茅；2014 年艺术科高考，13 名考生中有 11 名上本科线。学校先后获得平安校园、文明学校、治安保卫先进单位等荣誉称号。

福安市德艺学校

福安市德艺学校创办于 2004 年，是一所富有活力、蓬勃发展的高起点、高标准、现代化的九年制民办寄宿学校。学校占地 60 余亩，现有 61 个教学班（中学 36 个，小学 25 个），在校学生 3 200多人，教职工 250 多人，其中专任教师 173 人。小学实施中英文双语特色教学，中学实施学教做互动高效课堂，有效提高了课堂效率，效果明显。曾获福建省民办教育先进单位、福建省标准化学校、宁德市文明学校等荣誉。

4.1.6.3 Profiles of Major Private Schools

Ningde Municipal Experimental School

Its predecessor was Dongqiao Experimental School of Ningde City. In 2003 it was jointly established by Ningde No. 1 Middle School and the Affiliated Primary School of Ningde Normal University. In 2004 after permission by Ningde Municipal Bureau of Education, it was changed to a private school. In 2009 it merged with the Red Green Blue Education Group of Zhejiang Province and was upgraded to Ningde Experimental School with a total investment of over 100 million yuan and became a modern school that covers primary, secondary, elite and international education. Its location is at No. 8, Xingning Road, New District of Ningde City (behind the Municipal Government Center). It is directly under administration of the Municipal Education Bureau over the private education.

Jinqiao Middle School of Fuding City

It is a private middle school located on Fengjia Mountain. Its predecessors were Qiuxin Middle School and Wanchun Middle School of Fuding County. In January 2015, Fuding Municipal Government and the Municipal Education Bureau of Fuding City decided that the school cooperate with No. 1 Middle School of Fuding City which sends over the administrators to manage the school and the teachers to help teach there. The school covers an area of 130 mu with a constructed area of 12 000 square meters. It has 24 classes, over 1 200 students, 106 staff members, of whom 18 are senior teachers, and 29 are intermediate teachers. Since its establishment, it has achieved remarkable results. More than 50 students won in national and provincial competitions. Its enrollment rate onto national universities and senior middle schools tops those of Fuding City. In the national arts exams of 2014,11 out of 13 participants were up to the national university score demand. The school has been awarded honorable titles one after another like "Safe Campus", "Civilization School" and "A Model School with Its Security".

Deyi Middle School of Fu'an

It was established in 2004. It is a nine-year private boarding school that is vigorous, modern, highly started and standard. It covers an area of 60 Mu with 61 specialized teachers. It has 61 classes (36 are middle school educational classes, and 25 are primary educational classes) with more than 3 200 students and more than 250 staff members, of whom 173 are specialized teachers. Bilingual education of Chinese and English has been conducted in its primary school education, and its middle school education applies high efficient classroom teaching interaction teaching method so that classroom teaching efficiency has been improved greatly with obvious results. The school has been awarded honors like "Advanced Model School of Private Education of Fujian Province", "Standardized School of Fujian Province" and "Civilization School of Ningde City", etc.

第二节 体 育

4.2 Sports

一、体育设施建设

为迎接2018年十六届省运会在宁德市市举办和改善广大居民参与体育健身的需求，宁德市各级政府尽了最大努力，采取政府、社会、企业多方筹集资金，规划新建大量体育场馆及设施。县级及以下各级政府各部门、企事业单位、体育协会和社会各界集资建设的健身馆(站、点)、健身俱乐部、健身公园、健身广场、健身苑、活动中心等各类健身产地6 000余个。从2000年开始，建设全民健身活动中心3个，配备各种健身器材的全民健身路径190多条，在1 987个行政村建设了农民体育健身工程点1 987个、乡镇农民体育健身活动中心22个、县级青少校外体育活动中心10个、乡镇青少年校外体育活动场所89个。登山健身步道9条，城市社区多功能场35个，拆装式游泳池6个。为社区配备全民健身路径222条、为10个社区卫生服务站配备了体质监测器材各一套。2015年，建设15条健身路径，全市在建以及改造场馆项目共计9个(市体育中心体育馆、蕉城区综合体育场馆、周宁县体育馆、寿宁县体育馆、福安市体育中心综合馆、柘荣县综合体育馆、福鼎市十六中体育馆、霞浦县游泳馆)。

4.2.1 The Construction of Sports Facilities

In order to welcome the coming 16th Games of Fujian to be held in Ningde and also to meet the needs of all the citizens to do sports, all level governments are sparing no efforts to plan and build many gyms and sports facilities by raising money from governments, society and enterprises. The number of all kinds of sports facilities built by those governments, departments, enterprises and sports association below county level such as fitness gyms, fitness clubs, fitness parks, fitness square, activity centers, etc. has reached over 6 000. Since 2000, three fitness centers for all the citizens have been constructed and over 190 fitness paths with facilities have been built. In 1 987 villages, 1 987 fitness spots, 22 fitness centers for folks in villages and towns also have been established. The local governments also built 10 off-campus sports centers at county level, 89 sports centers at village or town levels, 9 climbing trails, 35 multi-functional community grounds, 6 dismountable swimming pools, etc. 222 paths have been also provided for the communities and ten of them have been equipped with physical check devices each. There are more than 8 000 fitness spots all together. In 2015, 15 fitness paths were constructed. The whole city is seeing 9 gyms under renewal or construction. They are Municipal Sports Gym, Sports Complex of Jiaocheng District, Zhouning County Gym, Shouning County Gym, Fu'an County Gym, Fu'an Sports Complex, Sports Complex of Zherong County, Gym of No. 16 Middle School of Fuding City, and Xiapu Indoor Swimming Pool.

二、群众性体育运动

让群众享受到体育事业发展的成果、提高人民身体素质、促进社会事业健康发展也是体育工作的终极目标。在全市各个公园、广场、社区,休闲散步、健身锻炼的人群随处可见,他们有的打太极,有的做健身操,有的打羽毛球,尽情享受着运动带来的健康与快乐。截至 2013 年,市级体育协会 15 个,县级以下的老体协、农体协和单项体育协会(俱乐部)2 100多个,健身气功和谐站点 20 个,全市 90%的行政村建立了老体协组织;培养了社会体育指导员 2 822人,培训健身气功辅导员 564人,培训第九套广播体操学员 560 多人,初步形成了市、县(市、区)、乡(镇、街道)、村四级的全民健身服务体系。

经常参加体育健身的人数达到 110 多万人,占总人口数(7 至 70 岁)的 34%,每天晨晚练人数 5 万人以上,参加体育健身项目也从传统的篮球、武术、羽毛球、乒乓球、跑步、游泳、太极拳、棋类等十几项,发展到现代时尚的瑜伽、跆拳道、健美操、网球、轮滑、气排球、广场舞、马拉松等四十余项,还有登山、山水游等健身与休闲为一体的活动。2013 年全市开展各种全民健身活动赛事有 1 200余场次。

4.2.2 Public Participation in Sports

In order to let all the citizens enjoy the fruits of the sports facilities and improve their physical condition as well as foster the healthy development of sports, Ningde City has made sports facilities available everywhere such as parks and communities for folks to walk and exercise so one can see guys do Taiji, aerobics, play badminton and enjoy the happiness of sports here and there. As of 2013, there were 15 municipal sports associations, 2 100 seniors sports associations, farmers sports associations and single sport event clubs, and 20 fitness qigong centers with 90% of the administrative villages covered. 2 822 instructors of sports have been trained and 564 coaches of qigong and 560 demonstrators of the ninth broadcasting aerobics have been trained so that a four-tier fitness service mechanism has been established that involves all the folks at the municipal, district and sub district and village levels

The number of folks who often participate in sports reached more than 1.1 million accounting for 34% of the whole population ranging from 7 to 70 years old. The number of people who exercise in the morning or evening was more than 50 000. The participated events widened from the traditional events like basketball, martial arts, badminton, table tennis, jogging, swimming, Taiji and chess playing, etc. to modern fashionable exercises like yoga, taekwondo, aerobics, tennis, roller skating, balloon volleyball, square dance, marathon, etc., over 40 kinds, besides there are other leisure events like climbing and tourism. In 2013, more than 1 200 activities were held that involved all types of folks.

三、竞赛成绩

近几年,(2010 年—2015 年 9 月)宁德市各类竞技体育竞赛成绩优异,共夺得 42 次国际、亚洲和全国冠军。其中包括:

翁巧珊,2010 年在韩国仁川第 17 届亚运会帆船帆板女子 RS:1 级的比赛中获得金牌。

李雪艳,2010 年分别在德国世锦赛和广州亚运会上夺得 6 枚金牌,还破了世界纪录。

2011 年在国际大赛中,闽东籍运动员获得 1 项冠军;在全国级别的比赛中,获得 9 枚金牌;

2012 年在国际大赛中,闽东籍运动员获得 2 枚金牌、2 枚银牌和 2 枚铜牌;在全国级别的比赛中,获得 11 枚金牌、6 枚银牌、1 枚铜牌。

2013 年在全国级别的比赛中,闽东籍运动员获得 3 枚金牌。

2014 年在国际大赛中,闽东籍运动员获得 3 枚金牌、1 枚银牌。

2015 年首届全国青年运动会宁德籍选手摘得 2 金 1 银 1 铜。第九届全国残疾人运动会上,宁德市 7 名残疾人运动员代表福建省取得了 4 枚金牌、1 枚银牌、2 枚铜牌,并取得打破一项世界纪录的骄人成绩。

4.2.3 Medals and Awards

Recent years(2010-September, 2015) have witnessed Ningde City winning medals and awards in all kinds of sports competitions including 42 international, Asian and national championships:

Weng Qiaoshan, won a gold medal in RS:1 Sailing Competitions at the 17th Asian Games held in Inchon, South Korea;

Li Xueyan won 6 gold medals and broke the world records in the World Championships held in Germany and the Asian Games in Guangzhou in 2010;

In the international competitions in 2011, the athletes from Mindong won 1 champion, and 9 gold medals in the national competitions;

In the international competitions in 2012, the athletes from Mindong won 2 gold medals, 2 silver medals, and 2 bronze medals as well as 11 gold medals, 6 silver medals and 1 bronze medal in the national competitions.

In the national competitions in 2013, the athletes from Mindong won 3 gold medals.

In the international competitions in 2014, the athletes from Mindong won 3 gold medals, and 1 silver medal.

In the first National Youth Games in 2015, the athletes from Mindong won 2 gold medals, 1 silver medal, and 1 bronze medal. In the Ninth National Paralympics Games, 7 athletes from Mindong on behalf of Fujian won 4 gold medals, 1 silver medal, 2 bronze medals and broke 1 world record.

四、宁德市体育明星

宁德市涌现出一批国际级、亚洲级和国家级的优秀运动员。黄世平,刘清华、李雪艳、阙志城、周传成、周斌、林忠仔、高传伟、郑雪萍等明星享誉中外。

黄世平,古田县人。1983 年进入国家射击队训练。在五运会上首次参赛就获得了冠军,1984 年获得洛杉矶奥运会铜牌,1985 年获国际级运动健将称号,1988 年汉城奥运会银牌,1990 年北京亚运会获得三枚金牌,之后退役。

陈新华,福安县人,1972 年进省乒乓球队,1974 年入选国家乒乓球集训队。1981 年全国乒乓球锦标赛获男子单打冠军。先后 4 次参加世界乒乓球锦标赛,担任中国队的主力队员,并获第 39 届男子单打第 3 名。1985 年获第 6 届世界杯赛男子单打冠军。1985 年获国际级运动健将称号,1981 年和 1987 年 2 次获国家体委颁发的体育运动荣誉奖章。

李雪艳,蕉城区漳湾镇增坂村人,1984 年出生,1997 年进入市青少年体校学习射击,2010 年进入国家射击队,截至 2014 年,她已获得国际、亚洲和全国级比赛金牌 15 枚。

刘美滨,宁德市蕉城区人。1997 年就读于宁德市蕉城区特殊教育学校。2007 年入选特殊奥林匹克运动会中国国家队队员。近五年来,刘美滨在特奥运动生涯中共获得了 17 枚省、国家、世界级的特奥金牌。

阙志城，男，古田人。1997 年进入福建省队，2002 年 11 月进入国家蹦床队。1998 年获全国蹦床冠军赛男团亚军，2001 年获九运会男团个人第三，2002 年获全国蹦床冠军赛个人冠军，2004 年获全国蹦床锦标赛男团冠军，2006 年获蹦床世界杯俄罗斯站比赛个人第二名（亚军），全国蹦床冠军赛个人、团体双冠军，第十五届亚运会男子蹦床比赛项目金牌（亚运会历史上第一枚蹦床男子冠军），2009 年第十一届全运会蹦床男团冠军

4.2.4 Sports Stars from Ningde

Some excellent competitors from Ningde came to the fore at international, Asian and national games. The sports stars like Huang Shiping, Liu Qinghua, Li Xueyan, Que Zhicheng, Zhou Chuancheng, Zhou Bin, Lin Zhongzai, Gao Chuanwei, Zheng Xueping, etc. are well-known at home and abroad.

Huang Shiping, a native from Gutian, Ningde, joined the national shooting team for training in 1983. In the fifth National Games, he first time participated in the Games and won the championship. In 1984 he won the bronze medal in the Olympic Games in Los Angeles. In 1985 he was awarded the title of "International Master Competitor of Sports". In 1988 he won a silver medal at the Seoul Olympic Games. In 1990 he won three gold medals at the Asian Games in Beijing and after that he retired.

Chen Xinhua, a native of Fu'an, joined the provincial table tennis team in 1972 and in 1974 was selected into the national team for training. In 1981 he won the champion at the national men's single competitions of table tennis. He participated in the world table tennis championships for four times and played as a major member of the Chinese team and won the third place of the Men's Single in the 39th World Table Tennis Championships. In 1985 he won the gold medal of the men's single at the world table tennis championships. In 1985 he was awarded the title of "International Master Competitor of Sports". In 1981 and 1987 he was awarded honorable medals of sports twice by the National Sports Committee.

Li Xueyan, a native of Zengban Village of Zhangwan Township of Jiaocheng District, was born in 1984 and in 1997 joined the Municipal Youth Sports School to learn shooting. In 2010 she joined the National Shooting Team. So far she has won 15 gold medals in international, Asian and national competitions.

Liu Meibin, a native of Jiaocheng District, was enrolled by the Jiaocheng Special Educational School of Ningde City in 1997. In 2007 she was selected by the National Team of Paralympics. In recent five years, she won 17 provincial, national and international gold medals of Paralympics games.

Que Zhicheng, male, a native of Gutian County, joined the Fujian Provincial Trampoline Team in 1997. In November 2002, he joined the National Trampoline Team. In 1998 he won the silver medal of the men's team trampoline events at the National Trampoline Championships. In 2001 he won the third place in the men's team trampoline in the Ninth National Games. In 2002 he won the gold medal at the National Individual Trampoline Championships. In 2004 he won the gold medal at the National Team Trampoline Championships. In 2006 he won the second place at the World Trampoline Championships in Russia. He was also champions at the National Team and Individual Trampoline Championships as well as a gold medalist at the Men's Trampoline Competitions of the 15th Asian Games and became the first male champion in the history of the Asian Games. In 2009 he became the champion at the Men's Team Trampoline Competitions of the 11th National Games.

第三节 医疗卫生

4.3 Health and Medical Care

一、建设成就

中华人民共和国成立初期，各县人民政府相继接管原民国政府县立卫生院。1950 年，全区各县立卫生院有卫生医疗人员 375 人，其中卫生技术人员 227 人，病床 38 张。如今(2014 年末)共有各类卫生机构 570 个(不含计生服务站及村卫生室)，其中医院 39 个，卫生院 106 个。卫生技术人员 14 247人，执业医师和执业助理医师4 614人，注册护士6 166人。有卫生机构床位12 696张。如今“海云工程”项目三期新增项目覆盖点 256 个，覆盖全市所有基层医疗卫生机构和行政村(人口在 800 人左右)的村卫生所，累计布点 894 个。项目所涉及村卫生所形成并有效管理电子健康档案 78.84 万份，累计为 8.46 万人进行了 28.36 万次各类医学检查。

2015 年还将投入1 093.42万元进一步实施“海云工程”项目四期推广，将通过项目点连接实现农村人口覆盖达 70%以上，通过乡医联办、乡镇卫生院业务延伸等方式，实现服务农村人口达 90%以上。“海云工程”是近几年宁德市农村卫生工作的重点，也是宁德市在全省乃至全国打造惠民工程的一个品牌。项目实施四年多来，为实现“小病不出村、大病及时转”的目标奠定了良好基础，受到社会各界广泛关注及各大新闻媒体重磅推荐，体现了党委政府对广大农民身体健康的责任担当。

4.3.1 Major Achievements

At the beginning of the founding of the People's Republic of China, the governments of different counties in Ningde one after another took over administration of the county hospitals of the Republic of China. In 1950, there were only 375 medical staff in all the hospitals in Mindong, of whom 227 were health specialists and there were only 38 wards. At the end of 2014, there were 570 health agencies of various kinds(not including the family planning stations or village clinics), of which 39 were hospitals and 106 were clinics. There were 14 247 health specialists, 4 614 executive doctors and assistant executive doctors and 6 166 registered nurses. There were 12 696 wards of health care institutions. Now Haiyun Medical Project(the Third Phase)newly increased 256 clinic spots covering all the medical organs and village clinics(with a population of about 800 persons). It was calculated that 894 spots had been set up. The targeted health clinics covered in this project effectively created and managed 788 400 digital heath files and provided 283 600 physical checks for 84 600 persons according to census. In 2015, 10.9342 million yuan was invested in the fourth phase to expand the Haiyun Medical Project so as to cover over 70% of the villages in the rural areas from one place to another. Village doctors were connected and village clinical service scope were extended so that over 90% of the rural population will be covered. “Haiyun Medical Project” is a highlight in the rural medical work in Ningde in recent years. It is also a favorable medical brand that Ningde Government is building around the province or nation. For 4 years since its implementation, a solid foundation has been laid for the goal that “patients with small diseases do not need to leave the rural areas for treatment while the patients with big disease are in time transferred to large hospitals”. The Project has received wide attention and highlighting publicity of the media, which indicates the responsibility shouldering of the Party Committees and the governments.

二、主要医疗机构

宁德市医院——福建宁德市蕉城北路 7 号

宁德市人民医院——宁德市蕉城北路 24 号

宁德市妇幼保健院——宁德市八一五中路

福州总医院第二附属医院——宁德市蕉城区蕉城南路 96 号

宁德市精神病院——宁德市蕉城北路大桥下 3 号

宁德市中医院——宁德市东湖路 16 号

宁德东韩整形医院——宁德市塔山路九龙商场(驿景大酒店旁)

福安市医院——福安市赛岐王厝

宁德市闽东医院——福安市城关区鹤山街 89 号

福安市中医院——福安市解放路 3 号

福安市妇幼保健院——福安市东风街 55 号

福安市民族医院——福安市石马街 97 号

福鼎市医院——福鼎市古城南路 93 号

福鼎市海军医院——福鼎市中山中路 164 号

福鼎市妇幼保健所——福鼎市前店 2 号

福鼎市中医院——福建省福鼎市富民路 22 号

寿宁县中医院——寿宁县胜利街 93 号

寿宁县医院——寿宁县鳌阳村

寿宁县妇幼保健所——寿宁县鳌阳镇解放街 195 号

霞浦县医院——霞浦县城西路 1 号

霞浦县妇幼保健院——霞浦县府前路 348 号

霞浦县中医院——霞浦县县西街 25 号

柘荣县中医院——柘荣县柳城南路 3 号

柘荣县医院——柘荣县上桥路 8 号

屏南县中医院——屏南县城南路

屏南县妇幼保健院——屏南县古峰镇文化路 27 号

屏南县医院——屏南县古峰镇文化路 4 号

古田县医院——古田县民主路 17 号

古田县中医院——古田县 614 路 3 号

古田县皮肤病防治院——福建省宁德市古田县 614 路 256 号

周宁县妇幼保健院——周宁县城关中华路 71 号

周宁县医院——周宁县城关东街 96 号

周宁县中医院——周宁县城关东市路 15 号

4.3.2 Major Hospitals in Ningde and Their Addresses

Ningde Municipal Hospital——7 Jiaocheng Bei Road, Ningde City

Ningde Municipal People's Hospital——24 Jiaocheng Bei Road, Ningde City

Ningde Municipal Maternity and Children Hospital——815 Mid Road of Jiaocheng District of Ningde City

No 2 Affiliated Hospital of Fuzhou General Hospital——96 Jiaocheng Nan Road of Jiaocheng District

Ningde Municipal Psychiatric Hospital——3 Bei Road of Jiaocheng District of Ningde City

Ningde Municipal Traditional Chinese Medicine Hospital——16 Donghu Road, Jiaocheng District of Ningde City

Ningde Donghan Plastic Hospital——at Jialong Mall on Tasha Road(by Yijing Hotel)

Fu'an Municipal Hospital——at Wangcuo, Saiqi Township of Fu'an City

Mindong Hospital of Ningde City——89 Heshan Street, Chengguan District of Fu'an City

Fu'an Traditional Chinese Medicine Hospital——3 Jiefang Road of Fu'an City

Fu'an Maternity and Children Hospital——55 Dongfeng Street of Fu'an City

Fu'an Ethnic Hospital——97 Shima Street of Fu'an City

Fuding Municipal Hospital——93 Gucheng Nan Road of Fuding City

Fuding Naval Hospital——164 Zhongshan Central Road of Fuding City

Fuding Women and Children Hospital——2 Qiandian of Fuding City

Fuding Traditional Chinese Medicine Hospital——22 Fuming Road of Fuding City

Shouning Traditional Chinese Medicine Hospital——93 Shengli Street of Shouning County

Shouning County Hospital——Aoyang Town of Shouning County

Shouning Maternity and Children Hospital——195 Jiefang Street of Aoyang Town, Shouning County

Xiapu County Hospital——1 Chengxi Road of Xiapu County

Xiapu Maternity and Children Hospital——348 Fuqian Road,Xiapu County

Xiapu County Traditional Chinese Medicine Hospital——25 Xianxi Street of Xiapu County

Zherong Traditional Chinese Medicine Hospital——3 Liucheng Nan Road of

Zherong County

Zherong County Hospital——8 Shangqiao Road of Zherong County

Pingnan Traditional Chinese Medicine Hospital——Chengnan Road of Pingnan County

Pingnan Maternity and Children Hospital——27 Wenhua Road, Gufeng Town, Pingnan County

Pingnan County Hospital——4 Wenhua Road, Gufeng Town, Pingnan County

Gutian County Hospital——17 Minzhu Road, Gutian County

Gutian Traditional Chinese Medicine Hospital——3,614 Road of Gutian County

Gutian County Dermatosis Prevention Hospital——256, 614 Road, Gutian County

Zhouning Maternity and Children Hospital——71 Zhonghua Road, Zhouning County

Zhouning County Hospital——96 Dongjie Street of Zhouning County

Zhouning Traditional Chinese Medicine Hospital——15 Dongshi Road of Zhouning County

三、主要医院简介

宁德市闽东医院

宁德市闽东医院(原名福建省宁德地区第一医院)位于福安市,隶属宁德市卫生局,建于1937年10月,是一所三级甲等综合性医院,是卫生部国际紧急救援中心网络医院、福建省交通事故救治定点医院、福建省高等医学院校临床教学基地、福建省全科医学临床培训基地。医疗范围辐射闽东及浙南地区。医院占地面积5.5万平方米,建筑面积约10.8万平方米,现有编制床位1 000张,员工约1 500多人。拥有高级专业技术人员一百多人,其中包括享受国务院政府特殊津贴专家、硕士研究生导师、兼职教授、副教授等,组成了专业技术群体。现有19个行政职能科室,24个临床一级科室,37个二级专业组和11个医技科室,其中骨外科、泌尿外科、神经内科、妇科、麻醉科、肾病学专业为重点专科。医院医疗设备先进,总值约1.5亿元。

宁德市医院

宁德市医院(福建医科大学附属宁德市医院)创建于1972年,现已发展成为一所集医疗、教学科研、预防保健及康复为一体的三级甲等综合医院。医院蕉城院和东侨新院总建筑面积32.9万平方米,医院现有编制床位1 000张,实际开放1 030张,设25个病区,29个临床专科,28个医技、药剂、功能检查科室,16个行政职能科室。心血管内科、呼吸内科、肾内科、眼科、产科 5 个重点专科。2013 年医院年门急诊病人 98 万人次，年出院病人 5.1 万多人次。现有员工 1 800多人，卫技人员中高级职称 126 人，博士 8 人，硕士 107 人；享受国务院政府津贴专家 3 人，全国名老中医药专家 1 人；教授 25 人，入选福建省"百千万人才工程"2 人。医院高端医疗设备更是日新月异，大型设备基本配备完毕并处于全市领先地位，医疗设备总值达 3.8 亿元。

4.3.3 Profiles of Major Hospitals

Mindong Hospital of Ningde City

It is located in Fu'an City (its former name was No. 1 Hospital of Ningde Prefecture), under administration of Ningde Municipal Health Bureau. It was established in October 1937 and is a 3A (highest level) comprehensive hospital as well as a joint hospital with the international aid center of the National Ministry of Health. It is also the designated hospital of the first aids for the traffic accidents in Fujian Province, as well as a clinical teaching base for medical higher learning institutions and a clinical training base covering all medical sectors in Fujian province. Its service area covers Mindong and the south region of Zhejiang Province. It covers an area of 55 000 square meters with a constructed area of 108 000 square meters. It has 1 000 sickbeds, about 1 500 staff members and over 100 senior medical specialists, of whom there are experts who enjoy the allowances of the State Council, postgraduate mentors, part-time professors, associate professors and so on.

Now there are 19 administrative departments, 24 Class-Ⅰ clinical departments, 37 Class-Ⅱ professional groups and 11 medical rooms, of which departments of orthopedics, urology, neurology, gynecology, anesthesia, nephrology are the key sectors. The hospital is equipped with advanced medical facilities worth about 150 million yuan.

Ningde Municipal Hospital

It is an affiliated hospital of Fujian Medical University and was established in 1972. Now it has become a 3A comprehensive hospital integrating medication, teaching and research, prevention, health care and rehabilitation and so on. It consists of two parts. One is in Jiaocheng District and the other in Dongqiao District. Its total constructed area is 329 000 square meters with 1 000 sickbeds(actually 1 030 sickbeds in service). It has 25 outpatients divisions, 29 clinical specialties, 28 medical tech divisions, pharmacies, and functional check departments, and 16 administrative departments as well. Its departments of cardiovascular medicine, respiratory medicine, nephrology, ophthalmology, obstetrics are the 5 key specialties. In 2013 it offered emergency treatment to 980 000 patients and over 51 000 patients are discharged. It has a staff member of over 1 800, among whom are 126 senior medical experts, 8 PhD degree holders, 107 masters, 3 experts enjoying the allowance by the State Council, 1 nationally well-know traditional Chinese medicine expert, 25 professors, 2 members of the "100/1000/1000 Talent Project of Fujian Province", etc. Its sophisticated and advanced medical facilities are improving daily and its large equipment has been set up completely, leading in the city with an total value of 380 million yuan.

宁德市中医院

宁德市中医院创建于 1978 年，是一所集教学、科研、预防、保健、急救为一体，具有中医特色并与现代医学技术相结合的二级甲等综合性中医院。地处宁德东侨经济开发区，占地面积 2.41 万平方米，建筑面积 1.05 万平方米。医院共有职工 214 人，卫生技术人员 191 人，其中高级职称 26 人，中级职称 85 人。医院科室配套齐全，设有三个门诊部，住院床位 200 张，设有 20 多个临床科室，并确定骨伤科、针灸推拿、结石科、肛肠科、脾胃科为重点专科，并开设 19 个独具中医特色的专科专病门诊。医院医技辅助科室齐全，有功能检查科、放射科、检验科等 20 多个。

福州总医院第二附属医院

福州总医院第二附属医院位于宁德市蕉城区，是闽东地区唯一一所驻军医院。该院成立于 1979 年，是一所集医疗、预防、保健、康复为一体的现代化二级甲等综合性医院。拥有总值达 2 000万余元的高、新、尖医疗设备，开放床位 300 余张，手术室 4 间。

该院有博士后 1 名，博士 3 名，硕士 7 名，是宁德市区唯一拥有医学博士后和博士的医院。医院开设有 14 个临床科室，10 个医技科室。依托南京军区福州总院长期派驻我院的专家和我院原有的高级人才形成了消化内科、普外科、骨科、泌尿外科、手足外科、妇产科等特色专科。医院转隶至南京军区福州总医院后，依托其完善的医疗设备和雄厚的技术实力，实现了医疗资源更大范围的共享，建立了疑难病例会诊绿色通道。

宁德市康复医院

宁德市康复医院（前身为宁德地区第三医院）是一所精神病防治、教学与科研为一体的专科医院，目前按"二级甲等医院"规范实施管理。诊疗范围主要包括精神科、心理科、老年护理科、中西医内科。2005 年 10 月，经省卫生厅批准，"宁德市精神卫生中心"在医院挂牌成立，确立了闽东精神卫生的主导地位。医院占地面积

32 亩，建筑面积7 500平方米，3 000平方米的新病房大楼，专科设备齐全，是目前省内同类专科医院中设计较先进、设施较完善的精神病专科病房。

医院内设一个女病区、两个男病区，还有一个老年康复病区，提供24小时保姆式服务。室外开辟有一个近800平方米的病人活动场，为患者提供新、绿、亮、洁的就医环境。全院现有工作人员142人，卫生技术人员100人，其中高级职称6人，中级职称28人。年门诊量4.8万人次，开放床位180张，年住院床数5万张。目前，医院诊疗范围已从单纯的精神病防治发展到了包括精神、心理、康复中西医内科在内的多学科综合诊治，精神科也从过去单一的重症精神疾病治疗发展到了对心理、精神障碍的研究与防治。

Ningde Municipal Traditional Chinese Medicine Hospital

Established in 1978, it is a 2A comprehensive TCM hospital that integrates teaching, research, prevention, health care, first aid and combines TCM features with modern medical technology. It is located in Dongqiao Economic Development Zone and covers an area of 24 100 square meters with a constructed area of 10 500 square meters. It has 214 staff members, of whom there are 191 medical professionals, 26 senior experts, 85 intermediate experts. The hospital is rather complete with its different departments. There are three clinical departments, 200 sickbeds, over 20 clinic divisions, etc. with departments of orthopedics and traumatology, acupuncture and massage, calculi, anorectum, spleen and stomach as key specialties. It also sets up 19 outpatients clinics with unique characteristics of traditional Chinese medicine. Its medical tech departments are quite complete with more than 20 departments of functional checks, radiology, clinical laboratory and others.

No. 2 Affiliated Hospital to Fuzhou General Hospital

Located in Jiaocheng District and established in 1979, it is the only military hospital in Mindong area. It is a modern and comprehensive 2A hospital that integrates medication, prevention, health care, and rehabilitation. It has some advanced, new and sophisticated facilities with worth over 20 million yuan as well as 300 sickbeds and 4 operation rooms. It has 1 post-doctorate, 3 PhDs, 10 masters, and is the only hospital that has post doctorate and doctorate staff in Ningde City. It runs 14 clinical divisions and 10 medical tech sections. Relying on the constant support of experts from Fuzhou General Hospital of Nanjing Military Region and its own senior staff, the specialties of gastroenterology, general surgery, orthopedics, urology, hand and foot surgery, obstetrics and gynecology have been formed. After the hospital was put under administration of Fuzhou General Hospital of Nanjing

Military Region, it has been realized that both medial resources have been shared wider and fast and efficient channels for consultations of difficult cases have been set up by relying on the complete medical equipment and strong technical strength of the military hospital.

Ningde Rehabilitation Hospital

Ningde Rehabilitation Hospital (formerly known as No. 3 Hospital of Ningde Prefecture) is a specialized hospital that integrates psychiatric prevention, treatment, teaching and scientific research. Now it is managed according to the "2A Hospital Standard". The scopes of its diagnosis and treatment mainly include psychiatric, psychological, geriatric care, internal medicines of the traditional Chinese medicine and the western medicine. In October 2005, approved by the Provincial Health Department, Ningde Municipal Mental Health Center was formally established in the hospital, which establishes the dominant status of the center in Mindong; the hospital covers an area of 32 mu with a constructed area of 7 500 square meters. It is complete with specialty equipment. The 3 000-square-meter new ward building is comparatively advanced and complete one for psychiatrics patients among its counterparts in other hospitals of Fujian.

Inside the hospital there is one ward for women patients and two wards for men patient. In addition, a senior rehabilitation ward provides 24-hour nursing service. Besides there is a 800-square-meter outdoor playground for them to be treated in a new, green, bright and clean open environment. The hospital has 142 staff members and 100 are medical specialists, of whom there are 6 doctors with senior professional academic titles, and 28 doctors with intermediate professional academic titles. The annual visits of the outpatients are 48 000. The hospital has 180 sickbeds and its annual inpatients reach 50 000 persons. At present, the hospital has expanded its treatment scope from the single curing and prevention service for psychiatrics patients to the integrated medical treatment with mental, psychological and rehabilitation methods. Its Psychiatrics Department also has widened its single treatment of the severe psychiatric patients to the research and prevention of the psychological and mental barriers.

第五章 文化特色

Chapter 5 Culture in Ningde

第一节 宁德特色文化

5.1 Distinctive Ningde Culture

一、宁德文化历史

宁德历史悠久，人杰地灵，文化源远流长，积淀深厚，拥有全国重点文物保护单位8处18个点，省级文物保护单位64处。既有霞浦黄瓜山遗址(距今3 500年历史)、福鼎南广古窑址、马栏山遗址、霞浦大京等古城堡，蕉城中兴紫国师塔、福安倪下石塔、兴云寺舍得塔、古田吉祥寺塔等名胜古迹，又是著名的革命老苏区、福安柏柱洋闽东苏维埃政府驻地，全国著名的畲族人口聚居区，畲族风情丰富多彩。还拥有木拱桥营造技艺，漳湾水密隔舱福船建造技艺，柘荣剪纸等3项世界级非物质文化遗产；国家级非物质文化遗产14项；蕉城霍童、古田杉洋、屏南双溪等3个国家级历史文化名镇；福安廉村，屏南漈下、漈头，福鼎仙蒲，周宁浦源，霞浦半月里等6个国家级历史文化名村等。其中，最具有代表性的是畲族文化、民间信俗文化、木拱桥文化、海洋文化、茶文化、红色文化、传统技艺文化等，形成了习近平总书记誉为的闽东之光。

宁德话，属于福州方言，或称之闽东方言。闽东方言可分为两个片区，南片区包括今天的福州市和宁德市的古田、屏南两县；北片区包括蕉城区、福安、周宁、柘荣、寿宁、福鼎、霞浦等7市(县)。整个闽东方言以福州话为代表，而北片区当以福安话为代表。福州话在南片区可自由交际，北片区各市(县)人也能基本听懂福州话。福安话在北片区的周宁、寿宁、柘荣等县可自由交际，霞浦、福鼎人也能基本听懂福安话。

5.1.1 Cultural History of Ningde

Ningde not only has a very long history with abundant resources and many talents, but also possesses deep cultural significance. Ningde boasts many historical sites: eighteen scenic spots scattered over eight major national historical and cultural sites and sixty-four provincial historical and cultural sites, including ancient forts like Cucumber Mountain historical site in Xiapu county(with 3 500 years of history), Nanguang Ancient Kilns in Fuding City, Malanshan Relics, Dajing Fort of Xiapu County, Zhongxingzi Pagoda in Jiaocheng District, Nixia Stone Pagoda in Fu'an city, Shede Pagoda in Xingyun Temple and Pagoda of Jixiang Temple in Gutian County. In addition, Ningde is also known as the Soviet-style revolutionary base in Mindong. The former Soviet-style Government is located in Bai Zhuyang, Fu'an City. As a famous populated area of the She ethnic people, Ningde enjoys rich and colorful She customs. What's more, Ningde owns three international intangible cultural heritages: carpenter techniques of covered wooden arch bridges, ship building skills of water-tight bulkhead in Zhangwan Port and Zherong paper-cutting; fourteen national intangible cultural heritages; three state-level historical famous towns: Huotong Town in Jiaocheng District, Shanyang Town in Gutian County, Shuangxi Town in Pingnan County; and six state-level historical famous villages: Jixia Village and Jitou Village in Pingnan County, Xianpu Village in Fuding City, Puyuan Village in Zhouning County, Banyueli Village in Xiapu county. Distinctive cultures such as the She ethnic culture, the culture of customs, beliefs and worships, the covered wooden arch bridges culture, the maritime culture, the tea culture, the red culture, traditional skills culture and so on helped form Ningde Culture which was described by Chinese president Xi Jinping as "the Glories of Mindong(East Fujian)".

Ningde dialect belongs to Fuzhou dialect, or "Mindong dialect", which can be divided into two main regions: the southern and the northern regions. The southern part covers current Fuzhou City, Gutian and Pingnan County in Ningde City; the northern part covers other seven cities or counties in Ningde: Jiaocheng District, Fu'an City, Zhouning County, Zherong County, Shouning County, Fuding City and Xiapu County. Generally speaking, Mindong dialect is represented by Fuzhou dialect, which can be used to communicate in the southern region without difficulty, and people from the northern region can basically understand it; while the northern region is represented by Fu'an dialect, which is the common language in Zhouning, Shouning and Zherong Counties, and people from Jiaocheng District, Xiapu County and Fuding City can basically understand it.

二、宁德市十大名片

宁德市十大名片分别是环三都澳、闽东北亲水游(含太姥山、白水洋、周宁鲤鱼溪)、中国电机电器城(福安)、中国食用菌之都(古田)、中国太子参之乡(柘荣)、中国大黄鱼之乡(蕉城)、畲族(宁德是全国最大的畲族聚居地)、"临水夫人"陈靖姑、木拱廊桥、宁德茗茶(含福安坦洋工夫茶、福鼎大白茶、宁德绿茶)。当选名片涵盖了宁德市政治、经济、历史、文化生活的各个领域。

5.1.2 Ten Highlights of Ningde

There are ten highlights in Ningde: Circum-Sandu Bay Region, Waterside Tour in the Northeast Fujian (including Mount Taimu, Baishuiyang River Square and the Carp Brook), China's Motor Electric City (Fu'an), Capital of Edible Fungi (Gutian County), producing area of Taizi Ginseng (Zherong County), Hometown of Large Yellow Croaker (Jiaocheng District), the She ethnic group (the largest residential area for the She ethnic group in China), Lady Linshui (Goddess Chen Jinggu), the Covered Wooden Arch Bridge, Ningde Teas (including Fu'an Tanyang Kungfu Black Tea, Fuding White Tea and Ningde Green Tea). These ten highlights cover various sectors of politics, economy, history and culture in Ningde City.

(一)畲族文化

畲族语言

畲族自称山哈,意为居住在山里的客人,有自己的语言,没有本民族的文字,通用汉字。他们也有借用汉字而赋予新的意义,或者干脆利用汉字部首创造新字。

畲族人与汉族交往时,说当地汉语方言或汉语普通话,畲族内部交际时,说本族内部通行的畲语。一种是居住在广东省博罗、增城、惠东海共1 200多人,自称"活聂"(山人)的畲族人使用的畲族语言,另一种是分布福建、浙江、江西、安徽等省以及广东省凤凰山区的潮州、丰顺等地,占全国畲族总人口的99%以上的畲族人使用,叫作"山哈话"。闽东畲族内部交际时就是使用这种语言,境内畲语当以福安畲语为代表,受当地汉语方言影响较小,保留的古成分也较多。目前除古田、屏南县多数畲民已不讲畲语外,其他县(市、区)畲族内部交际时都使用本族通行的畲语。

5.1.2.1 Culture of the She Ethnic Minority

Language

The She ethnic people call themselves as “Shanha”, which suggests guests living in mountains. They have their own language but no written language, so their current commonly-used written language is Chinese. Sometimes they render new meanings to the characters of Chinese, or even create new characters with Chinese character radicals.

Local Chinese dialect or mandarin are the common language for She people to socialize with the Han people, while the She language is the common language among their own minority group. There are two main She languages nowadays, one of them is in common use by more than 1 200 She people, who call themselves Huonie(mountain people). They reside in Boluo, Zengcheng and Huidonhai in Guangdong Province; The other is called Shanha dialect, which is in common use by more than 99% of She people in China from Fujian, Zhejiang, Jiangxi, Anhui Provinces and Chaozhou, Fengshun in Phoenix Mountain area of Guangdong Province. Represented by Fu'an She dialect, Shanha dialect is also the common language used by the Mindong She ethnic people. It preserved a lot of elements from the ancient language, and was barely affected by local Chinese dialect. At present, lots of She people still use their language for communication within their groups, except for some She people from Gutian and Pingnan Counties.

畲族民俗风情

每年农历二月二、三月三、封龙节、端午节、七月七、中秋节、重阳节等,都是畲族的传统节日。这些日子里青年男女对歌盘歌,篝火狂欢通宵达旦,气氛极为热烈壮观。

畲族婚礼是畲族人民又一独特的民族风俗,畲族青年男女通过对歌认识后,男方托媒说亲,经媒人撮合,女方(畲族称少娘)就要出嫁了。畲族少娘出嫁不管愿意与否,在梳妆前都要以歌当哭,两天两夜的哭嫁后举行多种仪式进轿,抬入男家。拜堂中的男跪女不跪更显畲族婚礼之独特,闹新房时男女盘歌,文明而不失诙谐,热烈又不失高雅,如一场引人入胜的赛歌会。

畲族的宗教信仰主要是祖先崇拜。祖图,又称盘瓠图,是畲族信仰的主要标志之一。畲族把有关始祖盘瓠的传说画在布上,制成约 40 幅连环画式的图像,代代相传,称为祖图。

畲族女子有其独特的装束打扮,称为凤凰装。凤凰装在头饰发型及服装上都随着年龄的变化而变化，可分为小凤凰装、大凤凰装、老凤凰装等。

畲家人崇尚银饰，畲族妇女的首饰有银项圈、银链、银手镯等。畲族姑娘出嫁时佩戴传统银凤冠头饰，以示吉祥如意，也显示畲族崇凤敬女的特有习俗。

Folk Customs

The She people celebrate many traditional holidays, such as the second day of the second lunar month, the third day of the third lunar month, Lantern Festival, Dragon-boat festival, the seventh day of the seventh lunar month, Mid-Autumn Festival, Double-Ninth Festival and others. Young people would sing duets or in antiphonal style around the bonfire all night, the atmosphere is extremely spectacular!

Weddings are also very special for the She people. Usually young people get familiar with each other through duets. When a young man falls in love with a girl, he would send a matchmaker to the girl's home. After the engagement is settled, the girl (called "Shao Niang" in the She custom) is ready to get married. Whether willing to or not, the young bride must cry in singing before dressing and makeup (to show unwillingness to leave). Such crying marriage rituals will last two days before the bride is carried to the groom's house by sedan chair. There is also a very unique custom with the She wedding: When performing the wedding ceremony, the groom kneels down while the bride stands. In particular, people would sing on the wedding night, making it a civilized, joyful, fervent and elegant folk singing competition.

The She Nationality believes in the power of ancestors. The legend of their original ancestor, Panhu is painted on a piece of cloth in about 40 picture strips, and passed onto each generation. The cloth is referred to as Zutu (Painted Picture of the Ancestor). Zutu or Pictures of Panhu are the main signature for the She people's religious belief.

The She women like to wear their particular dressing—the Phoenix Set, which usually changes in headdress, hair style and clothes according to different ages. This set can be divided into small Phoenix set, large Phoenix set and old Phoenix set and so on.

The She people adore silver ornaments, especially for women. They own silver necklaces, bracelets and others. On her wedding day, a She bride will wear a phoenix coronet held in place by silver hairpins, which not only indicates auspiciousness and happiness, but also the exclusive custom of "Phoenix worship and respect for women".

（二）陈靖姑信俗文化

据史载，陈靖姑为唐代大历年间人，24岁时毅然施法祈雨抗旱，为民除害而献身于古田，后被广大百姓尊崇为救产、护胎、佑民的女神，又有临水夫人、顺天圣母等封号。广大信众为纪念这一女神而建立的临水宫距今也有1 200多年历史，成为海内外奉祀陈靖姑的祖庙。现在，其信众遍布华人地区，各地分灵宫庙4 000多座，信众有8 000多万人，其中台湾分庙300多座，信众达2 000多万人。2008年被列入国家非物质文化遗产保护名录的陈靖姑信俗是海峡两岸共同的民俗文化，闽台两地陈靖姑文化交流持续不断，每年都有近万名台胞在内的数十万海内外信众通过各种方式回到祖庙进香朝拜，陈靖姑文化已成为连接两岸亲情的特殊纽带。古田临水宫，2009年被列为国家涉台文物重点宫庙，2013年被列为全国重点文物保护单位。

5.1.2.2 Belief in Chen Jinggu

It is recorded that Chen Jinggu was born in the Dali period of the Tang Dynasty. When she was 24 years old, she performed rituals to pray for rain, and finally sacrificed her own life to fight against demons. She is widely regarded as the protection goddess of " childbirth, fetus and people", also known as "Lady Linshui", "The Holy Mother". Believers set up a Linshui Temple to memorize this goddess. With more than 1 200 years of history, Linshui Temple has been worshiped as the ancestral temple for Goddess Chen Jinggu. Nowadays there are more than 4 000 temples, and more than 80 million believers, scattering over Chinese-speaking communities. In particular, Taiwan boasts more than 20 million believers, with more than 300 temples. In 2008, the custom of "Belief in Goddess Chen Jinggu" was listed as a national intangible cultural heritage. As a common folk culture for both sides of the Taiwan Strait, it has brought incessant cultural communication between Fujian and Taiwan. Every year tens of thousands of believers at home and abroad come back to the ancestral temple to worship through various ways, even including tens of thousands of Taiwan compatriots. The custom of "Belief in Goddess Chen Jinggu" has become a very special bond that tightly connects kinship between both sides of the Taiwan Strait. Linshui Temple of Gutian County was listed as a national Taiwan-related key temple in 2009, and a major national historical and cultural site for protection in 2013.

（三）闽东红色文化

闽东苏维埃政府所在地——柏柱洋

柏柱洋位于福安溪柄东南。1926 年冬，施霖和张少廉、张宝田从福州返回柏柱洋，发动家乡一带的农民组织农会，柏柱洋及远近村庄的农民纷纷响应，闽东最早的农民革命运动从此蓬勃发展。1931 年 4 月，邓子恢和马立峰一道领导溪柄和柏柱洋一带群众的抗租抗债斗争，掀起了闽东农民革命运动的新高潮。随后，陶铸、叶飞、曾志等同志，进一步领导闽东地区的革命斗争。1933 年 12 月闽东红带总队在柏柱洋狮峰寺正式成立，人数最多达十万之众。

1934 年初，闽东苏区创建于席卷闽东大地的工农武装暴动的硝烟中。柏柱洋成为暴动的指挥中心，并创建了在我国南方颇有影响的闽东苏区，发展成为中央红军长征前全国八大革命根据地之一。9 月，中国工农红军闽东独立师成立，全师有 1 600余人，并与畲族、汉族人民相结合，经过艰苦斗争，把闽东各县的小块根据地连成一片，形成了以福安、连江为中心，面积 1 万余平方千米，拥有近 100 万人口的农村革命根据地。1934 年 10 月，国民党调集重兵，对闽东苏区进行分进合围，实施五光政策，还派飞机轰炸柏柱洋，妄图一举扼杀红色政权。闽东临时特委和苏维埃政府带领人民群众开展惨烈的保卫苏区战斗。在敌我力量过于悬殊的情况下，闽东苏区首府柏柱洋终告失守。此后，闽东特委领导人民转入艰苦卓绝的三年游击战争。

5.1.2.3 Mindong Red Culture

Bai Zhuyang Village—Former Location of Mindong Soviet-Style Government

Bai Zhuyang is located in Southeast Xibing, Fu'an County. In the winter of 1926, in order to organize local villagers to participate in the peasant association, Shi Lin, Zhang Shaolian and Zhang Baotian returned from Fuzhou to Bai Zhuyang. They received a warm response from local villagers, and the earliest peasant revolution in Mindong began to make a glorious development. Deng Zihui and Ma Lifeng led local people from Xibing and Bai Zhuyang to participate in resistance movement against rent and debt, which set off a new upsurge of Mindong peasant revolution. Later on, Tao Zhu, Ye Fei, Zeng Zhi and other comrades were sent to lead unbearable Mindong peasant revolution by higher Party organizations. In December 1933, with more than one hundred thousand members, "Mindong Red Army with Sleeve Ribbons" was officially established in Shifeng Temple, Bai Zhuyang.

At the beginning of 1934, armed uprisings of peasants and workers spread all over Mindong area, and then Mindong Soviet-style Zone was reestablished, and Bai Zhuyang became the command center of these uprisings. In addition, Mindong Soviet-Style Zone was set up, and developed into one of the eight revolutionary bases before the Long March. In September, the Independent Division of the Red Army of Mindong was established. With more than 1600 people, they fought together with local She people and Han people, successfully merged several small revolutionary bases in Mindong, and finally formed Fu'an and Lianjiang-centered rural revolutionary base, which covered a total area of more than ten thousand square kilometers, with more than a million people. In October 1934, Kuomintang Party deployed massive forces and laid siege to Mindong Soviet-Style Zone and adopted Five Cruel Policies against the base. What was worse, they bombed Bai Zhuyang in order to destroy the red political power. Led by Temporary Special Party Committee and Soviet-style government, local people started a fierce fight against enemies to defend the new government. But the capital of Mindong Soviet-Style Zone (Bai Zhuyang) was lost due to great disparity in power between the enemy and the red army. Ever since then, Mindong Special Party Committee had to lead the people in an extremely hard and bitter guerrilla war for three years.

闽东红色旅游线路

闽东红色旅游线路被列入福建省红色旅游经典线路。据了解,闽东红色旅游线的主要景点包括马尾船政文化景区、福建省革命历史纪念馆、林则徐纪念馆、蕉城区中国工农红军闽东独立师旧址,福安市中共闽东特委旧址、牙城苏维埃政府旧址、百克医院、霍童暴动旧址支提寺等。

Mindong Red Tourism Routes

Mindong Red Tourism Routes were listed as the Red Tourism Classic Routes of Fujian Province, which cover Mawei Shipbuilding Cultural Scenic Spots, Fujian Province Revolutionary History Memorial Museum, Lin Zexu Memorial Museum, former site of Independent Division of the Chinese Workers' and Peasants' Red Army of Mindong in Jiaocheng District, former site of Mindong Special Committee of the CPC in Fu'an city, former site of Soviet-Style Government in Yacheng County, Baike Hospital and Huotong Uprising at Zhiti Temple and so on.

(四)闽东茶文化

闽东茶叶历史文化

闽东茶叶历史文化悠久而灿烂,可追溯至古老的西晋温麻县治时期,据考古发掘,早在西晋时期,闽东就有饮茶习俗,唐代已有"比屋皆饮"之说,陆羽《茶经》里就有闽东产茶的记载。入宋又盛行"斗茶",以后历经元、明、清代,茶叶生产进一步得到发展,清咸丰、同治年间,"坦洋工夫"红茶脱颖而出,并于1915年荣获巴拿马国际博览会金奖,曾被英国王室指定为御用专供茶,产品远销英国、荷兰、东南亚等多个国家和地区;现在的福安已成为中国最大的绿茶、花茶主产区。除了福安以外,宁德还有被称为中国白茶之乡的福鼎。福鼎白茶是风靡海外的保健茶,素有"世界白茶在中国,中国白茶在福鼎"的美誉。同时,闽东茶叶对外贸易十分活跃,1889年三都澳开埠之后,即成为福建省最重要的茶叶输出港口,全省约有50%的茶叶经此销往世界各地,被誉为海上茶叶之路的起点。

5.1.2.4 Mindong Tea Culture

Historical Culture of Mindong Tea

The time honored and splendid Mindong Tea culture can be traced back to Wenma County jurisdiction of Western Jin Dynasty. According to archaeological excavations, Mindong people started drinking tea in the Western Jin dynasty. It is said that nearly everyone drinks tea in the Tang dynasty. We can also find the evidence of tea production in Mindong region in *Cha Jing* (*Tea Classics*), written by Lu Yu. In Song Dynasty, tea competition became quite popular, then tea production received further development after the Yuan, Ming and Qing Dynasties. During the Xianfeng period and Tongzhi period, the representative of black tea—Tanyang Kungfu Tea stood out, and won the gold medal at the Panama Expo in 1915. It was once appointed as the exclusive tea supply for British royal family, its products have been sold to many countries and regions, such as England, Holland and Southeast Asia. Nowadays Fu'an has become the biggest producing area of green tea and scented tea in China. In addition, Fuding was praised as Hometown to White Tea in China. Famous for its function of health protection, Fuding White Tea also earns a good reputation that "The white tea of the world comes from China while the white tea of China is in Fuding". Meanwhile Mindong Tea was exported to other countries as well. Ever since its opening in 1889, Sandu Bay became the most important port for tea export, and also the starting point of the Maritime Tea Road, with about 50% of Fujian tea shipped to the whole world through Sandu Bay.

闽东最早的茶文化交流(空海法师将闽东茶文化带回日本)

唐贞观二十年(公元 804 年),日本佛教真言宗创始人空海法师等 23 人乘船入唐,因遭遇飓风侵袭,船破人乏,被迫在霞浦赤岸海口登陆,在赤岸的那段日子里,空海法师与当地民众频频往来,还曾到访建善寺。当时,建善寺周遭遍植茶树,官府民家僧寺均以茶相敬。这让来自东瀛的空海第一次品饮到了闽东茶,领略到了闽东茶的独特魅力,并为之深深吸引。据美国威廉·乌克思所著《茶叶全书》记载,僧侣弘法大师(名空海)又从中国研究佛法归去,对茶树非常喜爱,携大量茶籽,分植各地,并将制茶常识传布日本国内。陈椽教授编著的《茶业通史》亦有平城天皇大同元年(公元 806 年),空海弘法大师又引入茶籽及制茶方法的记载。空海法师在结束大唐之行的时候,带回了茶籽和制茶技术,成为中日茶文化交流的使者。闽东是空海法师踏上大唐土地的第一个落脚点,也是空海法师接受中国茶文化熏陶的第一块土地。1994 年,日本佛教真言宗信徒捐资在霞浦赤岸建立了空海大师纪念堂,此后每年都有多批日本进香团前来朝拜,从闽东追寻日本茶道的历史渊源。

The Earliest Tea Culture Exchange in Mindong (Master Konghai, i.e. Kukai) brought Chinese tea culture back to Japan)

In the 20th year of Zhenguan Period in Tang Dynasty (804AD), Master Konghai, the founder of the Japan's Shingon Buddhism, and other 22 people took a voyage westward to China by boat. However, they were forced to land at Chi'an seaport in Xiapu County due to great damage done by a rampant hurricane. During their stay in Chi'an, Master Konghai often communicated with local people, and paid a visit to Jianshan Temple. At that time, many tea trees were planted around Jianshan Temple, and tea had already become an important communication medium not just for officials, but also for local people and temples. This was the first time for Master Konghai to have a taste of Mindong Tea; he was deeply attracted by its unique charm. This experience was also recorded in *All About Tea*, written by William Ukers: "Master Kukai returned to Japan with his studies on Chinese Buddhism and his hobby for tea trees as well. He brought back many tea seeds, and planted them around the country, and spread tea production techniques." Similar recordings can also be found in *General History of Tea*, written by Chen Chuan, "Tea seeds and tea production techniques were introduced to Japan by Master Konghai in the first year of the Datong period, Emperor Heizei's reign (AD806)". By doing so, before the end of the trip, he had already become the envoy of tea culture exchange between Japan and China. Since Mindong is the first stop of Master

Konghai's visit to China in the Tang Dynasty, and the first place of his tea culture edification in China as well, believers of Japan's Shingon Buddhism donated property to establish Memorial Hall for Master Konghai in Chi'an, Xiapu County. Every year many pilgrims would visit the Memorial Hall and trace the historical origin of Japan's Tea Ceremony from Mindong.

(五)闽东海洋文化

温麻船屯与温麻县的设立：早在旧石器时代晚期，境内即有人类活动的遗迹。三国时期，约公元 3 世纪中叶，孙吴政权在今霞浦沿海开设了造船工场温麻船屯。闽东迈向海洋，揭开了有志可考的历史。

王审知开辟黄崎港：唐末、五代时期，王审知闽王从 898—925 年统治福建近 30 年。福建真正的开发从他开始。王审知治闽的主要举措之一就是大力发展福建的对外联系与对外贸易，为此他十分重视海港与航道建设。

5.1.2.5 Mindong Marine Culture

The setup of Wenma Shipyard and Wenma County: the existence of humans in Ningde can date back to the late period of the Paleolithic Age. During the three kingdoms period, about the middle of the 3rd century AD, Kingdom Wu established a ship building yard "Wenma Shipyard" in the coastal area of Xiapu County. Mindong began to step into a new period with recorded history.

Wang Shenzhi's exploitation of Huangqi Port: At the end of the Tang Dynasty and Five-Dynasties Period, the king of Kingdom Min, Wang Shenzhi started his reign over Fujian for nearly 30 years(898-925AD). The actual development of Fujian started from his governance. He attached great importance to the construction of ports and channels. During his governance, one of his main measures was to spare no efforts in developing outbound relations and foreign trade.

三都澳的历史与今天

三都澳历史上就是中国对外贸易港口之一。早在唐朝以前，三都澳就已开发。此后到五代闽王王审知执政时期，由于他重视港口建设和对北方的海上沟通，三都澳得到进一步的发展。明代开辟了运粮航线，1452 年，明朝廷在此设河泊所管理渔课。1684 年，清政府在三都澳设了宁德税务总口，下辖九个口岸，每年征税达 12 000两银子。1898 年，清廷将三都澳辟为福建的三个商埠之一(前两个是福州和厦门)。1899 年，清廷在三都成立福海关，三都澳正式开放为对外贸易港口。当时有 13 个国家的 21 个公司在三都澳设立洋行、分公司等。三都岛一度因设福海关、建洋行而畸形繁荣，又由于其本身军事、经济的特殊战略地位，直至日军侵华被炸，福海关于1949年正式关闭，黯然谢幕。

如今，随着高速公路、高铁交通网、港口码头等基础设施的建成及完善，三都澳又迎来了一轮大发展的契机。2005年，福建省委、省政府做出建设海峡西岸经济区的战略构想，宁德位于福建东大门，是海峡西岸经济区的重要组成部分，且是福建省的四大港口之一。宁德市委、市政府按照港口、产业、城市三位一体、互动发展的总体思路，以及向海、临海、跨海三步走的发展步骤，加快推进宁德中心城市建设，形成港城互动的一体化发展格局，逐步建设环三都澳海湾城市。

The Past and Present of Sandu Bay

As one of the foreign trade ports, Sandu Bay had been exploited before the Tang Dynasty. Then during the governance of Wang Shenzhi, he paid great attention to the construction of the ports and maritime communication to the north, therefore Sandu Bay received further development. A maritime route for grain shipping was set up in the Ming Dynasty, and the official river taxation inspection bureau was established to collect fishery tax by the court in 1452. Later Ningde Administration of Taxation was established in Sandu Bay by the Qing Government in 1684 (the 23rd year of Kangxi period, Qing Dynasty), which had jurisdiction over 9 ports, and could collect as much as 12 000 liang (unit of weight equal to 50 grams) silvers. In 1898, the Qing Government designated Sandu Bay as one of the three trading ports (the other two were Fuzhou and Xiamen). In 1899, the Qing Government set up Fuhai Custom there, indicating the formal establishment of Sandu Bay as a foreign trade port. At that time, 21 companies from 13 countries set up foreign firms and branch companies in Sandu Bay, hence an unhealthy prosperity appeared due to Fuhai Customs and numerous foreign firms. However, Sandu Bay was bombed by the Japanese invaders due to its special strategic position both in military and economy, as a result, Fuhai Customs was shut down and disappeared from the historical stage in 1949.

Nowadays, with the construction and betterment of infrastructures, such as expressways, high-speed railway networks, ports and wharves, Sandu Bay has received another chance for further development. In 2005, in order to build the Western Taiwan Strait Economic Development Zone, a strategic conception was brought up by the Fujian provincial Party committee and Fujian provincial government. As an important part of Western Taiwan Strait Economic Development Zone, Ningde is located in eastern Fujian, and is one of the four largest ports in Fujian province. The Ningde municipal Party committee and municipal government stick to its general concept of interactive development by combining the port, industry and city together, and insist on following the three-step development strategy of "towards the bay, by the bay and across the bay", while accelerating the central city construction of Ningde, so that an interactive development pattern of port and city integration can be formed, and the Sandu Bay City can be built up.

霞浦黄瓜山古人类遗址

黄瓜山遗址位于霞浦县南部海岸边一座相对孤立的山丘之上(海拔 50 米)。大约距今 3 000 至 4 000 年,为一处青铜器时代遗址,总面积约 6 000平方米。该遗址是 1987 年福建省文物普查中发现的,是闽东地区迄今发现的唯一一处贝丘遗址。经考古专家鉴定,所采集到的陶片、石器、兽骨和贝壳标本相当于中原夏、商、周时期的福建东北部地方文化遗存。在其后的野外考察中,专家在沙江、柏洋、崇儒、牙城、水门、州洋等 7 个乡镇陆续发现了 31 处类似的贝丘遗址,占地面积约 84 620平方米,后经推断,属新石器晚期至青铜器时代(约公元前 3000 至 3500 年)的古遗址。

贝丘遗址是古代人类居住遗址的一种,以包含大量古代人类食剩抛弃的贝壳为特征。贝丘遗址多位于海、湖泊和河流的沿岸,在贝丘的文化层中夹杂着贝壳、各种食物的残渣以及石器、陶器等文化遗物,还发现房基、窖穴和墓葬等遗迹。根据贝丘的地理位置和贝壳种类的变化,可了解古代海岸线和海水温差的变迁。

Ancient Human Site of Xiapu Cucumber Mountain

The Relics Site lies in a relatively isolated mountain on the South Coast of Xiapu County(altitude: 50 meters). With a long history of 3 000 to 4 000 years, this site belongs to the Bronze Age and has an area of 6 000 square meters. It was first discovered in a national archaeological survey in 1987, and identified as the only shell mound relic discovered in Mindong region. Pottery pieces, stone implements, animal bones and shell specimen were collected, and archaeologists claimed that these remains belong to cultural remains of people living in the northeast Fujian in the periods of Xia, Shang and Zhou Dynasties. Later in their field study, other 31 similar shell mounds were discovered successively in 7 towns and counties: Shajiang, Baiyang, Chongru, Yacheng, Shuimen and Zhouyang. The whole sites boast an area of 84 620 square meters. From the evidences archaeologists concluded that these were ancient sites from the late period of the Neolithic Age to the Bronze Age (3000-3500BC).

Shell mound is one type of the ancient sites of human habitation, signified by shell debris of human leftovers. Generally speaking, shell mounds are mostly located in coastal zones, river banks and lake shores. In the cultural layer, many shells, food residue, cultural remains of stone implements and potteries are found. In addition, traces of house foundation, caves and tombs have been discovered as well. What's more, we can fully understand the ancient coastline and temperature change of the sea, based on the geographical location of shell mound and the species change of shells.

(六)木拱廊桥廊桥文化

木拱廊桥是人类智慧的结晶,是历史变迁的缩影,更是优秀传统文化的珍宝。据了解,全国现存木拱廊桥140多座,大量分布于闽东北和浙西南两地。在福建,目前只有寿宁、屏南、周宁、古田、政和等地有。寿宁是国内现已发现的在以县为单位的区域内木拱廊桥数量最多地方之一。境内现存的木拱廊桥共有21座,年代序列最齐,从清乾隆、嘉庆、道光、同治、光绪至中华民国,乃至1949年后还在建造,这在全国极为罕见。由于寿宁的木拱廊桥数量众多,被誉为"世界木拱廊桥之乡"。其中有6座被列入国家重点文物保护单位,更有3座列入中国世界文化遗产预备名单申报点。寿宁的木拱廊桥,大多搭建于深沟高涧之上,与村民日常生活紧密相连,成为乡村文化的集散地,是人们生活中休闲的好去处。

屏南境内现存较好的古代木拱廊桥13座,其中,万安桥、千乘桥、百祥桥为国家重点文物保护单位,广福桥、广利桥为省级文物保护单位。境内的木拱廊桥除本身的巨大艺术价值外,还蕴含着许多颇值细述之文化亮点。如廊桥与地方民俗、信仰,与史实、传说故事,与桥名、碑记,与楹联、书法,等等。可以说,每一座木拱廊桥,都闪耀着文化的光芒。如万安桥,取义万民平安,万事平安;百祥桥意为桥纳百祥,吉祥如意,还有千乘桥、广福桥、广利桥、惠风桥、清晏桥、劝农桥、连升桥等廊桥,桥名直白而又蕴含良好祈愿,是儒家文化的具体化,给人以美妙之遐思。2006年,万安桥、千乘桥、百祥桥与闽东北其他9座廊桥捆绑,被国务院公布为第六批国家重点文物保护单位。

5.1.2.6 Covered Wooden Arch Bridge Culture

Covered wooden arch bridge is the quintessence of human wisdom, the epitome of historical changes and a treasure of excellent traditional culture. It is said that there are more than 140 existing covered wooden arch bridges nowadays, most of them scattered over the northeast of Fujian Province and the southwest of Zhejiang Province. In Fujian, one can only find covered wooden arch bridges in Shouning, Pingnan, Zhouning, Gutian and Zhenghe Counties, among which Shouning owns the most covered bridges (in units of counties) in China. Currently there are 21 covered wooden arch bridges with a complete chronology, originated from the periods of Qianlong, Jiaqing, Daoguang,Tongzhi, Guangxu of Qing Dynasty to the Republic of China, even after 1949, which is extremely rare in China. As a result, Shouning was named as "Hometown of the Covered Wooden Arch Bridges" due to its large number. Six of them have been already listed as Key National Historical and Cultural Sites, 3 of which were listed on the UNESCO World Intangible Heritage List. In Shouning County, covered bridges were usually built over a deep ravine or brook where local people grew up, they are tightly connected to the daily life of local villagers. Covered bridges have not only become the center of local culture, but also a good place for entertainment.

There are altogether 13 comparatively intact covered wooden arch bridges in Pingnan County, among which Wan'an Bridge, Qiancheng Bridge and Baixiang Bridge were listed as Key National Historical and Cultural Sites, and Guangfu Bridge and Guangli Bridge were listed as Key Provincial Historical and Cultural Sites. Except for its great value in art, these covered bridges also contain a lot of cultural highlights that were worth mentioning in details, such as local customs, belief, historical events, legendary story, name of the bridge, tablet inscription, couplets and calligraphy and so on. It is not an exaggeration to say that every single covered bridge is glittering with its insight into culture. For example, Wan'an Bridge was named because it symbolized peace and safety to everyone; Baixiang Bridge was named for its indication of good fortune. Other bridges were also named with good wishes, but easier to understand, such as Qiancheng Bridge, Guangfu Bridge, Guangli Bridge, Huifeng Bridge, Qingyan Bridge, Quannong Bridge and Liansheng Bridge and other covered bridges in the northeast of Fujian. Such names are the embodiment of Confucianism, which provides people with fascinating reveries. In 2006, together with other 9 covered bridges, Wan'an Bridge, Qiancheng Bridge, Baixiang Bridge were announced amid the sixth batch of National Major Historical and Cultural Sites by the State Council.

(七)传统技艺文化

福船是福建、浙江沿海一带尖底古海船的统称。而所谓"水密隔舱",就是用隔舱板把船舱分为互不相通的舱区,舱数有 13 个,也有 8 个。这一船舶结构是中国在造船方面的一大发明,具有提高船舶的抗沉性能,又增加了远航的安全性能。这一传统手工技艺,至今已有600多年历史。

宁德漳湾福船承其衣钵,特征鲜明,一脉尚存。如今,它已是一种濒将消亡的民间手工技艺,堪称中华绝活之一,造船的用料,需选择既轻便、坚固,又耐水的木材。一艘漳湾福船的制造,从备料、立龙骨到上画油漆,全都是手工操作,所造的福船船型多样,尤以一种当地称作三桅透(三桅三帆)的最具代表性。它的制作过程相当复杂,要经过安竖龙骨、配搭肋骨、钉纵向构件舷板、搭房、做舵等工序,最后油灰工塞缝、修灰、油漆上画,才完成全船。

2008年6月,福船技艺被列入第二批国家级非物质文化遗产名录;2010年11月,被联合国教科文组织列入《急需保护的非物质文化遗产名录》。

5.1.2.7 Traditional Skills

Fuchuan is the general name for ancient boats with sharp bottoms along the coastal area of Fujian and Zhejiang provinces. The "Water-tight bulkhead" is to divide the cabins into several small units sealed from each other, usually 13 or 8 units. With more than 600 years of history, such construction is one of China's great inventions on ship building, which not only enhances unsinkability of the boat, but also its safety in oceangoing voyages.

As the last category that still exists, Zhangwan Fuchuan well kept distinctive features and inherited the advantages of Fuchuan manufacturing skills. Nowadays, as an endangered folk art, Zhangwan Fuchuan can be called one of the Chinese forte skills. All construction materials are composed of light, strong and water-proof timbers. In order to build one boat, every step has to be done by manual operation, from material preparation, keel setting-up to painting. There are many kinds of shapes for Fuchuan, and only one stands out the most, called "Sanweitou"(three masts and three sails) by local people. The manufacturing procedure is very complicated, the whole boat has to be processed through the following steps: to place the keel and the frames first, nail the vertical component-plates, build the cabin, finish the rudder; in the end, workers would stuff up the cracks and paint the boat.

Fuchuan was listed as the second batch of national intangible cultural heritages in June 2008, and an intangible cultural heritage in need of urgent protection by UNESCO in November 2010.

第二节 民间艺术

5.2 Folk Arts

一、戏剧

闽东戏剧活动始于宋代，兴于明代。较具地方特色的剧种有四平戏、北路戏和平讲戏。

5.2.1 Opera

Mindong Opera originated from the Song Dynasty, and flourished in the Ming Dynasty. The most representative ones include Siping Opera, Beilu Opera and Pingjiang Opera .

(一)四平戏

"四平戏"俗称"庶民戏"，是一古老剧种，源于屏南、蕉城等地。明末，从江西传入屏南龙潭村，至今已有300多年的历史。

早期的四平戏，行当只有生、旦、净、末、丑、贴、外等七个。清初发展成为"九角头"。艺人自称"梨园弟子"，供奉戏神"田公元帅"。四平戏以四平腔为主，前台干唱，后台帮腔。脸谱继承宋元南戏化装传统，以红、白、黑为基本色调，线条简单明朗。

清光绪年间，四平戏的行当又有新的发展。生分正生、小生、武生、贴生、老生，旦分正旦、小旦、花旦、武旦、丑旦、彩旦，净改称大花，末改称二花，丑改称三花。演出剧目数量也大大增加，相传下来的"总本"有80多个。四平戏多为家族祖业，世代相传，所以300多年来始终保持古朴的风貌。

5.2.1.1 Siping Opera

Siping Opera, also known as "Opera for Shumin (ordinary people)", is an ancient opera originating from places like Pingnan County and Jiaocheng District. In the end of the Ming Dynasty, it was introduced from Jiangxi province to Longtan Village of Pingnan County, which has been in existence for more than 300 years.

The early Siping Opera features seven main types of performers, namely

Sheng, Dan, Jing, Mo, Chou, Tie and Wai, which developed into "nine roles" in the Qing Dynasty. Performers call themselves as "Operatic Disciples", and they worship Marshal Tiangong—the god of operas. Siping Opera is represented by Siping tone; performers only sing on the stage, with vocal accompaniment backstage. Their facial masks inherited the makeup tradition of Nanxi (Southern Opera) in the Song and Yuan Dynasties. With clear and simple lines, their basic colors cover red, white and black.

During Guangxu period in the Qing Dynasty, Siping Opera gained new development. Sheng was divided into Zhengsheng, Xiaosheng, Wusheng, Tiesheng and Laosheng, while Dan was divided into Zhengdan, Xiaodan, Huadan, Wudan, Choudan and Caidan, Jing was changed into Dahua, Mo Erhua, and Chou Sanhua. What's more, with the increase of performances, more than 80 Zongben (scripts) were handed down to generations. Most of Siping Operas are family-related business, and passed from generation to generation, so that the primitive feature can be well kept for more than 300 years.

(二)北路戏

"北路戏"俗称"乱弹"。由于主要乐器为长膜笛,故又名"横哨戏",流行于寿宁、古田、屏南、福安、蕉城、周宁等地。

北路戏道白唱词都用普通话。唱腔以西秦腔和吹腔为主,在长期流行中,又吸收乱弹、徽调、汉调音乐,综合形成一个多声腔的戏曲剧种,但其主要唱腔仍由西秦腔和吹腔发展出来的"平板"为基本调。清光绪以后,京剧盛行,北路戏又吸取皮黄唱腔。

5.2.1.2 Beilu Opera

Beilu Opera, commonly known as "Luantan (Free Style)", is also known as "Hengshao Opera" for its major instrument. It is very popular in places like Shouning, Gutian, Pingnan, Zhouning Counties, Fu'an City and Jiaocheng District.

Beilu Opera is commonly performed in Mandarin. Based on Western Qingqiang Tune and Chuiqiang Tune, absorbing the essence of Luantan, Anhui Tune and Handiao Tune, an opera with multiple tunes was formed. However, the basic tune of Beilu Opera is still Pingban (Flat Tune), deriving from Western Qingqiang and Chuiqiang Tunes. Peking Opera prevailed after the Guangxu period in the Qing Dynasty, so the Pihuang Tune was absorbed into

Beilu Opera.

（三）平讲戏

平讲戏源于明末清初的“驮故事”，又称“肩头棚”。表演时，小演员化装成戏中角色，由成人驮在肩上，敲锣打鼓边走边演。清嘉庆年间，江湖班多为本地演员，舞台语言也渐趋地方化，出现纯用当地方言演唱的剧种，道白“平白如讲”，故称“平讲戏”。平讲戏角色分为小生、小旦、老生、大花、二花等行当，着重于小生、小旦和老生，故有“三小戏”之称。唱腔以江湖调为主，后期还吸收梆子曲调。主要乐器有管弦、笛子、京胡、渔鼓、手鼓、手锣等。

5.2.1.3 Pingjiang Opera

Pingjiang Opera originated from "Carrying Story" or "Shoulder Tent" in the late Ming Dynasty and the early Qing Dynasty. During a performance, a little actor was carried by an adult and would perform to the beating of gongs and drums. In the Jiaqing period of the Qing Dynasty, performers were mainly local people, and stage language gradually tended to become local dialect. Since the opera was performed in local dialect, and sung in a nearly speaking style, it was called "Pingjiang Opera". This opera features in the following types of performers: Xiaosheng, Xiaodan, Laosheng, Dahua and Erhua and so on. Since Xiaosheng, Xiaodan and Laosheng are the three major types of performers, it was called "Sanxiao Opera". Folk songs were adopted as major tunes, and Bangzi was also absorbed in the later period. Major instruments cover orchestra, flute, Jinghu, Yugu, tambourine and hand gong and so on.

二、曲艺

清代中叶，闽东便有以“祝福生财、祈祥纳吉”为彩头的民间说唱艺人在城乡活动，尤其每年春节至元宵期间，其说唱活动更是到处可见。区内曲艺种类主要有评话、嘭嘭鼓、说书等。20 世纪 50 年代后又有快板、相声等，其中流行最广的首推评话和嘭嘭鼓。

5.2.2 Folk Art Forms

In the middle of the Qing Dynasty, many folk singing artists were active in the urban and rural areas of Mindong regions; normally they performed for blessings, prosperity, auspiciousness and good fortune. Especially from Spring Festival to Lantern Festival, they could be found everywhere. The most common folk art forms include Pinghua, Pengpenggu, Story-telling and others.

In the late 1950s, Allegro and Cross Talk appeared, but Pinghua and Pengpenggu plays still remain as the most prevalent ones in Mindong.

(一)评话

闽东评话始于清代中期,流行于霞浦、福鼎、福安、宁德、柘荣、古田、周宁等地,至今已有100多年的历史。

清光绪年间,霞浦县柏洋乡吴阿照首创霞浦方言评话,讲述《铁刀记》《甘国宝》《乾隆下江南》《陈美人告天状》《海棠花》等书目,蜚声福宁(霞浦)、福安、柘荣(当时霞浦辖区)等县山村。评话代代相传,至今尚有数十名的柏洋评话员为群众演出。

5.2.2.1 Pinghua

It is a kind of vivid story-telling. With more than 100 years of history, Mindong Pinghua originated in the middle of the Qing Dynasty, and is popular in Xiapu, Zherong, Gutian and Zhouning Counties, Fuding, Fu'an and Jiaocheng District.

In the Guangxu period of the Qing Dynasty (1875-1908), Wu A'zhao from Baiyang Village, Xiapu County created Pinghua in Xiapu dialect. Some plays, such as *Story of an Iron Knife*, *General Gan Guobao*, *Adventures of Emperor Chien Lung*, *the Imperial Appeal and Crabapple*, were renowned in villages of Funing (Xiapu), Zherong County (under jurisdiction of Xiapu at that time) and Fu'an City. Since Pinghua was handed down from generation to generation, dozens of Pinghua performers from Baiyang Village are still active today.

(二)嘭嘭鼓

明末,一种叫"莲花落"的民间曲调流传到福鼎、霞浦等地。这一曲种逐渐与福鼎秦屿一带的闽南话歌谣相结合,形成用闽南话演唱的嘭嘭鼓。因每段帮腔中都有衬词"牡丹花",所以也叫"牡丹花调"。

5.2.2.2 Pengpenggu Opera

At the end of the Ming Dynasty, a special opera tune "Lianhualao" was introduced to Fuding City and Xiapu County, which gradually combined with local Minnan ballads along the areas of Qinyu, Fuding City. As a result, Pengpenggu Opera performed in Minnan dialect was formed. Since the word "peony" served as padding syllables in every vocal accompaniment, it is also called "A Tune of Peony".

三、音乐与舞蹈

5.2.3 Music and Dance

(一)畲族山歌

畲族山歌多为七言一句或五言一句,有歌颂畲族始祖功绩的史歌,有歌颂生活的颂歌,有倾吐男女之间爱慕之情的情歌,有反映勤耕苦种的种田歌。演唱形式有独唱、对唱、齐唱和独特的双条落二声部盘唱形式。演唱方法有假声、真声和真假声结合三种,其中假声的唱法最有民族特色。闽东畲族歌言有拦路对歌、蚕里来客对歌、做表姐对歌、做亲家伯对歌等一系列罕见的盘歌习俗及定期定点规模大、群众性广的歌节歌俗。

5.2.3.1 Folk Songs of the She Ethnic Minority

Most of the She folk songs are seven or five words in one sentence; there are various types of the She music: epics that praise great achievement of the She people's ancestors; odes that sing of their daily lives; love songs that confide affection to each other; farming songs that reflect their hardworking in the field. Several singing forms cover solo, antiphonal singing, duet and unique two-part singing " Shuangtiaoluo". Among three singing methods—falsetto, true voice and combination of them, falsetto possesses the most national characteristics. Mindong She music features both series of rare antiphonal singing customs, such as "Road Blocking Songs", "Visitors Antiphonal Songs", " Songs at being Cousins" and "Songs at being Uncles-in-Laws" and so on; as well as music festivals and customs with large-scale, mass participation that have regular organizations at regular time.

(二)畲族的舞蹈

畲族的舞蹈按其内容和形式分为三类,即祭祀性舞蹈、农事庆典舞蹈和社交娱乐性舞蹈。

畲族巫舞

畲族巫舞《奶娘催罡》是闽东畲族巫师进行驱鬼镇妖活动中的一段祭祀舞蹈,分净坛、请神、踩罡三个章节,通过日常生活情节和生产活动的若干画面,塑造陈十四娘(又称奶娘,即民间传说中的妇幼保护神陈靖姑)这个驱妖镇魔的女神形象。相传,明朝中期宁德地区就有巫师表演的祀福舞蹈,至今已有四百多年的历史。

5.2.3.2 Dances of the She Ethnic Minority

There are three kinds of She dances according to the content and form, ritual dance, ceremonial dance and entertainment dance.

Sorcery Dance of the She Ethnic Minority

"Nai Niang Cui Gang(Goddess Chen Jinggu performs rituals)" is a typical ritual dance, performed by the Mindong She sorcerers to expel the evil spirit. In the dance, there are altogether three chapters: enshrine the altar, invoke the deities and jump on the handle of the big dipper. Through images from daily life and production activities, the goddess image of Chen Sister Fourteen (also known as Nai Niang and Chen Jinggu who is the goddess for women and children protection in folklore) was established. It is said that the She dance with sorcerers asking for blessings in Ningde region has been in existence for more than 400 years.

打枪担

打枪担,由畲族人上山砍柴草劳动活动转化的。上山时,畲族人边唱山歌,边用力敲击枪担,逐渐演变为打枪担。表演时,参加者腰佩刀鞘(俗称割吊),一手握柴刀,一手持枪担,且敲且舞。以柴刀击枪担、刀鞘,以刀柄、枪担撞地,清脆悦耳,节奏分明,整齐中富于变化。它还吸收了畲拳畲棍中的拔、挑、架、劈等对打动作,融体育、武术、舞蹈为一体。

目前,在宁德市被挖掘整理有《龙头舞》《香花舞》《祈福舞》《龙伞舞》《迎亲舞》《铃刀舞》《猎捕舞》《奶娘催罡》《巫舞》《打地狱》《对灯》等数十个畲族舞蹈。

Daqiangdan(Performance with Carrying-Poles and Choppers)

Daqiangdan derived from the She people' activity of cutting firewood in the mountains. They would strike their carrying poles on each other's while singing their local folk songs, which later evolved into "Daqiangdan" (performance with carrying-poles and choppers). In the dance, with a scabbard(normally known as Gediao) buckled to his/her waist, a performer with a chopper in one hand, and a pole in the other hand, would hit together and dance. Sometimes, he or she would use the chopper to hit the pole and scabbard, or use the handle of the chopper and the pole to hit the ground, which makes a crystal sound and clear rhythm. The whole dance is the combination of sports, martial arts and dance, neat and rich in variations. In addition, it absorbed some fighting movements of the She martial arts, such as pulling, lifting and splitting and so on.

Nowadays dozens of She dances have been discovered and collected, such as Dragon-head Dance, Fragrant Flowers Dance, Dance of Asking for Blessing, Dragon Umbrella Dance, Wedding Ceremony Dance, Lingdao Ritual Dance, Hunting Dance, Goddess Chen Jinggu Performs Rituals, Sorcery Dance and so on.

畲族二声部山歌双音

畲族二声部山歌双音，流传于宁德市的蕉城区八都镇猴盾畲族村及其周边的畲村，是畲族文化遗产中的瑰宝、是我国畲族山歌中唯一幸存的畲族二声部山歌歌种，于 2009 年被认定为国家非物质文化遗产。

畲族二声部山歌双音的主要表现形式：首先表现为二声部山歌双音属清唱，演唱形式，每个声部至少 1 人，每个声部的演唱人数可多可少，不论声部的男、女性别演唱，亦可两声部都由同性别演唱，但演唱情歌就一定要男、女各唱一声部。其次是二声部山歌双音词律歌词结构基本是七字一句，四句体，四句为一条。

"Shuangyin"—Double-Vocal Folk Singing

It was popular in Houdun Village and other She Villages in Badu Town, Jiaocheng District, Ningde City. As the only surviving Double-Vocal Folk Singing, it is the gem in the She cultural heritage, and was listed as national intangible heritage in 2009.

There are several major features for Shuangyin. First of all, Shuangyin itself belongs to a cappella. In Double-Vocal Folk Singing, there is no restriction on the number or the gender for performers, except for each part, there must be at least one person, and the love song must be performed by the male and female in separate parts. Secondly, as for the lyrics, there are mainly seven characters in one sentence, four sentences in one stanza, and four stanzas in one passage.

(三)畲族诗歌

畲族文学基本上是民间口头文学，多以畲语歌唱的形式表达。在长篇叙事诗歌中、最著名的就是《高皇歌》，又称《盘古歌》等。这是一首长达三四百句的七言史诗，以神话的形式，叙述了畲族始祖盘瓠立下奇功及其不畏艰难繁衍出盘、蓝、雷、钟四姓子孙的传说，反映了畲族的原始宗教信仰和图腾崇拜。畲族人还把这一传说绘成连环画式的画像，称祖图，即在一幅十来丈长的布帛上，用彩笔把这一传说的 40 多个画像连环式地绘在画卷上，世代珍藏。

5.2.3.3 Poetry of the She Ethnic Minority

The She literature is mainly of folk oral literature, and delivered by singing. In the long narrative poems, the most famous one is the Song of

Emperor Gaohuang, also known as Song of Panhu, it is a seven-character epic that lasts as long as three to four hundreds sentences. The epic describes the legend of the ancestor of the She people—Panhu, who was fearless of danger and difficulty, and his bringing up of his descendants surnamed Pan, Lan, Lei and Zhong. This poetry reflects the She people's primitive religious belief and totemism. In particular, the legend of their original ancestor, Panhu is painted on a piece of a hundred feet long cloth in about 40 picture strips, and this cloth is well preserved from generation to generation. This colorful cloth is called Zutu.

四、武术与杂技

畲族武术分为拳术和棍术两种，流派繁多，最为流行最具特点的是畲家拳和打柴棒，经千百年传承，已形成独具一格的民间武术。

5.2.4 Martial Arts and Acrobatics

The She martial arts are composed of many schools in two different categories: Chinese boxing and cudgel play. The most popular and characteristic ones are Shejia Quan (the She-Style Boxing) and Dachai Bang (Carrying-Poles Fighting), which have formed into folk martial arts with unique charm after hundreds of years of development.

(一)畲家拳

畲家拳有十余种套路，流行于福安县颇负盛名的武术之乡的金斗洋畲村。据传，畲族武术是在吸取南少林精华的基础上融汇而成，具有步稳势烈，发力短、猛、狠，攻守严谨，进攻多用指法、掌法等特点。

5.2.4.1 Shejia Quan(The She Ethnic-Style Boxing)

With more than ten series of skills and tricks, Shejia Quan is quite popular in the Hometown of Martial Arts—Jingdouyang She Village, Fu'an City. It is said that the She martial art is practiced based on the essence of Southern Shaolin Temple School of Boxing, with certain characteristics, such as steady footsteps, powerful aura, quick, powerful and fierce physical strength, tight offense and defense, the adaption of fingering and palm in defense and so on.

(二)打柴棒(盘柴槌)

打柴棒，又称盘柴槌，是流行于闽东畲族地区的一种民间棒术。由于使用的柴棒长短不一、功用不同,打柴棒,又分为两种:一种棒长 1.2 丈,一人耍弄,有攻有拦,叫中拦;一种棒长 0.7 丈,两人对打,互相攻防盘击,叫盘杖槌,也称齐眉杖。棒术的路数花样繁多,有三步进、三步退、四步半、五步跳、七步、九步、猴子翻身、双头槌、公牛转栏、金鸡啄米、老蛇吐吞、天观地测等。

5.2.4.2 Dachai Bang(Carrying-Poles Fighting)

Dachai Bang, also known as Panchai Chui, is a folk cane fighting in the She regions in Mindong. Due to different lengths and functions, Dachai Bang can be divided into two types: the first one is called Zhonglan, with a 4 meters long cane, it can only be practiced by one person; the second one is called Panzhang Chui, also known as Qimei Zhang, with a 2.3-meter-long cane; it is usually practiced by two people attacking and offending each other. There are many movements in Dachai Bang: three-step forward, three-step back, four and a half steps, five-step jump, seven steps, nine steps, monkey turn over, strike both fists, bull turn to parry, golden rooster stands on one leg and point stick, and so on.

(三)霍童线狮

霍童线狮,又称霍童抽狮,现留存于宁德霍童镇,当地人称之为打狮,是一种独特的民俗游艺表现形式,也是一种具有独特风格的民俗的杂技节目,已有 1 300 多年的历史。据历史传说,隋代谏议大夫、开山大祖黄鞠公曾为霍童灌溉村田,造福子民,当地以举办二月二灯会的方式来纪念他。其中,线狮表演就是该灯会中最具有特色的一个节目。自明朝中后期开始,霍童线狮已经逐渐发展成为当地节庆文化中的一个重要组成部分。如今,作为非物质文化遗产的霍童线狮,已经超越了传统民俗节庆二月二灯会的范畴,成为霍童人民日常生活中不可或缺的一部分。2006 年被列为第一批国家级非物质文化遗产名录。

5.2.4.3 Rope-Controlled Lion Dance in Huotong Township

Rope-Controlled Lion Dance in Huotong Township, also known as Huotong Puppet Lion Dance, is currently preserved in Huotong Township, Ningde City in Fujian Province. It is called “Dashi” by local people, is a very unique embodiment of folk culture and recreation. Meanwhile as an acrobatic performance with its unique charm, Rope-Controlled Lion Dance in Huotong Township has a long history of more than 1 300 years. It is said that Huang Ju, imperial remonstrator for the emperor in the Sui Dynasty, built an irrigation project to benefit local people. In order to commemorate his contribution, local people held lantern fairs on the second day of the second lunar month. At that time, puppet lion dance was the most unique performance at the lantern fairs. Nowadays as an intangible cultural heritage, Huotong puppet lion dance has transcended the traditional lantern fairs, and become an absolutely indispensable part in Huotong daily life. It was listed as the first batch of national intangible cultural heritage in 2006.

五、工艺与技艺

宁德民间手工艺历史悠久、名扬中外，主要有柘荣剪纸、纸札、香亭、竹编、贝雕、白茶制作技艺、畲族银器制作技艺、铁技、线香龙舞、高跷等工艺与技艺，极富地方特色。

5.2.5 Arts and Handicrafts

The folk handicrafts in Ningde have a very long history, and are well known at home and abroad, such as Zherong paper cutting, paper binding, incense pavilion, bamboo weaving, shell carving, processing technique of white tea, silver production of the She nationality, iron processing skill, rope-controlled dragon dance, stilts and other techniques, which are full of regional features.

(一)剪纸工艺

闽东的剪纸最为著名的当数柘荣剪纸，该县因剪纸的广泛性、艺术性和传承性而荣获国家文化部授予的“民间艺术(剪纸等)之乡”的荣誉。

柘荣剪纸始于明末清初，其剪纸手法主要有平铺式、对称式、多折式和网络式。风格独特，具有鲜明的地域个性，既承传了中原剪纸的写意、质朴、浑厚，又融合了南方剪纸的严谨、细腻、秀丽。2009 年 10 月，柘荣剪纸被联合国教科文组织列入《人类非物质文化遗产代表作名录》。

5.2.5.1 Paper Cutting

When it comes to paper cutting in Mindong region, Zherong paper cutting is surely the most famous for its universality, artistry and continuity, therefore Zherong was awarded “Hometown of Folk Arts” by the National Ministry of Culture.

Originated in the late Ming Dynasty and the early Qing Dynasty, Zherong paper cutting is varied in techniques of flat-cutting, symmetric-cutting, multifaceted cutting and network-cutting. With distinctive styles and regional characteristics, Zherong paper cutting inherited the causality, simplicity and vigor of Chinese paper cutting, while combined with the preciseness, tenderness and beauty of the southern paper cutting. In October 2009, it was listed as UNESCO Intangible Cultural Heritage.

（二）纸札工艺

纸札：纸札源于明代，属于灯技艺术。宁德洋中把纸札踩街活动称为迎灯。纸札融木偶、竹札、木雕、彩灯、绘画、缝纫、灯光为一体，应用物理原理制作成机关，景物立感巧妙，水火逼真，人物活动栩栩如生。

5.2.5.2 Paper Animation Art

Originated in the Ming Dynasty, this is a lantern-making technique. Parade activities with lantern presentations is called "Yingdeng (lantern parade)" in Yangzhong Township, Ningde City. With the combination of puppet, bamboo art, wood carving, colored lamp, painting, sewing and lights, machine-operated paper lantern was made according to applied physics principles, so that visitors can enjoy three dimensional scenery with rather realistic effect and vivid activities of characters.

（三）香亭工艺

在闽东木雕艺术中，最能见其地域特色和艺术功力的当数木雕香亭。香亭是民间秋斋迎神祭祀活动时使用的供奉物。造型繁杂，工艺精巧。香亭高约2米，宽1米，结构以四层为多，下有四方形镂花底座；第二层的四个支架上各雕一尊兽面，或龙或狮。支架上是香亭柱有雕龙缠绕，亭顶的飞檐也有兽形雕刻。每个香亭的最上层各不相同，有的是两人托镜，有的木雕装饰顶。

香亭多采取透雕与浮雕方式，采用凿、雕、刻、磨、铲等十几道工序制作而成，雕刻内容多为飞禽走兽、花鸟人物和各种装饰图案，色调金碧辉煌。香亭这一民间工艺美术品如今在闽东亦不多见。其中最负盛名的是古田县晒谷村的五件清代制作的香亭，它比较完整地体现出清代南方木雕艺术的风格，有较高的观赏和研究价值。

5.2.5.3 Incense Pavilion

Wood-carving incense pavilion embodies the most representative regional features and earns the highest artistic level in Mindong wood-carving arts. It is used to enshrine and worship gods during the traditional sacrifice-offering activity "Qiuzhai" in the fall. At two meters high, and one meter tall, the incense pavilion is very complicated in the whole sculpture, and exquisite in skills. The whole structure is composed of one square base with ornamental engraving and another four layers above the base. An animal face (usually a dragon or lion) is engraved on the four holders on the second layer. Timber columns are placed on the holders, and entwined by carved dragons. In addition, cornices on the roof are also engraved with animal carvings. Generally speaking, the decoration on the top layer of every pavilion usually differs from one another: sometimes it is the scene of two people holding a mirror, sometimes it is simply wood carving decoration.

By adopting embossment and openwork carving, an incense pavilion has to be processed by dozens of procedures, such as chiseling, carving, engraving, grinding, spading and so on. The contents of sculptures on the pavilion are usually birds and animals, flowers and persons and other decoration patterns with splendid colors, incense pavilion is not common nowadays in Mindong, among which five incense pavilions made in the Qing Dynasty are the most prestigious. They are kept in Shaigu Village, Gutian County. Since they completely represent the Southern wood-carving style of the Qing Dynasty, they still enjoy a high value of appreciation and research.

(四)竹编工艺

传统竹编技艺在闽东各地均有流传,以古田竹编最具典型代表。该技艺相传起于清末。传统竹编制作过程先是破竹抽丝、刮削磨光,将竹子剖削成一根根厚薄匀净、韧性十足的竹条,小的仅两三毫米宽。之后,用水将这些竹条浸泡上几分钟,使之变得柔软。接着便是编织,这是竹编工艺中最难的一个环节,通过对竹条的挑压交织,编织出千变万化的图案及各种精巧的生活日用品。此后再经染色、上油、晾晒等工序,一件竹编制品便大功告成。

早在1959年古田竹编的花篮、花筐、提盒等被编入《福建工艺美术选集》。现在的产品有瑰丽花篮、竹蝶、角目提篮、猫盒、玉青花插等近百种。编工精制,典雅美观。产品已在十几个口岸出口,远销欧美亚等地区,深受欢迎。

5.2.5.4 Bamboo Weaving Handicraft

Gutian bamboo weaving handicraft is the most typical representative of the traditional bamboo handicraft in Mindong. It is said that this handicraft originated at the end of the Qing Dynasty. In the traditional procedure, the bamboo craftsmen cleave the bamboo, cut one section and split it into vertical halves, then smooth the bamboo joints, when they cleave the halves into flat or thin bamboo strips with average size, the small but firm strips can be as thin as only two or three millimeters width. Later soaking in the water for several minutes is required to soften the thin strips. Next procedure is weaving. As the most difficult procedure, weaving is adopted to make different patterns and various exquisite daily necessities through several steps with the bamboo strips, such as pulling, pressing and interweaving. Last but not least, a piece of bamboo product has to be done by other procedures like dyeing, oiling and drying.

As early as 1959, some Gutian bamboo weaving products were compiled in *Fujian Handicraft Collections*, such as flower basket, flower crate and food carrier and so on. Currently there are nearly a hundred types of products, such as exquisite flower basket, bamboo butterfly, hand-woven basket, cat-shape carrier, green flower receptacle. With such delicate handicraft and elegant outlook, Gutian bamboo weaving handicrafts were exported to regions and countries of Europe, America and Asia from dozens of ports in China, and well received by the local peoples.

(五)贝雕工艺

贝雕,顾名思义就是把贝壳琢磨加工制成的工艺品。这一工艺是在发掘和继承我国古老的传统艺术的基础上发展而来的。闽东的贝雕种类主要有浮雕贝画、嵌贝漆器、贝雕插花、立体贝雕等数百种样式。

5.2.5.5 Shell Carving

Shell carving suggests a handicraft of polishing and processing shells. Based on discovering and inheriting of traditional crafts in ancient times, Mindong shell carving includes hundreds of patterns, such as embossed shell painting, shell-embedded lacquer, shell carving vases, three-dimensional shell carving and so on.

(六)福鼎白茶制作技艺

福鼎白茶制作技艺是创制福鼎白茶的中心工序,具有自然、科学、优质的特点,拥有高超的制作方法,独具科学艺术魅力。在传承古老制茶法的基础上,以萎凋和干燥两道工序为主,技术制作工序流程呈水线形式进行,在我国茶类制作技艺中占有重要而独特的地位,其价值和影响意义深远。该制茶技艺已列入第三批国家级非物质文化遗产名录中。

5.2.5.6 White Tea Manufacturing Craft of Fuding City

Natural, scientific and excellent, Fuding White Tea manufacturing craft is the key to Fuding White Tea, which possesses unique charm of science and art with superb manufacturing skills. On the basis of traditional tea manufacturing process, the whole procedure is conducted with a linear process, featuring two main manufacturing processes: withering and drying. With great value and deep significance, Fuding white tea was listed in the third batch of national intangible cultural heritages for its unique and important role in tea manufacturing crafts.

(七)福安畲族银器制作技艺

以珍华堂为代表的福安畲族银器制作工艺,传承了盛唐宫廷银匠千年绝艺,在银雕工艺上,至今仍沿用祖传秘方来处理银器的表面光泽,确保银雕作品不失千年本色。在工艺品五大技艺——操、凿、启、解、披上日臻成熟,有效避免了传统工艺的重复性和粗糙感,作品独具匠心。在中国矿冶学史上占有很高的地位,为畲族文化的传承留下了特殊物证,是研究畲族传统文化的珍贵资料。已列入第三批国家级非物质文化遗产名录中。

5.2.5.7 Silverware Manufacturing Craft of the She Ethnic Minority in Fu'an City

Zhehua Hall (treasure hall) represents the silverware manufacturing skills of the She Ethnic Minority in Fu'an; they preserve the extremely excellent skills of royal silverware manufacturers in the most prosperous Tang Dynasty. To ensure the integrity of the silver carving ornaments, manufacturers nowadays still adopt secret prescriptions from their ancestors to polish the surface of silverwares. In order to avoid the repeatability and roughness of traditional skills, and to present unique genuineness of the silverwares, major skills have gradually been improved over time such as drilling, chiseling, wielding, engraving and so on. Fu'an silverware manufacturing craft was listed in the third batch of national intangible cultural heritage. It not only occupies a high position in the history of metallurgy, but also preserves valuable evidence for the research of the She culture.

(八)闽东铁技

铁技又称台阁。明崇祯年间有迎春妆台阁的记载,至今仍流行于屏南、寿宁、福安等县。铁技是以锻铁、铁条、钢管为骨架,将儿童扮作传统戏剧人物或神话人物,按故事情节小型由一人顶在肩上,大型由数人抬扛(今已用车)乐队伴奏,沿街进行游行的一种民间表演艺术。有立于剑稍,有卧于树枝,有悬于半空,有驾雾腾云。技艺巧妙、隐蔽、惊险、令人心悬。2008 年 6 月,蕉城霍童铁技、福鼎沙埕铁技、屏南双溪铁枝会合各地以抬阁(芯子、铁枝、飘色)项目,列入国家第二批非物质文化遗产名录。

5.2.5.8 Mindong Iron Acrobatics

Mindong Iron acrobatics, also called Taige Performance, is still popular in Pingnan, Shouning, Fu'an and Jiaocheng. Records prove the existence of decorating Taige to welcome spring. Iron acrobatics is a performing art, which use wrought iron, iron bars and steel tubes as the framework, dress children into the figures from a traditional opera or mythology. Generally speaking, if the performance is of a short story, only one child would be placed on the shoulder of a single person; if it is of an epic one, the children would be carried by several people (already replaced by vehicles), parading along the street. Sometimes they stand at the end of the swords, sometimes lie down on a branch, sometimes hang in mid-air, sometimes jump as if to appear on the clouds. Their skills are ingenious, concealed, thrilling and breathless. In June 2008, after the joint application of three major teams, namely Huotong Iron Acrobatics in Jiaocheng District, Shacheng Iron Acrobatics in Fuding City and Shuangxi Iron Acrobatics in Pingnan County, Taige Performance (also known as Xinzi, Tiezhi, Piaose) was listed onto the second batch of national intangible cultural heritage.

(九)高跷技艺

高跷流行于区内各地。表演者用四五尺长的木棍,中间嵌钉小托板,绑在腿上,扮演古装戏剧人物,边踩边歌。宁德有一种高跷高达一丈二尺,捆绑时要坐在屋顶上,可表演上台阶、下台阶、二人抬酒桶等动作,别具特色。寿宁高跷古称撬戏,清康熙时,便有立春日人扮撬戏相欢的记载。这种高脚戏高出人群,行动自如,引人注目。至今斜滩在农历正月十三时有演出。

5.2.5.9 Stilts Performance

Stilts Performance is popular in Mindong. A stilt is made by fitting a footrest on a long wooden stick. People tie the stilts onto the legs, then walk on the stilts and sing while dressed in the figures of costume dramas. There are a very special stilt in Jiaocheng; since it is as long as four meters, performers have to sit on the roof to tie the stilts to make special movements, such as walking up and down the steps, two folks carrying a wine barrel and so on. Stilts used to be called as Qiao drama in Shouning County. It is recorded that people dressed up to play Qiao drama for fun on the beginning day of spring in the Kangxi period of the Qing Dynasty. In such eye-catching performances, people walk on the stilts as if they were on the ground. Even at present, the stilts team could still be seen on the thirteenth day of the first month of the lunar calendar in Xietan, Shouning County.

(十)线香龙舞技艺

线香龙舞属于龙舞的一种。其龙身以稻草捆成,视长度插置木柄,由表演者擎举舞动。另札一龙球,由一人擎举舞动。表演时龙身龙球都密插点燃的线香,球在前腾舞,龙身随后前行,打击乐伴奏,迎舞大街小巷,别有风趣。20 世纪 50 年代初,线香龙舞停止了活动,近年又复起。

5.2.5.10 Burning-Incense-Sticks Dragon Dance

Burning-Incense-Sticks Dragon Dance is a branch of dragon dances, in which the dragon is made from rice straw with wooden handles insert into it . During the dance, one performer holds a dragon ball, the other performers hold the dragon body up by handles; both the body and the ball of the dragon will be inserted with burning incense sticks. Performers raise and lower the dragon making it dance, and chasing the dragon ball as they wind through streets according to the sounds of drums and gongs, which is a fabulous and interesting performance. However, Burning-Incense-Sticks Dragon Dance performance had stopped in the early 1950s, but it has re-appeared again in recent years.

第三节 民俗民风

5.3 Local Festivals

一、节俗

宁德传统的节俗有 4 个与各地类似的大节(春节、清明节、端午节、中秋节),4 个与全国各地大同小异的小节(元宵节、七夕节、重阳节、祭灶),还有许多宁德本地特色的节俗、习俗、农时节令和畲族重要的节日。其中具有宁德当地文化色彩的列举如下。

5.3.1 Major Festivals

Generally speaking, traditional festivals observed in Ningde include 4 major national festivals (the Spring Festival; Tomb-Sweeping Day; Dragon-Boat Festival and the Mid-Autumn Festival), 4 festivals sharing similar features as in other parts of the country but preserving some local features (the Lantern Festival; the Double-Ninth Day and the Kitchen God's Day). Besides there are many festivals, customs, important agricultural days and important holidays of the She ethnic people. The following are some of the typical local festivals:

(一)端午节

农历五月初五为端午节,又称端阳节,俗称五月节。旧俗,新嫁女的娘家于节前要给女儿送肚兜、巾、扇等物,由新媳妇分赠家中老小,连续三年,俗称送节。女婿则要给岳父母送节鱼(通常为黄花鱼)。五月初五端午节,在民间被视为是一个不吉利的日子,故有破五(泼污)之习。家家户户清洗门户,在宅院四周喷雄黄酒,在孩童耳、鼻、头额等处涂雄黄,燃雄黄香,在门两侧插艾草、菖蒲,门上或厅堂张贴钟馗或张天师像,午餐吃粽,喝雄黄酒,意即泼掉秽气,以避邪恶。端午节有赛龙舟活动,源于纪念楚国爱国诗人屈原。

5.3.1.1 Dragon Boat Festival

It falls on the fifth day of May of the lunar calendar. It is also called "Duanwu Festival" or "May Festival". The old custom went like this: Before the festival, the family that has newly married their daughter should give her belly vests, scarves, fans, etc., so that she could share with her new family members, either senior or junior, and this should be done for three years in a row. Traditionally this practice was called "gifts-sending". While the son-in-law should send his parents-in-law "festival fish" (usually yellow croakers). The Dragon Boat Day on May 5th is considered by folks as an unlucky day so there was a custom of "breaking the fifth", sounding in Chinese as "getting rid of the dirt". Therefore each family would have a general cleaning and sprinkle realgar wine around the house and yards. Besides parents would dot the realgar wine on the ears, noses, and foreheads of their kids, and burn realgar incense and hang up wormwoods or calamus on the door sides. Besides, they would also post some photos of the evil spirit expellers like Zhong Kui or Zhang Tianshi. Folks would eat Zongzi and drink realgar wine to indicate ridding of the dirty and evil spirit. And dragon boat races are held in memory of Quyuan, the patriotic poet of Kingdom Chu.

(二)祭灶神

宁德农村都是农历二十三祭灶神,而市区大部分是农历二十四祭灶神,供品有水果、糖等。民间传说农历二十四一过完灶神就要上天向玉帝汇报这家一年的行为来判断给予惩罚和奖赏。糖俗称"灶神糖",买糖是为了粘住灶神的唇让他上天时说好话,祭灶神是在晚饭后开始,把新的灶神画像粘在灶台上,旧的撕下连同元宝一起烧了。先把摆供品的地方擦拭干净后摆上供品、倒满酒。家中妇女点上香烛先祭拜天地,妇女会手拿着香对灶神说上几句好话比如"灶神您多吃多喝,到天上去时帮我家说好话。"后插香、点蜡烛、放鞭炮。过大概二十分钟后烧元宝,再说上几句好话,等元宝烧完后再放一次鞭炮送灶神上天。而后大家共享祭灶神的贡品。

5.3.1.2 The Kitchen God's Day

It falls on the 23rd of the twelfth month of the Chinese lunar calendar for the rural folks while it falls on the 24th for most of the urban dwellers. The sacrifices include fruits and candies etc. The candies are called Kitchen God's candies. The purpose of the candies is to sweeten the Kitchen God so that he would say good things in heaven. As legend goes after 24th, the Kitchen God would go to heaven to report on the family's annual behaviors to Emperor Heaven for his punishment or award for the family. The ritual starts after dinner. New Kitchen God's poster is to be stick on the kitchen wall and the old one torn down and burned with the paper money. The housewife would clean the kitchen table first and put on the sacrifice and fill the cups with wine. Then the housewife would light up some joss sticks to pay tribute to the heaven and the earth. Then with the sticks in hand, she would say some good words to the Kitchen God like "Please eat and drink more and say something good about my family when in heaven." Later on she would lay straight sticks and light up a candle for letting of firecrackers to start the ritual. After about 20 minutes she would begin to burn the joss paper money. After the burning is done, another round of firecrackers is to set off to see off the Kitchen God to heaven. Then the ritual wraps up and family members share the sacrifices.

(三)中元节

城关一般是从农历七月十一开始,一直到二十五为止,但时间绝不能超过白露这天,且祭祖的日子多选单日。农村,如虎贝一带,七月初一请祖翁,意即迎请祖宗回家过节。到了七月十五望日再祭。两次祭祀,时间都安排在下午申时(15—17时),稍有不同的是,初一供品较简陋,且不烧纸钱。对于逝世已过百日的死者,必须连续烧三年纸钱,称作头年纸、二年纸、三年纸,祭祀时间也会安排在七月初十以前。祭品、沿海地区人们多以弹涂鱼、章鱼、鲫鱼、红蟳、虾等海产品上桌,山区多以茄子、豆腐、豇豆、五花肉。七月半祭祖,必须有七层糕、蒸饭,祭到半途,开始焚烧纸钱,沿海一带焚烧锡仔,山区乡镇焚烧草纸制成的条状纸钱。

5.3.1.3 Zhongyuan(Ghosts) Day

It is also known as the 15th Day of the seventh month or Ghosts Day. It usually falls on 11th to 25th for the urban dwellers, but the time would not exceed the White Dew Day. Normally the odd days are chosen for worshiping ancestors. In the rural areas, like Hubei Village, folks would "invite ancestors back" on the first of the month and then on 15th once again offer sacrifices. The 2 sacrificial rituals are both arranged around 3 to 5 o'clock pm. The slight difference between the two rituals: the offerings at the first time are simpler and there is no paper money burning. For those diseased ancestors who had their 100th Day Sacrificial Rituals, their offspring should burn paper money for three years in a row during this period before the tenth of the month. The first,second and third year joss paper money is simplified as "the first year paper", "the second year paper" and "the third year paper". For those coastal folks, they would offer mudskippers, octopuses, crucial carps, and red crabs as sacrifices while the folks in the mountainous areas would present eggplants, tofu, beans and streaky pork etc. On the Ancestors Worshiping Day(on the 15th of the seventh month), there must be seven-tier cakes and steamed rice. In the middle of the ritual, paper money burning begins. Along the coastal areas, folks would burn tinned paper money while the mountainous folks would burn rough paper money out of wood pulp.

(四)三月三歌会

三月三是传统的踏青节,也是畲族的传统节日。在宁德畲乡,三月三又称乌饭节和对歌节。每年的这天,畲民们便三五成群聚集在一起,以独特的形式来庆祝:举办三月三盘歌会,吃乌饭,请巫师跳巫舞祭祀保平安,金斗洋武术竞技、喝宝塔茶等,这些都是不可缺少的节日内容。

5.3.1.4 Antiphonal Singing Day

The third day of the third month is a traditional Han national holiday for enjoying the green spring time as well as a traditional holiday for the She ethnic minority people. In the She ethnic villages, the day is also called "Black Rice Day" and Antiphonal Singing Day. On this day, the She ethnic folks would gather in groups and celebrate the holiday uniquely with antiphonal singing, eating black rice, inviting the sorcerers to perform sacrificial dances for safety, Jindouyang Martial Arts Competitions, drinking tea and so on. All these items are indispensable on such a day.

(五)补天穿

农历正月二十日为福安社口镇潘洋一带畲民的节日。这一天,畲民不下田,要做糯米糍补天。相传为纪念女娲娘补天之功,在正月二十日女娲生日这天做糍粑帮助她补天。这一习俗的起源有另一说法:古时每年正月阴雨连绵,影响春耕,是皇天漏雨的缘故。因此,这一天畲民都要做糍,供祭天皇,取意补天穿(破漏处)。

5.3.1.5 Patching-the-Sky-Hole Day

The 20th of the first month of the Chinese lunar new year is a holiday for the She ethnic people in Panyang Village of Shekou Township of Fu'an City. This day, the She Ethnic people do not labor in the fields; rather they would make sticky rice to patch the sky hole. As legend goes, such a day is in memory of the merits of the goddess Nvwa, who was born on this day and helped patch the sky hole in the ancient times, therefore the She Ethnic people also want to help her patch the sky hole too. Another legend goes that during the first month of the lunar year in the ancient times, the weather used to be very rainy, which casted negative impact on the spring plow. The reason for the wet weather was that the sky was leaking. Therefore the She ethnic people on such a day want to make sticky rice to offer to Emperor Heaven to patch the sky hole to stop the rain for the spring plow.

(六)蓝公节

农历正月初四是古田富达村畲族蓝姓村民的祭祖日。传说,蓝应潮之父蓝文卿曾为唐朝节度使,晚年隐居侯官东流境雪峰山下,舍家业建雪峰寺后,迁居古田县富达村。蓝应潮成为该村蓝姓始祖。村内在每年初四日抬迎蓝应潮塑像供祭,并上演神戏,直到正月十五日将塑像抬回蓝公殿祖祠内活动始结束。

5.3.1.6 Ancestor Lan's Day

The fourth day of the first lunar month is an ancestor-worshiping day for the She ethnic folks of the Lan's clan in Fuda Village of Gutian County. It is said Lan Yingchao was their ancestor. Lan Wenqin, Lan Yingchao's father, was once a chief commander of the army in the Tang Dynasty, but in his last years of life, he lived in solitude at the foot of Xuefeng Mountain within Fuzhou area. He gave up all his property to support the construction of the Xuefeng Temple and moved to Fuda Village of Gutian County. And then Lan Yingchao became the ancestor of the village. Each year on the fourth day of the first lunar month, folks in the village would carry his clay statue for worshiping. At the same time some plays of gods are performed till the 15th of the first lunar month when folks carry his statue back to Ancestor Lan's Temple.

(七) 迎祖节

迎祖节,又称请祖节,是宁德畲族祭祖节日,每年在农历正月十四日举行。迎祖时,抬迎着装有香案的香亭,全副执事仪仗,场面极其隆重。

5.3.1.7 Ancestors-Worshiping Day

It is also known as Ancestors-Welcoming Day or Ancestors-Inviting Day which is a day set for worshiping ancestors and falls on the 14th of the first lunar month each year. When the ritual group processes, the joss stick pavilion is being carried by a group of men in ritual uniforms and with props. The occasion is extremely grave and splendid.

(八)封龙节

为每年的农历五月,是畲族人民祷求风调雨顺、五谷丰登的娱乐性节日。这一天畲族群众不从事农活,人们穿上节日盛装,兴高采烈地赴舞会,在山坪、田垅对打山歌,歌词多歌颂劳动、喜庆丰收和表达爱情等,歌会的场面十分动人。

5.3.1.8 Fenglong Day

It is also known as Dragon-Conferring Day and falls in the 5th month of the Chinese lunar year. It is an entertainment festival for the She ethnic people to pray for smooth weather and good harvests. On such a day, the She ethnic people do not work in the fields. Instead they wear colorful festive uniforms and cheerfully attend the gatherings. On the mountain top or in a field, they sing antiphonally in a competitive way. Their songs mainly sing of their agricultural activities, their joy of harvests and their love. The occasion is very active and touching.

二、习 俗

5.3.2 Folk Customs

(一)闽东各地除夕习俗

5.3.2.1 Customs on the Eve of the Lunar New Year in Mindong

守岁:除夕夜家人团聚于炉前,通宵不寐,叙旧话新。近年来,城镇人家多于年夜饭后,围坐在电视机前观看中央电视台的春节联欢晚会节目。

Guarding the Eve: on the eve family members used to gather around a stove, stay awake all night chatting about the past and coming years. Nowadays, urban citizens would sit in front of TVs and watch the New Year Gala on CCTV after a big eve dinner.

祭祖与年饭:除夕日备年货菜肴、果品及米果、糕点等祭祀祖先。祭毕,家人团聚而食,称年饭或岁饭。

Ancestors worshiping and Eve Dinner: On the eve, families prepare dishes, fruits, rice cakes, crackers and so on for the ancestral worshiping rituals. After that, family members gather and eat, which is called "Year Dinner" or "Eve Dinner".

隔年饭:宁德俗,岁除炊半熟米饭,备新正日食,谓之隔年陈。有的地方还在饭上放两粒福橘,在春节食用,取有食有余之意。

Rice Crossing the Old and New Year: In Ningde there was a custom that on the eve of the new year, folks would cook some half-done rice and for eating on the first day of the new year, which was also called "rice crossing the old and new year". In some places, people also put oranges on the rice for eating in the spring festival, indicating they have extra food from the past year.

压岁钱:长辈在除夕或春节时给未成年后辈赐钱,称压胜钱,取压胜除邪之意。今民间仍盛行此俗。

Red Envelope Money or Lucky Money: Senior members in the family would give the younger generations or minors lucky money on the eve or during the spring festival, which is also called "overcoming money" indicating it would overcome evil spirit. Nowadays it is still very popular.

迎年:即在新春零点时刻,家家户户燃放鞭炮、焰火,宫庙则擂鼓、鸣钟,以接年。

Welcoming the New Year: At the twelve o'clock of the eve of the lunar new year, each family lets off firecrackers or fireworks, and the temples would strike drums or hit the bells to welcome the new year.

做年茶,食年饭前,按长次入席,由辈分最小的媳妇泡冰糖茶水依次敬奉,还要多出一盏,称添丁茶。寿宁先喝橘皮糖水,再吃瓜果,谓之尝甜。霞浦、宁德先吃糍汤。

Preparing the Year Tea: Before the eve dinner, each is seated by their seniority. Then the youngest daughter-in-law in the family is to offer sweet tea to the family members based on their seniority. And she would need to leave one more glass which is called "New Kid Tea" indicating new year and new kid(s). In Shouning County, folks would drink sweet tea with some orange skin, and then eat some fruits. In Xiapu County and Jiaocheng District, folks would eat tangyuan (glue pudding).

(二)寿庆

寿庆俗称做寿,大体分为贺寿、拜寿与寿宴。以五十岁为初寿,六十岁为下寿,八十岁为中寿,百岁为上寿,故也称做寿为做十。一般五十开始做寿,但也有特例,如寿宁、宁德有做九的习俗,即担心十关难过,先在四十九、五十九、六十九时先做过九预庆,至十再庆。贺寿,又叫过寿、送十。在腊月十五日或年前,知情亲友给寿者送礼品,视亲缘关系而定送礼轻重,如猪蹄、红联、寿匾、糕果等。以女婿礼品为最,除送匾、联外,还得送给岳父一套新衣。

各县拜寿与寿宴的时间不同,宁德、福鼎在正月初二到初十,寿宁、周宁、柘荣、福安在正月初一,霞浦是正月初二。届时,亲朋好友一路鸣炮前来拜寿,寿宁等地祝寿者到达门口要与寿家赛炮,然后开门请入。寿堂一般设鼓乐队,拜寿者到,均以鼓乐相迎。拜寿时,下辈人给寿者叩头、鞠躬,寿者则分发红包,也称拜寿包。拜寿时也伴以鼓乐。拜寿毕,寿家办寿宴,宴请送寿礼者。如今,各县农村庆寿在形式上多沿袭旧俗。福安、周宁、柘荣、寿宁等地寿家正月里常自费请龙狮队或戏班来村表演助兴,包一场电影或录像招待邻里或亲朋,城镇则多办酒宴祝寿。

5.3.2.2 Longevity Celebrating Custom

Longevity celebrations used to consist of congratulations, kowtow and a longevity banquet. Folks used to begin celebrating their primary longevity at 50, lower longevity at 60, medium longevity at 80 and upper longevity at 100. Therefore celebrating longevity used to be called celebrating one's ten's each, like 50, 60,70, or 80. Folks used to begin to celebrate longevity at 50, but there were exceptions. For example in Shouning County or Jiaocheng District, folks had a custom to celebrate one's nine like 49 or 59 because they were worried to pass their ten's. So they would celebrate longevity when they were 49, 59 or 69 so as to warm up for the longevity celebrations when they reach their 50, 60 or 70. On the 15th of the 12th lunar month or before the Chinese lunar new year, those informed relatives or friends would send their gifts. And the price of the gifts depend on the relations. Some gifts can be pig legs, red couplets, plaques, cakes and dried fruits etc. Of all gift senders, the sons-in-law would send the most valuable gifts; beside plaques and couplets, they were supposed to send their fathers-in-law a new suit.

Offering Birthday Felicitations and Birthday Banquets : Their dates differ in different counties. They would be held from the second to the tenth of the first month of the lunar new year in Jiaocheng District or Fuding County. Folks in counties of Shouning, Zhouning, Zherong, Fu'an would hold the celebrations and dinners on the first day of the lunar new year while the folks in Xiapu County would do on the second day. At that time relatives and friends would celebrate to offer their birthday felicitations along the way with letting of firecrackers. Men in Shouning County would compete in letting off firecrackers with the hosts outside their gates. After that hosts would open the doors and allow guests in. In the hall of the hosts a band of drums used to be invited to welcome the guests when they arrive. When offering birthday felicitations, the juniors would kowtow or bow to the one who celebrates his or her longevity. In return, they would get red envelope money from the hosts. During this time the band would accompany with loud music. After that the hosts would hold a longevity banquet to treat the gifts senders. Nowadays, the celebrations in the rural areas of Ningde remain the former practice. Those in Fu'an, Zhouning, Zherong or Shouning would pay by themselves to invite some dragon dance troupes or some drama players to celebrate the occasion. They even may rent a movie or video to treat their neighbors or friends. In the urban areas most guys would host longevity banquets at restaurants.

(三)周宁鲤鱼溪鱼葬习俗

相传郑氏八世祖晋十公的孙子偷鱼,并被当场抓住,郑氏八世祖晋十公在宗祠前吊打孙子,自甘认罚,宴请村人三日。开宴前,他还让村人立下誓言:无溪中鲤鱼,则无浦源村人。就这样,浦源村人自此不吃鱼,鲤鱼溪的鱼自此不怕人,演绎了八百年来人羡鱼休唱钓鱼歌和鱼闻人声而来,见人影而聚的奇妙人文景观。但鱼也有大限,因此就形成了独特的鱼葬习俗。

鱼葬的程序如下:在一位司仪的宣布下,鱼葬开始了。先是由领队者将得享天年的鱼安放在祭台上,并对其进行净香、上酒,顶礼膜拜,接下来由村中德高望重的族人宣读祭文:奈何天不永年,遽尔云亡,人非草木,焉能忘情,衔悲忍痛,还招尔魂。此后,将鱼隆重地葬于洞穴中,点香、烧纸钱以表纪念。其情其景,丝毫不次于为亡故亲人下葬。这就是鲤鱼溪流传了八百多年的鱼葬习俗。

5.3.2.3 The Carp Funeral at the Carp Brook of Zhouning County

The legend goes like this: a grandson of Jin Shigong (the tenth son) of the 8th generation of the Zheng's clan stole a carp in the brook and was caught red-handed. So Jin hung him up in front of the clan temple and voluntarily accepted punishment by treating the village folks for three days. Before the banquets he also made the folks swear: No carps in the brook, no Puyuan Villagers. This way, the Puyuan villagers would not eat the carps which as a result would not be afraid of the folks, which for over 800 years showcases the amazing humanity cultural scene where "folks admire that the carps would hear the fishermen's song no more" and "the carps would gather when they hear folks coming or see their shadows". However the carps also have limited life so that there developed unique custom of the carp funeral.

The procedure of the carp funeral: first a master of ceremonies would announce the start of the carp funeral. Then a group leader would place the passed-away carp on the sacrificial alter, offer incense sticks and wine, and kowtow. After that, a senior folk of the clan in the village would read out the funeral oration: "How sorrowful that nothing could ever last in this world and you were no exception. We aren't weeds and how can we keep emotionless at your decease? We just constrain the sorrow and pray to welcome your spirit back ..." Then gravely they bury the carp in the cave. Meanwhile they burn some incense sticks and paper money in memory of the carp. The scene and the emotion were not less than that for the deceased relative at a funeral. This is the carp funeral custom that has been going on for over 800 years at the Carp Brook.

(四)渔业生产习俗

渔民出海捕鱼吃饭时,"老大"要坐"上闷"——甲板上吃,伙计在"下闷"——二舱吃,"老大"没有举箸,别人不敢动嘴。通常烤鱼不翻过来,不吃鱼眼睛。渔民信奉妈祖和齐天大圣(少数人信天主教),认为妈祖就是海神,齐天大圣法力高强,要靠她(他)庇佑,才能在"水里求财",得到平安。渔民特别把龙王爷作为图腾膜拜。

霞浦渔民,正月初五要把龙王爷请出来迎街。宁德渔民,每年年初总要做一张祈平安的疏文,跪在龙王爷脚下喃喃祈祷。新船下水要大祭聚餐,渔船出海要祷祭,回船卸载又要“做福”。每年农历三月十三妈祖诞辰和九月初九日妈祖升天,都要大祭大庆。

渔民还有许多避凶求吉的习俗。如大船的船头两旁有两只大眼睛,叫作“船眼”,以“压”船头,取镇邪意。出船当日如遇死人,或人群吵闹凶打之事,有的改日启航,有的将船眼用红布罩住,不让“船眼”看到不吉利的事。船到海中如遇大鱼,“老舟代”要分辨出它是就来讨食的,还是来问路的。若就来讨食的就用米倒入海中喂它;就来问路的,就凭罗盘念出方向,让它泅去。如遇怪鱼“海和尚”出现时,则用“字纸符”撒到海中,予以镇邪。船到北茭(黄岐半岛)过弯道出海时都要烧香化楮(俗称棉衣、草鞋仔),叫作散发“买路钱”。

5.3.2.4 Fishermen's Customs

When fishermen went fishing outside, the captain would eat on the deck and other fishermen could only eat on the second deck. If the captain did not raise his chopsticks, the others dared not eat first. Usually the grilled fish would not be turned over (indicating the ship would not be turned over, either). Nor would the eyes of the fish be eaten. Fishermen believe in Goddess Mazu and Monkey King. A few fishermen believe in Catholism). Most fishermen think Mazu is the sea god and Monkey King is super powerful and fishermen need their protection so that they can be safe and prosper at the sea. They also worship Dragon King. The fishermen in Xiapu County on the fifth of the first lunar month would carry the statue of Dragon King for parades on the streets. And the fishermen in Jiaocheng would prepare an oration and bow down at the foot of Dragon King to pray in whisper. When new boats were launched, huge sacrificial rituals and a big feast were required. Before the fishermen set off to the sea, they must pray and offer sacrifices. When they returned they must celebrate too. Each year on the 13th of the third lunar month when Mazu was born and on the ninth of the ninth lunar month when Mazu rose to heaven, large scale sacrificial rituals and big celebrations were required.

The fishermen had many other customs to ward off bad luck and usher in good fortunes. For example, they would draw two big eyes on both sides of the bow and call them “boat's eyes” so as to keep the bow stable and overcome evil spirits. On the day for the boat to set off to the sea, if anything bad took place, for example, a person died, or the crew quarreled, the captain would change the itinerary. Some would cover the boat's eyes so that they would not see the unlucky things. If a boat in the middle of the sea encountered a huge fish, the captain would make sure if it came for food or for directions. If it came for food, they would pour rice onto the sea to feed it. If it came for directions, they would read out the directions on the compass so as to let it swim there. If they met with a strange fish like "a sea monk", they would use some magic paper to spread to the sea so as to conquer the evil. When their boats reached Beijiao waters (the Huangqi Peninsula), and just passed the bends to the ocean, they would burn incense sticks and some other coats and straw shoes, which was regarded as passing fee for the waters routes.

(五)狩猎习俗

狩猎是畲家男子的副业。狩猎时既有个人单独进行,也有集体行动。狩猎需要协同行动,即3～5人一帮、7～8人一组,事前做好分工。到达狩猎地点,有的随带猎犬搜山,有的守候在野兽必经之路,伺机身击。其行猎方式有土铳射杀、弩杀猛兽、竹枪杀兽、竹吊拴兽、木笼框兽、陷阱困兽、累刀刮兽等。

畲民出门行猎时,要拜猎神为田公元帅或为畲族始祖。获得猎物时,击中野兽第一铳者,可分得兽头、兽皮和部分兽肉。如第一铳击中,野兽仍在奔逃,由另一个人补铳后,野兽才死的,兽头兽皮归第一铳者,部分兽肉则与补铳者均分。其余兽肉按出猎者(含旁观者)人头平均分配。如猎到中等野兽(如野兔、雉鸡等),就推举出一人把猎物煮好,各户拿出一些酒来聚食。

5.3.2.5 Hunting Customs of the She Ethnic Minority

Hunting was a sideline for the She ethnic men. Hunting could be done individually or collectively. Hunting needs coordination in a group of 3-5 or 7-8. Before hunting, tasks were assigned. When folks arrived at the hunting spot, some were responsible for searching the mountain with hunting dogs; some guarded the unavoidable routes for beasts and looked for chances to shoot. The hunting methods included shooting and killing with local self-made explosive guns, or crossbows or bamboo spears. Some other trapping methods were also used like trapping animals with hanging bamboo baskets, or wooden cages, or dug traps so as to hunt them.

When the She hunters were to set out for hunting, they must bow to their Hunting God who was Marshal Tiangong or their ancestors. Whey the first hunter shot dead an animal, he would get the head, skin and share some meat of the animal. If he did not shoot dead the animal which was at large and was shot dead by another hunter, the sharing was different. The first shooter would receive the head and the skin of the animal. The meat would be shared with the second shooter. The remaining meat would be shared equally among all the hunters present or even onlookers. If just some medium animals like rabbits or pheasants were hunted, then a folk would be recommended to help cook them. And other members would bring some wine to eat together.

三、农时节令

5.3.3 Agricultural Seasonal Customs

（一）二月二

农历二月二日相传是土地的节日。土地原称社神,民间以为田地劳作的丰歉由土地神管理,故祀之虔诚,将二月二作为一年农事开始的节令。乡村劳动人民为祈求当年五谷丰登,各家各户都舂米时作米果,祭祀土地神,有的乡村举行集体会餐,以示祝福。

5.3.3.1 The Second Day of the Second Lunar Month

It is said this is a day set for the land god. The folks believe that harvests on the land were decided by the management of the land god so they worship it devoutly with sacrifices. They regarded this day as the beginning of the yearly agricultural activities. All the rural folks for the sake of the yearly harvests, would make sticky rice cakes to worship the land god. Some villages also hold collective banquets to convey blessings.

（二）四月八

农历四月八日是牛节,民谚有“人歇五月五,牛歇四月八”。传说牛是被玉皇贬到人间的大神,玉皇仅许它四月八吃馒头,他日只能吃草。故每年四月八日天刚亮,牛主就将牛赶到高山上等吃玉皇撒下的馒头,并鸣炮或放铳以庆贺牛节。

5.3.3.2 The Eighth Day of the Fourth Lunar Month

It is a day set for the buffalos or Buffalos Day. The folk saying goes: “Folks rest on the fifth day of the fifth lunar month while the buffalos rest on the eighth day of the fourth lunar month”. It is said the buffalo was a big god expelled from the heaven by the Emperor of Heaven who only allowed it to eat bread on that day and on the other days it could only eat grass. Therefore at the dawn of the day, owners of buffalos would drive them to the tops of the mountains waiting for the bread dropped by Emperor Heaven. Meanwhile they would let off firecrackers or self-made explosive guns to celebrate Buffalos Day.

(三)立夏

立夏是农事小节日。闽东农村立夏当日,家家户户总要买上几块光饼和一些肉供祭土地神,酬谢他保护麦子收成,并祈求夏季无虫害。寿宁俗,家家户户吃立夏糊,用米浆伴上韭菜、豌豆、目鱼、肉等煮成糊,俗称焙立夏,寓立夏雨期勿太久之意。

5.3.3.3 Beginning Day of Summer

It is an agricultural solar term (the 7th). On the day, all the rural folks would each buy some guangbing cakes and some meat to worship God of Land expressing their thanks to him for his protection of the good harvest of the wheat and praying that there would be no pest harm in Summer. In Shouning County each household would eat "puree for the beginning of summer", which is cooked with leeks, peas, squids and meat. The puree is also called "Baking the Beginning of Summer" indicating that the rain season during the solar term would not last too long.

(四)冬节

冬节是民间的重要节日。旧民间有冬至日,粉米为丸,荐拜祠堂及粘门楣之俗,这和今日的搓丸相似。冬节前一晚,全家老少围坐搓冬节丸。大人教小孩搓冬节丸,以贺佳节团圆。

5.3.3.4 Winter Solstice Day

It is an important folk festival. Formerly in the rural areas there was a custom that on Winter Solstice Day, folks would use rice powder to rub little balls and offer to the temples and also stick couplets on the doors. This is the similar holiday of "Rubbing Balls Day" today. On the eve of Winter Solstice, all the family members both senior and junior would sit around to rub winter solstice pills. The seniors would teach kids how to rub the balls to celebrate the family union.

四、信俗

宁德民间比较有影响的信俗主要有陈靖姑信仰、城隍信仰和马仙信仰。

5.3.4 Traditional Beliefs and Worships

The most influential traditional beliefs in Ningde are beliefs in Goddess Chen Jinggu, in Town God and in Goddess Maxian

(一)古田临水宫请香接火仪俗

古田临水宫请香接火仪俗始于宋代,盛于明清,经数百近千年传承,已成为福建及世界各地华人社区颇具影响的世界文化现象,是具有鲜明地方特色和深远影响力的非物质文化遗产,具有重要的保护价值。

古田临水宫请香接火仪俗与奥运圣火传递有着相近的文化意味。各地信众以社区或村落为单位组成仪队,在福首的引领下,随带道师长途跋涉至临水祖宫祭拜最信仰的陈靖姑,以求消灾祈福,平安吉祥。届时,锣鼓喧天、鼓乐齐鸣,各路精彩的戏曲剧目竞相上演,各种雕塑、雕刻美轮美奂,俨然是盛大的民间文化艺术节。请香接火仪队回到村后,举行大规模的巡境分香活动,仪队沿村社全境逐条街巷挨家挨户巡游,所到之处,家家户户男女老少守候门前路口,摆香案迎圣火。仪队巡游到本村宫庙举行下马供仪式,将请回的香火供于宫庙神龛上。接火仪式结束后,村里举办平安宴,全村男女老少欢聚一堂,共享平安,共庆神诞,共同期盼新一年幸福安康,国泰民安。

5.3.4.1 The Incense Fire Relay Ceremony from Lady Linshui Temple, Gutian County (Belief in Chen Jinggu)

It started during the Song Dynasty and prevailed in the Ming and Qing Dynasty. After hundreds-of-year inheriting, it has become quite an influential cultural phenomena among Chinese in Fujian and the world. It is an intangible cultural heritage with distinctive local features and far-reaching influence, which is significantly valuable for protection.

The ceremony has similar cultural connotation to the torch relay of the Olympic Games. All the believers in different communities or villages would organize themselves into teams and under the leadership of their team leaders, they would drive over a long distance and overcome obstacles to reach Linshui Temple to worship their most believed Goddess Chen Jinggu so as to ward off disasters and to pray for happiness, security and luck. At that time, drums and gongs are hit and various wonderful plays are performed one after another. All types of sculptures and carvings are beautifully paraded. It becomes a splendid folk cultural art festival. After the incense fire relay team comes back to their own villages, they would hold large scale distribution of the incense and parade door to door in the villages. Everywhere they go, each member of the families there would line up in front of their doors and set up incense altars to welcome the holy fire. When the team reach their village temple, they would hold a dismounting ceremony to welcome the incense into their temple shrines. After the ceremony is done, the whole village would have a banquet for peace. All the villagers, both male and female, young or old, gather together and enjoy peaceful and prosperous times as well as to celebrate the birth of Goddess Chen Jinggu, and pray for health and happiness for themselves and security and stability for the nation in the new year.

(二)柘荣县马仙信仰

马仙,又称马氏天仙、马元君等,与妈祖、陈靖姑并称“福建三大女神”。马仙信仰始于唐中叶,源自浙南,盛行闽浙,影响赣粤、台港澳乃至东南亚,迄今1 300多年,信众上千万。唐肃宗、宋太宗、宋真宗、元英宗、明正德帝都曾敕封马仙,封号多为马氏护国夫人、护国嘉佑真仙、灵泽感应真人等。柘荣是民间马仙信仰中心地带与发祥地,信俗活动最为典型、影响最大,遍布闽、浙、赣、粤和台湾,及东南亚等地,信众达1 000多万人,形成了独具特色的马仙信俗文化,最具代表性的是柘荣十三境每年一度的接仙民俗文化活动。仪俗由接仙、献祭、游境、醮仪、送仙五大部分组成,期间穿插着丰富多彩的民间文艺活动,前后历时一个月,是闽浙边界最隆重的马仙信俗活动之一。马仙信俗自宋朝传入柘荣后,成为弘扬孝德精神的载体乃至民众祈祷健康平安的精神寄托。目前,柘荣县马仙信俗已成为福建省唯一列入民俗门类的第四批国家级非物质文化遗产代表性项目名录。

5.3.4.2 Belief in Goddess Maxian

Goddess Maxian, also known as Heavenly Goddess Ma and Yuanjun Ma, is regarded as one of three major goddesses in Fujian Province with Goddess Mazu and Goddess Chen Jinggu. The custom began in the middle of the Tang Dynasty from the south of Zhejiang Province, prevailed in Fujian and Zhejiang, and influenced Jiangxi, Guangdong, Taiwan, Hong Kong, Macau and even the Southeast Asia for over 1300 years with more than 10 million believers. Emperors Shuzong and Taizong of the Tang Dynasty, as well as Emperor Zhenzong of the Song Dynasty and Emperor Yingzong of the Yuan Dynasty, and Emperor Zhengde of the Ming Dynasty all conferred her titles as “Protective Mrs. Ma”, “True Protective Goddess”, and “True Spiritual Goddess” and so on. Zherong County had become a central and spreading area of the custom of belief in Goddess Maxian. Its belief activities are the most typical, and the most influential covering areas of Fujian, Zhejiang, Jiangxi, Guangdong, Taiwan, Hong Kong, Macau and the Southeast Asia with more than 10 million believers. A unique and distinctive Goddess Maxian Culture has been developed and the most typical is the annual welcoming activities for Goddess Maxian in Zherong. The ceremonies include welcoming Goddess Maxian, offering sacrifice, parade, Taoist rituals and seeing off Goddess Maxian.

During this time many folk artistic performances are carried out for over a month, forming the most splendid folk activity of belief in Goddess Maxian around the borders of Fujian and Zhejiang. Since the belief custom was introduced to Zherong in the Song Dynasty it has become an important platform to publicize filial spirit and to pray for health and happiness. Nowadays, the custom of belief in Goddess Maxian in Zherong County has become the only folk custom listed into the fourth batch of the national intangible cultural heritages in Fujian Province.

五、食俗

5.3.5 Dietary Customs

(一)酒宴

宁德的传统酒宴通常有十道菜,象征十全十美,开席前桌上陈列有:白酒、葡萄酒、全家福拼盘(一般均为卤味类)、水果拼盘、水果罐头和花生、瓜子、糖果、蜜饯,供大家品尝。开席时第一道菜一般是芙蓉鱼翅,最后一道菜以一道甜汤作为整个酒席的结点,寓意甜甜蜜蜜。若是办婚宴要有大枣、花生、桂圆、莲子,取其谐音,祝福新人早生贵子,中间还有炒干贝、对半煎蟹、清蒸大龙虾、爆炒章鱼、清蒸石斑鱼、鸽蛋鲍鱼、海螺拼盘、鱼唇酸辣汤、甜点。大约开席3~5菜时,父母要领新郎、新娘到各席向前来祝贺的亲朋好友致谢敬酒。

5.3.5.1 Banquets in Ningde

The traditional banquet in Ningde usually consists of ten dishes symbolizing perfection in Chinese culture. Before the banquet, things placed on the table are: liquor, wine, a plate of assorted cold dishes, and a plate of assorted fruits, canned fruits, peanuts, watermelon seeds, candies, preserved sweet for guests to enjoy. When the banquet begins, the first dish is usually Shark's skin soup, and the last dish normally is a sweet soup as a wrap up of the banquet to indicate the happy and sweet life. In a wedding banquet, dates, peanuts, longans and lotus nuts would be included to use their Chinese sounds to wish the new couple would have a baby as early as they can. There are other dishes like fried dried mussel meat, grilled crab in half, steamed lobster, fried octopus, steamed grouper, abalone soup with pigeon eggs, assorted conches and shells, spicy and sour soup of fish lips, and dessert. After enjoying 3 or 5 dishes, the parents of the bride and groom would lead them to various tables to toast and thank the congratulating guests.

(二)四季小吃

宁德味小吃丰富多样,一年四季常食的点心有肉丸、牛肉粉、芋头面、酸菜水粉、肉菜面、扁肉、煎包、海蛎包、牛肉丸子、锅边糊、鱼丸、大肠粉扣、江南丸、芦叶(菅)棕(畲族特色食品)等。夏季常食的点心有药膳小肠汤、火烧仙草蜜、红豆汤、鸳鸯面、美容豆汤、凉拌绿竹笋、豆腐脑、泥钉冻,绿豆糕等。

5.3.5.2 Snacks in Ningde

Ningde boasts plentiful snacks. The snacks available around the year are: meat balls, beef noodles, taro noodles, sour vegetable noodles, meat and vegetable noodles, wonton, grilled meat balls, grilled oyster balls, beef balls, puree, fish balls, noodles with pig intestines, south China balls, dumplings in reed leaves(the She ethnic food). The summer snacks are: herbal soup with small intestines, herbal honey jelly, red bean soup, yuanyang noodles, green bean soup, cold mixed bamboo shoots, tofu jelly, sea worm jelly, green bean cake etc.

(三)肉丸

宁德的肉丸是最出名的特色小吃之一,既是一道饮宴不可缺的常菜。主要是取圆字寓意团圆、圆满。圆谐音缘,尤其适合喜宴,如以鱼、肉两圆混合上席,更有成双、有余的吉兆。肉丸最大的特点在于肉丸的皮是由地瓜粉揉芋泥作外壳,外表看起来晶莹剔透,以鲜肉、豆腐干、葱花、酱油、味精作馅,煎熟或蒸熟即成,醇香可口。

5.3.5.3 Round Meat Ball

It is one of the most delicious and distinctive snacks in Ningde. It is a common dish but indispensable at banquets too. The significance about the snack is its round shape which implies reunion, satisfaction, luck and destiny, especially fit for wedding banquets. If it goes with fish, it means double happiness and extra prosperity. Its distinctive feature is its wrapper which is made of sweet potato starch and mashed taro, looking like crystal. It is stuffed with fresh meat, dried tofu and onion leaves. Either fried or steamed, it tastes delicious.

第六章 宁德旅游

宁德依山傍海，风光秀丽，旅游资源独具特色，融“山海川岛湖林洞”于一体，既有“奇特景观”白水洋、“海上仙都”太姥山、“南国天山”嵛山岛、“榕枫盈眼”杨家溪、“人鱼同乐”鲤鱼溪、“碧波如镜”翠屏湖、“洞天福地”支提山、“海上天湖”三都澳等各具特色的自然景观，也有“燧人氏造火”、“黄帝造霍”、“尧帝封太姥”、“顺天圣母”陈靖姑等传说，也有被称为桥梁“活化石”的木拱廊桥、畲族民歌、闽东革命等文化遗产，是中国大陆海岸线上保留下来的一块没有受破坏和污染的生态休闲旅游胜地。

Chapter 6 Traveling in Ningde

Ningde, lying by mountains and the coast, enjoys beautiful scenery and rich unique tourism resources that feature mountains, seas, rivers, islands, lakes, forests and caves. There are unique natural scenic spots boasting various characteristics like Baishuiyang River Square (“a unique scene”); Mount Taimu (“a coastal fairyland”); Yushan Mount Island (another “Mount Heaven in South China”); the Yangjiaxi River (“a coastal Shangri-la of banyans and maples”); the Carp Brook (folks and the fish having fun together); Cuiping Lake (“green crystal”); Mount Zhiti (“a blessed land for the Taoists”; Sandu Bay(“a sky lake”) and so on. Besides there are legends like “Ancestor Suiren made fire”, “Emperor Huangdi built Mount Huo”, “Emperor Yao conferred the title of Mount Taimu”, “Chen Jinggu, a Holy Mother Obedient to the Heaven”, etc. In addition, there are cultural heritages like the Covered Wooden Arch Bridge praised to be “a living fossil of bridges”; folk songs of the She Ethnic People; revolutionary history in East Fujian and so on. Ningde is an eco-friendly, primitive, leisure tourism resort along the coast of China.

第一节 风景名胜

6.1 Scenic Spots and Places of Historical Interest

一、宁德风景名胜

6.1.1 Scenic Spots and Places of Historical Interest in Ningde

(一)屏南鸳鸯溪(5A)

鸳鸯溪,5A级国家重点风景名胜区,位于屏南县东北部,距县城30千米,处屏南、周宁、政和三县交界,总面积78.8平方千米,溪长14千米,是我国目前唯一的鸳鸯鸟保护区。每年秋季有数百上千只鸳鸯从北方飞来越冬,故有"鸳鸯之乡"之美誉。

鸳鸯溪共分白水洋、鸳鸯溪、叉溪、水竹洋——考溪、鸳鸯湖等5个游览区。白水洋游览区最让人称绝的是面积达8万平方米的"十里水街"。鸳鸯溪游览区,以野生动物鸳鸯、猕猴和稀有植物为特色,融溪、瀑、峰、岩、洞、潭、雾等山水景观为一体。其中最有特色的是"百丈漈水帘洞",为全国五大水帘洞之首。叉溪游览区位于鸳鸯溪下游,它以数千亩原始次森林为主,辅以丰富多彩的河谷景观。水竹洋-考溪游览区位于叉溪游览区西面,它以险峰、幽谷和黄山松为主要特色。鸳鸯湖游览区位于双溪镇,以湖光、小岛、鸳鸯、野鸭群及四季杜鹃花和寺庙、古塔等组成。

6.1.1.1 The Mandarin Duck Stream of Pingnan County (5A)

The Mandarin Duck Stream is a five-A national key scenic spot. It's located in the northeast of Pingnan County, 30 kilometers away from the county proper, and in a junction area of three counties of Pingnan, Zhouning and Zhenghe. It covers a total area of 78.8 square kilometers, and is 14 kilometers long. It's the only protection zone for mandarin ducks in China at present. There are hundreds of mandarin ducks flying from the north to hibernate each fall; therefore it enjoys a reputation of "homeland of mandarin ducks".

It has five sightseeing zones: the Baishuiyang River Square, the Mandarin Duck Stream, the Chaxi Stream, the Shuizhuyang-Kaoxi Stream and the

Mandarin Ducks Lake. The unique sightseeing spot in Baishuiyang is the "five-kilometer street of water" on three rocks covering an area of 80 000 square meters. In the scenic spot of the Mandarin Duck Stream, the features are of the wild mandarin ducks, rhesus monkeys and rare plants, which lie side by side with the streams, waterfalls, peaks, rocks, deep ponds and fog. Among them, the "Baizhangji Waterfall Cave" is the most characteristic, and stands out among the five similar caves in the nation. The scenic spot of Chaxi Stream lies in the lower reaches of the Mandarin Duck Stream, with thousands of acres of primitive forest as the main scene as well as the colorful views of rivers and valleys. The scenic spot of Shuizhuyang—Kaoxi Stream is in the west of the Chaxi Stream, with its perilous peaks, deep and secluded valleys and Pinus taiwanensis as the main features. The scenic spot of Mandarin Ducks Lake is in Shuangxi Township and composed of lake views, small islands, mandarin ducks, wild ducks and azaleas in the four seasons, temples and ancient pagodas forming a charming view.

(二)屏南白水洋(5A)

白水洋,5A级国家重点风景名胜区,2010年与福鼎市太姥山、福安市白云山联合列为宁德世界地质公园。白水洋位于宁德市屏南县境内,园区由白水洋、宜洋、水竹洋、棋盘顶和双溪五大景区组成,总面积达77.34平方千米。其中最具特色的是"十里水街",它是由三块平坦的巨石铺于水底而成的,最大的一块达4万平方米,总面积达8万平方米。河床布水均匀,水深没踝,阳光下,洋面波光粼粼,一片白炽,故称之为白水洋。因其奇特的地质地貌现象而被誉为"天下绝景,宇宙之谜",前国务院副总理吴仪游玩白水洋后题"奇特景观"。

6.1.1.2 The Baishuiyang River Square of Pingnan County (5A)

The Baishuiyang River Square is a five-A national key scenic spot. In 2010, it became a part of Ningde Global Geoparks with Mount Taimu of Fuding City and Mount Baiyun of Fu'an City. It's located in Pingnan County of Ningde City, and is composed of five scenic zones of the Baishuiyang River Square, Yiyang Water, Shuizhuyang Water, Qipan Peak and the Shuangxi River, with a total area of 77.34 square kilometers. The most characteristic of the scene is "the five-kilometer street of water" on three flat rocks with the largest one covering an area of 40 000 square meters, and the whole 3 rocks covering 80 000 square meters. The water distribution on the river bed is balanced and on ankle deep. Under the sunshine, the waves on the river bed glisten and look white; therefore the river square is called Baishuiyang(White Water) River Square. Because of its unique geological landforms, it is praised as "a unique scene in the world and a mystery of the universe". The former Chinese Vice-Premier Wu Yi inscribed "A Unique Scene" for it after her visit.

(三)福鼎太姥山风景区(5A)

太姥山,5A级国家重点风景名胜区,2010年与屏南县白水洋、福安市白云山联合列为宁德世界地质公园。景区位于福鼎市境内,观赏面积有92.02平方千米,保护面积为200平方千米,有太姥山岳、九鲤溪瀑、晴川海滨、福瑶列岛、桑园翠湖等5个景区和冷城古堡、瑞云寺2个景点。其中,太姥山岳是整个风景名胜区的精华所有,以降险、石奇、洞异、雾多四绝名震遐迩54峰:笔架峰、仙药峰、莲花峰、拔云峰、仙女峰、神羊峰、石虎峰、天柱峰、天圭峰等。各种形态的石景360多个,如夫妻峰、"九鲤朝天"、"二佛谈经"等,各种各样的洞100多个,若想遍历诸洞,需时28天,这些洞各具特色,而在诸洞中最神奇的,首推一线天、七星洞、将军十八洞。

6.1.1.3 Mount Taimu of Fuding City (5A)

Mount Taimu is a five-A national key scenic spot. In 2010, it became a part of Ningde Global Geoparks with Baishuiyang River Square of Pingnan County and Mount Baiyun of Fu'an City. It's located in Fuding City with a sightseeing area of 92.02 square kilometers, and a protected area of 200 square kilometers. There are six scenic zones in it, namely, Taimu Mountain, Nine Carp Brook Waterfalls, Qingchuan Beach, Fuyao Islands, Mulberry Field and Cuihu Lake, plus two historical sites of Lengcheng Fort and Ruiyun Temple. Among them, Taimu Mountains are the highlight of the whole scenic spot, where there are 54 peaks such as Bijia Peak, Panacea Peak, Lotus Peak, White Cloud Peak, Fairy Peak, Shenyang Peak, Stone-Tiger Peak, Sky Pillar Peak, Tiangui Peak and so on, which are famous for their four wonders of "breath-taking peaks, unique rocks, secluded caves and frequent fog". Besides, there are more than 360 rock scenes in various figures, such as The Couple Peak, "Nine Carps Looking at the Sky","Two Buddha's Talk about the Scriptures", etc. And there are more than 100 various caves. It takes 28 days if one wants to travel through all of the caves. They are distinctive, and the most magical ones are Yixiantian (A Narrow Opening of the Sky), Seven-Star Cave and the Eighteenth Cave of the General.

（四）福安白云山（5A）

白云山，国家重点风景名胜区，2010 年与屏南县白水洋、福鼎市太姥山联合列为宁德世界地质公园，近些年更发现了大规模古冰川遗迹——冰臼群。白云山位于福安市西北部，距市区 55 千米，因白云缠绕而得名。风景区总面积为 95.88 平方千米，由白云山、九龙洞、龙亭峡谷、金钟山及黄兰峡谷等 5 个景区组成。景区主峰缪仙峰海拔 1 448米，为闽东第一峰。山上白云凝秀，气候独特，除千变万化的云海奇观时常可见外，在仙顶峰还可看到罕见的“佛光”。

白云山后峰西坡有始建于明正德四年（1509）的“冷水寺”，后毁，1987 年重建，寺前有“天池”，盛产午时莲。该莲十分奇特，每日午时伸出水面开花，花开时噼啪有声，花呈白色。传说是王母娘娘座下七仙女经常来此天池沐浴戏耍，所以天池中长出了稀世的午时莲花，莲花平时都深藏水中，只有到午时才浮露出水面，亭亭玉立、皎洁无比，午时过后，莲花又慢慢沉入水中，所以福安县旧志里称为“午时莲花”。

6.1.1.4 Mount Baiyun of Fu'an City (5A)

Mount Baiyun (White Cloud) is a national key scenic spot. In 2010, it became a part of Ningde Global Geoparks with Baishuiyang River Square of Pingnan County and Mount Taimu of Fuding City. In recent years, large-scale ancient moulin clusters have been found in the scenic spot. It's located in the northeast of Fu'an City, 55 kilometers away from the downtown area, and named after the winding white clouds around the mountain. The whole scenic spot covers 95.88 square kilometers, and is composed of five zones of Mount Baiyun, Nine-Dragon Cave, Dragon Pavilion Valley, Mount Jinzhong and Huanglan Valley. The main peak of the spot is Miaoxian Peak, No. 1 in East Fujian, with an elevation of 1 448 meters, where white clouds are beautiful, and the climate unique. Besides, one can often see the ever-changing sea of clouds and the rare “Buddha Light” on top.

There's “Lengshui Temple” built in the fourth year (1509AD) during the reign of Emperor Zhengde in the Ming Dynasty on the western slope of the back peak of the Mountain. Later it was destroyed, and rebuilt in 1987. There's a “Heaven Pond” in front of the temple with lots of lotuses booming at noon. The lotuses are unique, and stretch out of the water and bloom at noon every day with a splashing sound. Their flower looks white. It is said that the seven fairy girls of Heavenly Queen used to come here to bathe and play, as is the reason the pond grows rare lotuses that bloom at noon. They usually hide in the deep water, and only come out of the water at noon. They are graceful and pure. In the afternoon, the lotuses gradually sink into the water. Therefore they are called "noon-time lotuses" in the old *Chronicles of Fu'an County*.

(五)周宁九龙祭瀑布群

九龙漈瀑布是省级风景名胜区,位于周宁县城东南 13 千米处的危峰断峡之中。瀑布总落差 300 多米,在长达 1 000米的流程中连续九级不同的落差穿过峡谷,形成奇绝的飞瀑深潭,被誉为"中国少有""福建第一""华东第一瀑"。2013 年 8 月九龙漈瀑布被批准为国家 4A 级旅游景区。第一级瀑布最为壮观,瀑高 46.7 米,宽 76 米,丰水期可达 83 米、巨瀑右上方还有一个直径 14 米的潭穴,镶嵌瀑间,人称"龙眼"。第六级至第九级是瀑瀑相接,人称"四叠瀑"。4 级瀑布流程 629 米。瀑间遍布怪石,形态各异、神奇逼真。九龙漈瀑布群四周群山耸立,峰奇石异、栩栩如生、有"鸽子峰""金鱼峰""腾龙峰""骆驼峰""蟾蜍爬壁""石猴观瀑"等。

6.1.1.5 The Nine-Dragon Waterfall of Zhouning County

It's a provincial-level scenic spot, and located in the breath-taking valley, 13 kilometers away from the southeast of Zhouning County proper. The total drop is over 300 meters. Along its 1 000-meter fall, there are consecutively nine stages at different levels, forming unique flying falls and deep ponds. It is known for being "No. 1 in Fujian", "Rare in China" and "No. 1 in East China". In August of 2013, it was approved as a 4-A national tourist attraction. The first stage of the waterfall is the most spectacular with a height of 46.7 meters and a width of 76 meters which can be expanded to 83 meters in rainy seasons. There's a deep pond of 14 meters in diameter in the upper right of the great waterfall, and is called a "dragon eye". The sixth to the ninth stages are connected one after another and are called "four-stage waterfall". The fourth stage waterfall flows a path of 629 meters, among which there are exotic and vivid rocks in different shapes. Around the fall, the mountains rise high with fantastic peaks and vivid rocks such as "Pigeon Peak", "Goldfish Peak", "Hovering Dragon Peak", "Camel Peak", "A Rock with Toad Climbing the Wall" and "A Rock of Monkey Viewing the Waterfall", etc.

(六)宁德周宁鲤鱼溪

周宁鲤鱼溪位于周宁县城西五千米处的浦源村中,曾被评为"福建最美的乡村",是我省十大旅游风景区之一。鲤鱼溪源自宋代,历经八百年,2008 年以"三个世界唯一"(鱼冢、鱼葬、鱼祭文),收录吉尼斯——"年代最久的鲤鱼溪"。鲤鱼溪源于海拔1 448米的紫云山麓，汇数十条山涧清泉奔流而下，峰回水转，至浦源村口水势顿减，五弯六曲穿村缓流而过。溪流贯村而去，长一华里，宽数米。溪中悠然遨游着七、八千尾彩色斑斓的大鲤鱼，“闻人声而至，见人形而聚，竞相觅食”，水深及膝，清澈见底，鲤鱼满溪，故而得名“鲤鱼溪”。浦源鲤鱼溪不仅以神奇锦鲤闻名遐迩，且村景幽雅，名胜古迹保护完好。

6.1.1.6 The Carp Brook of Zhouning County

The Carp Brook, five kilometers away from the west of Zhouning County proper, is located in Puyuan Village which was rated as "the most beautiful village in Fujian Province", and is one of the top ten tourism scenic spots in Fujian. The Carp Brook originated in the Song Dynasty(960-1279 AD)and has a history of 800 years. In 2008, with its three unique characteristics in the world (only fish mound, only fish burial service and only fish eulogy), it was listed into the Guinness World Records as "a carp brook with the longest history". It derives from the Ziyun foothill with an altitude of 1,448 meters, collecting dozens of mountain springs as it runs down. The flowing of the water slows down when it arrives at the entrance of the village and winds slowly through the village. The brook is 500 meters long and several meters wide. There are seven or eight thousand colorful big carps freely swimming in the brook. They approach and gather when hearing or seeing people and compete for food. The brook is a knee deep, clean and clear and full of carps, from which it gets its name. It's not only famous for miraculous fancy carps, but also known for its quiet and elegant village scenic spots and well-protected historic sites.

(七)古田翠屏湖(3A)

翠屏湖，省级风景名胜区，位于福建省宁德市古田县城东郊，距城区 3 千米。1958 年，国家在此兴建“一五”计划重点工程、我国第一座地下水电站——古田溪水电站，筑起长 412 米、高 71 米的大坝蓄水，淹没了逾千年历史的古田旧县城，形成了水域面积达 37.1 平方千米、蓄水量为 6.41 亿立方米的福建省第一大人工淡水湖。因湖背靠翠屏山，遂名“翠屏湖”。这里四周群山环抱，四季如春，湖面烟波浩渺，空气清新，水质碧澄，素有“福建太湖”“福建千岛湖”之美誉。湖中三十六个大小岛屿隔水相峙：有群鹭翔栖被誉为“爱情之岛”的白鹭岛，建于百年前的湖心岛欧式别墅，后垄岛上富有地方特色的溪山书画院以及深藏在山腹中迷宫般的地下发电厂等景点。

6.1.1.7 Cuiping Lake of Gutian County (3A)

Cuiping Lake is a provincial-level scenic spot located in the eastern suburb of Gutian County, 3 kilometers away from the downtown area. In 1958, the Gutianxi River Power Station was built here. It was a national key project of the First Five-Year Plan of China and also the first underground hydro-power station in China. A dam of 412 meters long and 71 meters high was built to store water which submerged the old town of Gutian with a history of more than one thousand years, as a result creating the largest artificial freshwater lake in Fujian Province with a water area of 37.1 square kilometers and a storage capacity of 641 million cubic meters. Because the lake locates against Mount Cuiping, so it's named after the mountain and is called "Cuiping Lake". It's surrounded by mountains and enjoys spring-like weather all the year. The surface of the lake is vast and misty with crystal clear fresh water; it's known as "The Taihu Lake of Fujian Province" and "The Thousand-island Lake of Fujian Province". Thirty-six islands of different sizes are scattered there. Among them there are scenic spots like the Egret Island known as "Love Island" for the perching of egrets, the European-style villas built on the Central Island of the lake 100 years ago, the Xishan Calligraphy and Painting Academy on the Houlong Island full of local characteristics; and the labyrinthine underground power plant hidden deeply in the mountains and so on.

(八)三都澳

三都澳又名三沙湾,位于宁德市东南部,为中国1.84万千米黄金海岸线的中点。距宁德市区3千米,为闽东沿海的"出入门户,五邑咽喉",是世界级天然深水良港。素有"海上明珠"之称。三都澳旅游区景点多集中在三都澳东南部,可分为斗姥景区、福海关遗址景区、青山景区、笔架山景区和鸡公山景区五个部分,此外还有海上渔城全国农业旅游示范点,三都军港观赏和海上景观游赏等三大游览点。澳内有许多形态各异的礁石岸坞,峰奇石怪,景色优美,每年吸引众多游人前去观光。

6.1.1.8 Sandu Bay

Sandu Bay, also called Sansha Bay, is located in the southeast of Ningde City in the midpoint of the golden coastline of 18,400 kilometers in China, three kilometers away from the downtown of Ningde City. It's an important exit and pivotal access to five counties along the coast of East Fujian as well as a world-class natural deep harbor. It has been known as "a coastal pearl". The tourist attractions are mainly located in the southeast of Sandu Bay in five zones, namely Doumao Scenic Spot, Fuhaiguan Customs Historical Site, Mount Qingshan, Mount Bijia and Mount Jigong. Besides, there are another three tourist spots, namely, Sea-Farming Town on the Sea, which is a national demonstration site of agricultural tourism, the navy base of Sandu Port as well as the seascape around Sandu Port. There are reefs of various shapes and exotic peaks and rocks with beautiful views in the bay and each year they attract many tourists.

(九)福鼎嵛山岛

福鼎嵛山岛,古称福瑶列岛,意即“福地、美玉”,位于霞浦三沙5海里,是闽东最大的列岛,中国最美的十大海岛之一。嵛山岛由大嵛山、小嵛山、鸳鸯岛、银屿等11个岛屿、4个礁石组成,陆地面积28.3平方千米,海岸线长30.12千米。大嵛山岛直径5千米,面积21.22平方千米,最高处纪洞山海拔541.3米,为闽东第一大岛。在海拔200米处,有大小两个湖泊,人称大、小天湖。湖周围群峰环拱,其状似盂,嵛山岛也有由此得名,大天湖面积1 000多亩,小天湖200多亩,两湖相隔1 000多米,各有泉眼,常年不竭,水质甜美,清澈见底。湖畔多有野生乌龟出没。湖四周山坡平缓,有“南国天山”之誉的万亩草场。小嵛山岛为一无人岛,面积3.28平方千米,沿岸因被海水冲刷风化,基岩裸露,礁石林立,海蚀地貌十分突出,构成奇特的景观。小岛海拔仅50米,岛上植被茂密,栖息着成千上万只海鸥和其他候鸟,乍然飞起,十分壮观。

6.1.1.9 Yushan Mount Island of Fuding City

Yushan Mount Island was called Fuyao Archipelagoes in the ancient times, meaning “a blessed land and a beautiful jade”. It is located about 5 nautical miles away from Sansha of Xiapu County. It's the largest archipelago in East Fujian, and one of the ten most beautiful islands in China. It is composed of four reefs and 11 islands like Bigger Yushan Mount Island, Smaller Yushan Mount Island, Yuanyang Island, Yinyu Island and so on. The land area is of 28.3 square kilometers with a coastline of 30.12 kilometers. Bigger Yushan Mount Island is 5 kilometers in diameter, and covers an area of 21.22 square kilometers and its highest point is Mount Jidong at an elevation of 541.3 meters. It is the largest island in East Fujian. On the island, at an altitude of 200 meters, there are two lakes called Bigger and Small Tianhu Lakes. Mountains surround the lakes and they look like a jar(Yu). That's why they are called Yushan Islands. Bigger Tianhu Lake covers an area of about 1 000 mu, and Smaller Tianhu Lake is more than 200 mu. They are about 1 000 meters apart and each gets spring outlets which perennially keep flowing with sweet and crystal water. Round the lake there often appear wild turtles. The surrounding slopes are flat, and there is a grassland over 10,000 Mu like a mini Tianshan Mountain in Xinjiang, thus called the "Tianshan Mountain in South China". Smaller Yushan Mount Island has no inhabitants and covers an area of 3.28 square meters. The seacoast of the island is being scoured by seawater and weathered, so the bedrock is exposed. Besides there are reefs around and the marine abrasion landform is quite obvious, which constructs a unique scene. The island is just 50 meters above the sea level with dense vegetation, and there are thousands of seagulls and other migratory birds perching here. When they suddenly fly, the view is spectacular.

(十)霞浦杨家溪

杨家溪,位于宁德市霞浦县境内,原名南洋坪,相传北宋名将杨文广在此平定南蛮十八洞之一,并留杨家将士在此驻守。杨家溪又名九鲤溪、七里溪,1988 年 8 月经国务院批准,杨家溪属国家级风景名胜区太姥山五大景区之"九鲤溪瀑景区",素有"海国桃源"之美誉。景区约 35 平方千米,由九鲤溪景区、龙亭瀑布景区、钱大王村区、青龙寺区、杨家溪村景区、下坪洋村区、半岭亭区、渡头村区和雉溪龟山村区等九个小区构成。杨家溪畔有两片相距不远,总面积有 250 亩的枫香林,约有 1 100多棵枫树。秋末冬初,枫叶黄里秀红,犹如绯云停驻;在两片枫香林之间的间隔地带有 17 丛古榕群,树龄最长者已有 800 多年,其中一株"榕树王",树干周长 12.6 米,冠幅直径 51 米,高 30 米,树干中空,有 7 个洞口,洞内可容数人。据说这是全球纬度最北的一片古榕林,近处百亩桃树林,春暖花开,景色更佳,春夏绿叶如茵,秋冬白花遍野。

6.1.1.10 The Yangjiaxi River of Xiapu County

It's located in Xiapu, Ningde City and was formerly known as Nanyangping Grassland. It's said that in the Northern Song Dynasty, Yang Wenguang, a great general, pacified one of the 18 southern tribes of ethnic people, and asked his troops to station here and that's why it got its name(the Yang's). It's also called the Nine-Carp Brook and the Qilixi River. In August of 1988, approved by the State Council, it became a part of the Nine Carp Brook Waterfall Scenic Spot, one of the five scenic zones of the national scenic spot of Mount Taimu and has been known as "a coastal Shangri-la". It covers an area of about 35 square kilometers, and is composed of nine small zones, namely the Nine-Carp Brook, Dragon Pavillion Waterfall, Qian Dawang Village, Qinglong Temple, Yangjiaxi Village, Xiapingyang Village, Banling Pavilion, Dutou Village and Zhixiguishan Village. There are two maple forests not far away from each other along the river and they cover a total area of 250 Mu with more than 1 100 maple trees. In the deep Autumn and early Winter, the maple leaves are yellow mingled with red, like dark-red clouds lingering on there. At the interval zone between the maple trees, there are 17 groups of old banyans, of which the oldest is over 800 years old. One of them was called "king of the banyans" having a trunk with a circumference of 12.6 meters, a diameter of 51 meters and a height of 30 meters. And it is hollow in the tree trunk with 7 holes and can hold several persons inside. It is said that this banyan forest occupies the most northern latitude in the world. Nearby, there are one hundred Mu of peach trees. The scenery is super when they blossom in spring. In the scenic spot all the leaves turn green in spring and summer and in fall and winter white flowers can be seen everywhere.

（十一）大京海滩

大京海滩位于霞浦县长春镇东南部，东冲半岛近陆端，素有"福建夏威夷"、"闽东北戴河"之美誉。沙滩长3 000米，宽200多米，并有明代古城堡等名胜古迹和神话传说相衬托。大京海滩的迷人之处是沙龙岗的外面是一个斜度很缓的斜坡，海水浸不到，干燥的沙子雪白雪白的，由于吸收了阳光的热量，踏上去温而不烫，沿着斜坡往下，沙子渐渐潮润起来，沙地也就坚实起来。由于海水的凝聚力，踩下去，整个脚板陷下去，感觉与在雪地上行走无异。再往下，沙地就更坚实了，就算负重的车子行过，也不过留下淡淡的车辙。沙龙岗的另一侧，有一条纵深约百多米的清一色木麻黄的风沙防护林。这是福建省第一条大面积的木麻黄人工风沙防护林。林中地面全是细砂，间有耐旱的杂草点缀，加上木麻黄枝叶遮天蔽日，营造出一片浓浓的绿荫，故而被称为"情人的天堂"。在大京沙滩的东北部有一条不足百米长的鹅卵石滩，由于海浪的冲刷摩擦，鹅卵石已没有棱角，全由优美的弧线构成。

6.1.1.11 Dajing Beach of Xiapu

It's located in the southeast of Changchun Township, Xiapu County at the near end of Dongchong Peninsula. It has been known as "Hawaii in Fujian" and "Beidaihe Beach of East Fujian". The beach is 3 000 meters long and 200 meters wide. There are places of historic interest like the ancient forts of the Ming Dynasty and myths and legends. The fascinating scene here is the mild slope outside the Shalonggang Mound, The slope is not soaked in seawater, and the dried sand is of snow-white color. Because the sun heat is absorbed, so the sand is warm but not hot when people stand on it. Down the slope, the sand is gradually moist, and becomes solid. Because of the cohesive force of the seawater, when walking down, one's whole feet will sink like walking on snow. Walking down further, people feel the sand gets more solid and there won't be obvious tracks left even it is passed by heavy vehicles. On the other side of Shalonggang Mound, there's s a protective forest belt of sand barrier casuarina over about one hundred meters long. This is the first large area of planted forest of casuarina sand barrier in Fujian Province. The area is covered with thin sand and dotted with drought resistant weeds, plus the casuarina leaves making a lot of shade in summer, so it's called "a paradise for lovers". In the northeast of the beach, there's a cobblestone belt less than hundred meters long, and because of the scour and friction of the waves, the cobblestones have become smooth, and shaped as beautiful arches.

(十二)台山列岛

台山列岛隶属福鼎市太姥山镇，是福建省距离大陆最远且有人居住的唯一列岛，是中国四大天然厚壳贻贝保护繁殖基地之一，距福鼎沙埕港约 18 海里，福鼎沙埕港及台山岛有客船通航。台山列岛由西台、东台、南船屿、南屿等 15 个岛屿及 22 个礁石组成，分布在方圆 5 平方千米范围内。15 个岛屿中西台岛最大，面积约 1.2 平方千米，最高点海拔 130 米，东台岛次之。两个岛相距 1 000多米，是 15 个岛屿中有人居住的两个岛。东台与西台岛之间的西南面入口处，横亘着列岛中的第三大岛——南船屿。其他的岛屿和礁石则分布在东西长 6 千米、南北宽约 4.5 千米的东海上。台山列岛未经开发，至今还是个原始的海岛风光，岛上礁石奇特，洞穴幽秘，有"一线天""天桥""千堆雪""海底隧道""鸟岛"等原生态景色，还有"雨伞礁"和"犀牛礁"，犹如两个忠实的卫士一南一北守卫着主岛的入口处。长久以来，它们一直被岛上渔民视为庇护当地风调雨顺保平安的吉祥物。在那里你可以观东海日出日落、潮涨潮退，捉海边小生物，拾贝壳，看成群的海鸟。游泳，海钓，潜水，体验渔家生活，观赏湛蓝海水，徒步环绕群岛，参观台山战役遗留防御工事等。

6.1.1.12 Taishan Archipelagoes

They are parts of Taimushan Township of Fuding City and are located the furthest distance from the mainland of all inhabited archipelagoes in Fujian and one of the four protected natural breeding bases of thick shell mussels in China. They are 18 miles away from Shacheng Port of Fuding. There's a ship route between Shacheng Port and Taishan Archipelagoes. They are composed of 15 islands of Xitai, Dongtai, Nanchuan, Nanyu etc. and 22 reefs scattered within a range of 5 square kilometers. Among the 15 islands, Xitai Island is the largest one, with an area of about 1.2 square kilometers. Its highest point is 130 meters above sea level. Dongtai Island is the second largest one. The two islands are about 1,000 meters apart and the only inhabited among the 15 islands. In the southwest entrance between Dongtai and Xitai Islands, there's the third largest island—Nanchuan Island. The other islands and reefs are distributed on the East China Sea within a range of 6 kilometers long from east to west and 4.5 kilometers wide from north to south. The Taishan Archipelagoes remain natural and keep the original island scenery with unique reefs and secluded caves. There are primitive scenes like "A Narrow Opening of the Sky", "Heavenly Bridge", "Thousand Piles of Sand Snow", "Subsea Tunnel" and "Bird Island", etc. Besides there are views like "Umbrella Reef" and "Rhino Reef". They look like tow loyal guards defending the north and south entrances of the main islands. For a long time, the local fishermen have considered them as a refuge and mascot that can ensure smooth weather for the crops and keep the area safe. One can enjoy the sunrise and sunset and the tide in the East China Sea, catch little sea creatures, pick up shells, and watch a flock of sea birds. One can also swim, go fishing and diving, experience the fishermen's life there, appreciate the blue sea water, walk around the islands and visit the remaining battle sites of Taishan Island and its fortifications, etc.

(十三)牛郎岗海滨沙滩

牛郎岗海滨沙滩,位于福鼎市秦屿镇东南方,距国家级风景名胜区太姥山23千米,海滨沙滩依山面海,与嵛山岛隔海相望。这里气候冬暖夏凉,素以"碧海金沙好消夏"而吸引各地游客慕名而至。景区分为海滨浴场区、高科技农业园区、垂钓区、鸟岛保护区等18处游览观赏项目。牛郎岗海滨沙滩平坦、明净,环山绿树成荫,周围礁石造型各异,有鸳鸯礁、织女洞、海上一线天等自然景观,是一处集休闲、旅游、海滨度假为一体的旅游新景区。

6.1.1.13 Niulanggang Beach

It's located in the southeast of Qinyu Township of Fuding City and 23 kilometers away from the national scenic spot of Mount Taimu. It lies by the mountains and faces the sea, standing here with the Yushan Mount Island across the sea. The climate here is fairly mild in winter and rather cool in summer. So it has been known for "the blue sea and golden beach for a cool summer", therefore it attracts many tourists. The scenic spot consists of 18 zones for sightseeing, namely, beach swimming area, high-tech agricultural park, fishing zone and bird-protection area, etc. The beach is flat, bright and clean and the surrounding trees provide pleasant shade in summer. Besides the nearby reefs are in different miraculous shapes, becoming natural scenes like Mandarin Duck Reef, Weaving Girl Cave, A Narrow Opening of the Sky on Sea and so on. It's a new tourist resort for leisure, travel and coastal vacationing.

(十四)支提山

支提山,位于宁德市区西北50千米处。"支提"为梵文"聚集福德"之意,共分4个游览区,即支提胜场、瀛洲击水、霍童洞天和那罗延窟。

支提寺是宋开宝四年(971)所建,寺内存有明永乐、万历御赐"千圣天冠"铁佛、"鎏金大毗卢"铜佛五爪金龙紫衣以及"北藏经"等稀世之宝。1983年4月9日经国务院批准,列为全国佛教重点寺院。支提寺所处的支提山,海拔800多米,周围耸立99峰,全山有700多个景点,被列为"支提胜场"景区。

瀛洲击水景区在2007年洪口水库修建蓄水时没入水下。那罗寺位于虎贝乡,始建于唐代,寺为木架两层结构,上无片瓦,实为岩中奇寺。附近有罗汉洞、古佛塔、狐猿叫月、五鸟攀枝、九龙盘、开法台、观音织布等景点,组成了"那罗延窟"景区。2007年,国家林业局批准设立"福建支提山国家森林公园"。支提山森林公园总面积2 299.93公顷,森林覆盖率达90%以上,森林公园分为平匋山景区、支提山景区、金山景区和白马山景区,各景区既各具特色,又互相映衬,由此构成了支提山森林公园融峰峻、林茂、谷幽、水秀、瀑奇于一体的独特自然景观,还有国家级珍稀保护植物,如桫椤、金毛撅、三尖杉群落等。

6.1.1.14 Mount Zhiti

It's 50 kilometers away from the northwest of Ningde City. "Zhiti" means "gathering of blessings and virtues" in Sanskrit. It has four sightseeing zones, namely Zhiti Ritual Site, Single-Raft Surfing on the Yinzhou River, Taoist Huotong Mountain and Nryana Cave.

Zhiti Temple was built in the fourth year (971AD) of the Kaibao period in the Song Dynasty. It keeps rare royal gifts of 1 000 iron Buddhas and a purple coat with a five-claw golden dragon and a copper Buddha as well as "the Beizang Scriptures", etc. during the reign of Emperors Yongle and Wanli of the Ming Dynasty. On April 9th of 1983, it was listed as a national key temple of Buddhism approved by the State Council. Mount Zhiti stands at an altitude of more than 800 meters and has 99 peaks and more than 700 scenic spots. They constitute a zone of scenic spots of the Buddhist rituals.

The scenic spot of the Single-Raft Surfing on the Yinzhou River disappeared because of the construction and water storage of Hongkou Reservoir in 2007. Nryana Temple in Hubei Village was built in the Tang Dynasty. It has a two-tier structure of timber frame and there's no tile on the top. It's actually a unique temple in the rocks. Nearby, there are Arhat Cave, Ancient Buddhist Pagoda, Fox and Ape Rocks Shouting at the Moon, Five-Bird Rocks Flying to the Branches, Nine Mingling Dragon Rocks, Religious Ritual Stage, Goddess Guanyin Weaving, etc. All these form a scenic zone of "Nryana Cave". In 2007, the State Forestry Ministry approved the establishment of "the National Forest Park of Mount Zhiti in Fujian". The total area of the forest park is of 2 299.93 hectares with a forest coverage rate of more than 90%. The forest park is divided into scenic spots of Mount Pingtao, Mount Zhiti, Mount Jinshan and Mount Baima. These scenic spots are distinctive and mutually enhance each other's scenery, so that they constitute unique natural scenes of high peaks, luxuriant forests, quiet valleys, crystal water and unique falls. Besides there are also some national rare and protected plants, such as spinulose tree fern, cephalotaxus and fortunei, etc.

(十五)霞浦建善寺

建善寺,位于霞浦县城北龙首山东段华峰秀谷下,始建于南齐永明元年(483),至今达1 500多年,为福建省现存年代最早的寺院,有“八闽第一古刹”之称。是唐代五大禅宗之一的沩仰宗创始人灵祐禅师的祝发出家之地。在寺后橄榄树下,留有当年灵祐禅师坐禅灵石和禅堂断墙,至今善男信女拥挤香火益旺。建善寺院雄伟宽大,占地达2千多平方米,寺内风光佳丽,清幽明媚,寺前老榕交柯成荫,院中银杏挺立(有“活化石”之称的珍贵孑遗植物),寺后木棉苍劲。寺内还收藏有霞浦县许多历史珍贵碑刻等文物。

6.1.1.15 Jianshan Temple of Xiapu County

It is located in the beautiful valley of the east section of Mount Longshou in northern Xiapu County proper. It was built in the first year (483AD) of the Yongming period in the Nanqi Dynasty, over 1 500 years ago. It's the oldest temple in Fujian Province, and has a reputation of being "the first ancient temple in Fujian". It was the temple where Lingyou, the founder of the Weiyangzong Denomination, one of the five Zen Denominations in the Tang

Dynasty became monk and a Zen master. Under the olive tree in the backyard of the temple, there remains a sitting stone for his meditation and a broken wall of the meditation room. Up to now, devout men and women flood there to offer their incense. The temple, majestic and broad, covers an area of more than 2,000 square meters. Inside the temple, the scenery is beautiful, quiet, radiant and enchanting. In front of the temple, the old banyan trees intersect. The gingko stands upright in the yard (a precious plant known as the "living fossil"). Behind the temple, the ceiba trees are strong and flourish. In the temple are kept some cultural relics like the precious historical inscriptions of the county.

(十六)宁德古田临水宫

临水宫,位于福建省古田县大桥镇中村临水,是一座风格别致的仿唐代宫殿建筑,始建于唐贞元八年(792),后经元明清历代重修扩建,至今已有1 200多年的历史,是分布国内外各地临水宫的祖殿,被福建省人民政府列为省级文物保护单位。

临水宫依山建筑,红墙绿瓦,参差错落,气势恢宏,全宫占地2 000多平方米,分前后左右四分殿:前殿南墙设两重仪门,越数级台阶达大院,院内存有古戏台、钟鼓楼、拜亭和正厅,以精雕细刻的廊柱、雕梁、画栋、斗拱扶摇而上,形成大小藻井。正厅中间供奉着相传以陈靖姑真身所塑造的神像;左殿是太保殿;右殿塑有三十六婆官像;后殿由陈母葛夫人殿、梳妆楼、三清宫组成。临水宫周围还散存着与陈靖姑身世相关的百花桥、梳妆桥、顺天府宫、夫人潭等10多处遗迹,是人们探幽访古,游览观光的胜地。近年来,许多美、英、法、荷兰、日本、马来西亚、新加坡、泰国等国家,以及港、澳、台等地区及大陆学者、专家、游客纷纷到临水宫考察旅游。

6.1.1.16 Lady Linshui Temple of Gutian County

It's located in Zhongcun Linshui Village of Daqiao Township, Gutian County of Fujian Province. It's a chic building that imitates the palace architecture in the Tang Dynasty, and was built in the eighth year (792AD) of the Zhenyuan period, then it was rebuilt and expanded in the dynasties of Yuan, Ming and Qing. It has a long history of more than 1 200 years. It's the oldest original temple of all Linshui temples in China and abroad, and listed as a protection site of provincial cultural relics by Fujian Provincial People's Government.

It's built on the mountain slope with red walls and green tiles and looks very spectacular. It covers an area of 2 000 square meters with four branch temples in its four directions. In the south of the front temple there are two ceremonial gates. One has to walk step by step upwards to get to the main yard where there are Ancient Stage, Bell and Drum Towers, Worship Pavilion and the main hall inside. There are sunken panels of big and small sizes of fine engraved and carved pillars, beams, painted rafters and brackets. In the middle of the main hall, there's a statue said to be the real appearance of Goddess Chen Jinggu. On the left, it's Guardians Hall. And there are 36 statues of midwives in the right wing. The back temple is composed of Mrs. Ge's (Chen's mother) Temple, Dress and Make-up Tower and Sanqing Temple. There are also kept more than 10 relics related to Chen Jinggu's life experience, such as Baihua Bridge, Dress and Make-up Bridge, Shuntianfu Temple and Lady Chen's Pond, etc. They are the sites for visits and looking back the ancient time. In recent years, Linshui Temple has been visited by many scholars, experts and tourists from home and abroad, including America, Britain, France, Holland, Japan, Malaysia, Singapore, Thailand as well as Hong Kong, Macao and Taiwan, etc.

(十七)东狮山

东狮山,形似狮而得名,位于福建省柘荣县城东 3 千米处,总面积 13.7 平方千米,海拔 1 480米,为太姥山脉的主峰。环山之中有谷、泉、洞、岩、峰、石等自然景观二百二十七处。1998 年 7 月东狮山被省政府批准为省级风景名胜区,由蟠桃映翠景区、百丈朝暾景区、仙人锯板景区、普悦洞天景区、龙井瀑布景区和仙都胜境景区 6 大景区组成。蟠桃景区洞奇石怪,洞幽寒彻,溪流清澈,雾纱轻绕,总给人几分神秘感。百丈景区绝岩峭壁,层峦叠嶂,冬季时这里四处冰凌高挂,玉树琼枝,一派北国风光。龙井景区曲折川流,水落深潭,飞流直下的瀑布,水雾迷蒙,荡涤着人们的心灵。仙都景区空谷幽兰,漫山杜鹃,春夏之交这里百鸟啭啼,山花烂漫,煞是可爱,还有宋时窑群遗址、明朝开国功臣袁天禄的义军练兵场、明湖广布政司游朴之墓,石亭、石坊等名胜古迹。寺观多达十多处,有普光寺、觉性寺、东峰寺、广福寺、白马宫、青云宫、马仙观、三清观等。

6.1.1.17 Mount Dongshi (Eastern Lion)

It looks like a lion, and so comes its name. It's located 3 kilometers away from the east of Zherong County proper, Fujian Province, and covers a total area of 13.7 square kilometers at an altitude of 1 480 meters. It's the main peak of the Taimu Ranges. There are 270 natural scenes of valleys, springs, caves, rocks, peaks and stones, etc. In July of 1998, it became a provincial-level scenic spot approved by the provincial government. There are six major scenic spots of Yingcui, Baizhang, Immortals' Masterpieces of Rocks, Puyue Caves, Longjing Waterfall and Xiandu Fairyland. The caves and stones in the Yingcui Scenic Spot are amazing and cool. The rivulets there are clean and crystal with fog circling around and producing a mystic feeling. In the Baizhang Scenic Spot there are exotic rocks and cliffs on multiple ranges of mountains. In winter the ice hangs highly on the trees making them look like a beautiful and snowy scene of North China. In the Longjing Scenic Spot the river flows circuitously into the deep pond and the waterfall produces mist that seems to refresh people's soul. In the Xiandu Fairyland Scenic Spot there are azaleas everywhere; birds sing and flowers bloom lovely and beautifully at the junction of spring and summer. In addition, there are also historical and cultural sites like the kiln relics of the Song Dynasty; the training ground of the volunteer army commanded by Yuan Tianlu, a meritorious founder of the Ming Dynasty; the Tomb of Youpiao, a minister of the Ming Dynasty as well as stone pavilions and memorial archways, etc. In addition there are more than ten Buddhist and Taoist temples, such as Puguang Temple, Juexing Temple, Dongfeng Temple, Guangfu Temple, Baima Temple, Qingyun Temple, Maxian Temple and Sanqing Temple, etc.

(十八)宁德东湖国家湿地公园

宁德东湖国家湿地公园是 2009 年 12 月底,经国家林业局批准设立。东湖国家湿地公园位于宁德市区以东 4 千米的大金溪河口,公园总面积为 623.8 公顷。宁德东湖国家湿地公园是福建省建设的第二个国家湿地公园。公园生物多样性丰富,已查明维管束植物有 48 科 88 属 98 种、野生脊椎动物有 31 目 79 科 226 种,共有鸟类 14 目 30 科 110 种,占福建省鸟类总种数的 20%,湿地特征典型,湿地景观和历史文化价值高。公园根据功能定位、湿地与鸟类的分布特点分为山、湖、岛、海 4 大景区,通过合理布局,突出独特的湿地生态旅游功能和景观效果,成为福建省著名的滨海湿地生态休闲游览胜地和生态科普教育的湿地公园。

6.1.1.18 National Wetland Park of Donghu Lake of Ningde City

It was established with the approval of the State Forestry Administration at the end of December, 2009. It's located at the estuary of the Dajinxi River, 4 kilometers away in the east from the downtown. It covers a total area of 623.8 hectares. It's the second National Wetland Park in Fujian Province. It's rich in biological diversity. There are vascular plants of 48 families and 88 genera and 98 species. There are 31 orders, 79 families and 226 species of wild vertebrates, and 14 orders, 30 families and 110 species of birds, accounting for 20% of bird species in Fujian Province. It boasts typical characteristics, scenes, and high historical and cultural values of wetlands. According to its functional orientations and the distribution of the wetland and birds, it has been divided into four scenic spots of hills, lakes, islands and sea. The well arranged layout of the park highlights the unique wetland ecotourism functions and scenery effect and the spot has become a famous provincial leisure resort of the coastal wetland as well as an ecological wetland park of popular science education.

(十九)上金贝畲村

上金贝畲村位于宁德市蕉城区金涵畲族乡,海拔 325 米,距离宁德市区只有十几分钟的车程,是近年来兴起的一个适宜观光休闲的社会主义新农村的代表与典范。其借助独有的历史遗迹和景观,并在政府的重视和有识之士的发掘下,从一个名不见经传的畲族小山村迅速发展成为一个清秀美丽的畲族新农村。在村边,走过一条 500 米的葡萄长廊,沿途垄间池塘中盛开的荷花随风摇曳。长廊的尽头是樱花园、蜜柚园、茶园等,构建起了一个“科技农业观光农庄”。村北半山腰上的丛林中有一座明代神秘古墓,经专家考证应是明代建文帝朱允炆陵寝,虽墓室被盗,但依然保留着其独特风采。游人可沿着登山步道,登上村后的八仙顶峰。山虽不高,但山上石峰耸立,林幽谷深,局部山峰仿佛有张家界之神韵。站在峰顶,可远眺附近村镇及宁德市区,天气好时,还可看见三都澳海阔天空。

6.1.1.19 Shangjinbei Village of the She Ethnic People

It's located in Jinhan, a village of the She Ethnic People in Jiaocheng District of Ningde, at an elevation of 325 meters, and only ten minutes' drive from the downtown. It's a representative example of the new socialist countryside suitable for sightseeing and leisure. With the help of the unique historical sites and scenes, and some capable scholars and the government, it has developed rapidly into a new beautiful and well-known village of the She Ethnic People. Walking through the grape vinery corridor of 500 meters long, one can see water lilies flourishing in the pond in summer. At the end of the corridor, there is an oriental cherry garden, a honey pomelo garden and a tea garden. These make the farm village a place to learn about science and agriculture. To the north of the village, halfway up the mountain in the forest, there's an ancient mystic tomb. According to research by experts, it is the mausoleum of Emperor Jianwen (Zhu Yunwen) of the Ming Dynasty. Though the tomb was pillaged, the unique style still can be seen. One can also walk along the mountain trail to climb to the peak of the Eight Immortals Mountain in the back of the village. Though the mountain is not very high, it has rising rocky crags, dense forests and deep valleys. Some parts of the mountain gain the charm similar to that of Zhangjiajie Scenic Spot in Hunan Province. Standing on the top of the mountain, one can see the nearby villages and towns and some parts of the downtown. On a sunny day, one can even see the Sandu Bay afar.

(二十)寿宁西浦村

西浦村位于闽浙边界,至今有1 100多年历史,是南宋特赐状元缪蟾的故乡,历史上出过18名进士,历代的举人、贡生、秀才等更是举不胜举,使西浦成为名副其实的"状元故里"。西浦的韵致在水,散布着各种各样的桥梁,木拱桥、石板桥、古碇步为国内罕见,它们建造年代不同,所用材质各异,具有一定的文物研究价值,被誉为"桥的博物馆"。古民居群等建筑文化经典与双溪交汇、状元树、滨水杨柳带、鲤鱼溪等自然景观完美结合,展示了西浦村"廊桥水乡,状元故里"的独特魅力,先后获得"全国生态文化村""海西十佳魅力乡村""省级园林村""省级文明村""宁德市十大最美乡村"等称号。

6.1.1.20 Xipu Village of Shouning County

It's located in the boundary area of Fujian and Zhejiang Provinces, with a history of over 1 100 years so far. It's the hometown of No. 1 Imperial Exam Scholar Miao Chan in the Southern Song Dynasty. There were 18 successful candidates in the highest imperial examinations in the history of the village. There were also numerous successful candidates in the imperial examinations at the provincial, county and town levels. Therefore Xipu is worthy of its name of "Home village of Imperial Exam Scholars". The river is an important special element in Xipu, and there are many kinds of bridges, namely wooden arch bridges, stone slab bridge and ancient stone-stool bridge. Though they were built in different times with different materials, they have research value as cultural relics, and Xipu is known as a "bridge museum". The ancient residence buildings are combined perfectly with the natural scenes of the Shuangxi River, No. 1 Scholar Tree, Willow Trees in Binshui and the Carp Brook, etc. They show the unique charm of a place that has been listed as one of the National Ecological Cultural Villages and called "one of the top ten charming villages in the west coast of the Taiwan Straits", "provincial garden village", "provincial civilized village", and "one of the top ten most beautiful villages of Ningde City".

二、宁德名人故居

6.1.2 Former Residences of Famous People in Ningde City

(一)甘国宝故居

甘国宝(1709—1776),清康熙四十八年(1709)生于古田县二十六都(今屏南小梨洋村),曾官至福建陆路提督,兼闽阅操大臣,是清代的一位名将。在四十余载戎马生涯中,甘国宝不但治军严饬,戍边尽责,威震一方,且体恤兵民,扶贫济困,恩泽黎民,对百姓视如父,爱如子深得百姓拥戴。尤其是他两度戍台,担任挂印总兵,为保卫和建设台湾、维护国家领土完整,做出不可磨灭的历史贡献。2007 年,中国国民党荣誉主席连战先生为纪念甘国宝戍台 240 周年时,欣然题写"超凡入圣"四个隶字,精辟地概括了这位清代名将护国爱民的非凡一生。

甘国宝故居,位于甘棠乡小梨洋村,为清代民居,宅占地面积约 300 平方米,坐西北向东南,由门前埕、大门、照壁、正厅、后座楼房组成,正厅前有左右下廊、马弄,现皆毁,楼上正厅悬挂有甘国宝中试后上司赠给的"会魁"金字匾。甘潈下村上祠堂,悬有乾隆皇帝御赐"福"字金匾,为甘国宝于清乾隆三十三年(1769)十二月省亲进带回。2001 年甘国宝故居被列为县级文物保护单位。

6.1.2.1 Former Residence of Gan Guobao

Gan Guobao (1709-1776) was born in the 48th year (1709AD) of the reign of Emperor Kangxi of the Qing Dynasty in No. 26 Village of Gutian County (now called Xiaoliyang Village of Pingnan County). He had been the provincial commander-in-chief and minister in charge of army training. He was one of the great generals in the Qing Dynasty. In his forty-year military career, he was sublime because of his strict training and responsible guard of the border, but also because of his sympathetic treatment of people and soldiers. He helped the poor, brought people grace, considered them as the family, and loved them, so he was respected and supported by people. He was twice stationed in Taiwan, and was a general commander and made an indelible historical contribution to defending and safeguarding the national territorial integrity. In 2007, Lien Zhan, honorary chairman of the Chinese Nationalist Party in Taiwan inscribed four Chinese characters of "Extra Ordinary and Holy" to celebrate the 240th anniversary of Gan Guobao's stationing in Taiwan, which brilliantly summarized the contribution of his extraordinary life in defending and loving the nation and people in the Qing Dynasty.

His former residence is located in Xiaoliyang Village of Gantang Township. It's a folk house in the Qing Dynasty and covers an area of about 300 square meters. It lies in the northwest but faces to the southeast. It is composed of the front field, gate, sky light well and main hall and the back building. In the front of the main hall, there used to be lower corridors and a horse lane. There's a gilded plaque inscribed "Top Exam-Taker" hanging in the main hall that was given by the authorities after he passed the exam. In the ancestral temple of Ganjixia Village, there's a gilded plaque inscribed "Blessings" from Emperor of Qianlong which was brought back by Gan Guobao when he came back to visit relatives in December of the 33rd year(1769) of Emperor Qianlong's reign. In 2001, it was announced that the residence would be as a county-level cultural relic unit for protection.

(二)薛令之故居遗址

薛令之(683—756),长溪廉村(今属福安市溪潭镇)人,"开闽第一进士",史称其"文章破闽天荒",是福建历史上第一位进士,后官至太子侍讲,以清正廉洁而著世。唐肃宗即位后,感念他的清廉特赐他的故乡为"廉村",水为"廉溪"。这是中国历史上唯一由皇帝敕封以"廉"字命名的村庄。据史料描述,薛令之的出现,中国古代诗坛才有了福建籍诗人清晰的身影和声音,是他为福建写下了最为精彩的第一笔,并奏响了闽籍诗人文学创作的序曲。其生前所著《明月先生集》和《补阙集》,今已无存。《全唐诗》仅录其《自悼》和《灵岩寺》二诗。

廉村位于福安市溪潭镇,原名石矶津,是唐朝福建第一个进士薛令之的故乡。村里的后湖宫("明月先生")为祭祀薛令之的祠堂。祠前村道拐个弯,就到了薛令之故居遗址。廉村河对岸的城山村灵岩山,有一处薛令之年少读书地,人称"灵谷草堂"。草堂于唐咸通元年(公元 860 年)改建为寺,现存寺院建筑重修于民国初年。1999 年底,福建省人民政府授予廉村为全省首批历史文化名村。2004 年廉村先后被宁德市和福安市评为爱国主义教育基地以及廉政教育基地。

6.1.2.2 Former Residence of Xue Lingzhi

Xue Lingzhi(683-756)is from what was formerly called Liancun Village of Changxi County and now Xitan Township of Fu'an City. He was known as "the first successful candidate in the highest imperial exam history of Fujian Province", and it is recorded that "his articles enlightened the people of Fujian Province". Later he was appointed an official in charge of the education of the royal family. He was well known for his honesty and uprightness. After his enthronement, Emperor Suzong of the Tang Dynasty conferred honorary names to the hometown and river of Xue Lingzhi "Liancun Village" ("Incorruption Village" and "Lianxi River" ("Incorruption River") in memory of Xue's outstanding character. This is the only village named so by an emperor in the history of China. According to the historical records, Fujian poets began to be active in ancient Chinese poetry just because of Xue Lingzhi. He made a great contribution to the literary creation of Fujian poets. His works of *Collections of Mr. Bright Moon* and *Supplements of Mr. Bright Moon* were lost. There are only two of his poems that remain, "Mourning For Oneself" and "Ode to Lingyan Temple" and they are a part of *The Full Poem Collections of the Tang Dynasty*.

Liancun Village, the hometown of Xue' is located in Xitan Township of Fu'an City. Formerly it was called Shi Jijin. The Houhu Temple is the ancestral temple for worshiping Xue Lingzhi. Just take a turn in front of the temple, one will arrive at his former residence.

Across the Lianxi River, in Mount Lingyan of Chengshan Village there used to be a place where Xue Lingzhi studied. Folks call it "Linggu Cottage of Learning".

It was rebuilt as a temple in the first year (860AD) of Emperor Xiantong's reign in the Tang Dynasty, and the present temple was restored in the early years of the Republic of China. At the end of 1999, the Liancun Village was enrolled onto the first batch of historical cultural villages approved by Fujian Provincial People's Government. In 2004, Liancun Village was awarded by Ningde and Fu'an as a base for patriotic and incorruption education.

(三)圆瑛故居

圆瑛(1878—1953),光绪四年(1878)生于古田县平湖乡端上村农家。为当代爱国名僧,佛教领袖。圆瑛不仅佛学造诣精湛,且擅长诗文、书法,国内的主要禅林都留下他的遗墨,新中国成立后为中国佛教协会首任会长。

圆瑛故居位于平湖镇端上村,始建于明末崇祯年间。端上开祖文昌公,开村第一屋至今400多年,属明代样式二层木结构。主楼长10.5米,宽5.5米,计面积115.5平方米;其侧房为4×4米二层楼,计面积32平方米;总计面积147.5平方米。圆瑛居住此屋系圆公祖上遗产。只知圆公爷、父辈三代住进此屋。圆公是开村第十一代后裔,从出生至14岁在此屋居住,19岁在家养病,20岁即1897年,离开此屋不复返,距今112年。此屋此后交由堂侄吴贞玉看管、居住。贞玉于20世纪70年代搬出,此屋至今被闲置已有30余载。2008年对圆公故居进行修缮,并整理出圆公遗物如过冬棉袄、生活用茶筒、照明竹纸灯、自学课桌、石凳、石枕，以及圆母、元铨公政绩德行勋匾和圆公叔谋生用具等遗物。

6.1.2.3 Former Residence of Yuanying

Yuanying(1878-1953)was born into a peasant family in Duanshang Village of Pinghu Township of Gutian County in the fourth year (1878) of Emperor Guangxu. He's a famous patriotic monk and one of the Buddhist leaders. His accomplishments of Buddhism were exquisite, and he was also good at poems and calligraphy. The domestic main Buddhist temples still keep his works of calligraphy. He was the first inaugural President of the Buddhist Association of China after the founding of PRC.

The former residence of Yuanying is located in Duangshang Village of Pinghu Township and was built during the years of Emperor Chongzhen's reign in the late Ming Dynasty. It was the first house of his ancestor Wenchang in the village with a history of more than 400 years. It's a wooden structure of two stories from the Ming Dynasty. The main building is 10.5 meters long and 5.5 meters wide, and covers an area of 115.5 square meters. The attached house beside it has two stories of 4×4 meters with an area of 32 square meters. The total area of these two buildings covers an area of 147.5 square meters. The residence is his ancestral heritage and it's known that three generations of his have lived here. He's one of the eleventh generation descendants and lived here from his birth to 14 years old. At 19, he was recovering from poor health at home. At 20 (1897), he left the house and never came back. So far it has been 112 years. After Yuanying left, the residence was inhabited and taken care of by his nephew Wu Zhenyu. In the 1970s, Zhenyu moved out, so it has been uninhabited for more than 30 years. It was repaired in 2008, and his mementos have been collected such as his winter jacket, tea tin, bamboo paper lamp, self-study desk, stone bench, stone pillow, plaque of political achievement and virtues, living utensils and other mementos, etc.

(四)游朴故居

游朴(1526—1599)，柘荣县黄柏乡人。隆庆元年(1567)中举人，万历二年(1574)中进士后步入仕途。曾供职于吏部、刑部及四川、广东、湖广等地，政声卓著，在二十余载的为官生涯中，他清理冤狱、惩奸除恶、厉行改革、赈灾济困、兴修水利、清正爱民，深受百姓敬重和当朝赞许，《福建省志》称赞“三主法司，无一冤狱”。

游朴故居位于霞浦县松城街道俊星村曲井头府前路72-2号。始建于明万历年间(1573—1619),坐北向南,二进合院式,占地面积1 400平方米,依次由大门、前厅、天井、书房、卧室等组成。主体建筑为抬梁、穿斗混合式,悬山顶,砖木结构。大厅面阔7间、宽23米,进深7柱、深14米,大厅木构架采用减柱造,跨间10多米。屋顶檩下斗拱装饰,地面用方砖铺成。天井地面用青石条铺成,大门已毁。整座房屋用材硕大,极具明代风格,是霞浦县内唯一明代官宦人家建筑,2010年被霞浦县政府列入第八批县级文物保护单位。

6.1.2.4 Former Residence of Youpiao

Youpiao (1526-1599) is from Huangbai Village of Zherong County. In the first year (1567) of Emperor Longqing, he succeeded becoming a Juren (meaning a successful candidate in the imperial exams at the county-level). In the second year (1574) of Emperor Wanli, he succeeded being a Jinshi (meaning the successful candidate in the highest imperial examination) and began his political career. He had worked in the Ministry of Personnel Affairs, the Ministry of Justice, and in places of Sichuan, Guangdong and so on, making outstanding political achievements. During the 20 years of his official career, he was honest and upright and extraordinary at dealing with unjust verdicts, reform. He was relieving the people in disaster and giving them financial help, undertaking water conservancy projects. Because he was honest and upright he was respected and praised by the people and the imperial government for "not making a single wrong ruling in Three Terms of Office" as recorded in the *Chronicles of Fujian*.

His residence is located at No. 72-2 Fuqian Road, Qujingtou, Junxing Village of Xiapu County. It was initially built during the years of the Wanli period(1573-1619). Following the traditional Chinese architectural layout, it lies against the north of the land and faces the south. It's a courtyard type with two entrances, and covers an area of 1 400 square meters. It is composed of gate, well, front hall, study and bedrooms. The main structure is a mixed style of pillars and beams with an overhanging gable roof style. It's made of wood and brick. The main hall is 23 meters wide and 14 meters deep, and has 7 large rooms. The top of the roof is decorated with a system of brackets inserted between the top of a column and a crossbeam. The floor was paved with square bricks. The dooryard is paved with green slates. The front door was destroyed. Lots of building materials were used for the construction with obvious Ming Dynasty styles. It's the only remaining officer's building of the Ming Dynasty in Xiapu County. In 2010, it was listed on the eighth batch of county-level cultural relics for protection by Xiapu County Government.

(五)罗文藻故居

罗文藻(1616—1691),明万历四十年(1616)生于福安县罗江罗家巷里巷村,为中国第一任华籍主教,于崇祯六年(1633)秋领洗入教,1690年罗马教廷宣布在中国成立北京和南京两个主教区,与澳门分立,罗文藻为南京教区主教。其传教步伐遍布大江南北以及海内外,他又于顺治年间晋铎,成为一名多明我会会士,再成为主教,历经崇祯、顺治、康熙三代帝王,跨越两个朝代,一生为传教事业做出巨大的贡献。

罗文藻的故居为土木结构,厅堂正面中间挂着一张从书里翻拍出来的黑白照片。由于年久失修,故居一部分已十分破旧,无人居住;另一部分由罗文藻的后人拆后用红砖重建。

6.1.2.5 Former Residence of Luo Wenzao

Luo Wenzao (1616-1691) was born in Lixiang Village, Luojia Alley, Luojiang of Fu'an City in the 40th year (1616) of Emperor Wanli's reign in the Ming Dynasty. He was the first Chinese bishop and was baptized in the sixth year (1633) of Emperor Chongzhen's reign. In 1690, the Vatican announced to establish two episcopates in Beijing and Nanjing in China, parallel to Macao. Then he was appointed bishop of Nanjing Episcopate. His missionary work is all over the world. He was promoted during the years of Emperor Shunzhi and became a member of the Dominican Order. His serviced as bishop spanned two dynasties and encompassed the reigns of three emperors, Chongzen, Shunzhi, and Kangxi. He made an indelible contribution to missionary work.

Luo's residence is a structure of wood and soil. On the wall in the middle of the main hall hangs a likeness of him that was copied from a book. One part of the residence is uninhabited and has not been maintained for many years. Descendants of Luo have rebuilt the other parts of the residence with red brick.

第二节 宁德旅游线路

6.2 Traveling Routes in Ningde

一、宁德蕉城区旅游线路

线路1:天后宫(妈祖庙),南祭公园,宁德东湖国家湿地公园
线路2:天王寺景区,"中华畲族宫",戚继光公园
线路3:霍童宏街宫,支提山("天下第一山")
线路4:三都澳,斗帽岛

6.2.1 Inner Traveling Routes of Jiaocheng District

Route 1: Tianhou Temple(Temple of Goddess Mazu), Nanji Park, National Wetland Park of Donghu Lake
Route 2: Scenic Spot of Tianwang Temple, "the She Ethnic Palace of China", Qi Jiguang Park
Route 3: Hongjie Palace of Huotong Town, Mount Zhiti ("No.1 Mountain in China")
Route 4: Sandu Bay, Doumao Island

二、宁德市周边景点自驾游路线

6.2.2 Self-Driving Traveling Routes Around Ningde

(一)太姥山、霞浦杨家溪、福安白云山、三沙(嵛山)。

线路1:G15高速公路(沈海线、同三线),在太姥山互通口下高速,按指示牌行走,即遇两个环岛均向右,进入秦太旅游公路,再行15千米即到太姥山景区大门。
线路2:南面方向出发到福州后,一路向北,途经马尾、连江、宁德、福安、霞浦、三沙(嵛山)、牙城(杨家溪)、太姥山(秦屿)。
线路3:北面方向出发到温州后一路向南,途径瑞安、平阳、苍南、分水关、福鼎、八尺门、太姥山(秦屿)、牙城(杨家溪)。

线路4:从其他方向到福鼎太姥山自驾游路线,一般先到温州或福州,再按上述线路行走。

6.2.2.1 Mount Taimu, Yangjiaxi River in Xiapu County, Mount Baiyun in Fu'an City, Sansha (Yushan Island)

Route 1: Exit Expressway G15 (Tongjiang-Sanya Expressway) at Mount Taimu Exit and follow the signs from Qinyu to Mount Taimu. Drive another 15 kilometers to reach the scenic spot.

Route 2: From Fuzhou, drive north through Mawei District, Lianjiang County, Ningde City proper, Fu'an City, Xiapu County, Sansha (Yushan Island), Yacheng (the Yangjiaxi River) and Mount Taimu (Qinyu Township).

Route 3: Set out from Wenzhou City, drive south through Rui'an City, Pingyang, Cangnan, Fenshuiguan, Fuding City, Bachimen, Mount Taimu (Qinyu Township) and Yacheng (the Yangjiaxi River)

Route 4: After arriving in Wenzhou or Fuzhou, use the above routes.

(二)屏南白水洋、鸳鸯溪宜洋景区、古田临水宫、翠屏湖

线路1:浙江或江西入闽,双溪入屏、白水洋、鸳鸯溪宜洋景区、双溪镇、千乘桥、城关。

线路2:福州、三都澳、漳湾下高速、八都、白玉入屏、际头古村、城关、千乘桥、双溪、白水洋、鸳鸯溪宜洋景区。

线路3:福州、闽清、水口、古田翠屏湖、古田临水宫、吉巷、甘棠入屏、甘国宝故里、城关、千乘桥、双溪、白水洋、宜洋景区。

线路4:温州、福鼎、太姥山、宁德漳湾下高速、八都、白玉入屏、际头古村、城关、千乘桥、双溪、白水洋、宜洋景区。

线路5:宁德、虎贝、代溪入屏、九峰寺、甘国宝故里、城关、千乘桥、双溪、白水洋、鸳鸯溪宜洋景区。

线路6:从其他方向到屏南白水洋自驾游路线,可参考选择以上入屏后,再按上述线路行走。

6.2.2.2 The Baishuiyang River Square of Pingnan County, Mandarin Duck Stream of Yiyang Village, Lady Linshui Temple of Gutian County and Cuiping Lake

Route 1: From Zhejiang and Jiangxi provinces, begin scenic tour at Shuangxi Township of Pingnan County, and then visit Baishuiyang River

Square, Mandarin Duck Stream of Yiyang Village, Shuangxi Township, Qiancheng Covered Bridge and the county proper.

Route 2: From Fuzhou City, follow the expressway to Ningde City and exit at Zhangwan, continue through Badu and Baiyu Township to Pingnan County. Begin tour at Jitou Ancient Village, Qiancheng Covered Bridge, Shuangxi Township, Baishuiyang River Square and Mandarin Duck Stream of Yiyang Village.

Route 3: Set off at Fuzhou City, pass by Minqing City, Shuikou, Cuiping Lake of Gutian County, Lady Linshui Temple of Gutian County, Jixiang, arrive at Pingnan County from Gantang Township, Former Residence of General Gan Guobao, Qiancheng Covered Bridge, Shuangxi Township, Baishuiyang River Square, Mandarin Duck Stream of Yiyang Village.

Route 4: Set off from Wenzhou City, pass by Fuding City, Mount Taimu, exit the expressway at the exit of Zhangwan, Badu Township, arrive at Pingnan from Baiyu, Jitou Ancient Village, Qiancheng Covered Bridge, Shuangxi River, Baishuiyang River Square, Mandarin Duck Stream of Yiyang Village.

Route 5: Set off at Ningde City, pass by Hubei Village, get to Pingnan County from Daixi Township, Nine Peaks Temple, Former Residence of General Gan Guobao, Qiancheng Covered Bridge, Shuangxi Township, Baishuiyang River Square, Mandarin Duck Stream of Yiyang Village.

Route 6: From the other directions to Baishuiyang River Square one can drive to Pingnan County first and then follow the above directions.

(三)宁德三都澳

线路:可选择走沈海高速公路到"飞鸾、三都澳"出口,沿着城澳疏港公路到城澳码头,然后乘坐快艇到斗姥风景区。

6.2.2.3 Sandu Bay

Route: Exit the Shenyang-Haiko Expressway at Sandu Bay of Feiluan Township, then go along the coastal port road to Cheng'ao Pier, and take a speed boat there to the Doumao Scenic Spot.

(四)周宁鲤鱼溪、九龙漈瀑布

线路1:宁武高速、周宁鲤鱼溪、九龙漈瀑布。

线路2:福州、罗宁高速、福宁高速、宁武高速、周宁鲤鱼溪、九龙漈瀑布。

6.2.2.4 The Carp Brook and Nine-Dragon Waterfalls of Zhouning County

Route 1：Ningde-Wuyishan Expressway，the Carp Brook，Nine-Dragon Waterfalls.

Route 2：Set off from Fuzhou City，pass by Luoyuan-Ningde Expressway，Fuzhou-Ningde Expressway，Ningde-Wuyishan Expressway，the Carp Brook，the Nine-Dragon Waterfalls in Zhouning County.

（五）福安白云山、溪塔葡萄沟、九龙洞景区。

线路：福州、宁德、福安赛岐、廉村、穆阳镇——溪塔（全国第三大葡萄沟、畲乡文化）、蟾溪村（九龙洞上下两个主景区之间）、白云山莲花寺（或白云道观）。

6.2.2.5 Mount Baiyun of Fu'an City，Xita Grape Valley and the Scenic Spot of Nine-Dragon Caves

Route：Set off from Fuzhou City，pass by Ningde City，Saiqi Town of Fu'an City，Liancun Village，Muyang Township，Xita Village（the third largest grape valley in China and a village of the She Ethnic culture），Chanxi Village（between the main scenic spots of the upper and lower Nine-Dragon caves），Lotus Temple of Mount Baiyun（or the Taoist Temple of Mount Baiyun）.

（六）柘荣东狮山、九龙井、鸳鸯草场、流桥溪大峡谷

线路：福州、沈海高速、宁上高速、沈海复线福安至柘荣。

6.2.2.6 Mount Dongshi of Zherong County，Nine-Dragon Well，Mandarin Duck Meadow and Liuqiaoxi Grand Canyon

Route：Set off from Fuzhou City by way of Shenyang-Haikou Expressway，Ningde-Shangrao Expressway，branch of Shenyang-Haikou Expressway to Fu'an City and then to Zherong County.

第三节 宁德交通指南

6.3 Ningde Transportation Information

一、航空

宁德机场位于霞浦县，属于支线机场。根据海西经济区合理布局支线机场的要求，近期按4C飞行区等级，建设宁德霞浦机场民航扩建工程，能满足B737、A320、MD90等系列Ⅰ、Ⅱ类飞机起降，并有序开辟国内大中城市航线，积极拓展民航业务。

6.3.1 Air Transportation

Ningde Airport is located in Xiapu County and is a regional airport. It is constructed according to the layout requirements of the Western Taiwan Straits Economic Zone, 4C flight level, and the recommendations of the civil aviation expansion project of Xiapu and Ningde. It meets the take-off and landing requirements of aircrafts of Class Ⅰ and Ⅱ series like B737, A320, and MD90, etc. Efforts are being made to open up gradually aviation lines to large and medium-sized cities at home and to expand the civil air transportation business.

二、铁路

自2010年起，宁德已开通了温福铁路和合福高铁路宁德段。正在建设中的衢宁铁路与温福铁路形成"一横一纵"的格局。"十二五"期间，推进"三纵五横"铁路网建设，里程783千米。届时宁德人民通过铁路交通前往全国各地将非常方便。

宁德动车站(火车站)位于东侨新区，隶属南昌铁路局管理，现为二等站。有公交6、18、20、22到达市内各个方向。

6.3.2 Railway Transportation

Wenzhou-Fuzhou Railway and Hefei-Fuzhou High-Speed Rail have been in use since 2010. Quzhou-Ningde Railway is under construction, which will form a layout of "one horizontal and one vertical line" with Wenzhou-Fuzhou Railway in Ningde. The 12th Five-Year Plan, calls for a railway network of "three Vertical and five horizontal lines" with a mileage of 783 kilometers. Once it is completed, the people of Ningde will find it more convenient to travel around the nation by railway.

Ningde Railway Station is located in the new area of Dongqiao Economic and Technological Development Zone under the management of Nanchang Railway Bureau. It's a second-class station now. Buses No. 6, 18, 20, and 22 provide service to the station.

三、公路

宁德的公路交通十分便捷,可通往全国各地,主要有沈海高速(G15 高速)、宁武高速、福宁高速、沈海复线。

沈海高速公路是沈阳—海口国家高速公路,简称"沈海高速",编号为 G15,起点在沈阳,终点在海口,途经辽宁、山东、江苏、浙江、福建、广东、海南七个省,全长 3 710千米,是唯一 一条贯通中国东南沿海地区的高速公路。其中途经福建宁德段的福鼎市、霞浦县、福安市和蕉城区。

宁武高速公路宁德段起于沈海线福宁高速公路的湾坞枢纽互通,终于闽赣界的武夷山汾水关,与江西省路段衔接,全长 301.39 千米。经宁德福安、周宁等县、市,终于南平政和县,与南平段相接。其主线长约 62.1 千米,另建屏南高速公路连接线约 22.6 千米。设置设福安、白云山、周宁、屏南、白水洋等收费站 5 个。

宁德有两个长途汽车站既汽车南站位于万安西路 8 号,北站位于蕉城区建新路 21 号。

汽车南站问询电话:0593-7866907/0593-2926131

汽车北站问询电话:0593-282292/0593-2837845

6.3.3 Highway Transportation

Highway networks in Ningde provide convenient links to every part of the country. The main routes are Shenyang-Haikou Expressway (Expressway G15), Ningde-Wuyishan Expressway, Fuzhou-Ningde Expressway and Second Shenyang-Haikou Expressway.

Shenyang-Haikou Expressway is a national highway and numbered as G15. It was briefly called "Sheng-Hai Expressway". Beginning in Shengyang City and ending in Haikou City, it passes through 7 provinces of Liaoning, Shandong, Jiangsu, Zhejiang, Fujian, Guangdong and Hainan for a total of 3 710 kilometers. It passes through Fuding City, Xiapu County, Fu'an City and Jiaocheng District in Ningde City and is the only expressway along the southeast coastal areas of China.

Ningde-Wuyishan Expressway starts at Wanwu Interchange of Fuzhou-Ningde Expressway and ends in Fenshuiguan of Wuyishan City, the border of Fujian and Jangxi Provinces, and extends to Jiangxi Province. The total length is 301.39 kilometers. It goes through Fu'an City, Zhouning County and ends at Zhenghe County of Nanping City. The main line is about 62.1 kilometers long, and a branch line of 22.6 kilometers has been built to connect with Pingnan. And five toll gates in Fu'an, Baiyunshan, Zhouning, Pingnan and Baishuiyang River Square have been set up.

There are two long-distance bus stations in Ningde. The southern bus station is located at No. 8 Wanan West Street and the northern bus station lies at No.21 Jianxin Street of Jiaocheng District.

Inquiry phone number of the southern bus station: 0593-7866907/0593-2926131

Inquiry phone number of the northern bus station: 0593-282292/0593-2837845

四、水路

宁德港分为四个港区，分别为三都澳港区、赛江港区、三沙港区、沙埕港区，是福建省沿海港口的重要组成部分、也是福建省最早对外开放的港口之一。光绪二十九年，美、日开辟了三都澳至福州、温州、青岛、烟台、牛庄、宁波、苏门答腊等地的航线，1985 年与香港正式通航，1992 年开通直达香港、上海、广州、青岛等 9 条不定期的海上航线，2006 年获准为金门、马祖、澎湖直航货运口岸，并开通宁德漳湾—辽宁营口内贸集装箱航线，2014 年首次与阿尔巴尼亚通航。

6.3.4 Waterway Transportation

Ningde Port is divided into the four operational zones of Sandu Bay, Saijiang, Sansha and Shacheng. Being one of the first ports of the Fujian Province open to the outside world, it plays an important role. In the 29th year of Emperor Guangxu's reign of the Qing Dynasty, America and Japan opened shipping routes from Sandu Bay to Fuzhou City, Wenzhou City, Qingdao City, Yantai City, Niuzhuang City, Ningbo City and Sumatra, etc. Navigation between Ningde Port and Hong Kong began in 1985. In 1992, nine irregular shipping routes were opened to Hong Kong, Shanghai, Guangzhou and Qingdao, etc. Direct shipping and freight-transport to Jinmen, Mazu and

Penghu of Taiwan were approved in 2006. Meanwhile a container route for domestic trade from Zhangwan Port to Yingkou Port of Liaoning Province was opened. In 2014, the first navigation line with Albania began for the first time.

五、公交车

宁德的公交线路四通八达，十分便利。公交车以空调大巴为主，小型公共汽车为辅，空调大巴实行无人售票制，自备零钱，市区 6 条运距在 10 千米以上的公交线路，票价 2 元制，运距在 10 千米以下的票价一元制，夏天开空调，调整为 1.5 元。小型公交大部分是去人流量较少的郊区村镇，票价根据路程的远近在 3～5 元之间。

6.3.5 Public Bus Service

Ningde has convenient public bus service in all directions. Large air-conditioned buses run on the main roads and minibuses run through the back roads of the city or suburbs. Bus fares are paid by scanning a prepaid card or customers should pay with the exact amount of cash. The fare for 6 bus routes with a total route distance of 10 kilometers or more is 2 yuan. The fare for bus routes less than 10 kilometers is 1 yuan except in summer when the cost goes up to 1.5 yuan to offset the cost of air-conditioning. Most of the minibuses go to the suburbs and their ticket prices range from 3 to 5 yuan according to the distance.

第四节 宁德主要酒店

6.4 Major Hotels in Ningde

一、宁德主要五星级酒店

6.4.1 Major Five-Star Hotels in Ningde

(一)万达嘉华酒店

万达嘉华酒店是万达酒店及度假村管理集团旗下的五星级品牌酒店。主楼高

20 层，共拥有 290 间豪华舒适、设施齐备的客房与套房，餐饮设施包括可提供国际美食的全日制餐厅、环境幽雅时尚的中餐厅、特色餐厅和大堂酒廊，同时酒店设有 1 200平方米的无柱式大宴会厅和 6 个多功能厅，可承办国际性大型宴会的地标性场所。另外，酒店还设有室内恒温游泳池、健身中心及美容美发沙龙等康乐设施，旨在为宾客提供理想的休憩场所。

酒店地址：宁德市蕉城区天湖东路 1 号

酒店客服电话：0593-2511111-6601

周边环境：万达广场、兴业证券、沃尔玛、广电大厦。

交通信息：坐落于市内繁华都市商圈，距离宁德火车站、汽车南站、北站大约 10 分钟车程，距宁德国家湿地公园(南岸、北岸公园)、塔山公园仅 5～8 分钟车程。

6.4.1.1 Wanda Realm Ningde

It is a five-star hotel under the management of Wanda Realm Hotels and Resorts Group. Its main building has 20 stories with 290 comfortable and well-equipped guest rooms and suites. Its catering facilities include daily dining rooms of international food, cozy and trendy Chinese restaurants, distinctive dining rooms, large scale halls, and wine corridors in lobby. Additionally, the hotel provides a 1 200-square-meter and pillar-less hall and 6 multi-functional halls which can host large international banquets. The hotel is also equipped with constant warm indoor swimming pool, fitness center, and beauty salons making it an ideal place for guests to rest.

Hotel Address: No. 1 Tianhu East Road, Jiaocheng District, Ningde City

Hotel Telephone: 0593-2511111-6601

Nearby landmarks: Wanda Plaza, Xingye Securities, Wal-Mart, Broadcasting and Television Building.

Transportation Information: it is located in the downtown area and about 10 minutes' drive from Ningde Railway Station, South Bus Station, and North Bus Station. It is only 5 to 8 minutes' drive to Ningde National Wetland Park (Northern and Southern Park), and Tashan Pagoda Park.

(二)福鼎金九龙大酒店

金九龙大酒店是集商务客房、购物、休闲、娱乐、中西美食、商务、会议为一体的综合性公共建筑，定位为顶级国际商务酒店。酒店层高 23 层，拥有各类商务客房约 450 间(套)[主楼约 290 间(套)、副楼公寓房约 160 间(套)]，设有行政商务楼层。酒店内设中餐(闽菜、瓯菜、粤菜及各大菜系)、豪华宴会厅、西餐、日本料理、咖啡厅、大堂吧、室内游泳馆、健身中心、精品店、银行等，可同时容纳约 600 人设备先进的多功能国际会议厅、中、小型会议室及多媒体培训室，设施一流的酒店康体娱乐场所，拥有约 54 个 KTV 包间、约 38 个豪华桑拿包间、时尚演绎厅等项目。

酒店地址：桐南新城玉龙北路 66 号

酒店电话：0593-7666666　传真：0593-7666629

交通信息：距市中心 0.5 千米，距火车站 5 千米，距温州龙湾机场约 90 千米(车程约 70 分钟)，距汽车北站约 1 千米。

6.4.1.2 G-Kouloon Hotel(Fuding)

It is a comprehensive hotel that provides service for accommodation, shopping, leisure, entertainment, eastern and western cuisine, business conferences, and so on. It is a top-class international hotel of 23 stories with about 450 guest rooms and suites, of which 290 are rooms or suites in the main building and 160 are in the attached building. There are business and administration floors and restaurants of various cuisines of Fujian, Wenzhou, and Guangdong and other major cities, as well as luxurious banquet halls, western and Japanese restaurants, coffee bars, lobbies, indoor swimming pool, fitness center, boutiques, and banks etc. There are also well-equipped multi-function halls of various sizes that can hold 600 guests at a time for international conferences, seminars and multi-media training. There are 54 KTV rooms, 38 luxurious sauna rooms and fashion show halls.

Hotel Address: No. 66, Yulong Bei (North) Road, Tongnan Xincheng (New Town)

Hotel Telephone: 0593-7666666　　Fax: 0593-7666629

Transportation Information: It is just half kilometer to downtown of Fuding City, one kilometer to the north bus station, 5 kilometers to the train station and 90 kilometers to Wenzhou Longwan International Airport about 70 minutes' drive.

(三)福建东方帝景国际酒店(霞浦)

宁德霞浦帝景国际酒店是霞浦目前唯一一家五星级酒店，酒店楼高 13 层，拥有各类客房共 228 间，餐饮包厢 23 个及可容纳 100～300 人大型宴会厅 2 个。酒店提供专业会议室、棋牌室、游泳池、购物中心、音乐会所及大堂吧，还拥有 200 个停车位的免费停车场。

地址：霞浦县太康路 365 号(阳光城对面)

电话：0593-8799999　传真：0593-8769222

交通信息：距市中心 1 千米步行约 10 分钟可到酒店，距福宁长途汽车站直线

507 米,距北站直线 1.9 千米,距汽车站 2.3 千米,距火车站 3.3 千米。

周边景点:距杨家溪仅 20 分钟车程,太姥山 30 分钟的车程,所有的摄影点车程 5～10 分钟。

6.4.1.3 Oriental D.J. Royal International Hotel (Xiapu, Fujian)

It's the only five-star hotel in Xiapu. It is 13 stories high with 228 guest rooms, 23 dining rooms, and 2 large convention rooms that can accommodate 100 to 300 guests at one time. It also provides specialized meeting rooms, chess rooms, swimming pool, shopping center, music bar and lobby bar, etc. Free parking is available for 200 cars.

Address: No. 365 Taikang Road, Xiapu County Proper

Tel: 0593-8799999 Fax: 0593-8769222

Transportation Information: It is about 1 kilometer or about a 10 minutes' walk to the downtown. It's about 507 meters to the Funing Long-Distance Bus Station, 1.9 kilometers to the North Bus Station, 2.3 kilometers to the bus station of Xiapu and 3.3 kilometers to the train station.

Surrounding Scenic Spots: 20 minutes to the Yangjiaxi River, 30 minutes to Mount Taimu and about 5 to 10 minutes to all the beach photographing spots for photographers.

二、宁德主要四星级酒店

6.4.2 Major Four-Star Hotels in Ningde

(一)美伦大饭店

美伦大饭店,地处高速公路宁德市区的出口要道,是宁德市首家按四星级标准兴建的旅游涉外饭店,大饭店楼高 10 层,共有客房总数 179 间(套),标间面积 30 平方米,有中西餐厅及豪华餐饮包厢,聘请名厨主理,提供粤、闽及当地特色菜肴,有国际会议厅及会见厅等 5 个会议室,可按纳 10～350 人的各种类型会议,配有全省领先水平的高科技设施设备,智能化的会议保密系统及管理系统,专业的服务队伍,全方位地保障会议及各种宴会的顺利进行。大饭店地理位置得天独厚,交通便捷,风格独特。旅游景区、购物中心举步可至,是商务、旅游客人的首选之地。

地址:中国宁德市站前路 28 号

大饭店电话:0593-2929888

交通信息:距市中心 3 千米 7 分钟车程。距汽车南站约 1 千米,行车约 3 分钟,距汽车北站约 4.6 千米,行车约 15 分钟。

周边环境:距宁德国家湿地公园(南岸、北岸公园)、塔山公园仅10分钟车程。

6.4.2.1 Meilun Hotel

It is located near the exit of the expressway and was designed and built according to four-star international hotel standards. It is 10 stories high with 179 guest rooms and suites of 30 square meters each. There are eastern and western restaurants and luxurious dining halls. Well-known chefs are hired to provide Cantonese and Fujian and local cuisines. There are five international convention halls and other meeting rooms that can hold 10 to 350 guests at a time. The hotel is equipped with hi-tech facilities, smart secrecy and management systems as well as professional service teams so as to guarantee the smooth process of all the meetings and banquets. Its unique style enjoys an advantageous location with convenient transportation. Scenic spots and shopping centers are within walking distance which is an ideal choice for all the businessmen and tourists.

Address: No. 28, Zhanqian Road, Ningde City

Tel: 0593-2929888

Transportation Information: It is 3 kilometers for about 7 minutes' drive to the downtown area; about 1 kilometer for about 3 minutes' drive to the South Bus Station; and 4.6 kilometers about 15 minutes' drive to the North Bus Station.

Surrounding Scenic Spots: about 10 minutes' drive to Ningde National Wetland Park (North and South Parks) and the Tashan Pagoda Park.

(二)宁德山水大酒店

山水大酒店位于宁德市闽东路的商务黄金地,楼高15层,附楼高4层,按四星级标准设计装修,拥有157间各类高级客房,标间面积31平方米,三楼国际会议厅可容纳250人,五楼三个会议室分别可容纳30、40、120人。中餐厅可同时接纳600人用餐。咖啡厅、酒吧、夜总会、桑拿、保健中心、美容美发中心、健身房、网球场游泳池及票务旅游等完善的服务项目设施,是一座豪华型的综合性商务旅游酒店。

酒店地址:东侨区闽东中路18号(联通大楼旁)

酒店电话:电话:0593-2918888

交通信息:距市中心1千米,车程3分钟

周边环境:中国联通宁德分公司、建设科技大厦、地税局、高级中学,均为宁德标志性建筑物。

6.4.2.2 Ningde Landscape Hotel

It is located at the golden business section on Mindong Road of Ningde City proper. It is 15 stories high with an attached building of four floors. It was designed and decorated according to four-star hotel standards with 157 various guest rooms, double-bed rooms with 31 square meters each. On the third floor there is a convention room which can hold 250 guests. On the fifth floor there are three meeting rooms that can hold 30, 40 and 120 persons respectively. Its Chinese restaurant at a time can receive 600 guests. It is also equipped with coffee bar, night club, sauna, healthcare center, beauty salon, tennis court, swimming pool and ticketing and traveling service booths, etc. It is a luxurious and comprehensive hotel for business and travel.

Address: No. 18, Mindong Zhong Road, Dongqiao District (by the Unicom building)

Tel: 0593-2918888

Transportation Information: It is 1 kilometer away to the downtown area about 3 minutes' drive.

Surrounding Landmarks: Ningde Unicom Building, Hi-Tech Building of Construction, Local Taxation Bureau Building, and High School, etc.

(三)宁德东方国际大饭店

东方国际大饭店集餐饮、客房、会议接待、夜总会、桑拿休闲、超市购物为一体。饭店主楼高15层,客房总数160间(套),内配备各类规格的客房、套房及总统套房,同时设有各类大、中、小型会议室。餐饮方面由香港潮福城名厨主理,中餐厅提供美味粤菜、港式茶点、闽菜等,同时还有意式旋转餐厅。

酒店地址:宁德市蕉城区八一五中路1号(东方大厦对面)

大饭店电话:0593-2076666

交通信息:距汽车北站约0.46千米,汽车南站约3.17千米。

周边环境:东宁购物广场、东方康宁购物广场、宁德第一医院、建设银行、中国银行宁德分行、肯德基宁德餐厅、兰韵茶楼等。

6.4.2.3 Oriental International Hotel

It is a comprehensive hotel that provides catering, guestrooms, convention reception, night club, sauna, leisure and shopping service, etc. It is 15 stories high with 160 guest rooms including standard, suites, and a presidential suite. In addition, it is equipped with meeting rooms of large, medium and small sizes. The catering service is provided by famous chefs from Hong Kong Lucky

Full City Restaurant. Its Chinese restaurant serves delicious Cantonese cuisine and Hong Kong tea snacks and there is also a rotating Italian restaurant.

Address: No. 1, 815 Mid Road, Jiaocheng District proper of Ningde City

Tel:0593-2076666

Transportation Information: It is only 0.46 kilometer to the North Bus Station, and 3.17 kilometers to the South Bus Station.

Surrounding Landmarks: Dongning Shopping Mall, Dongfang Kangning Shopping Mall, No. 1 Hospital of Ningde City, Construction Bank, Ningde Branch of Bank of China, KFC, Lanyun Tea House and so on.

(四)宁德唐城金海湾大酒店

金海湾大酒店位于宁德市东侨区,毗邻市政府,揽东湖国家湿地公园的迷人风景。由主楼、附楼组成,总建筑面积约为39 000平方米,集住宿、餐饮与休闲娱乐于一体,配套设施齐全。酒店内有邮政服务、免费 WiFi、多种语言服务人员、旅游服务、专职行李员、免费停车场、前台贵重物品保险柜、公共区域闭路电视监控系统、商务中心、会议服务、取款机、茶室、商品部、大堂吧、残障人客房、咖啡厅、电子结账系统、大堂无障碍通道、中餐厅、西餐厅、宴会厅、棋牌室、卡拉 OK 厅、夜总会等。

酒店地址:宁德市东侨经济开发区闽东东路 3 号(市总工会附近)

酒店电话:0593-2577777

交通信息:距动车站仅 2 千米,汽车北站 4.9 千米,汽车南站 3.1 千米。

周边环境:市规划馆,国家湿地公园(宁德长江支队纪念亭)、宁德市会展中心、市体育中心、塔山等。

6.4.2.4 Golden Coastal Hotel of Ningde

It is located in Dongqiao District near the Municipal Government and overlooks the beautiful scenery of the Ningde National Wetland Park. It consists of the main and attached buildings for a total area of 39,000 square meters. It provides accommodations, catering, leisure and entertainment together with well-equipped facilities. It offers postal service, free WiFi, multi-lingual clerks, tourism guide, bell service and free parking, safes for valuables at the reception, public and closed-circuit monitoring, business center, convention halls, ATM's, tea house, shops, lobby bar, accessible rooms, coffer bar, e-billing system, accessible lobby, Chinese and western restaurants, banquet halls, chess rooms and Karaoke rooms, and night clubs, etc.

Address: No. 3 Mindong Dong (East) Road, Dongqiao Economic and Technological Development Zone of Ningde City (by the Workers' Union

Building)

Transportation Information: It is respectively 2 kilometers, 4.9 kilometers and 3.1 kilometers to the Train Station, the North Bus Station and the South Bus Station.

Surrounding Landmarks: Municipal Planning Hall, National Wetland Park (Memorial Pavilion for the Changjiang Branch), Municipal Expo Center, Municipal Sports Center, and the Pagoda Hill, etc.

(五)华尔道夫世鸿大酒店

酒店位于北岸公园正对面,是宁德市最大的酒店,更是宁德市形象工程。主楼高 9 层,客房总数 181 间(套),是集住宿、商务、旅游、会议接待、中西餐饮、娱乐休闲等功能于一体的豪华大型四星级旅游涉外酒店,建筑面积达 68 000平方米,总占地面积 75 亩。酒店内设有商务中心、会议服务、公共区域闭路电视监控系统、多功能厅、取款机、前台贵重物品保险柜、视听设备、茶室、西餐厅、中餐厅、宴会厅等,提供免费 WiFi、停车场、火车站往来班车服务。

酒店地址:东侨开发区北湖滨路 3 号(北岸公园正对面)

酒店电话:400-626-5577 (预约)

交通信息:距火车站 2.2 千米,汽车北站约 6 千米,南站约 2.52 千米。

周边环境:长江支队纪念亭、塔山、宁德市会展中心、市规划馆、国家湿地公园。

6.4.2.5 Waldorf Shihong Hotel Ningde

It is located in front of the Northern Lakeside Park. It is the largest and the exemplary hotel of Ningde City. Its main building is 9 stories high with 181 guest rooms and suites. The large 4-star luxurious hotel covers 68,000 square meters over a land area of 75 Mu. It provides comprehensive services include accommodations, business center, tourism assistance, convention center, eastern and western cuisines, entertainment and leisure center, public and closed-circuit monitoring systems, multi-functional halls, ATM's, safes for valuables, audio and video facilities, tea house, banquet halls, free WiFi, parking lots, and a shuttle bus to the train station.

Address: No.3 Bei (North) Hubin Road, Dongqiao Economic and Technological Development Zone (opposite the northern lakeside park)

Tel: 400-626-5577 (for reservation)

Transportation Information: It is 2.2 kilometers from the Train Station, 6 kilometers from the North Bus Station, and 2.52 kilometers from the South Bus Station.

Surrounding Landmarks: Memorial Pavilion for the Changjiang Branch, the Pagoda Hill, Municipal Expo Center, Municipal Planning Hall, Ningde National Wetland Park, etc.

(六)闽东宾馆

闽东宾馆位于蕉城繁华中心,宁德市区104国道汽车北站旁,宾馆层高9层,共有152间客房、占地面积30亩,按照四星级酒店标准,精心设计,装修打造出具有地方民族文化内涵的现代化商务酒店,交通便捷、环境幽雅。酒店提供免费WiFi、停车位,有商务中心,会议室,中、西餐厅,提供邮政服务,多种语言服务人员,旅游服务,茶室,商品部,大堂吧,公共区域闭路电视监控系统,无障碍通道,宴会厅,棋牌室等。

酒店地址:福建省宁德市蕉城区蕉城北路26号

酒店电话:400-620-1356;0593-7163333

交通信息:距汽车北站直线277米,汽车南站直线4.5千米,动车站约6.3千米。

周边环境:市公安局出入境办证大厅、汽车北站、新加坡商业步行街、建设银行等。

6.4.2.6 Mindong Hotel

It is located in the bustling downtown area near the north bus station on National Highway No.104. It is 9 stories high with 152 guest rooms and covers 30 Mu of land. It was designed and built according to a 4-star hotel standards and was furnished with local ethnic characteristics. The location is convenient and the layout is quiet and tasteful. The hotel provides free WIFI, parking lot, business center, convention halls, Chinese and western restaurants, postal service, multi-lingual clerks, tourism, tea house, shops, lobby bar, public and closed-circuit monitoring system, accessible paths, banquet halls, and chess rooms, etc.

Address: No. 26, Jiaocheng Bei Road, Jiaocheng District, Ningde City, Fujian.

Tel: 400-620-1356; 0593-7163333

Transportation Information: It is 277 meters from the North Bus Station, 4.5 kilometers from the South Bus Station, and 6.3 kilometers from the South Bus Station. Surrounding Landmarks: Exit and Entry Administration Hall of the Municipal Public Security Bureau, North Bus Station, Singapore Business Street and Construction Bank, etc.

三、宁德主要三星级酒店

6.4.3 Major Three-Star Hotels in Ningde

(一)宁德最佳西方财富酒店

宁德最佳西方财富酒店是美国最佳西方国际集团在宁德市的首家连锁酒店。酒店拥有148间多种风格、类型的客房,全面配置高品质的星级客用品、大屏幕数字电视等,环境雅致、舒适。

酒店同时为住客提供丰富的早餐品种和物美价廉的中晚商务套餐,内配设宽敞停车场,前台贵重物品保险柜、公共区域闭路电视监控系统、自动取款机、公共音响系统、非经营性客人休息区、多媒体演示系统、棋牌室、会议厅、商务中心、旅游票务服务、信用卡结算服务、商务服务、传真/复印,为商、旅宾客提供高性价比的住宿体验。

酒店地址:蕉城区蕉城南路39号(宁德一中对面)

酒店电话:0593-7167888 传真:0593-7167777

交通信息:步行距蕉城区人民政府814米,火车站6.8千米,市中心3.1千米,汽车南站约3.7千米。

周边环境:宁德一中、宁德蕉城区实验小学、建设银行、宁德市公安局、劳动大楼等。

6.4.3.1 Best Western Fortune Hotel Ningde

It is the first chain hotel in Ningde affiliated to the Best Western International Inc, USA. It's elegant and comfortable environment includes more than 148 guest rooms of various styles that are well equipped with such things as big screen televisions. It provides a quality breakfast, lunch, and supper at a reasonable price. In addition guests enjoy free and spacious parking lots, safes for valuables at the reception, public closed-circuit monitoring systems, ATM's, public music system, visitor rest zone, multi-media demo system, chess rooms, convention halls, business center, ticketing, credit card settling, business service, fax and copying.

Address: No. 39, Jiaocheng South Road, Jiaocheng District (Opposite No. 1 Middle School)

Tel: 0593-7167888 Fax:0593-7167777

Transportation Information: It is respectively 814 meters, 6.8 kilometers, 3.1 kilometers and 3.7 kilometers to the People's Government of Jiaocheng

District, the train station, the downtown area and the South Bus Station.

Surrounding Landmarks: Ningde No. 1 Middle School, Ningde Experimental Primary School, Construction Bank, Municipal Police Station, Municipal Labor Building, etc.

（二）锦江都城宁德蕉城酒店

锦江都城宁德蕉城于2014年6月正式加入锦江都城酒店，成为锦江国际集团旗下首批中高端轻艺术酒店。酒店位于宁德市蕉城区，坐落于万达广场。万达广场项目拥有约18万平方米的大型国际购物中心，吃、住、购物、娱乐一应俱全。酒店以4星级标准进行装修，共计154间精装修客房，配有会议室、行李寄存、商品部、安全消防系统、公共区域闭路电视监控系统、提供免费WiFi高速上网，免费停车、大堂免费报纸等等，能够满足所有商旅客人的住宿需求。每年接待宾客近10万人次。

酒店地址：蕉城区天湖东路1号万达广场3号楼

酒店电话：0593-2255666

交通信息：距火车站约5千米，汽车南站约3千米，汽车北站约3千米。

周边环境：沃尔玛、兴业证券、广电大厦、南岸公园、北岸公园等均在酒店2千米范围内。

6.4.3.2 Metropolis Jinjiang Hotel, Jiaocheng District, Ningde

It officially joined Metropolis Jinjiang Hotels and became one of the first medium and high-end hotels of light music. The hotel is located in the 180 000 square meter Wanda Plaza and guests enjoy the convenience of food, shopping, and entertainment. It was designed and furnished according to a 4-star hotel standards with 154 exquisitely decorated rooms and equipped with convention rooms, luggage rooms, shops, security and firefighting systems, public and closed-circuit monitoring system, free WiFi, free parking, newspapers in lobby to meet the needs of guests. Each year nearly 100 000 guests are received.

Address: No. 3 Building, Wanda Plaza, at No. 1 Tianhu Dong Road, Jiaocheng District.

Tel: 0593-2255666

Transportation Information: It is 5 kilometers to the train station, 3 kilometers to the south bus station, and 3 kilometers to the north bus station.

Surrounding Landmarks: Wal-Mart, Industrial Securities Building, Broadcasting and Television Building, South Lakeside Park, North Lakeside Park within 2 kilometers.

（三）宁德星程（原驿景）大酒店

星程大酒店店位于宁德市东侨开发区塔山路2号邮政大厦旁。88米高的20层主楼与院内25 800多平方米的大型花园温情相拥。酒店拥有各类客房共109间（套），可俯瞰宁德全城的迷人景致，配备KTV包厢30个，有2个不同规格的会议室以及能够容纳50多个车位的大型停车场。无限时免费上网宽带、独立控制的中央空调系统、专用的豪华客梯、监控系统、消防报警系统等一应俱全。

酒店地址：塔山路2号邮政大楼，宁德邮局旁边（东侨开发区）

酒店电话：0593-2226668

交通信息：距市中心1.6千米，火车站4.9千米，汽车南站4.6千米，汽车北站6.9千米。

周边环境：万达广场、沃尔玛商业中心（步行10分钟）、工商银行、广电大厦、逸涛社区等。

6.4.3.3 Xingcheng Hotel (formerly Postal Hotel) of Ningde City

It is located at NO. 2 Taishan Road, Dongqiao Economic Zone beside the Postal Building. The hotel has 20 stories, stands 88 meters high and contains 109 rooms overlooking the city. A 25 800 square meter garden located behind adds elegance to the splendid environment. It is equipped with 30 KTV rooms, various meeting rooms and a large parking lot that can hold 50 cars. The hotel provides internet access, individually controlled central air conditioning, luxurious elevators, monitoring, and firefighting systems.

Address: No. 2 Taishan Road beside the Postal Building in Dongqiao Economic Zone

Transportation Information: It is 1.6 kilometers from downtown, 4.9 kilometers from the train station, 4.6 kilometers from the South Bus Station, and 6.9 kilometers to the North Bus Station.

Surrounding Landmarks: Wanda Plaza, Wal-Mart (10 minutes' walk), Industrial and Commercial Bank of China, Broadcasting and Television Building and Yitao Community.

四、其他三星级酒店

（一）星程酒店宁德汽车北站店

地址：蕉城区蕉城北路29号（新佳坡步行街）

电话：0593-2372333

（二）宁德一品假日酒店（蓝天店）

地址:蕉城区京都商贸区银兴路 1 号
电话:0593-2291111
传真:0593-2359111
(三)宁德唯依主题酒店
地址:蕉城区蕉城南路 40 号
电话:0593-7187999
传真:0593-2512111
(四)宁德东方国际威悦大酒店
地址:蕉城区环城路 21 号(附小旁)
电话:0593-8993666
(五)宁德财富假日酒店
地址:蕉城区东侨经济开发区
电话:0593-2396999

6.4.4 Three-Star Hotels in Ningde

6.4.4.1 Xingcheng Hotel(A Branch near the North Bus Station)

Address: No. 29 Jiaocheng Bei Road, Jiaocheng District (in Xinjiapo Walking Street)

Tel: 0593-2255666

6.4.4.2 Yipin Hotel (Lantian Branch)

Address: No. 1 Yinxing Road, Jingdu Commercial Zone, Jiaocheng District

Tel: 0593-7187999

Fax: 0593-2512111

6.4.4.3 Ningde Weiyi-Theme Hotel

Address: No. 40 Jiaocheng Nan Road, Jiaocheng District

Tel: 0593-7187999

Fax: 0593-2512111

6.4.4.4 Oriental International Junyue Hotel

Address: No. 21, Huancheng Road (by the Attached Primary School)

Tel:0593-8993666

6.4.4.5 Fortune Holiday Hotel of Ningde

Address: Dongqiao Economic Development Zone of Jiaocheng District

Tel: 0593-2396999

五、宁德主要经济型酒店

宁德速 8 酒店(汽车南站):宁德市蕉城南路 98 号-2

如家快捷酒店(宁德后岗国防教育中心店):宁德市蕉城区站前路 12 号

宁德一家大酒店:宁德市蕉城区蕉城南路 103 号

宁德锐思特汽车酒店(宁川店):宁德市蕉城区宁川南路

宁德城市快捷酒店:宁德市蕉城区宁川北路城东花苑 7 号楼

宁德蕉城时尚旅酒店:宁德市蕉城区天湖东路 1 号万达广场

聚商音乐连锁酒店:宁德汽车南站店(原京港如家),东侨经济开发区万安西路 1 号

汉庭酒店(宁德南环路商业街店):宁德市蕉城区蕉城南路 8 号

汉庭酒店(宁德万达店):蕉城区宁川北路 2 号

宁德华容快捷酒店:蕉城区闽东中路郦景阳光大门口 1 号楼

6.4.4.5 Major Budget Hotels in Ningde

Super 8 Hotel (by the South Bus Station): No.98-2 Jiaocheng South Road, Ningde;

Home Inn (inside the National Defense Education Center Building): No.12 Zhanqian Road, Jiaocheng District, Ningde;

Yijiada Hotel of Ningde: No.103 Jiaocheng Nan Road, Jiaocheng District, Ningde;

Rest Motel Ningde (Ningchuan Branch): Ningchuan Nan Road, Jiaocheng District;

City Fast Service Hotel: Building 7, Chengdong Huayuan Community, Ningchuan Bei Road, Jiaocheng District;

Vogue Hotel of Jiaocheng District of Ningde: No. 1 Tianhu Road, Jiaocheng District (near Wanda Plaza);

Jushang Music Hotel: by the South Bus Station at No.1 Wan'an Xi Road, Dongqiao Economic and Technological Development Zone;

Hunting Inn (Nanhuan Business Street Branch): No. 8 Jiaocheng Nan Road, Jiaocheng District;

Hunting Inn(Wanda Branch): No.2, Ningchun Bei Road;

Huarong Fast Service Hotel: No. 1, Lijing Yangguang Gate, Mindong Zhong Road, Jiaocheng District.

第五节 美食特产

闽菜是全国八大菜系之一，以闽东、闽南、闽西、闽北、闽中、莆仙地方风味菜为主形成的菜系。以闽东和闽南风味为代表，闽东风味，以福州菜为代表，主要流行于闽东地区，调味偏于甜、酸、淡，喜加糖醋，各县市最具有特色的菜有炒干贝（"瑶柱"，满金山）、泥钉冻、福鼎"澎海"、古田"火麒麟"、屏南米烧兔、畲族乌米饭，爆炒章鱼等。

闽东风味小吃有元宵丸、肉丸 、芋蛋面、鼠曲糍、三沙粿、寿宁米糕、乌蛋粿，煎海蛎、土豆糕、古田盒面（卤面）、鸳鸯面（即苦椎面）、继光饼、泥鳅面、"三糍"（糯米糍、粳米糍、马铃薯糍）、"蛋燕"、魔芋糕、芦叶（菅）棕、八宝芋泥等。

6.5 Gourmet Foods and Local Products

Fujian Cuisine is one of the eight major cuisines of China and has developed its local characteristics based on the flavors from all over the province. Flavors of East and South Fujian have the strongest influence. The East Fujian flavor is represented by Fuzhou Cuisine and popular in East Fujian (Mindong). The flavor tends to be sweeter and more sour due to the addition of sugar and vinegar but less salty. Typical dishes from different parts of Ningde include: Fried Mussel Meat with Water Chestnuts, Sea Worms Jelly, "Penghai" Seafood Broth in Fuding, "Fiery Kylin" Dessert in Gutian, Roast Rabbit over Rice in a Wok in Pingnan County, Black Rice of the She Ethnic People, and Fried Octopus, etc.

Ningde has many snacks to offer such as Lantern Festival Balls, Meat Balls, Mashed Taro Noodles, Cudweed Rice Cake, Shansha Sticky Rice Cake, Rice Dumpling of Shouning County, Fried Oyster Cake, Potato Cake, Braised Noodles of Gutian, Mandarin Duck Fruit Noodles, Jiguang Cake, Loach Noodle, three kinds of cakes (of sticky rice, japonica rice, and potatoes), Sweet Potato Noodles, Konjac Cake, Dumplings in Reeds, Eight-Ingredient Mashed Taro, etc.

一、宁德美食

6.5.1 Ningde Local Gourmet Foods

(一)炒干贝("瑶柱"满金山)

宁德酒席的必备菜,因为干贝炒出为黄色,蛋炒出也是黄色,寓意着充满财富象征和富贵气息。主料:干贝。辅料:荸荠(或地瓜)、五花肉(取其第2层或第4层的猪油肥肉)、鸡蛋五六个、葱白、适量盐巴和料酒。先将干贝蒸熟或煮熟,隔着纱布搓成丝,再加入蛋液,荸荠末,也有人会加上一些肥肉丁,混合起来一起炒。

6.5.1.1 Fried Mussel Meat with Water Chestnuts

It is a must for banquets in Ningde because it looks golden which indicates prosperity and fortune. The main ingredient: mussels. The additional ingredients include water chestnuts (or sweet potato), streaky pork of which the second or fourth tier's oil is extracted, 5 or 6 eggs, onion root, some salt and rice wine. Cooking methods: First, steam mussel meat or boil it. Then smash it in a filter cloth. Fry it with some eggs, water chestnuts and some diced meat.

(二)福鼎"澎海"

福鼎"澎海"是一道羹汤,凡是婚宴、寿宴、乔迁酒等各类宴席必上"澎海",而且是第一道,宾客们也能据此猜出其整场筵席的档次。这道羹汤用料很讲究,有档次较高的鱼翅、海参、螃蟹肉、土丁、鱼唇等。制作步骤:一是将主料切成丁或丝;二是在锅中倒入汤,主料下锅烧开后,放入辅调料;三是煮沸后,用湿淀粉勾芡;四是在沸锅中均匀淋上预先准备好并调拌成白色的蛋清,上桌前放一点葱花即可。

6.5.1.2 "Penghai" Seafood Broth in Fuding

It is a broth that is served as the first dish and a must at dinners of wedding, longevity and house-moving celebrations. Just according to this dish, guests can guess how much money is needed for the whole banquet. The broth has high standards for the ingredients, which include shark skin, sea cucumber, crab meat, sea worms, fish lip meat, etc. Cooking procedures: Firstly chop the ingredients into small or thin slices; secondly pour soup into the wok and then the main ingredients and some seasoning; thirdly, after the broth boils, thicken the soup with some wet starch; fourthly, pour the prepared egg white on the boiling broth and then put some onion leaves on it before serving.

(三)古田火麒麟

火麒麟是酒席上的甜食。由煮熟的槟榔芋加入猪油、白糖和炒过的黑芝麻、红枣,装饰成银灰色的小山丘,用一小杯烧酒,在"山脚"均匀地浇绕一圈,用火柴将烧酒点燃,顿时像一座火焰山,就着烧酒点燃的火光,从"山顶"上吃起,可谓"闽东一绝"。

6.5.1.3 "Fiery Kylin" Dessert in Gutian

It is a dessert unique to East Fujian (Mindong) which is served at banquets. It is made from cooked sliced taros with lard, sugar, fried sesames, and red dates inside. Arrange the ingredients into a small "mound". Then pour a little cup of Chinese liquor around the foot of the mound and light it. Suddenly the dessert will look like a fiery mound. The desert is eaten from top to bottom and the taste will vary throughout.

(四)畲族乌米饭

畲族乌米饭自唐朝以来就是畲族同胞"三月三"过节的传统食品,它来自大自然乌稔树(也叫乌饭树)的绿色树叶泡制而成的色香味和开脾健胃驱湿膳疗作用。二十世纪末经宁德市畲族乌米饭加工坊开发,现已成福建九地市和浙南等地设宴的佳肴,分别有红鲟乌米饭、竹桶乌米饭、太极乌米饭、荷叶乌米饭、菠萝乌米饭、草包乌米饭、乌米卷、八宝乌米饭(甜、咸)等品种。

6.5.1.4 Black Rice of the She Ethnic People

It is a traditional food of the She Ethnic people dating back to the Tang Dynasty and is served on the "March 3rd" festival. The black color of the rice comes from natural Black Rice Tree leaves and traditional Chinese medicine states the rice is good for stomachs and spleens and drives "dampness' from the body. At the end of the 20th Century, the She Ethnic people set up black rice workshops to develop more varieties and now they have become delicious dishes at the banquets in the major cities of Fujian and even around the south of Zhejiang province. The varieties include Black Rice Covered with Red Crabs, Black Rice Cooked in Bamboo, Tai Chi Black Rice, Lotus Leaf Black Rice, Pineapple Black Rice, Grass Wrap Black Rice, Black Rice Rolls, Black Rice with 8 Ingredients(both sweet or salty).

(五)爆炒章鱼

爆炒章鱼是福建省的汉族传统名菜,也是宁德酒席上必不可少的一道大菜。

章鱼含有丰富的蛋白质、矿物质等营养元素，并还富含抗疲劳、抗衰老，能延长人类寿命等重要保健因子——天然牛磺酸，营养丰富，口感鲜嫩。

6.5.1.5 Fried Octopus

It is a traditional and famous dish in Fujian and also a must at banquets in Ningde. Octopus contains rich protein and other nutrient mineral as well as a key gene of natural taurine that can fight against fatigue, ageing and prolong life. It is indeed nutritious and tastes fresh and tender.

（六）屏南米烧兔

米烧兔是屏南最有特色的美食之一，色味俱佳，油亮的兔皮呈米黄色，兔肉溢出阵阵米香，让你未食先流涎水。制作工艺独特，先在铁锅里放入大米，再用竹架托住宰杀的兔子，烧起微火让锅温慢慢烘干兔肉大部分水分，同时让米香逐渐渗入肉中。用餐时，将米烧兔切成细块，佐以糟姜、葱蒜以及摩芋丝等炒煮即可。

6.5.1.6 Roast Rabbit over Rice in a Wok in Pingnan County

It is one of the special gourmet foods in Pingnan County which looks and tastes good. The bright oily skin of the rabbit looks rice yellow and the rabbit meat emits a mouth-watering fragrance. The cooking process is unique. Put rice into the wok and hang the rabbit over the rice.

（七）泥钉/土丁冻

泥钉，生活于滩涂表层，刚出土时呈土褐色，榨压洗净后呈灰白色。制作时把洗净的“泥钉”放入锅里煮熟后加入水和适当的食盐。待水烧滚后把“泥钉”连同浓浓的汤汁装入碗中，八至十二小时后，整碗的汤汁就冻结起来了。味道鲜美，营养丰富，含有丰富的蛋白质和胶原蛋白，既美味又养颜。凡吃过“泥钉冻”的人都交口称赞其为“闽东第一冻”。

6.5.1.7 Sea Worms Jelly

The worms live in the muddy shores. When they first get out of the mud, they look brown. After they are washed, they look gray and white. Cooking methods: put the washed sea worms into the wok to be cooked, and then add some water and salt. After the water is boiled, pour the worms and the soup into bowls. After 8 to 12 hours, the whole bowl of soup will jell. It is fresh and nutritious with protein and collagen and looks good. Those who tried praise it as the “No.1 Jelly of Mindong”.

参考文献
References

[1]福建省宁德地区地方志编纂委员会.宁德地区志[M].北京:方志出版社,1998.
[2]宁德编委会.宁德[M].福州:福建人民出版社 ,2000.
[3]宁德市地方志编委会.先行的脚步[M].海峡摄影艺术出版社,2009.
[4]宁德市委宣传部,宁德市公安消防支队.走进闽东[N].(宁)新出〔2009〕内书第 36 号.
[5]宁德市统计局.国家统计局宁德调查队.宁德统计年鉴 2014[Z].北京:中国统计出版社,2014.
[6]宁德市统计局,国家统计局宁德调查队.宁德统计年鉴 2015[Z].北京:中国统计出版社,2015.

电子文献:

[1]佚名.宁德概览.宁德方志委网.[2013-01-15].http:/www/ndfzw.com/ndkk/.
[2]宁德市统计局,国家统计局宁德调查队.2014 年宁德市国民经济和社会发展统计公报.宁德网.[2015-03-18].http://www.ndwww.cn/news/ndwnews/201503/527116_6.html.
[3]宁德市统计局,国家统计局宁德调查队.2013 年宁德市国民经济和社会发展统计公报.宁德网.[2014-03-18].http://www.ndwww.cn/news/ndxw/201403/451225.html.
[4]胡善安.宁德核电 3 号机组正式进入运行状态.新华网福建频道.[2015-03-11].http://www.fujian.gov.cn/ztzl/zdxmjs/jsdt/201503/t20150311_919483.htm.
[5]佚名.大唐宁德公司:全面扭亏为盈.火力发电网.[2014-03-10].http://news.bjx.com.cn/html/20140310/495680.shtml.
[6]宁德市人民政府招商中心.投资宁德在线.http://nd.investnd.gov.cn/.
[7]佚名.宁德市医院大全.99 健康网.http://yyk.99.com.cn/ningde/.
[8]陈薇.前进中的宁德体育事业 群众体育蓬勃发展.东南网 .2012-10-28.http://nd.fjsen.com/2012-10/28/content.9696035.htm.
[9]陈小妹.宁德市加快体育事业发展综述.蕉城在线.2013-10-20.http://www.ndnews.cn/xwpd/sdjc/201310/250198.html.
[10]佚名.宁德土特产与工艺品简介.新浪旅游.http://travel.sina.com.cn/china/2009-08-05/153699603.shtml.
[11]佚名.宁德市重点推出民族传统工艺美术品参加文博会.福州新闻网.[2013-09-27].http://news.fznews.com.cn/zt/2013/wbh6/xmqy/2013-9-27/2013927KFrPEtJWBB113956.shtml.
[12]福建省情资料库—地方志之窗.[2014-7-06].http://ndfzw.com/xszhi/.

[13]佚名.教育.中国宁德.[2015-07-13].http://www.ningde.gov.cn/cms/www2/www.ningde.gov.cn.

[14]佚名.宁德市幼儿园基本情况(2013 年).中国宁德.[2013-09-11].http://www.ningde.gov.cn/cms/www2/www.ningde.gov.cn.

[15]古田县政协文史委.国家非物质文化遗产——临水宫请香接火仪俗.宁德市政协网.[2010-09-22].http://www.ndzx.gov.cn/xxbk/wszl/201009/154216.html.

[16]佚名.福鼎白茶制作技艺晋升第三批国家级非物质文化遗产名录.宁德网.[2010-07-20].http://www.ndnews.cn/xwpd/zbxw/fdzx/fdyw/201007/130478.html.

[17]周邦在.宁德城市总体规划(2009—2030)草案出炉.东南网.[2011-12-07].http://nd.fjsen.com/2011-12/07/content_7096946_2.htm.

[18]宁德市加快推进环三都澳区域发展的实施意见.福建招商网.[2014-08-23].http://fj.zhaoshang.net/2014-08-23/197388.html.

图书在版编目(CIP)数据

福建应用翻译大全. 宁德分册:汉英对照/龚帆元主编. —厦门:厦门大学出版社,2019.5
(福建省高校“一带一路”跨文化研究丛书/林大津总主编)
ISBN 978-7-5615-7107-1

Ⅰ.①福… Ⅱ.①龚… Ⅲ.①福建—概况—汉、英②宁德—概况—汉、英 Ⅳ.①K925.7

中国版本图书馆 CIP 数据核字(2018)第 258868 号

出 版 人 郑文礼
责任编辑 王扬帆 高奕欢
封面设计 李嘉彬
技术编辑 许克华

出版发行 厦门大学出版社
社 址 厦门市软件园二期望海路 39 号
邮政编码 361008
总 编 办 0592-2182177 0592-2181406(传真)
营销中心 0592-2184458 0592-2181365
网 址 http://www.xmupress.com
邮 箱 xmupress@126.com
印 刷 厦门市万美兴印刷设计有限公司

开本 787 mm×1 092 mm 1/16
印张 20.5
插页 2
字数 460 千字
版次 2019 年 5 月第 1 版
印次 2019 年 5 月第 1 次印刷
定价 68.00 元

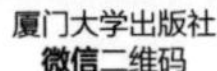
厦门大学出版社
微信二维码

厦门大学出版社
微博二维码